Street by Street

MIDDLES

DARLINGTON, HARTLEPOOL, STOCKTON-ON-TEES

Billingham, Bishop Auckland, Ferryhill, Great Ayton, Guisborough, Newton Aycliffe, Redcar, Saltburn-by-the-Sea, Sedgefield, Shildon, Spennymoor

1st edition May 2001

© Automobile Association Developments Limited 2001

This product includes map data licensed from Ordnance Survey® with the permission of the Controller of Her Majesty's Stationery Office. © Crown copyright 2000. All rights reserved. Licence No: 399221.

All rights reserved. No part of this publication may be reproduced, stored in a retrieval system, or transmitted in any form or by any means– electronic, mechanical, photocopying, recording or otherwise – unless the permission of the publisher has been given beforehand.

Published by AA Publishing (a trading name of Automobile Association Developments Limited, whose registered office is Norfolk House, Priestley Road, Basingstoke, Hampshire, RG24 9NY. Registered number 1878835).

Mapping produced by the Cartographic Department of The Automobile Association.

A CIP Catalogue record for this book is available from the British Library.

Printed by G. Canale & C. S.P.A., Torino, Italy

The contents of this atlas are believed to be correct at the time of the latest revision. However, the publishers cannot be held responsible for loss occasioned to any person acting or refraining from action as a result of any material in this atlas, nor for any errors, omissions or changes in such material. The publishers would welcome information to correct any errors or omissions and to keep this atlas up to date. Please write to Publishing, The Automobile Association, Fanum House, Basing View, Basingstoke, Hampshire, RG21 4EA.

Ref: MD104

Key to map pages ii-iii

Key to map symbols iv-1

Enlarged scale pages 2-9

Street by Street 10-153

Index – towns & villages 154

Index – streets 155-185

Index – featured places 186-190

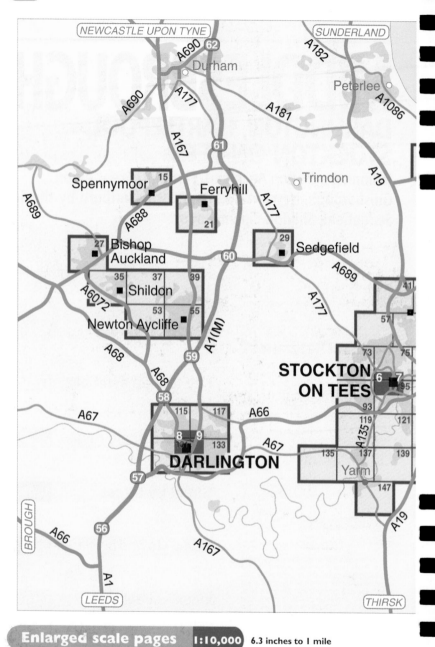

Enlarged scale pages   1:10,000   6.3 inches to 1 mile

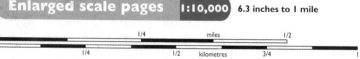

| 0 | | 1/4 | | miles | | 1/2 |
| 0 | 1/4 | | 1/2 | kilometres | 3/4 | 1 |

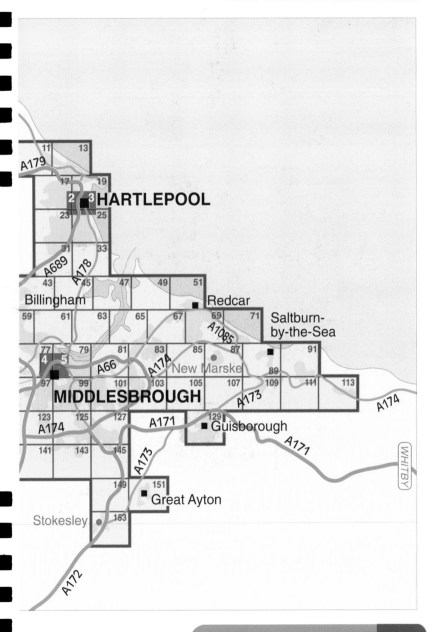

11 13
A179
17 19
2 3 HARTLEPOOL
23 25
31 33
A689 A178
43 45 47 49 51
Billingham   Redcar
59 61 63 65 67 69 71 Saltburn-
A1085   by-the-Sea
77 79 81 83 85 87 91
4 5 A66 A174 New Marske
97 99 101 103 105 107 109 111 113
MIDDLESBROUGH   A173   A174
123 125 127 A171 129
A174 A173   Guisborough A171
141 143 145
149 151
153 Great Ayton
Stokesley
A172
WHITBY

4.2 inches to 1 mile   **Scale of main map pages   1:15,000**

0   1/4   miles   1/2   3/4   1
0   1/4   1/2   kilometres 3/4   1   1 1/4   1 1/2

iv

Junction 9	Motorway & junction	P+🚌	Park & Ride
Services	Motorway service area	🚌	Bus/coach station
	Primary road single/dual carriageway		Railway & main railway station
Services	Primary road service area		Railway & minor railway station
	A road single/dual carriageway	⊖	Underground station
	B road single/dual carriageway	⊖	Light railway & station
	Other road single/dual carriageway	++++++++	Preserved private railway
	Restricted road	LC	Level crossing
	Private road	•—•—•—	Tramway
← ←	One way street	----------	Ferry route
	Pedestrian street	....	Airport runway
----------	Track/ footpath	—·—·—··	Boundaries- borough/ district
	Road under construction	ⱯⱯⱯⱯⱯ	Mounds
]====[	Road tunnel	**93**	Page continuation 1:15,000
P	Parking	7	Page continuation to enlarged scale 1:10,000

River/canal lake, pier	Toilet with disabled facilities
Aqueduct lock, weir	Petrol station
465 ▲ Winter Hill — Peak (with height in metres)	**PH** Public house
Beach	**PO** Post Office
Coniferous woodland	Public library
Broadleaved woodland	**i** Tourist Information Centre
Mixed woodland	Castle
Park	Historic house/ building
Cemetery	Wakehurst Place NT — National Trust property
Built-up area	**M** Museum/ art gallery
Featured building	† Church/chapel
⎍⎍⎍⎍ City wall	Country park
A&E Accident & Emergency hospital	Theatre/ performing arts
Toilet	Cinema

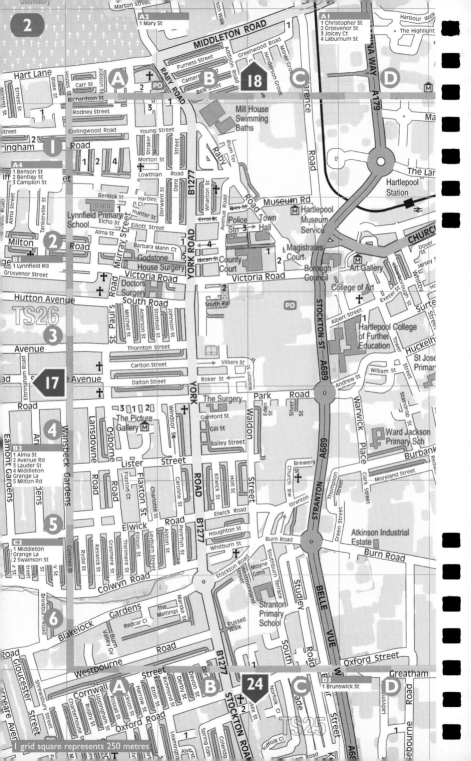

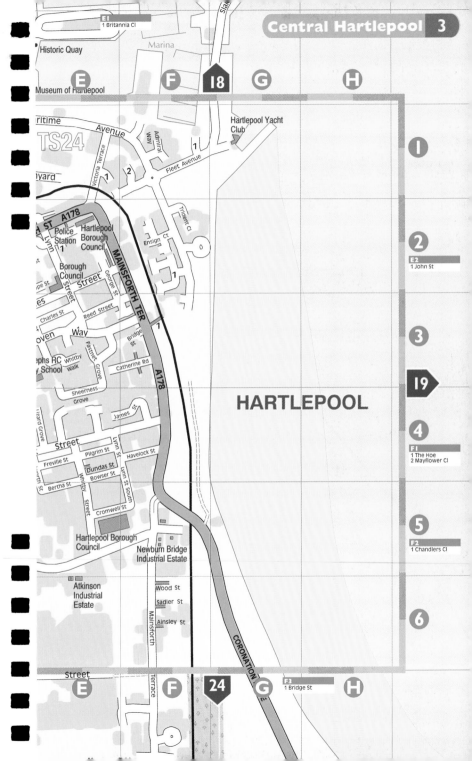

E1
1 Britannia Cl

Historic Quay

Marina

Museum of Hartlepool

E   F   **18**   G   H

Maritime   Avenue

TS24

...yard

Victoria Terrace

Admiral Way

Fleet Avenue

Hartlepool Yacht Club

1

2

E2
1 John St

...D ST A178

Police Station

Hartlepool Borough Council

Lynn

MAINSFORTH TER

Borough Council   Street

...es   Street

Charles St

Reed Street

George St

Ensign Ct

Trident Cl

...ope St

3

...oven   Way

...phs RC ...y School

Whitby Walk

Bridge St

Fastnet Grove

Catherine Rd

A178

19

Sheerness Grove

HARTLEPOOL

James St

Lizard Grove

Street

Pilgrim St

Lynn St

Havelock St

Freville St

Dundas St

Bowser St

4

F1
1 The Hoe
2 Mayflower Cl

...rth St

Bertha St

Whitby Street

Lynn St South

Cromwell St

Hartlepool Borough Council

Newburn Bridge Industrial Estate

5

F2
1 Chandlers Cl

Atkinson Industrial Estate

Wood St

Sadler St

Mainsforth

Ainsley St

CORONATION

6

Street

E   F   **24**   G   **F3**
1 Bridge St   H

Terrace

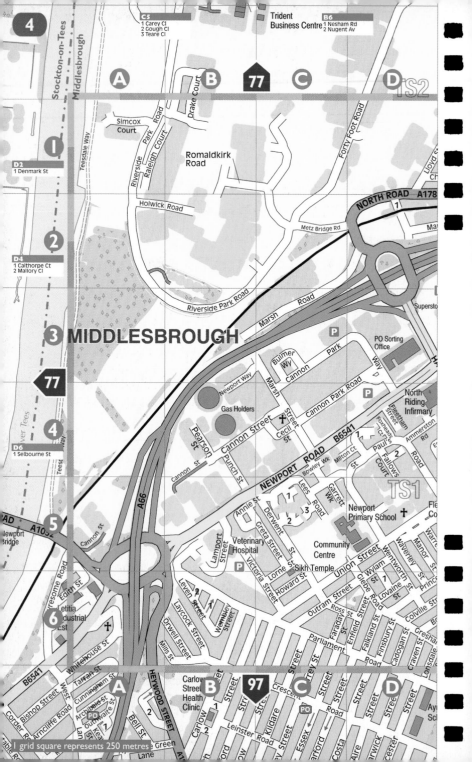

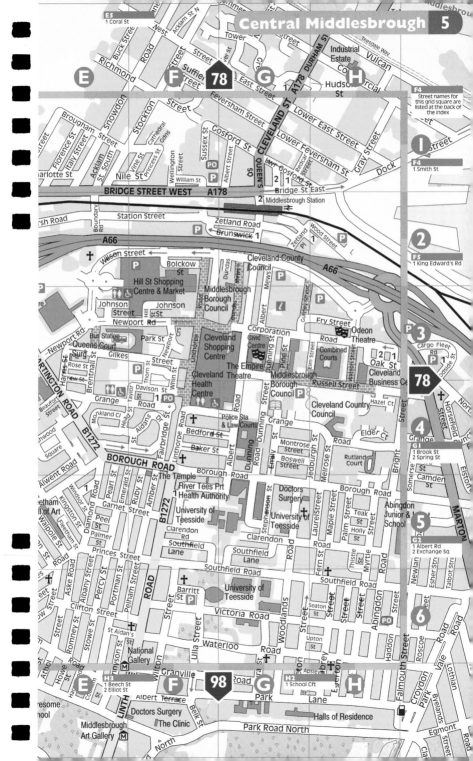

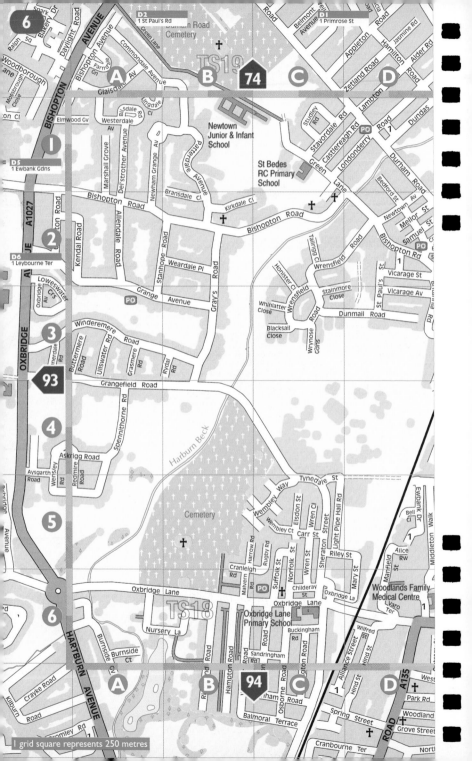

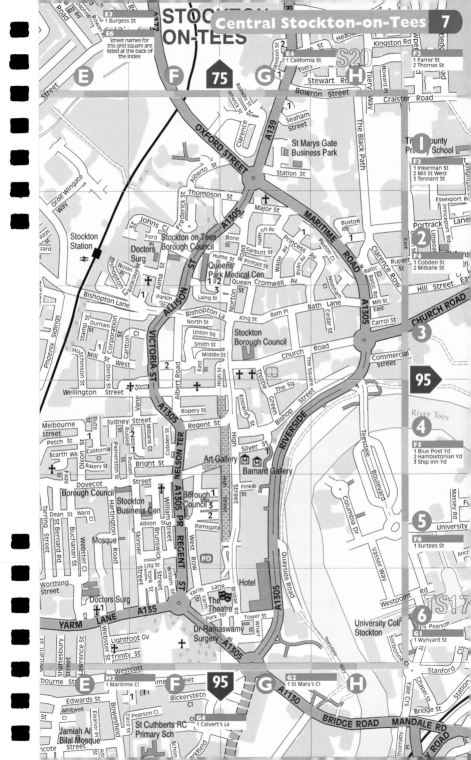

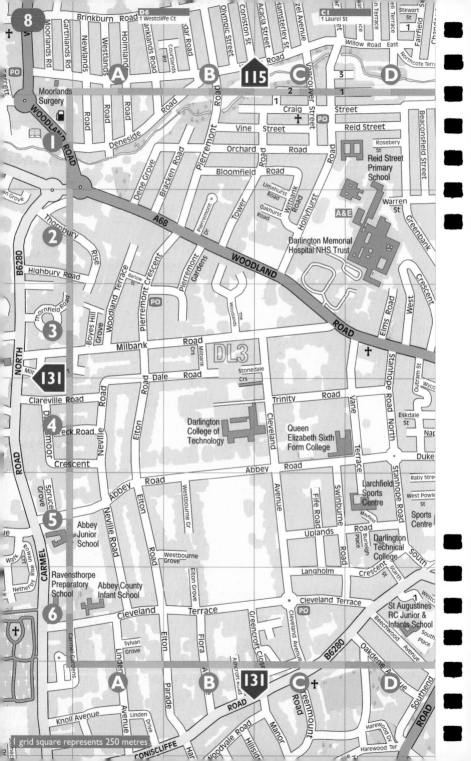

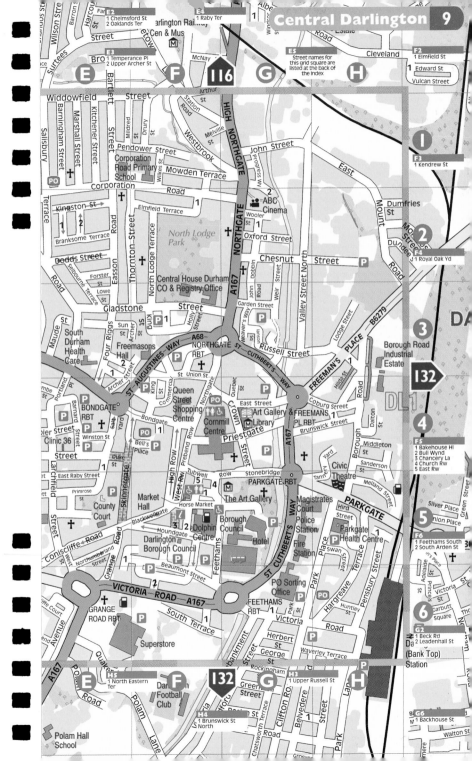

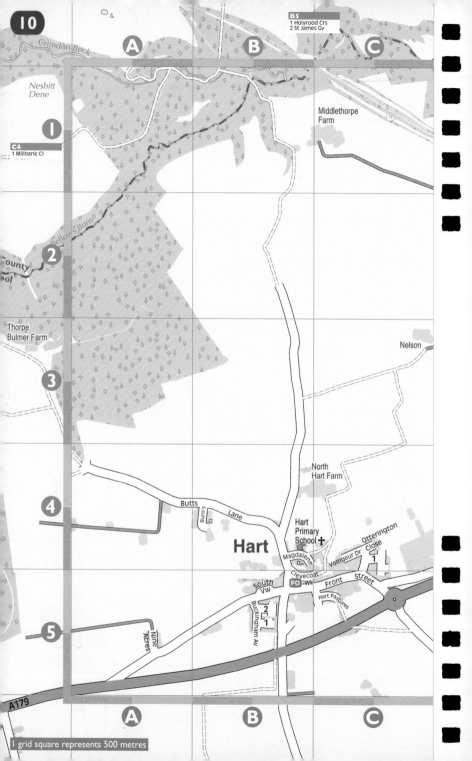

Grimdon Beck

B5
1 Holyrood Crs
2 St James Gv

A
B
C

Nesbitt Dene

Middlethorpe Farm

1

C4
1 Millbank Cl

Fellows Burn

2

County ol

Thorpe Bulmer Farm

Nelson

3

North Hart Farm

4

Butts Lane

Burn's Cl

Hart Primary School †

Otterington Close
1

Hart

Magdalene Dr

Voltigeur Dr

Clevecoat Wk

South Vw

PO

Front Street

Hart Pastures

Buckingham Av

2
1

5

Nine Acres

A179

A
B
C

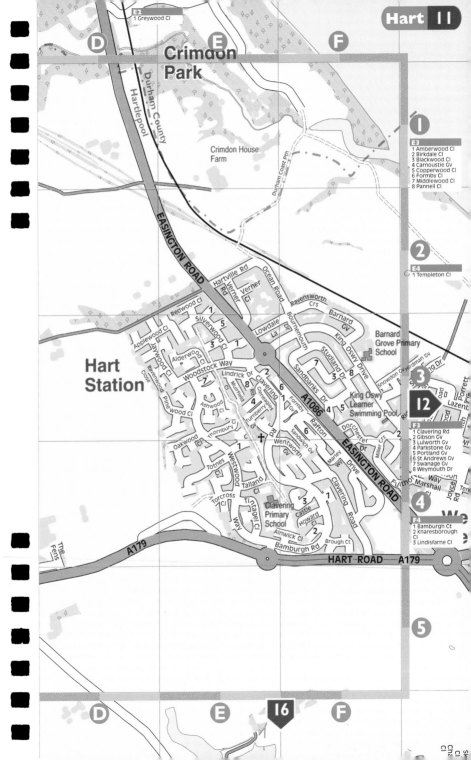

Crimdon
Park

E2
1 Greywood Cl

Durham County
Hartlepool

Crimdon House
Farm

Durham Coast Pth

1

E3
1 Amberwood Cl
2 Birkdale Cl
3 Blackwood Cl
4 Carnoustie Gv
5 Copperwood Cl
6 Formby Cl
7 Middlewood Cl
8 Pannell Cl

2

E4
1 Templeton Cl

Hart
Station

EASINGTON ROAD

Hartville Rd
Verner Rd
Verner Cl
Ocean Road
Lowdale La
Ravensworth Crs
Bournemouth
Barnard Gv

Redwood Cl
Silverwood
Applewood Cl
Jaywood Cl
Alderwood Cl
Ravenswood Close
Pinewood Cl
Woodstock Way
Lindrick Dr
Clavering
Sandbanks Dr
Studland Dr
King Oswy Drive

Barnard
Grove Primary
School

Snowdon Gv
Wordman Gv
Birtley Dr
Lazenby

3

12

Ashwood Cl
Thornbury
Turnberry
Gleneagles
Formby Cl
Rafton
Dorchester Dr
Miller Crs
Fulthorp

King Oswy
Learner
Swimming Pool

F3
1 Clavering Rd
2 Gibson Gv
3 Lulworth Gv
4 Parkstone Gv
5 Portland Gv
6 St Andrews Gv
7 Swanage Gv
8 Weymouth Dr

Oakwood Cl
Westwood
Totnes
Tintagel Cl
Talland
Torcross Cl
Way

Wentworth Gv
Sandwich Gv
Marley Dr
Clavering Road

Way
Marshall
Joyce

4

We

Clavering
Primary
School

Castle
Howard
Alnwick Cl
Bamburgh Rd
Brough Ct

F4
1 Bamburgh Ct
2 Knaresborough Cl
3 Lindisfarne Cl

The Fens

A179

HART ROAD   A179

5

12

A4
1 Butterwick Rd
2 Dobson Pl

A   **B**   **C**

1

B4
1 Nesbyt Rd

2

B5
1 Bradshaw Ct
2 Bulmer Pl
3 Clifford Cl
4 Harrison Pl
5 Hastings Pl
6 Horsley Pl
7 Pounder Pl

Golf Links

Hart Warren

North Sands

Barnard Grove Primary School

arnard Gv

King Oswy Drive

3

Dalton Gv Hirdman Gv

Speeding Dr

King Le Swim

II

C5
1 Rawlings Ct
2 Surgery La

Ridlington Way

Howden Road

Hood

Lazenby Road

Goldsmith Av

Porrett Close

Hiltone

Pert Rd

Whitrout Road

Henry Smith Secondary School

EASINGTON ROAD

Miller Dr

Fulthot Cl

Nicholson Way

Joycel

Marshall Cl

1 PO

King Oswy Drive

Tempest Rd

2

St John Vianny RC Primary Sch

Dickens Steet

Gilberti Pl

Rogeri Pl

Dowson Rd

1

Bruntoft Av

Lamberd Rd

West Vw Rd

4

ugh Ct

Clavering Road

West View

West View Road

A1049 **WEST VIEW ROAD**

West Vw Rd

Cemetery

Annandale Crs

Davison Drive

Skelton St

Emerson 1

Ellett Ct

3

Carrick St

Bruce Crs

Miers Av

Winterbottom

PO

WEST VIEW

Smyth

Sedgewick Cl

Hartlepool Borough Council

Purves Pl

Garside Drive

Arkley Crs

HART ROAD — A179 —

EASINGTON ROAD

Hartlepool Old Boys R F C Mayfield Park

Jones Road

Jowitt Rd

6 4 5

7

Runciman Rd

Sharp Crs

West View Primary School

Warren Road

Warren

2

Wells Avenue

Skerne Rd

Skerne Road

Doctors Surgery

Road

5

Middle Warren

Lightfoot Crs

1

7

4

3

A   **17**   **B**   **C**

A179

Ha lepool Hospital Management Committee

Hartlepool & Peterlee Hospitals NHS Trust

Thames Av

Holdforth

Holdforth Road

Oakeswa

stonech

eldfare

Thompson

Warren

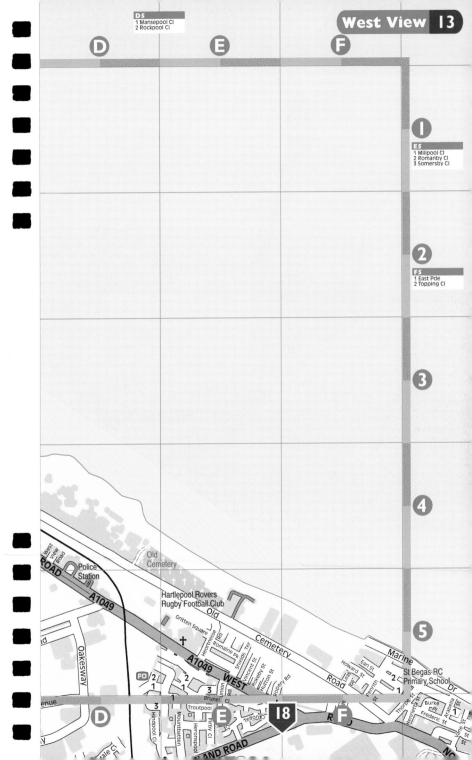

D
E
F

D 5
1 Mansepool Cl
2 Rockpool Cl

1

E 5
1 Millpool Cl
2 Romanby Cl
3 Somersby Cl

2

F 5
1 East Pde
2 Topping Cl

3

4

Old Cemetery

West View Road

Police Station

Hartlepool Rovers Rugby Football Club

Old Cemetery Road

Gritten Square

Heortnesse Rd

Romaine Pk Ter

Shields Ter

Vincent St

Roseby St

Hutton St

Robery Rd

A1049

A1049 WEST

PO

Brunel Cl

Oakesway

Mountbatten

Firby Cl

Heronspool

Hippolpool Cl

Troutpool

Telford Cl

D
E
18
F

Howard St

Earl St

Penrith

Marine Dr

St Begas RC Primary School

Thorpe St

Henrietta St

Frederic St

Burke Pl

Arabella

5

ROAD

NORTHERN ROAD

avenue

14

A   B   C

B1
1 Keldmere

4   5
Gervaulx
Court
Winchester
Carr
Glastonbury
Close
Cane
Close
2

Carr

5   2   3   7
Thirlmere   Glenmere   Lane
Buttermere   Grasmere
Kentmere   Carr   Birchmere
Hazelmere   8
4   6   Tangmere
Kirkdale   Farndale
Rosedale   Westerdale   Bransdale
Glaisdale

I
Witworth Hall
B4
1 Duncombe Cl

Burton Beck
Farm

Oxclose
Primary
School

2
C1
1 Burnmere
2 Caldermere
3 Ellesmere
4 Langmere
5 Mossmere
6 Rossmere
7 Troutbeck Cl
8 Windermere

Carr
Street
Dunelm Street
North

DL16

3
C3
1 Princess St

Whitworth Road

Rosa Street
Primary School

Carr
Street
Rose Street

SPENNYMOOR
St Paul's
Flora St
St Paul's   Edward St
Vyner St
Craddock Street
Strat

4
C4
1 Robert St

Bishop's
Close

Spennymoor
Comprehensive
School

Belle Vue
7
Villa
Street
Victoria
Close
Lothianna
Osborne
Road
View Drive

Page Grove
Westmoor
Close
Whitworth
Close
7

Inglesgarth
Court
Chestnut Avenue
Ash Grove
Victoria
Greens

Thistle
Close
Bluebell
Drive
Primrose Cl
Lilac Close

West
Terrace
Whitworth
Road
Hawthorn
Rd

Whitworth
School
Beech Avenue

**Middlestone
Moor**

Grayson
Heather
Grove
North
Drive
Briar Cl
Central Drive
Heath
Road
Thorn
Cl
Fern
Grove
Rock
Road
South View

Cemetery
Spennymoor
Comprehensive
Lower School
A688

5

Albion St
Hirst Cl
Moorside
Lyne Road

PO
Willow
Rd
Durham Street
Gibbon
Wood
St
Hancroft
Garth
Road
Durham
Whitworth

A   B   C

Middlestone
Moor County
Junior Sch
South View
So   Court
Nanny Pop
Lonnen

A688

I grid square represents 500 metres

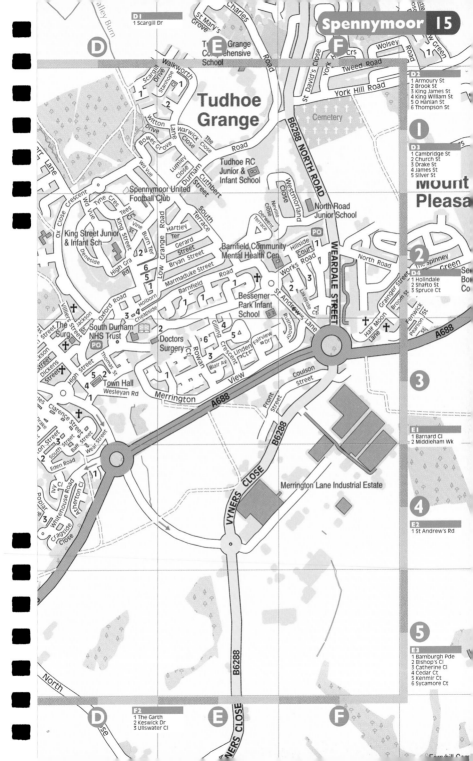

D1
1 Scargill Dr

St Mary's Grove

Charles Road

D

E

Grange Comprehensive School

F

Wolsey

Walkworth Road

Scargill Drive

Stanhope

Witton Drive

Bowes Grove

West Lane

Lumley Close

Warwick Close

The Close

Durham Close

Cuthbert

Tudhoe Grange Road

Tudhoe Grange

Wd Vue

Tweed Road

York Hill Road

Cemetery

B6288 NORTH ROAD

St David's Close

York H Crs

D2
1 Armoury St
2 Brook St
3 King James St
4 King William St
5 O Hanlan St
6 Thompson St

I

D3
1 Cambridge St
2 Church St
3 Drake St
4 James St
5 Silver St

Mount Pleasa

Tudhoe RC Junior & Infant School

Westmorland Close

North Road Junior School

Spennymoor United Football Club

Wd Close Crescent

Tyne Cres

King Street

Vine

Burn Ter

South Terrace

Hartley Ter

Gerard Street

Bryan Street

Neville Close

Derwent Terrace

Barnfield Community Mental Health Cen

Hillside Court

PO

Ox Close

King Street Junior & Infant Sch

Tees Crs

Deneside

High Gra Rd

Low Grange Road

Marmaduke Street

Barnfield Road

Works Road

3

Lakeside Terrace

North Road

The Spinney

Green

2

Grainger Street

Broom St

1 Holindale
2 Shafto St
3 Spruce Ct

Sea Bo Co

Villiers Street

Oxford Road

Holborn

Cheapside

4

5
7

Bessemer Park Infant School

St Andrew's Lane

Risonmoor

Fenwick

Pearson St

Half Moon Lane

A688

Jackson Street

The Surg

South Durham NHS Trust

PO

Doctors Surgery

6

5
4

Cilling Crescent

Linden Ct

Fairview Dr

Rowan Ct

Blair Av

View

Dickens Street

High Street

5 2
4
1

Town Hall

Wesleyan Rd

Thomas St

Merrington

A688

Coulson Street

Front Street

3

E1
1 Barnard Cl
2 Middleham Wk

Clarence Street

Drake

St

South Street

Bar Street

Wear Street

Eden Road

7

Ivy Cl

Atherton Cl

Whitehouse Road

Poplar

3

Cragside Close

VYNERS CLOSE

B6288

Merrington Lane Industrial Estate

4

E2
1 St Andrew's Rd

5

E3
1 Bamburgh Pde
2 Bishop's Cl
3 Catherine Cl
4 Cedar Ct
5 Kenmir Ct
6 Sycamore Ct

North

D

E

VYNERS CLOSE

F

F2
1 The Garth
2 Keswick Dr
3 Ullswater Cl

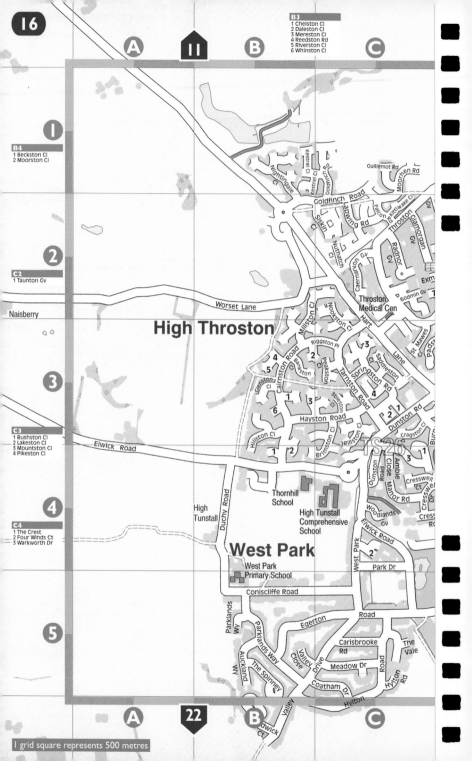

B3
1 Chelston Cl
2 Daleston Cl
3 Mereston Cl
4 Reedston Rd
5 Riverston Cl
6 Whinston Cl

A II B C

I

B4
1 Beckston Cl
2 Moorston Cl

Guillemot Rd

Moorhen Rd

Kestrel Cl

Nightingale Cl

Goldfinch Road

Kittiwake Cl

Throston Gv

Clamorgan Gv

2

C2
1 Taunton Gv

Naisberry

Siskin Cl

Nuthatch

Lapwing Rd

Falcon Ct

Radnor Gv

Exm

Worset Lane

Caernarvon Gv

Bodmin Gv

High Throston

Throston Medical Cen

St. Mawes

pads

3

C3
1 Bushston Cl
2 Lakeston Cl
3 Mountston Cl
4 Pikeston Cl

Elwick Road

Carnston Road

Millston Cl

Nookston Cl

Hart

Lane

Riggston Pl

Peakston

Saddleston Cl

Springston Rd

3

4

5

Lolenston Gv

Bankston

Tarnston Road

Siderston

Haxton Road

Hilston Cl

Brimston Cl

Rilston Cl

Dunston Rd

2 7

2 5

Cragston Cl

Bur

4

C4
1 The Crest
2 Four Winds Ct
3 Warkworth Dr

High Tunstall

Duchy Road

Thornhill School

High Tunstall Comprehensive School

Dunston

TS26

Amble Close

Cresswell Ct

3 1

Cress

Woodlands Gv

Manor Rd

Pear

Elwick Road

West Park

West Park Primary School

Coniscliffe Road

West Park Road

Park Dr

2

5

Parklands Wy

Auckland Wy

Parklands Way

The Spinney

Valley Close

Egerton

Valley Drive

Carisbrooke Rd

Meadow Dr

Coatham Dr

Road

Road

Hylton Rd

The Vale

A 22 B C

Elwick Ct

Valley

Hylton

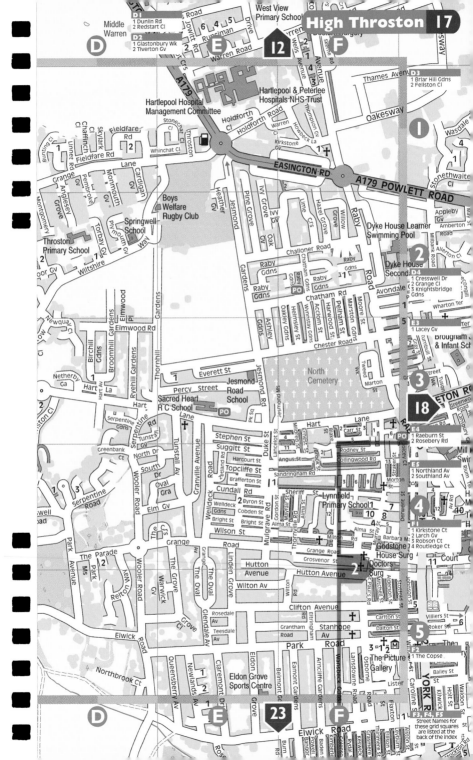

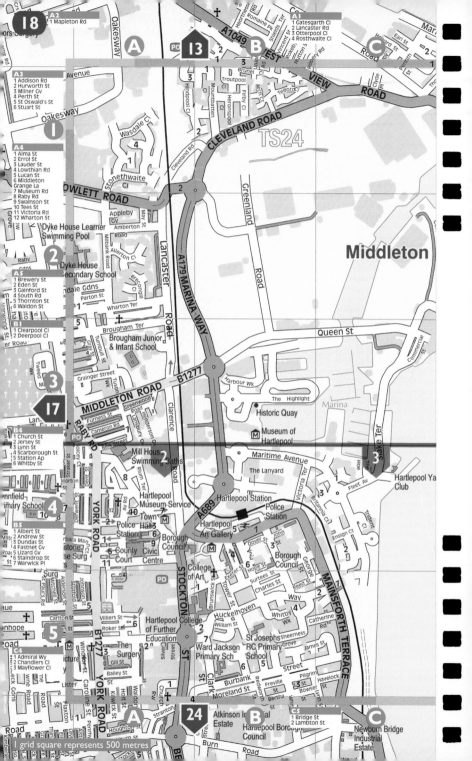

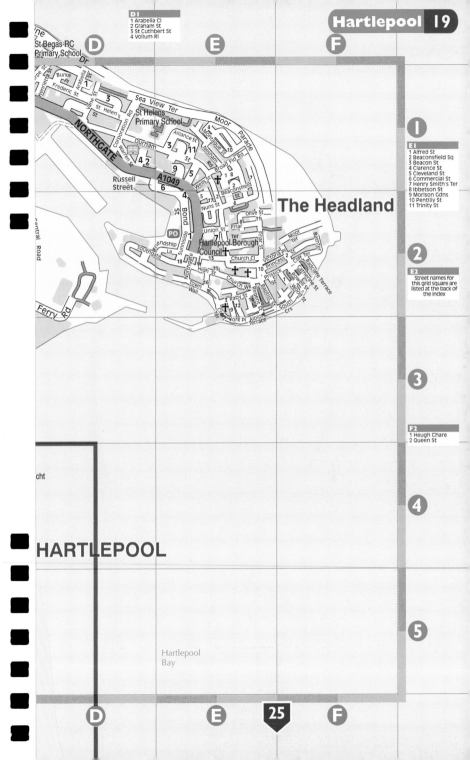

D

E

F

I

2

3

4

5

The Headland

St Begas RC
Primary School

Sea View Ter

St Helens
Primary School

Moor
Parade

NORTHGATE

A1049

Russell
Street

Hartlepool Borough
Council

Beaconsfield

Nuns St

Union St

Olive St

Church Cl

Church Wk

Town
Wall

York Pl

Central
Road

Ferry Rd

HARTLEPOOL

Hartlepool
Bay

25

D

E

F

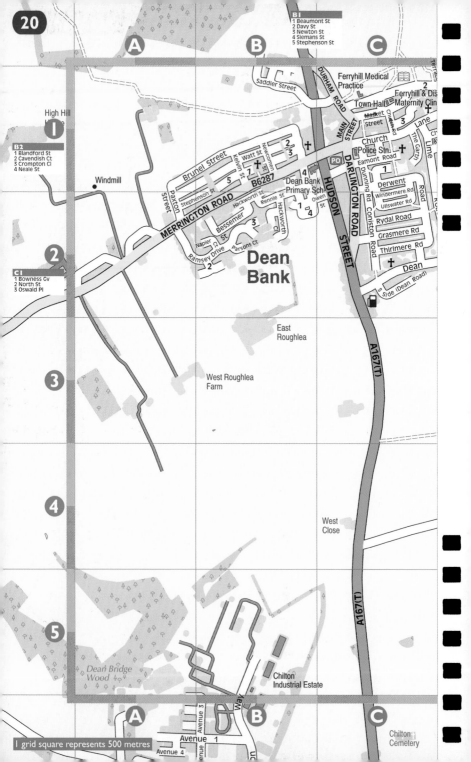

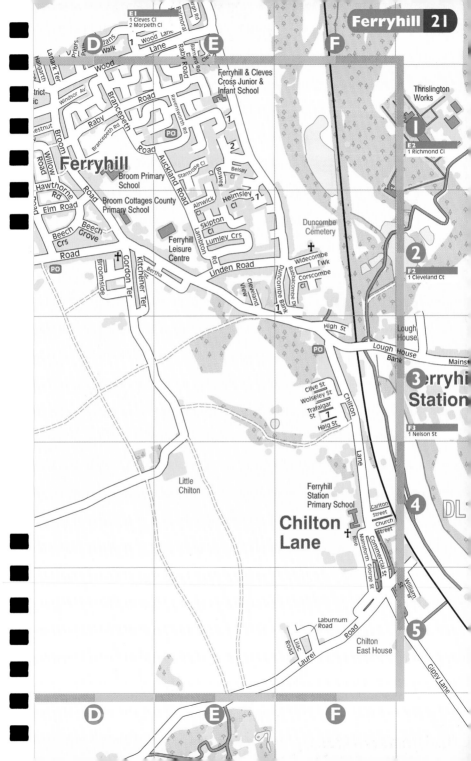

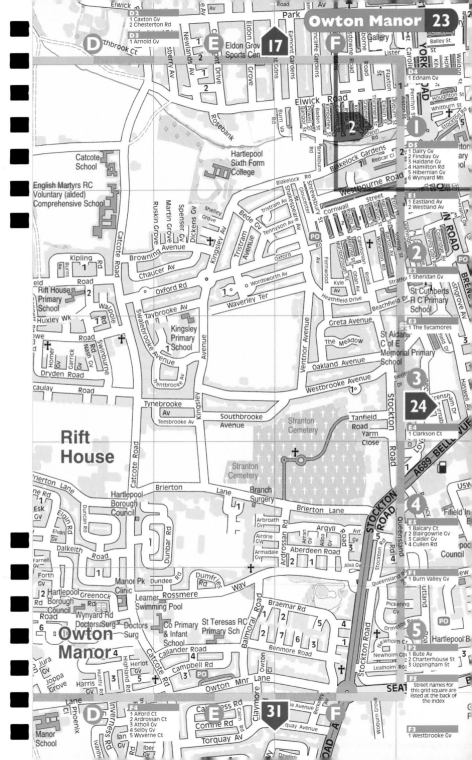

Rift House

Owton Manor

Catcote School

English Martyrs RC Voluntary (aided) Comprehensive School

Hartlepool Sixth Form College

Rift House Primary School

Kingsley Primary School

St Aidans C of E Memorial Primary School

St Cuthberts R C Primary School

Stranton Cemetery

Stranton Cemetery

Branch Surgery

Hartlepool Borough Council

Hartlepool Borough Council

Manor Pk Clinic

Rossmere Swimming Pool

Co Primary & Infant School

St Teresas RC Primary Sch

Doctors Surg

Doctors Surg

Manor School

Eldon Grov Sports Cen

17

24

31

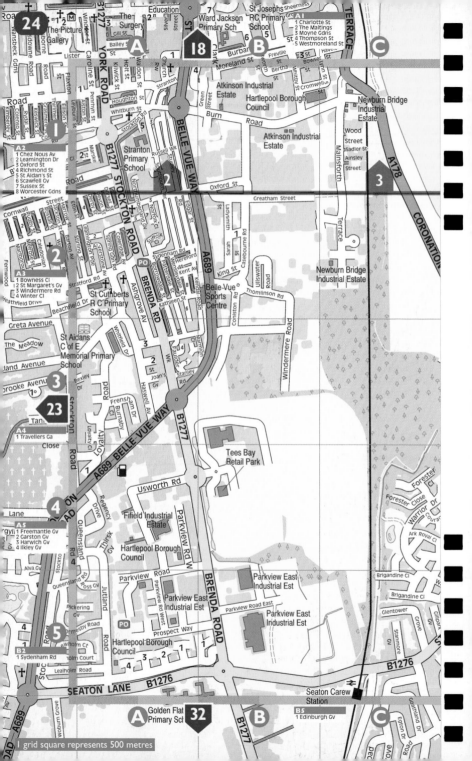

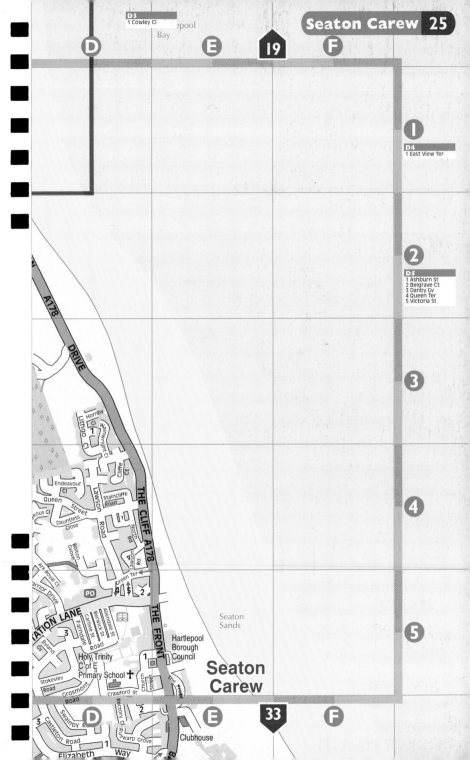

D **E** 19 **F**

D3
1 Cowley Cl

Hartlepool
Bay

1
D4
1 East View Ter

2
D5
1 Ashburn St
2 Belgrave Ct
3 Danby Gv
4 Queen Ter
5 Victoria St

3

A178

DRIVE

Hornby
Cl
Lithgo
Cl
Wainwright Cl

Cliffe
Ct

4

Endeavour
Cl
Queen
Street
Lawson
Road
Staincliffe
Road

North
Rd

Dauntless
Close

Courageous Cl

THE CLIFF A178

Bolton
Grove

Queen Rd

Green Ter

5

AK-Royal Cl

Warrior Drive

PO
5 2

Seaton
Sands

STATION LANE

Carlisle St
Farndale
Berwick St.

Allendale St
Road

Hartlepool
Borough
Council

Byland

3

Stokesley
Road

Holy Trinity
C of E
Primary School

THE FRONT

Church
Street

Crosmont
Road

Crawford St

The Front

**Seaton
Carew**

D **E** 33 **F**

Swainby Rd

Castleton
Road

3

1

Rectory Cl

Ruswarp Grove

Clubhouse

Elizabeth
Way

A

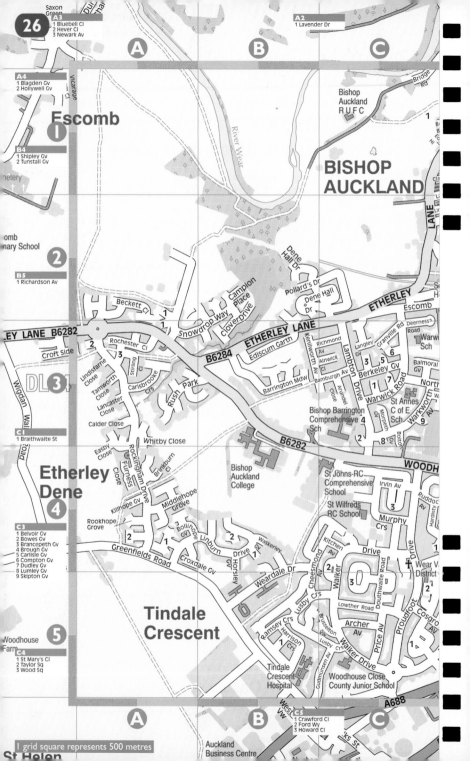

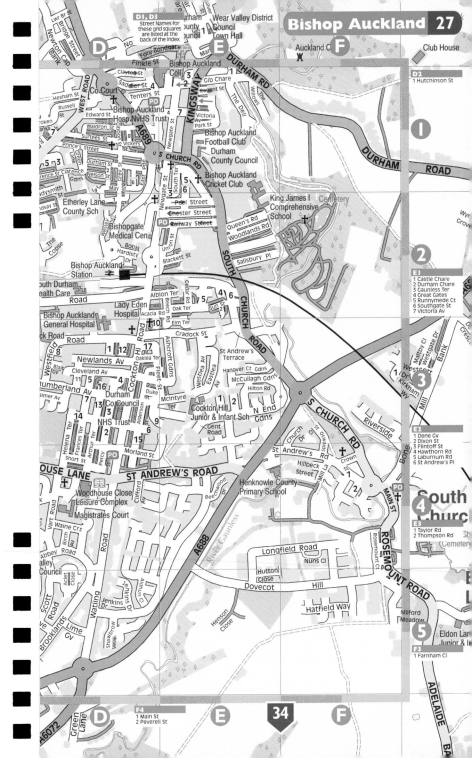

D1, D3
Street Names for these grid squares are listed at the back of the index

Wear Valley District Council Town Hall

Auckland C

Club House

D2
1 Hutchinson St

DURHAM ROAD

Lwr Br
Bridge Street
Newton Cap
Fore Bondgate
Finkle St
Bishop Auckland Coll
Gib Chare
Regent St

Clayton St
Saddler St
Tenters St
Victoria
Ayk
Park St

Co.Court
West Road
Hexham St
Russell St
Edward St
Waldron St
Surtees St
Vickers
Prince's Street
Durham St
Nelson St
May St
Clarence St
Clarence Gdns
Ladysmith
Lindsay Rd

Bishop Auckland Hosp NVHS Trust

A689

Bishop Auckland Football Club
Durham County Council

Bishop Auckland Cricket Club

Peel Street
Chester Street
Railway Street

Queen's Rd
Woodlands Rd

King James I Comprehensive School

Cemetery

Wyn Grove

Etherley Lane County Sch

Bishopgate Medical Cen

Bob
Hardisty
Dr

Blackett St

Salisbury Pl

CHURCH RD

SOUTH CHURCH ROAD

Bishop Auckland Station

South Durham Health Care
Road

The Copse

Albion Ter
Cedar Rd
Beech Rd
Oak Ter
Acacia Rd
Elm Ter

Sun
2

Lady Eden Hospital

Bishop Auckland General Hospital
k Road

Cradock St

St Andrew's Terrace

Hanover Ct Gdns
McCullagh Gdns
Hilton Rd

Riverside

Westfield
Newlands Av
Cleveland Av
Cumberland Av
Palmer Av

Oaklea Ter
Ashcroft Gdns
Fleet St
Duke St
McIntyre Ter

Westlea Av
Eastlea

N End Gdns

Cockton Hill Junior & Infant Sch

Gent Road

St Oswalds Rd

Church Dr

Crown
St

Mattby Cl
Westgate Dr
Westcott Dr
Kirkham Wy

E1
1 Castle Chare
2 Durham Chare
3 Gaunless Ter
4 Great Gates
5 Runnymede Ct
6 Southgate St
7 Victoria Av

Bone

Mill

E2
1 Dene Gv
2 Dixon St
3 Flintoff St
4 Hawthorn Rd
5 Laburnum Rd
6 St Andrew's Pl

Helena Ter
Frances Ter
Arthur Ter
Percy
Short St
Durham
Co.Council
NHS Trust
Alderson
Morland St

St Andrew's Rd
Hillbeck Street

St

PO

South Churc

E3
1 Taylor Rd
2 Thompson Rd

HOUSE LANE
ST ANDREW'S ROAD

Woodhouse Close Leisure Complex
Magistrates Court

Clifford
Beechwood

Henknowle County Primary School

Main St
Rosemount Ct

Rosemount Road

alley
Council
Adcot
Close
Scott Road
Waine Crs
Abbey Road
Brooklands
Lime Gv
Var Road
Birch Av
Jenkins Dr
Alnum Rd
Shawcrow
Vew

A688
River Gaunless

Longfield Road
Nuns Cl
Hutton Close
Dovecot
Hill
Hatfield Way

Adelaide Ba

Milford Meadow

Eldon Lan
Junior & In

F3
1 Farnham Cl

A6072
Green Lane

F4
1 Main St
2 Peverell St

34

D   E   F

D   I   2   3   4   5

28

A   B   C

1

Knotty
Hill

Green
Knowles

Low
Hardwick

2

Hotel

A177

3

Hardwick Hall
Country Park

4

Brakes Farm

Sandy   Bank
A689

St
OL

5

Sands
Hall

Sands Farm

Sedgefield
Racecourse

A   B   C

1 grid square represents 500 metres

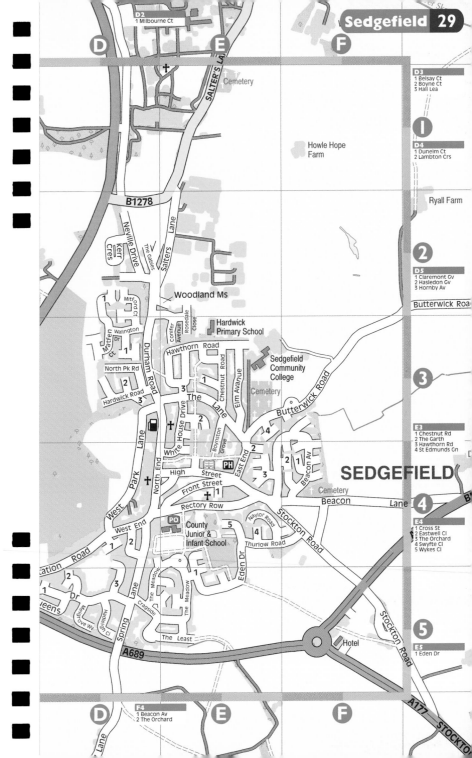

Sedgefield **29**

D2
1 Milbourne Ct

D3
1 Belsay Ct
2 Boyne Ct
3 Hall Lea

Howle Hope Farm

Ryall Farm

B1278

Butterwick Roa

D5
1 Claremont Gv
2 Hasledon Gv
3 Hornby Av

Woodland Ms

Hardwick Primary School

Sedgefield Community College

Cemetery

E3
1 Chestnut Rd
2 The Garth
3 Hawthorn Rd
4 St Edmunds Gn

SEDGEFIELD

Cemetery

Beacon Lane

E4
1 Cross St
2 Eastwell Cl
3 The Orchard
4 Swyfte Cl
5 Wykes Cl

County Junior & Infant School

PO

Hotel

Stockton Road

E5
1 Eden Dr

A689

A177 STOCKTO

F4
1 Beacon Av
2 The Orchard

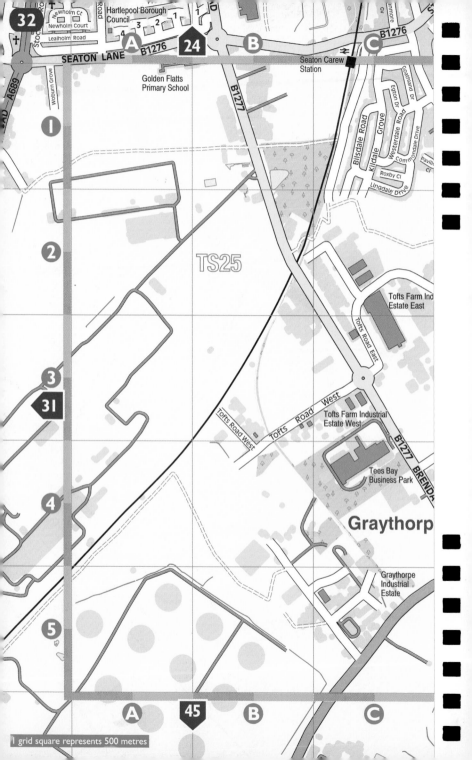

Holy Trinity
Stokesley Road
Byland
Road
D1
1 Castleton Rd
2 Deacon Gdns
3 Ingleby Rd
Hartlepool
borough
Council

Church Street
The Front

Seaton Carew 25

Grosmont Road
Crawford St

D School ✝

E

F

Rectory cl
Rushwarp Grove
2

Swainby Rd

Castleton Road
3
1
Elizabeth Way

A178

Clubhouse

Grace Cl
The Links
The Wickets

Seaton Carew Cricket Club

Headingley Ct
Headingley Court

1

2

ustrial

TEES ROAD

ROAD

Golf Course

Hartlepool Power Station Visitor Centre

D

E

46

F

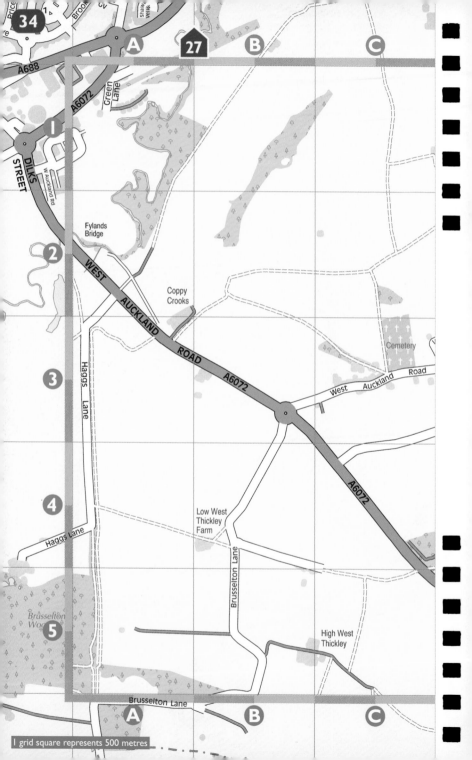

34

27

A688

A6072

Green Lane

DILKS STREET

W Auckland Rd

1

Fylands Bridge

2

WEST AUCKLAND ROAD

Coppy Crooks

A6072

Haggs Lane

3

West Auckland Road

Cemetery

4

Haggs Lane

Low West Thickley Farm

Brusselton Lane

A6072

Brusselton Wood

5

High West Thickley

Brusselton Lane

A

B

C

1 grid square represents 500 metres

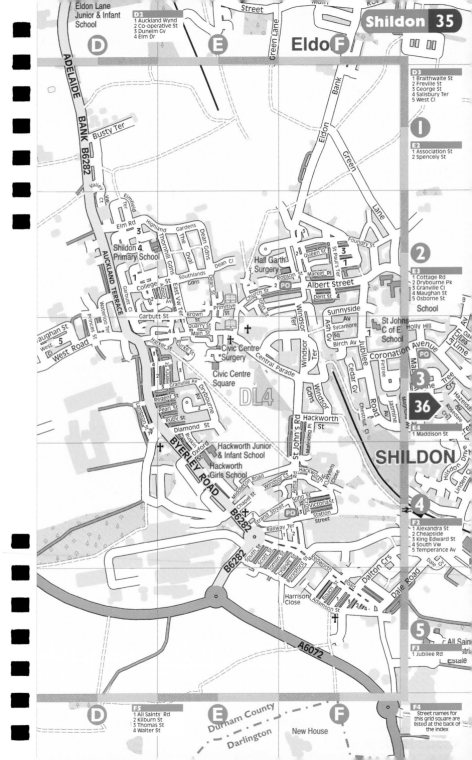

Shildon **35**

Eldo**F**

D2
1 Auckland Wynd
2 Co-operative St
3 Dunelm Gv
4 Elm Dr

D3
1 Braithwaite St
2 Freville St
3 George St
4 Salisbury Ter
5 West Cl

E2
1 Association St
2 Spencely St

E3
1 Cottage Rd
2 Drybourne Pk
3 Granville Cl
4 Maughan St
5 Osborne St

E4
1 Maddison St

36

SHILDON

DL4

F2
1 Alexandra St
2 Cheapside
3 King Edward St
4 South Vw
5 Temperance Av

F3
1 Jubilee Rd

F5
1 All Saints' Rd
2 Kilburn St
3 Thomas St
4 Walter St

Durham County
Darlington

New House

F4
Street names for
this grid square are
listed at the back of
the index

Eldon Lane
Junior & Infant
School

ADELAIDE BANK B6282

Busty Ter

Shildon
Primary School

AUCKLAND TERRACE

Hall Garth
Surgery

Albert Street

St Johns
C of E
School

Coronation Avenue

Civic Centre
Surgery

Civic Centre
Square

BYERLEY ROAD

Hackworth Junior
& Infant School

Hackworth
Girls School

B6282

A6072

All Saints
Estate

36

A

B

A3
1 Rowan Av
2 Weardale Wk
3 Westerdale Gdns

C

Old Eldon

Moor Lane

1

A4
1 Tynedale Wk

Bank

een Lane

Foundry St

St Paul's Ter

3
1

2

B3
1 Baysdale Gdns

St

4

Sunnyside Av

Sycamore

Birch Av

Jubilee

Cedar Gv

Sunnydale Comprehensive School

St Johns C of E School

Holly Hill

Coronation Avenue

PO

Maple Avenue

Pine Tree Crs

Magnolia Wy

3

35

Larch Av

Oak Gea

Yewtree Av

Lime Gv

Queensway

3

Cleveland Av

1

Eskdale Gdns

Farndale Gdns

Glaisdale Gdns

Hazeldale Av

Rosedale Crs

Teesdale Wk

Crescent

Spout Lane

Middridge Lane

Middridge

1

Jubilee

2

1

Hilsdon Drive

Linden Cl

Shildon Station

SHILDON

4

East Thickley

Dale Gv

Dale Road

Dale Road Trading Estate

Dalton Crs

5

All Saints Industrial Estate

Hawthorn House

A

52

B

C

I grid square represents 500 metres

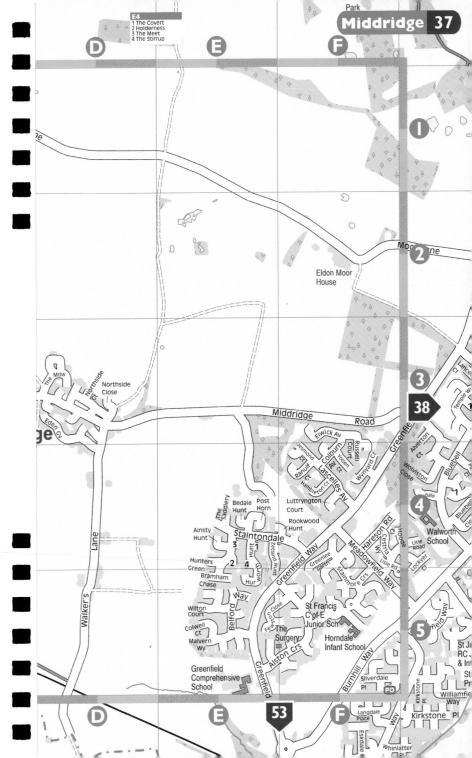

Park

D   E   F

I

E4
1 The Covert
2 Holderness
3 The Meet
4 The Stirrup

Moor Lane

2

Eldon Moor
House

3

38

Lance Ct

Temple Ct

The Mdw
Northside
Ct
Northside
Close

Middridge   Road

Greenfie

Elwick Av

Coburn Av
Russell Court
Jesmond
Ranulf Ct
Lascelles Av
Yoden Ct
Hambleton Ct
Wynyard Ct

Alverton
Ct

Wolviston
Close

Bluebell

Eden Gv

ge

The Saddlery
Bedale
Hunt
Post
Horn

Luttryngton
Court

Rookwood
Hunt

dale

4

Walworth
School

Bluebell
Way

Ainsty
Hunt

Staintondale
3   1
Hunt
2   4   Zetland Hunt

Hareson Rd

Hoode

Lisle Rd

Lisle
Road

Lockyer
Ct

Walker's   Lane

Hunters
Green
Bramham
Chase

Greenfield Way

Greenlee
Garth

Greenlee
Garth

Stanmore Crs

Meadowfield Way

Cestria Wy

5

field Way

Wilton
Court

Belford   Way

Hur

Cocks Close
Fewston

St Francis
C of E
Junior Sch

Colwell
Ct
Malvern
Wy

The
Surgery

Alston Crs

Horndale
Infant School

St Jo
RC
& Inf

St
Pr

Greenfield
Comprehensive
School

Greenfield

Burnhill Way

Silverdale
Pl

PO

Kirkstone
Pl

Williamfie
Way

D   E   53   F   Langdale
Place

Kirkstone

Way

Esksdale

Whinlatter
Pl

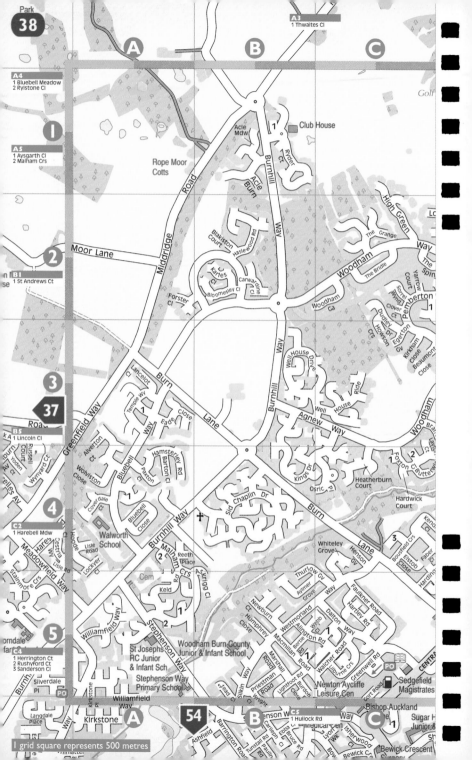

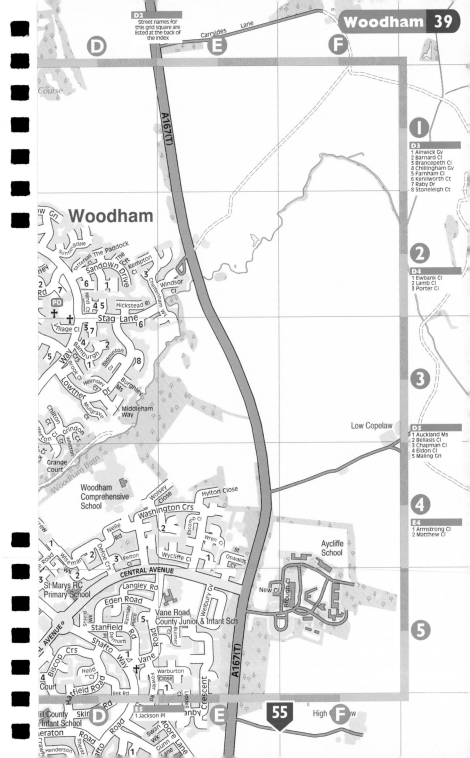

Course

Woodham

Carrsides Lane

D   **E**   **F**

I

2

Sunningdale
Tattersall The Paddock
Sandown Drive
The
Crt
Kempton
Cheltenham Wk
Windsor
Cl

PO
Hickstead Rl
Hind Cl
Stag Lane
Village Cl
Bamburgh
Brook Cl
Badminton
Gv
Burnley
Way
Helmsley
Dr
Burghley
Ms
Lowther
Mulgrave
Middleham
Way
Chilton
Grindon
Whitton
Grange
Court
Woodham Burn

3

Low Copelaw

Woodham
Comprehensive
School
Wolsey
Close
Hylton Close
Washington Crs
Nelle
Rd
Defoe Crs
Escomb
Cl
Wren Cl
St
Oswalds
Ct
Wycliffe Cl
Felton
CENTRAL AVENUE
St Marys RC
Primary School
Wiseman
Langley Rd
Eden Road
AVENUE
Stanfield
Shield
WK
Ramsay
Place
Denham
Vane Road
County Junior & Infant Sch
Vane
Road
Welbury Gv
Burner
Biscop
Crs
Shafto
Way
Heild
Cl
Warburton
Close
Court
Hatfield Road
Fowler Rd
Bek Rd
Liddell Cl
Crescent

4

Aycliffe
School
New Cl
Brough Cl

5

County
Infant School
Skinner
eraton
Road
Shafto
Road
Granby
D   **E**
swan
Moore Lane
Gunn
Lane
Henderson
Crawl

55

High Cow

F

A167(T)

CS
1 Ashcombe Cl
2 Calder Cl
3 Hazelmere Cl
4 Humber Gv
5 Lowther Cl
6 Ribble Cl

A B C

I

The Wynd

ington Drive

COAL LANE

A689

Samsung Av

2

Futhorpe Rd

Mountstewart

The Wynd

3

Warren
Farm

Wynyard

4

Wynyard Road

Sandy Lane

A19(T)

Wolviston Mill

6

Eden Way

St Pauls
RC
Primary
School

5

Wilmire
House

4

Severn Gv

2

White
House
Farm

1

White

Avon Gv

Rudston

3

Lenham Cl

A B C

Knapton Av

Ganton Cl

Skipton

6

House

Hart

Tanton

2

3

1 grid square represents 500 metres

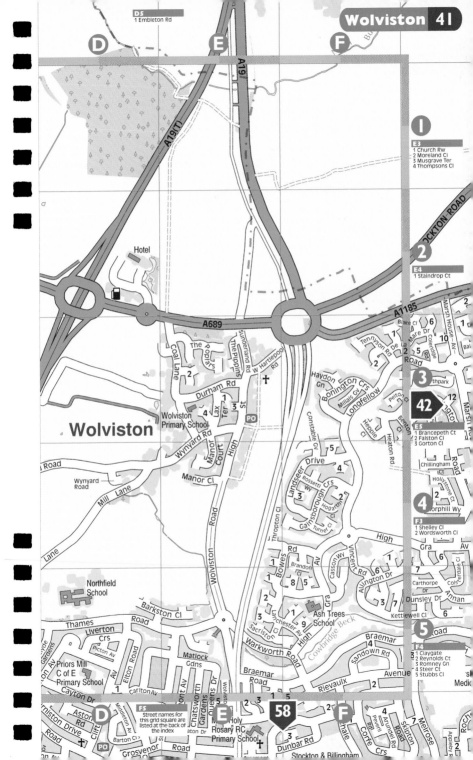

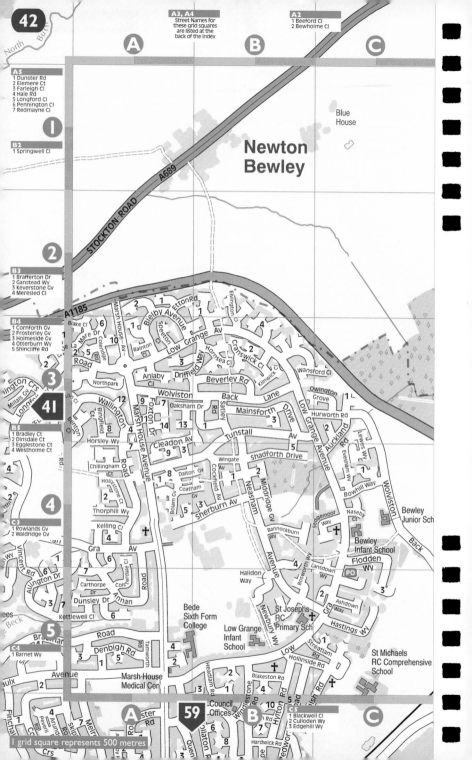

42

A3, A4
Street Names for
these grid squares
are listed at the
back of the index

A2
1 Beeford Cl
2 Bewholme Cl

North Burn

A **B** **C**

A5
1 Dunster Rd
2 Elemere Ct
3 Farleigh Cl
4 Hale Rd
5 Longford Cl
6 Pennington Cl
7 Redmayne

Blue
House

1

**Newton
Bewley**

B2
1 Springwell Cl

A689

STOCKTON ROAD

2

B3
1 Brafferton Dr
2 Ganstead Wy
3 Keverstone Gv
4 Meresied Cl

A1185

Etton Rd

Bielby Avenue

B4
1 Cornforth Gv
2 Frosterley Gv
3 Holmeside Gv
4 Otterburn Wy
5 Shincliffe Rd

Blake Cl

Mare Dr

Coleridge

Speeton

Low Grange Av

Bainton

Cranswick Cl

Hornsea Cl

Wansford Cl

Anlaby
Cl

Drifield Wy

Beverley Rd

Kilnwick

Northpark

Wolviston

Back

Lane

Owington
Grove

3

Millais Gv

Longford

41

Wallington

Foxton
Cl

Marsh House Avenue

Oaksham Dr

Mainsforth

Drive

Low Grange Avenue

Hurworth Rd

Auckland Rd

Lewes Wy

Evesham Wy

Wolviston

Benson

Bingfield

Horsley Wy

8

14 **13**

Tunstall

Cleadon Av

9 **3**

Shadforth Drive

5

Bowhill Way

B5
1 Bradley Ct
2 Dinsdale Ct
3 Egglestone Ct
4 Westholme Ct

Chillingham

Hollystone Ct

Dalton Gv

Coatham

Wingate
Av

Cockfield Av

Neasham

Midridge Gv

Naseby

Bewley
Junior Sch

Thorphill Wy

Bolam Gv

Sherburn Av

Back

C3
1 Rowlands Gv
2 Waldridge Gv

Kelling Cl

Bannockburn
Wy

Sedgemoor
Way

Bewley
Infant School

Gra

Av

Vincent Rd

Allington Dr

Carthorpe

Cols

Ferdale Cr

Annan

Road

Halidon
Way

Bosworth Wy

Newbury Wy

Avenue

Lansdown

Flodden
Wy

PO

Dunsley Dr

Kettlewell Cl

Ashdown
Way

Hastings Wy

Bede
Sixth Form
College

Low Grange
Infant
School

St Josephs
RC
Primary Sch

5

Braemar

Rees Beck

C4
1 Barnet Wy

Road

Denbigh Rd

Tamworth

Headlam Rd

Windlestone

Blakeston Rd

Hollinside Rd

Streatlam Rd

Low

Hylton Rd

St Michaels
RC Comprehensive
School

Marsh House
Medical Cen

Avenue

Aster
Rd

A **59** **B** **C**

Council
Offices

C5
1 Blackwell Cl
2 Culloden Wy
3 Edgehill Wy

Quen

Dilaton

Redworth

Hardwick Rd

I grid square represents 500 metres

Meadows

D E 30 F

I

Field
House
Farm

2

3

44

Hartlepool
Stockton-on-Tees

4

A1185

ool

Cemetery

5

Fore
Marsh

Lane

LC

Cowpen
Bewley

Cowpen Lane

Marsh

Lane

D Royce Av E 60 F

Bentley Av

Avenue

Cowpen Bewl

Lag
Ro

1

D E **32** F

I

Works

A178

TEES ROAD

2

Hartlepool

Stockton - on - Tees

3

46

River Tees

4

5

A178

SEATON CAREW ROAD

D E **62** F

46

A   33   B   Hartlepool Power Station Visitor Centre   C

Seaton-on-Tees Channel

1

2

Hartlepool
Stockton - on - Tees

3

45

4

5

Seal
Sands

A   63   B   C

I grid square represents 500 metres

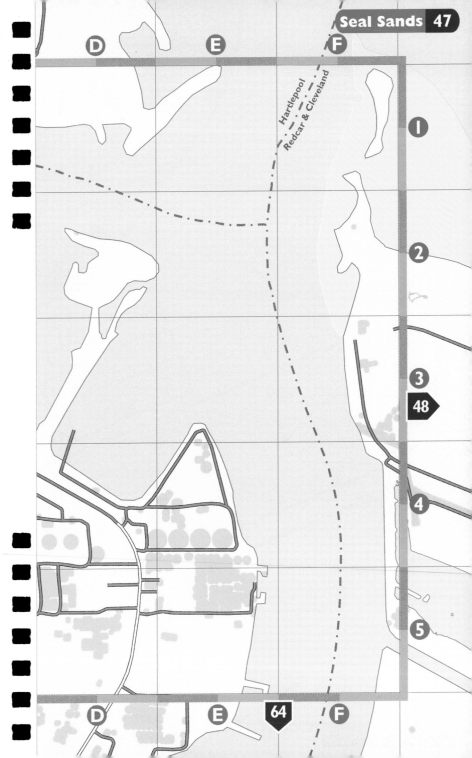

A   B   C

1

Bran
Sands

2

3
47

4

5

A   65   B   C

1 grid square represents 500 metres

D E F

I

2

Coatham
Sands

3

50 ▶

War

4

Tod Point

5

C
M

Teesdale Way

D E 66 F

British Steel
Redcar Station

A B C

C4
1 Rocket Ter

C5
1 Hamilton Gv
2 Hornsea Gv

1

2

3

49

Golf
Course

4

Warrenby

Coath

Bridge Road

Snipe Street

Marina Av

High

St

Coatham C of E
Primary School

Church St

Tod Point Road

York Road

Harval Rd

Kirkleatham

1

1

2

Newland Communi
Mental Health Cen

Homleigh Gv

Priory Grove

5

Coatham
Marsh

Kirkleatham Lane

COR

Severn
Road

Gordon Road

Greta Rd

Derwent Rd

Forth Road

A

67

TRUNK ROAD

385

B

Lovat Avenue

Duncan Avenue

Atholl Gv

C

Teesdale Way

I grid square represents 500 metres

TS10

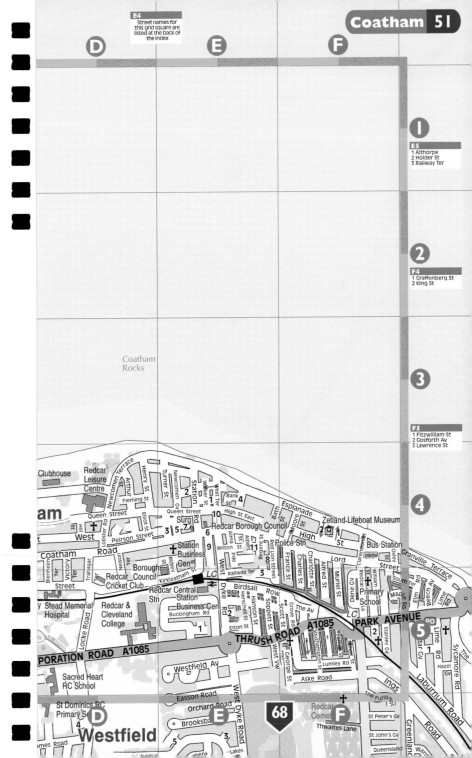

E4 Street names for this grid square are listed at the back of the index

D E F

I

E5
1 Althorpe
2 Holder St
3 Railway Ter

2

F4
1 Graffenberg St
2 King St

3

Coatham Rocks

F5
1 Fitzwilliam St
2 Gosforth Av
3 Lawrence St

4

Clubhouse
Redcar Leisure Centre
Newcomen Terrace
Henry St
Arthur
Turner St
Fleming St
Station
Walker St
West Ter
Bank St
Esplanade
Zetland Lifeboat Museum
Queen Street
Queen Street
High St East
Redcar Borough Council
Eliot St
Surg
Peirson Street
3 5 7 2
10
6
9
Police Stn
Bus Station
am
West
Coatham
Blenheim
Victory Ter
Trafalgar
Nelson Ter
Ridley
Ter
Station Business Cen
Wilton
Alma
Albert St
High St
France St
Charles St
Charlotte St
Lord
Alfred St
Muriel St
Cranville Terrace
Oxley Ter
South Ter
Beech Av
Elm Gv
Lime Gv
Road
Borough
Redcar Council Cricket Club
Kirkleatham
LC
Railway Ter
West
Redcar Primary School
William St
Maple Gv
y Stead Memorial Hospital
Locke Road
Redcar & Cleveland College
Redcar Central Stn
Business Centre
Buckingham Rd
Birdsall
Dyke Rd
Herschel St
Hanson St
Soppett St
Row
Scott St
Grove Rd
The Av
LC
Hazel Gv
1
2
1
Sacred Heart RC School
ORATION ROAD A1085
Westfield Av
Elton St
THRUSH ROAD A1085
George St
Southampton St
Lumley Rd
Yeoman St
PARK AVENUE
Stanley Gv
Laburnum Road
Sycamore Rd
bar Gv
The
St Dominics RC Primary S
Easson Road
Orchard Road
Brooksba
West VW
Aske Road
Ings
The Furlongs
Redcar Ceme
St Peter's Gv
St John's Gv
Queensland
Greenlan
Road
War
4
D
E
68
F
5
Westfield
ames Road
5
3
Lakes
Thwaites Lane

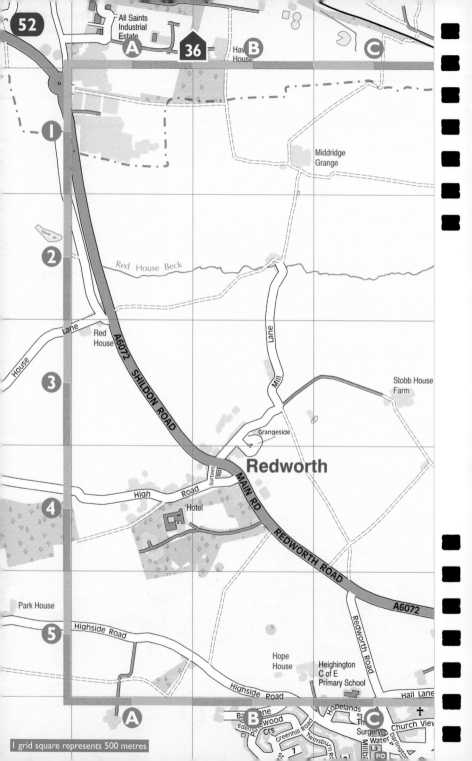

52

All Saints
Industrial
Estate

A

36

Hav
House

B

C

A6072

1

Middridge
Grange

2

Red House Beck

House Lane

Red
House

Lane

Mill

Stobb House
Farm

A6072 SHILDON ROAD

3

Grangeside

Redworth

High Road

Surtees Rd

Hotel

MAIN RD

4

REDWORTH ROAD

A6072

Park House

Highside Road

5

Hope
House

Heighington
C of E
Primary School

Redworth Road

Highside Road

Hall Lane

A

Ba Lane

B

Eden
Crs

Pinewood
Crs

Greenhill Road

Hopelands

Twinsburn Rd

Th
Surgery

Water
Millbk

Darlington

C

Church View

PO

1 grid square represents 500 metres

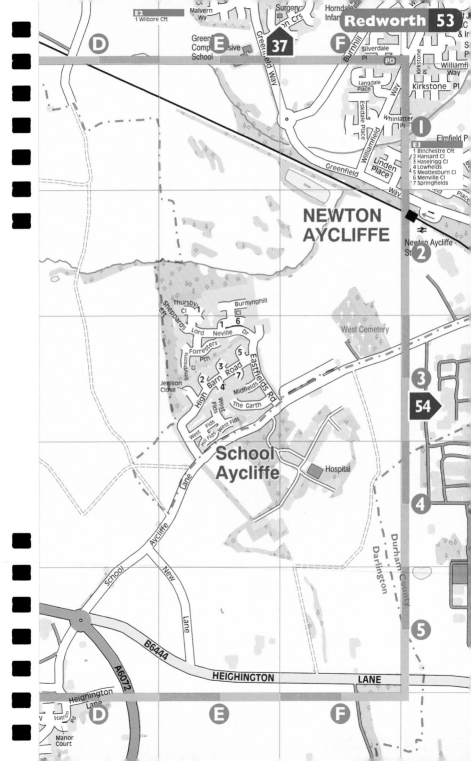

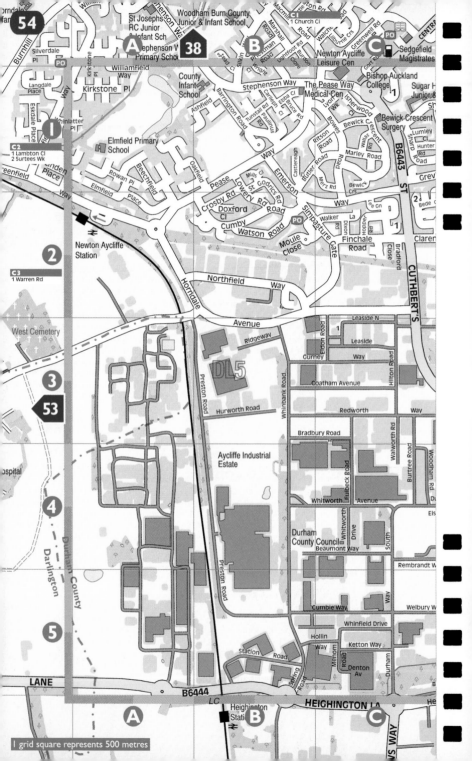

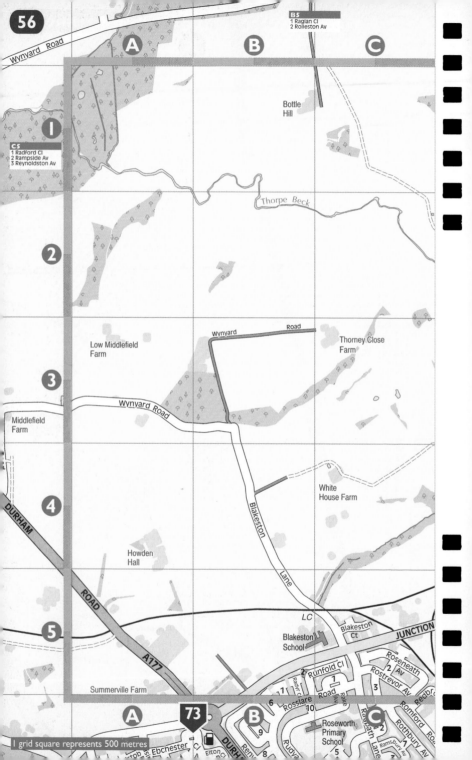

Wynyard Road

A   B   C

Bottle
Hill

1

Thorpe Beck

2

Wynyard   Road

Thorney Close
Farm

Low Middlefield
Farm

3

Wynyard Road

Middlefield
Farm

4

Blakeston Lane

White
House Farm

DURHAM

Howden
Hall

ROAD

LC

5

Blakeston
Ct

JUNCTION

Blakeston
School

A177

Roseneath

Rostrevor Av

Runfold Cl

2 Av

3

Raby Cl

Summerville Farm

Rosslare

Road

Rake Ln

Rudyard

Redbro

Romford Ro

Rothbury Av

A   73   B   C

Roseworth
Primary
School

Ebchester   Elton Cl   Renn   Rudy   Ramsbu

Lane

Av

2

5

8

9

10

6

7

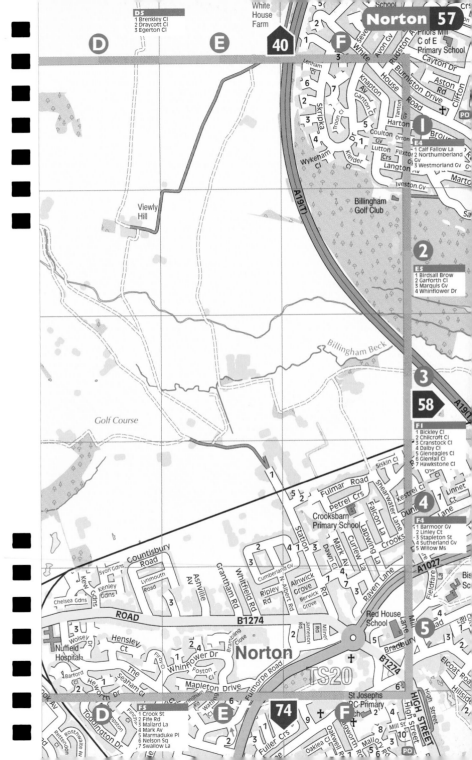

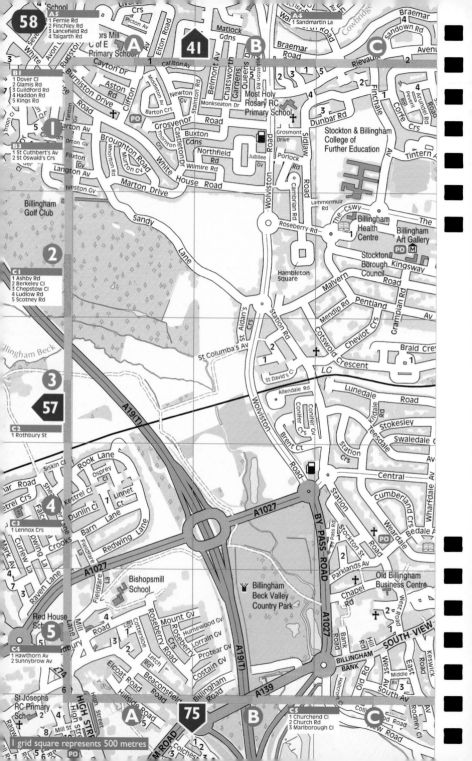

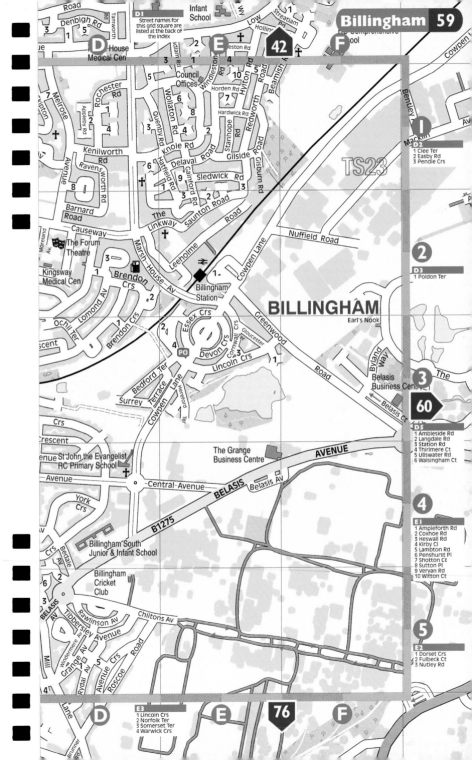

Billingham 59

TS23

BILLINGHAM

Earl's Nook

D1 Street names for this grid square are listed at the back of the index

D2
1 Clee Ter
2 Easby Rd
3 Pendle Crs

D3
1 Poldon Ter

60

D5
1 Ambleside Rd
2 Langdale Rd
3 Station Rd
4 Thirlmere Ct
5 Ullswater Rd
6 Walsingham Ct

E1
1 Ampleforth Rd
2 Coxhoe Rd
3 Heswall Rd
4 Kirby Cl
5 Lambton Rd
6 Penshurst Pl
7 Shotton Ct
8 Sutton Pl
9 Veryan Rd
10 Witton Ct

E2
1 Dorset Crs
2 Fulbeck Ct
3 Nutley Rd

E3
1 Lincoln Crs
2 Norfolk Ter
3 Somerset Ter
4 Warwick Crs

76

Haverton Hill 61

D5
1 Beech Ter
2 Holly Ter
3 Poplar Ter
4 Port Clarence Rd
5 Sycamore Ter
6 Willow Ter

Fore

Saltholme

Ash St
Oak St
Elm St
Clarence St

Lime Tree
Close

Fieldview
Cl
Saltholme
Meadowdale
Cl
Rugby Ter

Cambridge
Terrace

Community
Farm

Port Clarence

PO

High
Clarence
Primary
School

ROAD

Westlowt

SEATON CAREW ROAD

SEATON CAREW

62

A

45

B

C

SEATON CAREW ROAD

1

2

3

61

4

5

TS2

A

79

B

C

SEATON CAREW ROAD

1 grid square represents 500 metres

River Tees

Riverside Rd

Riverside Road

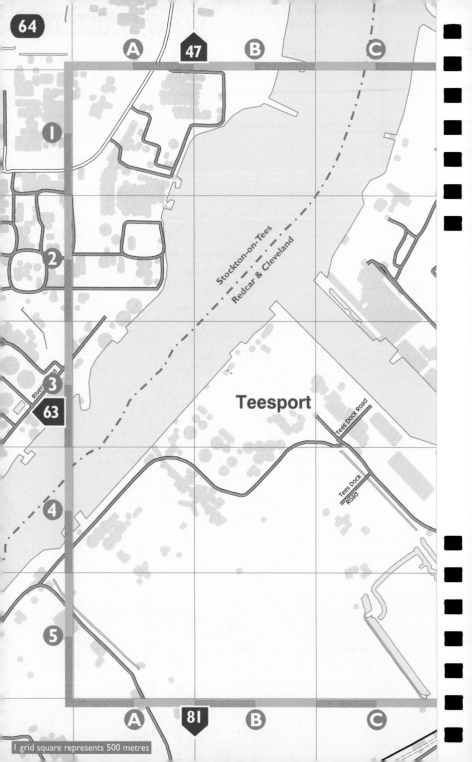

64

A 47 B C

1

2

Stockton-on-Tees
Redcar & Cleveland

River Rd
3
63

Teesport

Tees Dock Road

Tees Dock
Road

4

5

A 81 B C

1 grid square represents 500 metres

66

A
49
B
C

1

British Steel
Redcar Station

Limerick

2

Teesdale   Way

West Coatham   Lane

Wilton Avenue

Broadway West

3

65

A1085

4

TRUNK ROAD

5

A
83
B
C

1 grid square represents 500 metres

Wilton Works

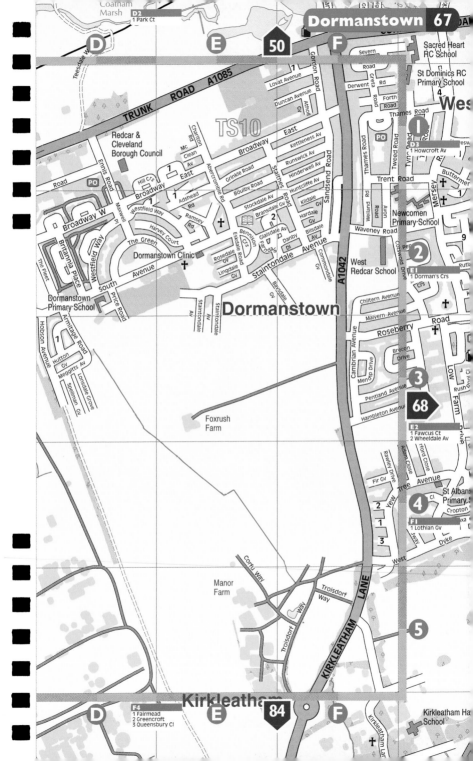

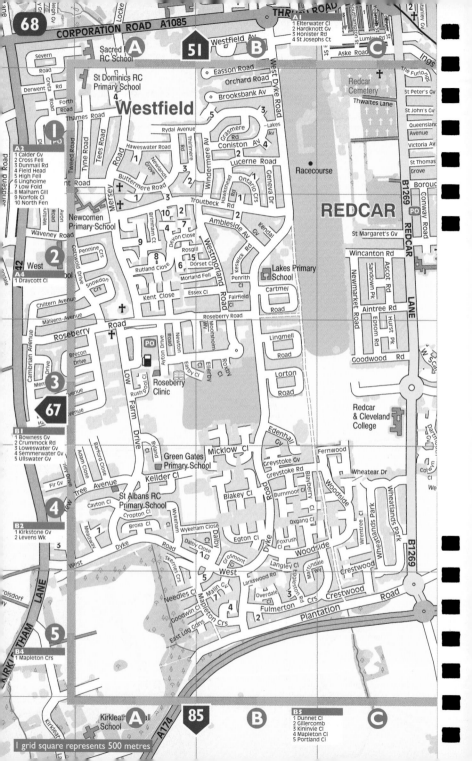

D1
1 The Larches
2 Malcolm Gv
3 The Willows

D2
1 Bolton Cl
2 Nottingham Dr
3 Rochester Dr
4 Skelton Dr

I

D3
1 Berkeley Dr
2 Conisborough Dr
3 Cormorant Dr
4 The Hampstead
5 Hayburn Cl
6 High Stone Cl
7 Homerell Cl
8 Lavernock Cl
9 Luff Wy
10 Rothesay Dr

2

D4
1 Kinmel Cl
2 Shoreham Cl
3 Torcross Wy
4 Wembury Cl

A108

E1
1 Salisbury Gv

3

70

E2
1 Alnwick Cl
2 Whitby Crs

MARSKE
THE-SEA

4

E3
1 Druridge Gv
2 Seaton Cl
3 Stoupe Cl
4 White Stone Cl

5

Redcar R

Ryan's

E4
1 St Ives Cl
2 Seaham Cl
3 Shaidon Cl
4 Sheringham Ct

Longbeck Station

A174   86

F5
1 Westfield Rd

F4
1 De Havilland Dr

Rye Hills
School

Redcar
East
Station

Primary
School

Warwick

Walworth Cl

Kilton Cl

The Leas

Greenstones

Primary
School

Chester Rd

PO

Kenilworth

Scalby Gv   The Strand

Filey

The Green

Trevarrian Dr

Redcar   Road

Grewgrass
Farm

Grewgrass Lane

Cat Flatt Lane

Green Lane

Redcar Road

Cleveland Vw

Green La

Coast Road

Laburnum Road

A1085

Lilac Grove

Chestnut Av

Oak   Road

Cypress Rd

Laurel Rd

Zetland Rd

Canterbury Rd

Ripon Road

Durham Rd

Winchester Road

Beverley Road

Norwich Rd

Durham Rd

A   B   C

A4
1 Folland Dr
2 Lancaster Dr

A5
1 The Landings
2 Lysander Ct
3 Spitfire Cl

B4
1 Mariners Ct
2 Wanstead Cl

69

B5
1 Greenacres Cl
2 Inglewood Av
3 Kerridge Cl
4 Raisbeck Cl
5 St Mark's Cl
6 Yeoman Ter

A1085 COAST ROAD

Scanbeck Howle

MARSKE-BY-THE-SEA

Bydales School

Marlborough Avenue

Churchill Drive

C4
1 Church St

Headlands

The Firlands

The Kirklands

St Germain's

Vickers Cl
Beardmore Av
Wallis Way
Brabazon Dr
Barnes
Woodford Close
Chartwell Cl
Churchill Drive
Wellington
Halifax Cl
Westgarth

Spencer

Blenheim Cl

Primary School

Dovecote Cl

Marske Clnc

The Garth

Church La
Valley

High St
The Wynd

Church
Vicarage Drive
Church
School

Primary School

Pennyman
Scanbeck Drive Wk
Kirkleatham

Hummershill

Marske Cricket Club

Zetland

Cleveland Vw
Redcar Road
Northfield Rd
Middlefield Rd
Eastfield Rd
Highfield Rd

Redcar Av

Ryan's Rw
The Dr

Falklands Cl
Driftswood Dr
Dene Wk
Sherwood

Wheatlands
Mickledales Dr
Epping

Grundales Dr
Fir Rig Dr

Fell Briggs

Redcar Road

Doctors Surg
PO

East St
Chapel St
Chapel Cl

HIGH STREET

Mt Pleasant Av
Southfield Rd
East Mdw

Hill Lane
Windy

Lavender

Meadow Road

Lane

Longbeck Station

87

Marske Station

C5
1 Adelaide Pl
2 Fitzwilliam Cl
3 Prospect Ter
4 St Germain's Gv
5 Scrafton Pl
6 Zetland Rd

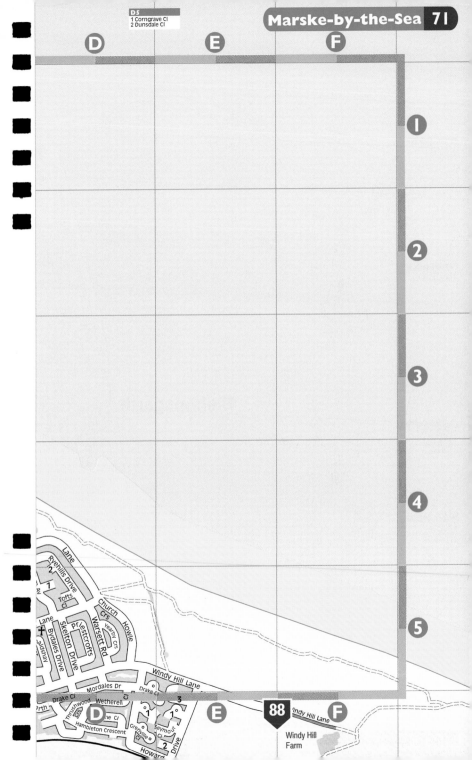

D5
1 Corngrave Cl
2 Dunsdale Cl

D

E

F

1

2

3

4

5

Lane

Ryehills Drive
2
1
Tofts Cl
Howle
Church
Crs
Priestcrofts
Warsett Rd
Yeasby Crs
Skelton Drive
Bydales Drive
Audshav
Westcrofts
Skelton Lane

Windy Hill Lane

Mordales Dr
Drake Cl
Drake Cl
Wetherell Cl
Drake Cl
3
Trushwood
ne Cl
1
Hambleton Crescent
Grenville Cl
Seymour
2
Drive

rth

88 Windy Hill Lane

Windy Hill
Farm

Howard

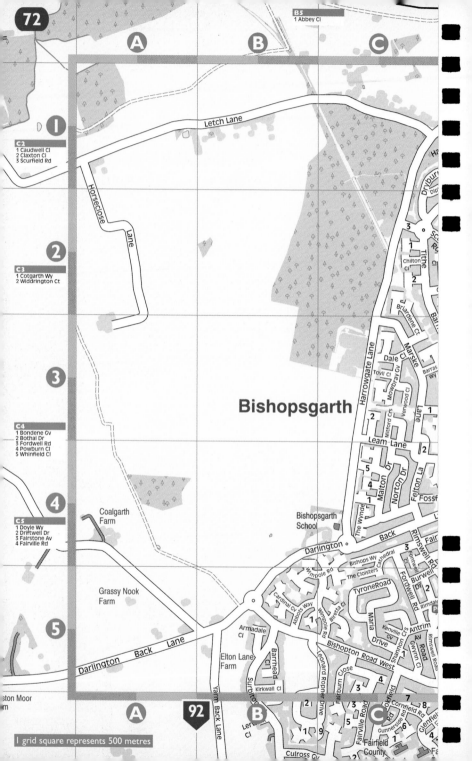

A   B   C

B5
1 Abbey Cl

1

C2
1 Caudwell Cl
2 Claxton Cl
3 Scurfield Rd

Letch Lane

Horseclose Lane

2

C3
1 Cotgarth Wy
2 Widdrington Ct

Dryburn

Har

Tithe

Chilton Cl

Briardene Ct

Harrowgate Lane

Dale Cl

Tovil Cl

Mowbray Gv

Verwood Cl

Marske Lane

Barras Wy

3

Bishopsgarth

C4
1 Bondene Gv
2 Bothal Dr
3 Fordwell Rd
4 Powburn Cl
5 Whinfield Cl

Mitford Crs

Leam Lane

Malton Dr

Norton Dr

Felton La

Fossf

4

Coalgarth Farm

C5
1 Doyle Wy
2 Driftwell Dr
3 Fairstone Av
4 Fairville Rd

The Wynd

Bishopsgarth School

Back

Darlington

Rimswell Rd

Fair

Bishops Wy

The Cloisters

Cathedral

Fordwell

Burwell Dr

Wimpole Rd

Tyrone Road

Fordwell Rd

Rimdale

Grassy Nook Farm

Cardinal Gv

Abbots Way

Wimpole Rd

Biretta Cl

Maria Drive

Kenville Crs

Shannon

Gwynn Cl

Antrim Av

Rimswell Road

5

Darlington Back Lane

Armadale Cl

Elton Lane Farm

Barmead

Surbiton

Kirkwall Cl

Leonard Ropner Drive

Bishopton Road West

Fairburn Close

Cockfield

Cornfield Rd

Glenfield

ston Moor

Yarm Back Lane

Len
Cl

Fairville Road

Fairfield County

Gunnerside Cl

A   **92**   B   C

Culross Gv

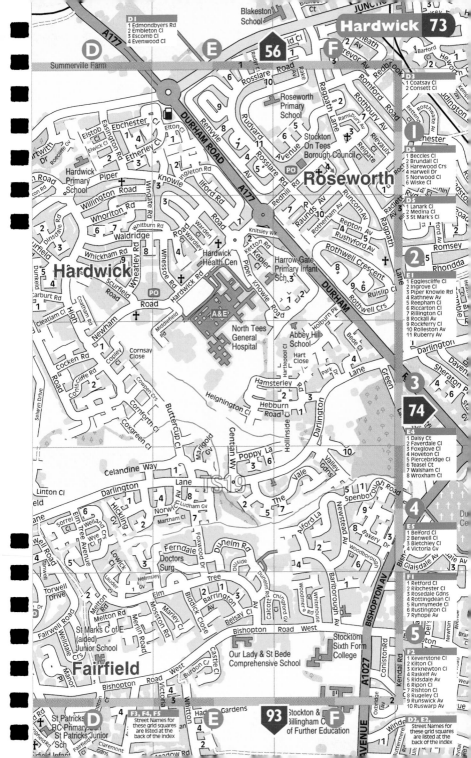

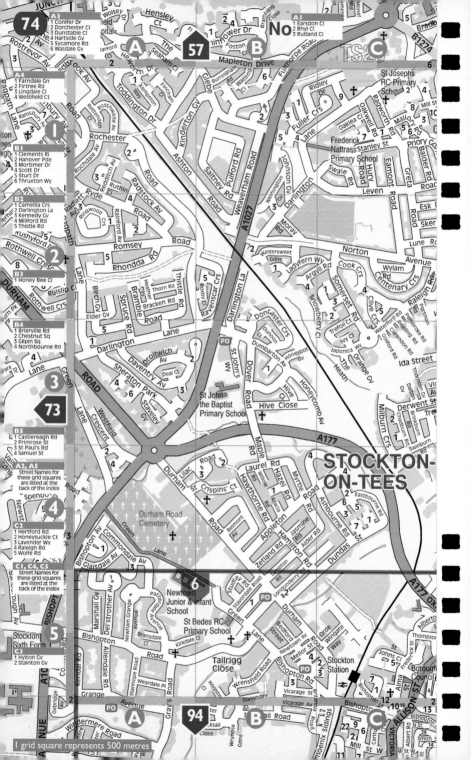

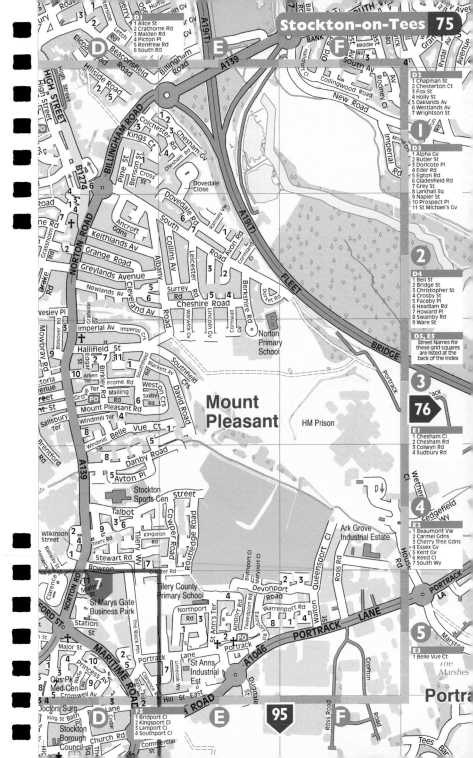

Mount Pleasant

HM Prison

Ark Grove Industrial Estate

Stockton Sports Cen

St Marys Gate Business Park

Tilery County Primary School

St Anns Industrial Est

Norton Primary School

Dovedale Close

Portrack

The Marshes

76

95

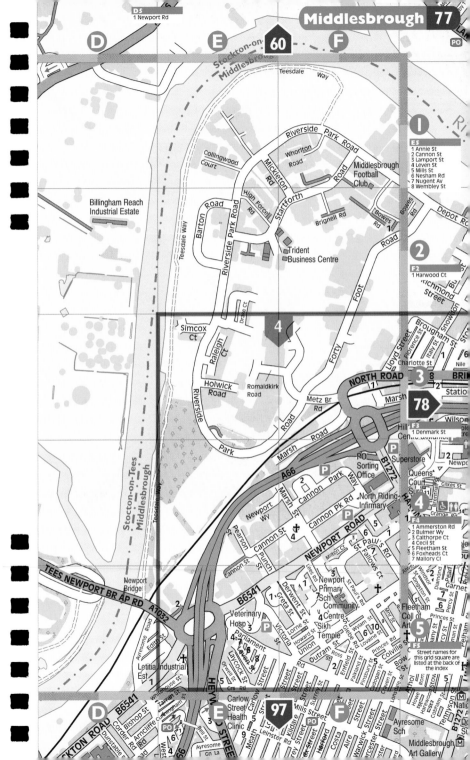

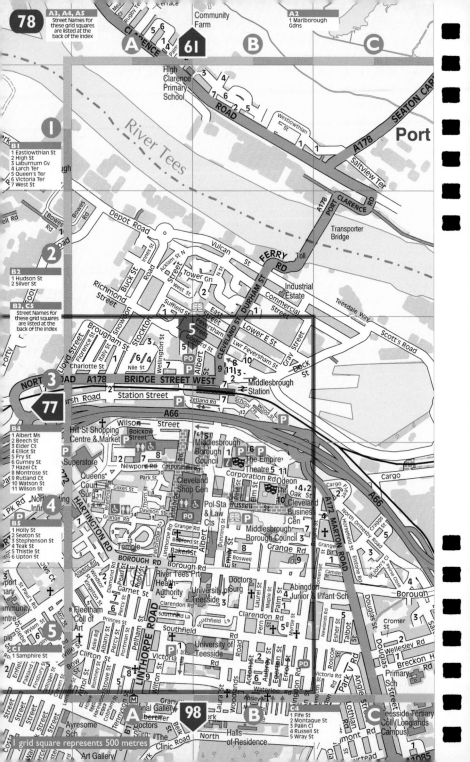

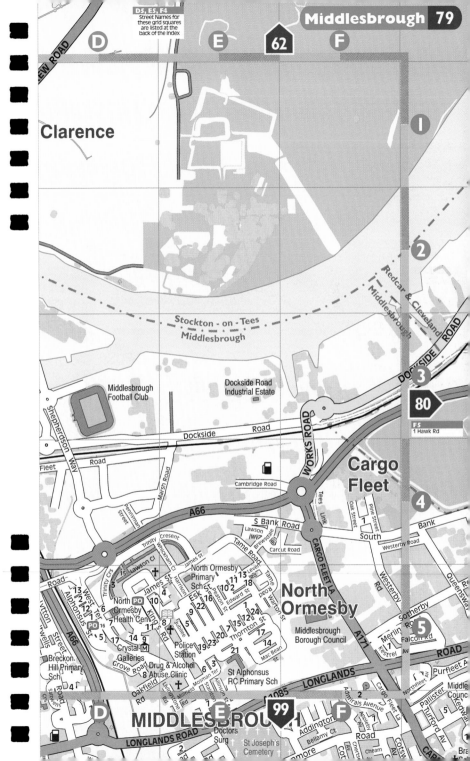

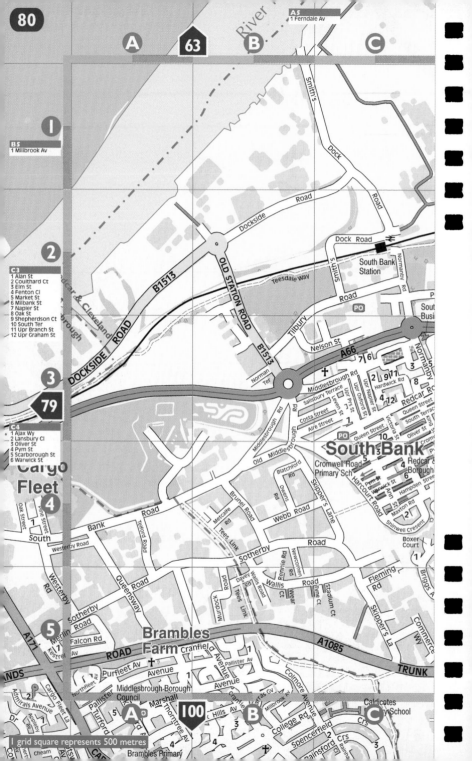

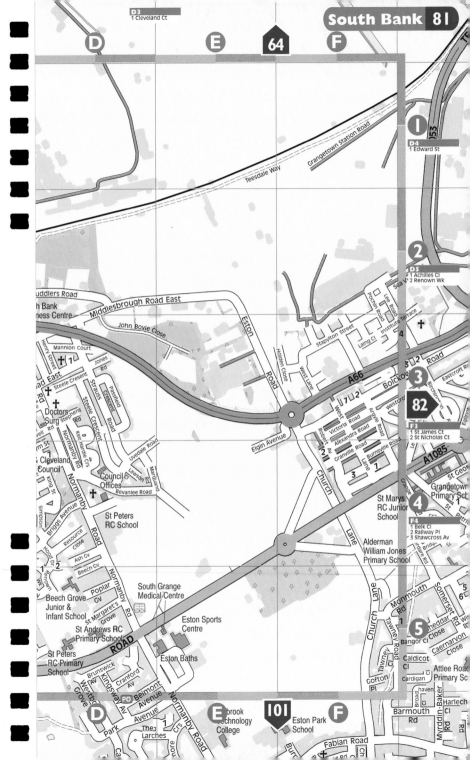

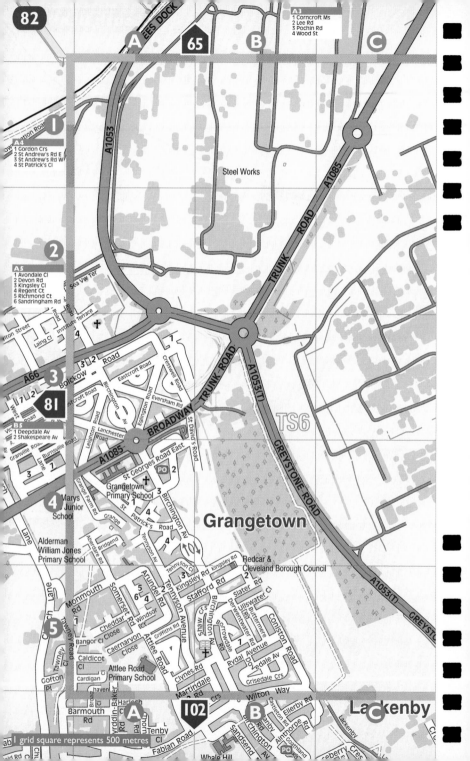

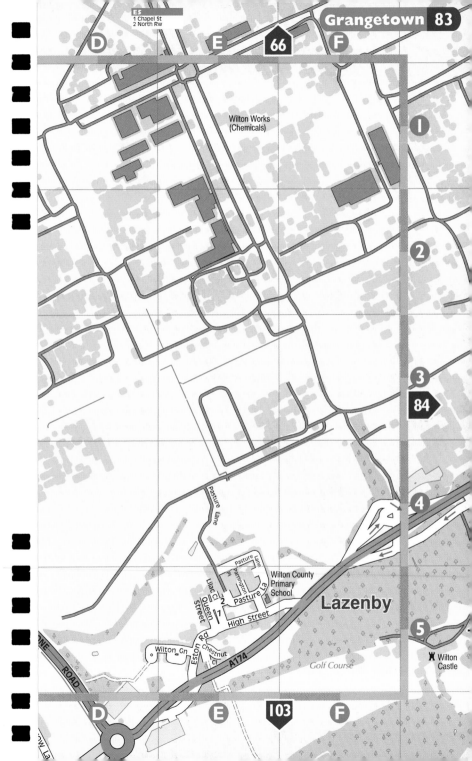

D

E

66

F

I

ES
1 Chapel St
2 North Rw

Wilton Works
(Chemicals)

2

3

84

4

Pasture Lane

Pasture Lane

Lilac Cl

Parrington

Pasture La

Wilton County
Primary
School

Queen Street

7

High Street

Lazenby

Eston Rd

Chestnut Cl

Wilton Gn

A174

Golf Course

5

Wilton
Castle

D

E

103

F

ROAD

W La

84

A **67** B C

Kirkleatham

Kirkleatham Old Hall
Museum Ⓜ

A1042

A174

Kirkleatham Lane

Troisd

KIRKLEATH

1

2

3
83

4

azenby

Wilton

Wilton

A174

Wilton Lane

Wilton Lane

5

☩
✠ Wilton
Castle

A **104** B C

1 grid square represents 500 metres

Bank Top
Farm

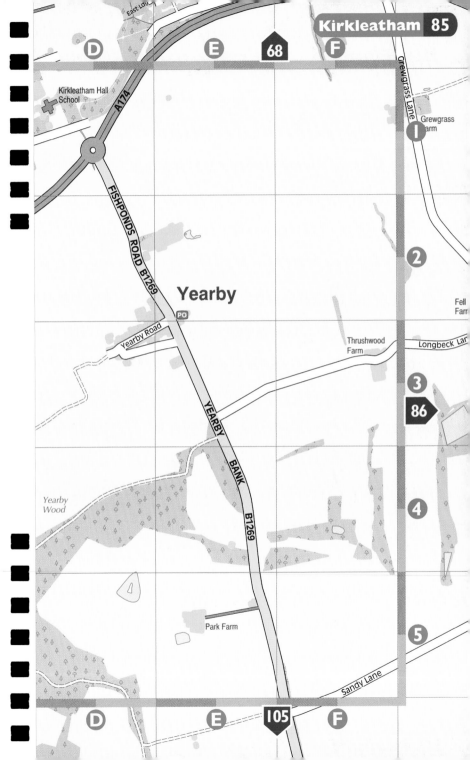

D   E   68   F

Grewgrass Lane

Kirkleatham Hall School

A174

Grewgrass Farm

1

2

Fell Farm

Yearby

PO

Yearby Road

Thrushwood Farm

Longbeck Lane

3

86

YEARBY BANK

B1269

Yearby Wood

4

Park Farm

5

Sandy Lane

D   E   105   F

86

A **69** B **C**

B3
Street names for
this grid square are
listed at the back of
the index

Cat Flatt Lane

A174

Grewgrass Farm

1

Gurney Street

Pontac Road

2

Fell Briggs Farm

Thrushwood Farm

Longbeck Lane

Victoria Cl

PO

Dale St

Beacon Dr

3

85

Merion Dr

Lindrick Road

Hartsbourne Crs

Fulford Gv

Birkdale

St Andrew's Rd

Gleneagles Rd

9 **12**
4
6
6
5

1
4

Kilbridge Cl

Sunningdale Rd

Brancepeth Cl

Parkstone Cl

4 **3**

8

13

2

Ashridge Cl

Moortown Rd

Sandmoor Road

3

Pinehurst Wy

Ryder Cl

Coxmoor Wy

10

Infant School

7

Primary School

St George's Crs

Carnoustie Rd

2
1

Kingsdown Wy

Harlech Gv

Hinscliffe Cv

Coombe Hl

1

5

Allendale Tee

Walmer Crs

7

Woodbrook Cl

Rosemount Rd

11 **7**

Turnberry Dr

Hillside Cl

4

New Buildings Farm

5

Sandy Lane

A **106** B C

I grid square represents 500 metres

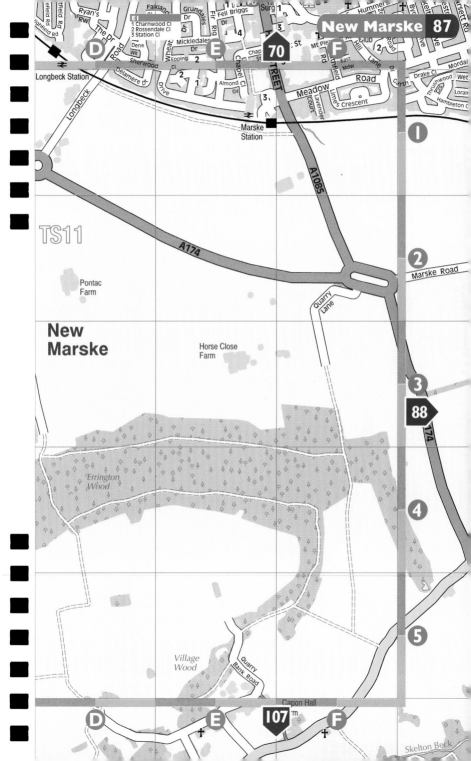

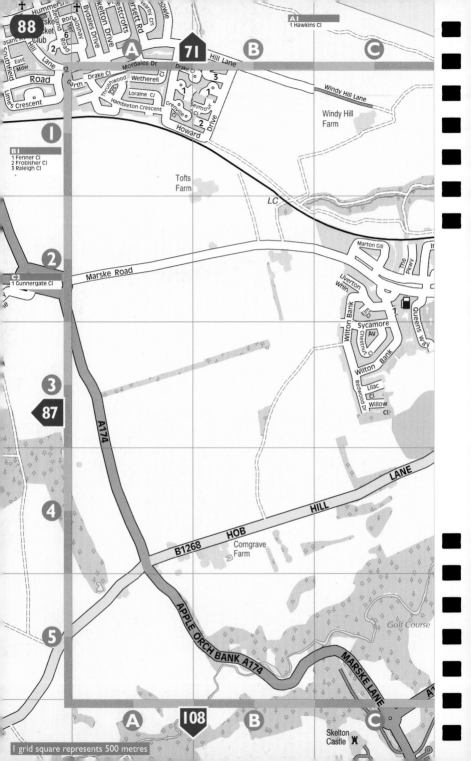

88

71

87

108

A   B   C

1   2   3   4   5

A1
1 Hawkins Cl

B1
1 Fenner Cl
2 Frobisher Cl
3 Raleigh Cl

C2
1 Gunnergate Cl

Hummershill

Zetland

Cricket Club

Bradshaw

Road

East Mdw

Southfield

Road

Lime's Crescent

Westcrofts

Dorsett Rd

Bowie

Skelton Drive

Bydales Drive

Hill Lane

Mordales Dr

Drake Cl

Wetherell

Trushwood

Loraine Cl

Hambleton Crescent

Grenville Cl

Seymour Cl

Howard   Drive

Hill Lane

Windy Hill Lane

Windy Hill Farm

Tofts Farm

LC

Marton Gill

The Pkwy

Liverton Whin

Wilton Bank

Elm Cl

Sycamore Av

Chestnut Cl

Wilton Bank

Redwood Dr

Lilac Cl

Willow Cl

Queens Way

Marske Road

A174

B1268

HOB   HILL   LANE

Corngrave Farm

APPLE ORCH BANK A174

MARSKE LANE

Golf Course

Skelton Castle

1 grid square represents 500 metres

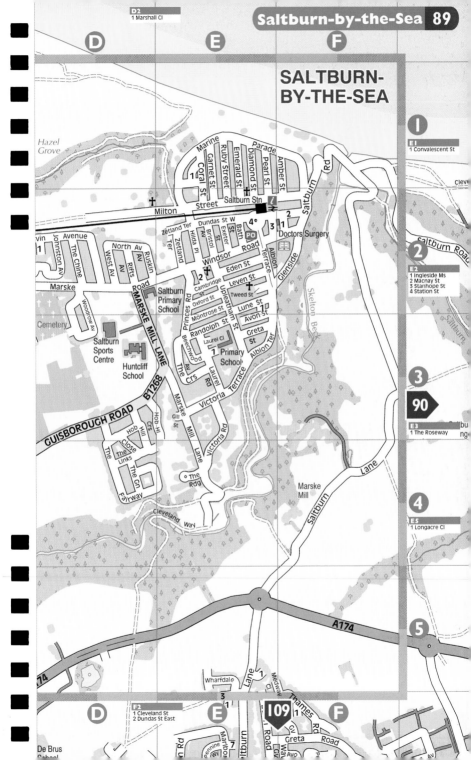

SALTBURN-BY-THE-SEA

D2
1 Marshall Cl

E1
1 Convalescent St

E2
1 Ingleside Ms
2 Macnay St
3 Stanhope St
4 Station St

E3
1 The Roseway

90

E5
1 Longacre Cl

109

F2
1 Cleveland St
2 Dundas St East

Hazel Grove

Marine
Coral St
Garnet St
Ruby Street
Emerald St
Diamond St
Parade
Pearl St
Amber St
Saltburn Rd

Milton Street
Saltburn Stn

Zetland Ter
Zetland Ter
Ruskin
Zetland
Hilda Pl
Bristol Ter
Dundas St W
Exeter St
Bath St
PO
Doctors Surgery
Glenside

Johnston Av
The Chine
vin Avenue
North Av
West AV
Rifts AV

Marske Road

Windsor Road
Cambridge St
Eden St
Leven St
Albion Terrace

Saltburn Primary School

Princes Rd
Oxford St
Upleatham St
Tweed St
Lune St
Avon St

Montrose St
Randolph St
Beechwood
Laurel Cl
Greta St
Albion Ter

Cemetery

Woodrow Av

Saltburn Sports Centre

Huntcliff School

MARSKE MILL LANE

B1268

GUISBOROUGH ROAD

The Crs
Laurel Rd
Marske Mill Lane
Gill St

Primary School

Victoria Terrace
Victoria Rd

Hob Hill
Hob Crs
Close
The Links
The Gn
Fairway

The Rdg

Cleveland Way

Skelton Beck

Marske Mill

Saltburn Lane

Saltburn Lane

A174

74

Wharfdale

Lane
Medway Rd
Thames Rd

Marlboro

Pennine

Greta Road

De Brus School

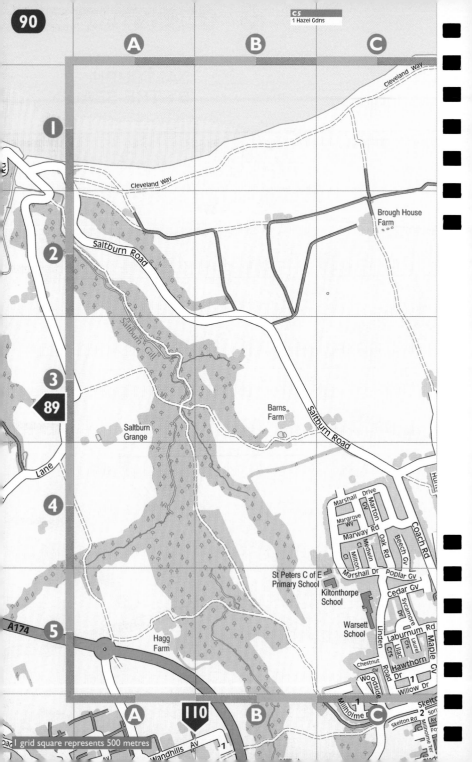

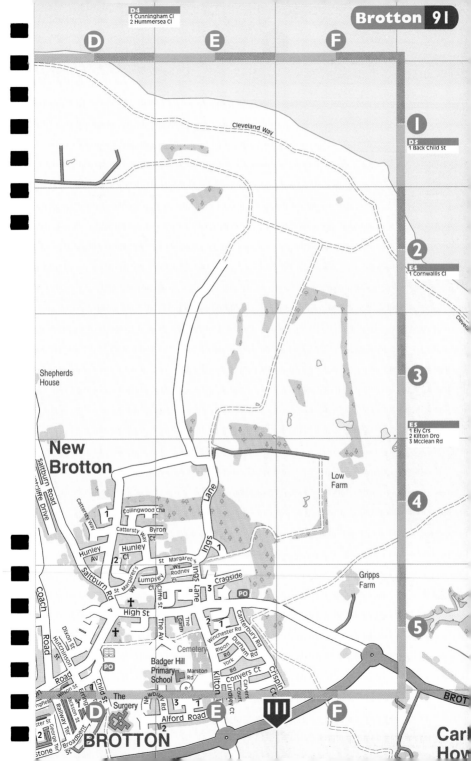

D4
1 Cunningham Cl
2 Hummersea Cl

Cleveland Way

①

D5
1 Back Child St

②

E4
1 Cornwallis Cl

Cleveland

③

Shepherds
House

E5
1 Ely Crs
2 Kilton Dro
3 Mcclean Rd

New Brotton

Low
Farm

④

Saltburn Road
Wycliffe Drive

Cattersty Way

Collingwood Cha

Byron Ct

Cattersty Way

Hunley AV

Hunley Cl

St Margaret's Wy

Rodney Cl

Lumpsey Cl

Ings Lane

Margaret's St

Saltburn Rd

Cragside

⑤

Gripps
Farm

PO

Coach Road

Cliffe St

Ings Lane

The Garth

The Av

Canterbury Rd

Winchester Rd

Durham Rd

Ripon Rd

York Rd

Conyers Ct

Crispin Ct

High St

Dixon St
Hutchinson St

Cemetery

Badger Hill
Primary
School

Marston Rd

Kilton

Carvers Court

Lindsey Ct

Crispin Ct

BROT

PO

Kingfield
Errington St
Jackson St
Wilson St
Child St

The
Surgery

Newbury Rd

Alford Road

D **E** **F**

BROTTON

Railway Ter
George Ter
Broadmeadows St

Carl
How

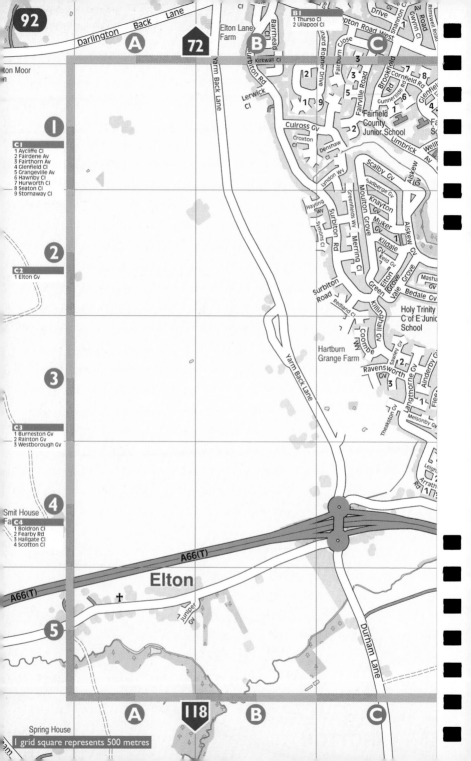

92

72

B1
1 Thurso Cl
2 Ullapool Cl

A   B   C

Darlington Back Lane

Elton Lane Farm

Kirkwall Cl

Surbiton Rd

Lerwick Cl

Culross Gv

Croxton Cl

Denshaw Cl

Fairfield County Junior School

Limbrick

Lyndon Wy

Scalby Gv

Sadberge Gv

Knayton Gv

Muker Gv

Alskew Gv

Kildale Gv

Keld Gv

Green Grove

Elton Vale

Bedale Gv

Masham

C1
1 Aycliffe Cl
2 Fairdene Av
3 Fairthorn Av
4 Glenfield Cl
5 Grangeville Av
6 Hawnby Cl
7 Hurworth Cl
8 Seaton Cl
9 Stornaway Cl

C2
1 Elton Gv

ton Moor

Havring Wy

Surbiton Rd

Symons Cl

Greenfields Wy

Merring Cl

Surbiton Road

Redland Cl

Killinghall Gv

Coombe Wy

Holy Trinity C of E Junior School

Hartburn Grange Farm

Sawler Gv

Ravensworth Gv

Langthorne Gv

Alnderby Gv

Theakston Gv

Meisonby Gv

Leigh

Arrathorne Rd

C3
1 Burneston Gv
2 Rainton Gv
3 Westborough Gv

Smit House Fa

C4
1 Boldron Cl
2 Fearby Rd
3 Hallgate Cl
4 Scotton Cl

A66(T)

Elton

A66(T)

Juniper Gv

Durham Lane

Spring House

A   118   B   C

1 grid square represents 500 metres

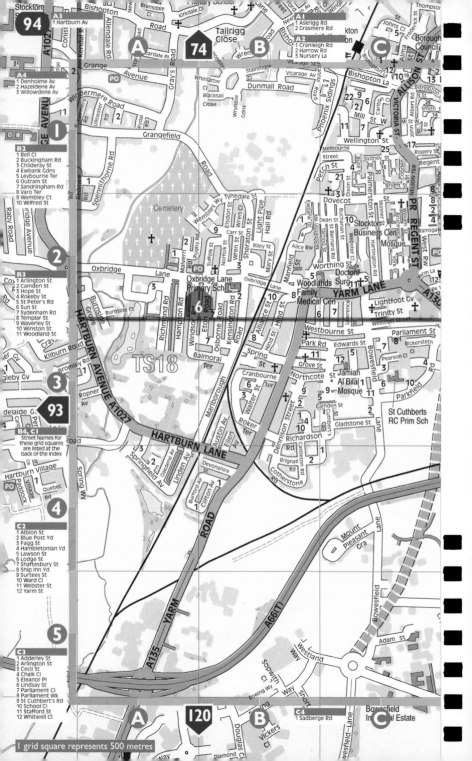

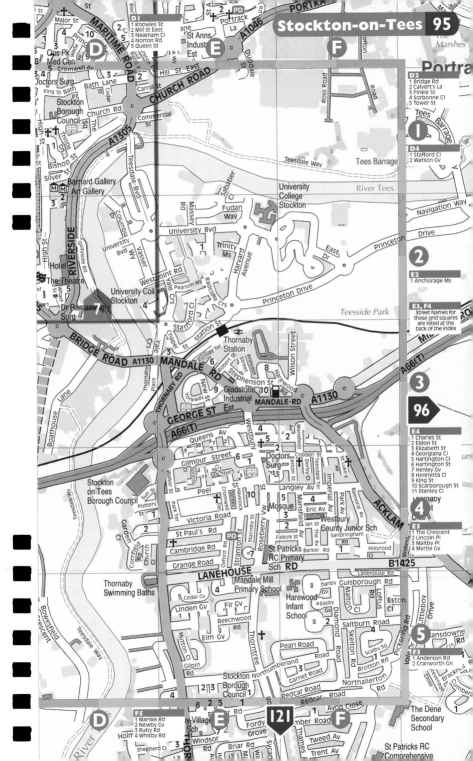

D1
1 Knowles St
2 Mill St East
3 Neasham Cl
4 Norton Rd
5 Queen St

D2
1 Bridge Rd
2 Calvert's La
3 Finkle St
4 Sorbonne Cl
5 Tower St

D4
1 Stafford Cl
2 Watson Gv

E2
1 Anchorage Ms

E3, F4
Street Names for
these grid squares
are listed at the
back of the index

E4
1 Charles St
2 Eldon St
3 Elizabeth St
4 Georgiana Cl
5 Hartington Cl
6 Hartington St
7 Henley Gv
8 Henrietta Cl
9 King St
10 Scarborough St
11 Stanley Cl

E5
1 The Crescent
2 Lincoln Pl
3 Maltby Pl
4 Myrtle Gv

F3
1 Anderson Rd
2 Cranworth Gn

F5
1 Marske Rd
2 Newby Gv
3 Ruby Rd
4 Whitby Rd

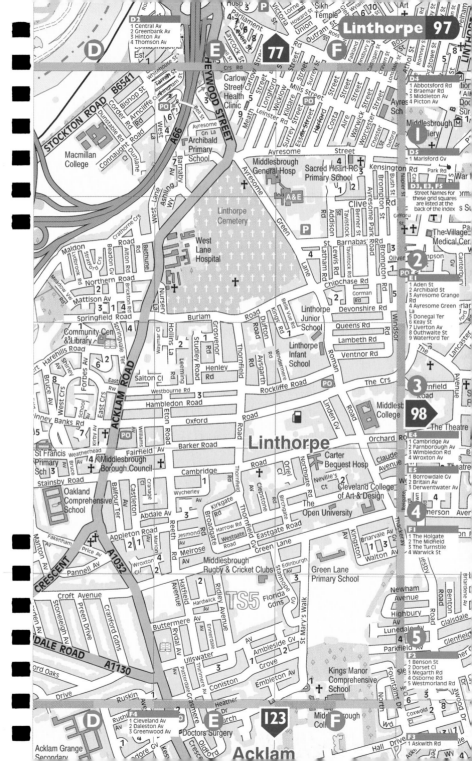

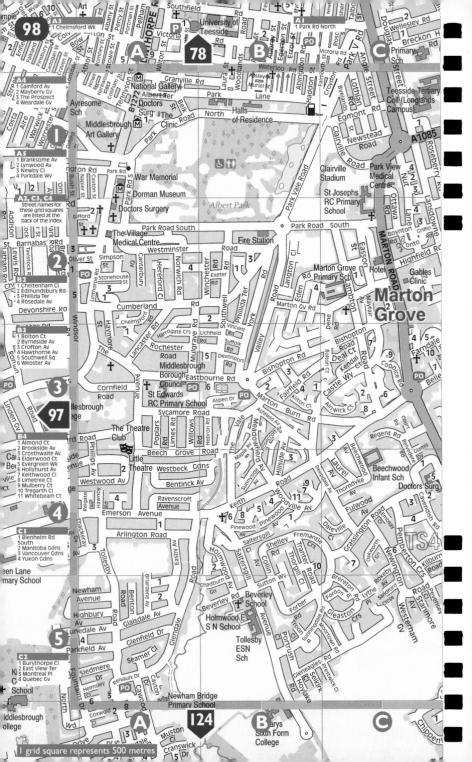

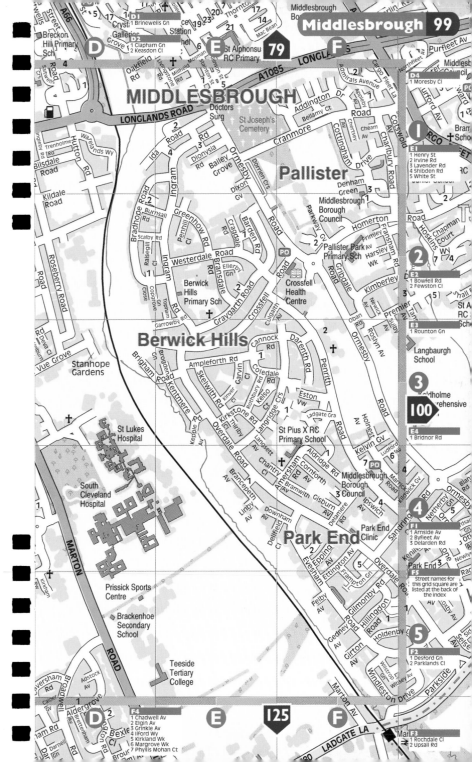

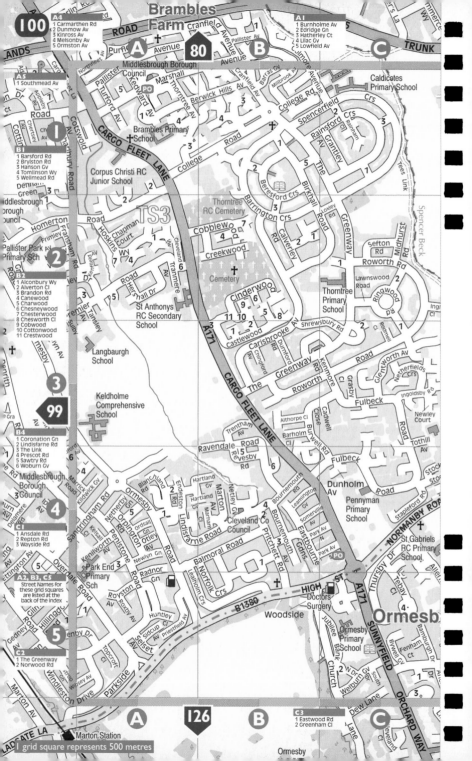

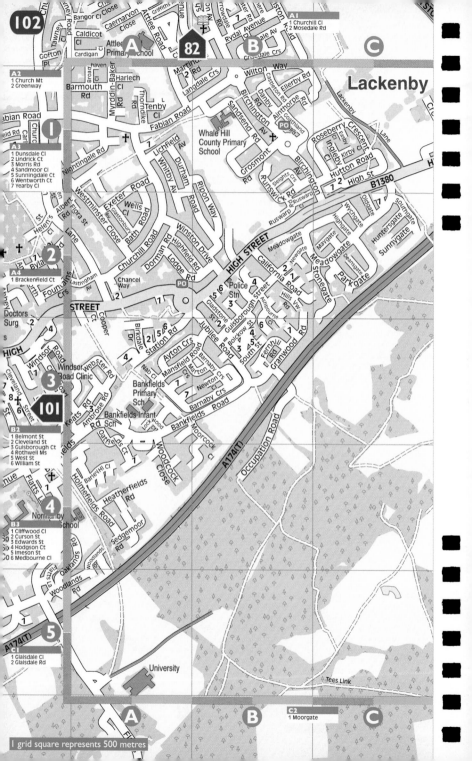

102

82

101

A1
1 Churchill Cl
2 Mosedale Rd

Lackenby

A2
1 Church Mt
2 Greenway

A3
1 Dunsdale Cl
2 Lindrick Ct
3 Morris Rd
4 Sandmoor Cl
5 Sunningdale Ct
6 Wentworth Ct
7 Yearby Cl

2

A4
1 Brackenfield Ct

3

B2
1 Belmont St
2 Cleveland St
3 Guisborough Ct
4 Rothwell Ms
5 West St
6 William St

4

B3
1 Cliffwood Cl
2 Curson St
3 Edwards St
4 Hodgson Ct
5 Imeson St
6 Medbourne Cl

5

C1
1 Glaisdale Cl
2 Glaisdale Rd

C2
1 Moorgate

Whale Hill
County Primary
School

Bankfields
Primary
Sch

Bankfields Infant
Sch

Normanby
School

University

Police
Stn

Windsor
Road Clinic

Doctors
Surg

HIGH STREET

B1380

A174(T)

Occupation Road

Tees Link

1 grid square represents 500 metres

Castle

D

Wilton Gn

Eston Rd

chestnut

E A174

83

Golf Course

F

1

2

3

104

4

5

ROAD

W Lane

H STREET

A174(T)

Lazenby Bank

Wilton Moor Plantation

Eston Moor

High Barnaby Farm

Tees Link

D

E

F

104

† Wilton Castl
✗ Wilton
Castl
A
84
B
C

1
Bank Top
Farm

Wilton Lane

2

Court
Green
Woods

3

◀103

4

Moordale Beck

High Barnaby
Farm

5

Poplar
Farm

A
B
C

1 grid square represents 500 metres

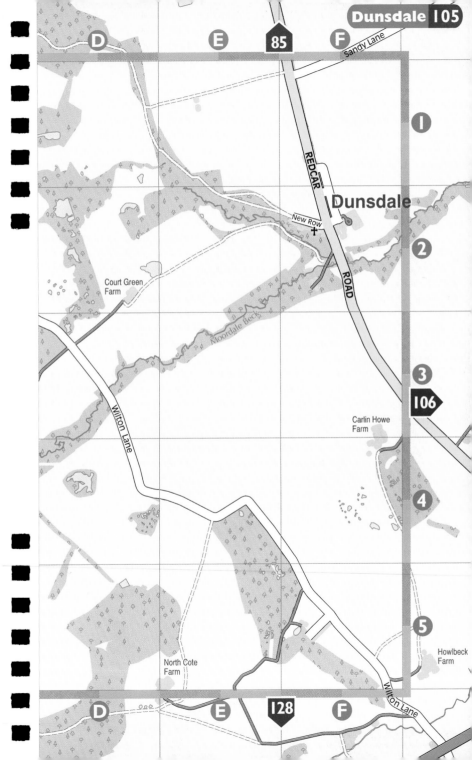

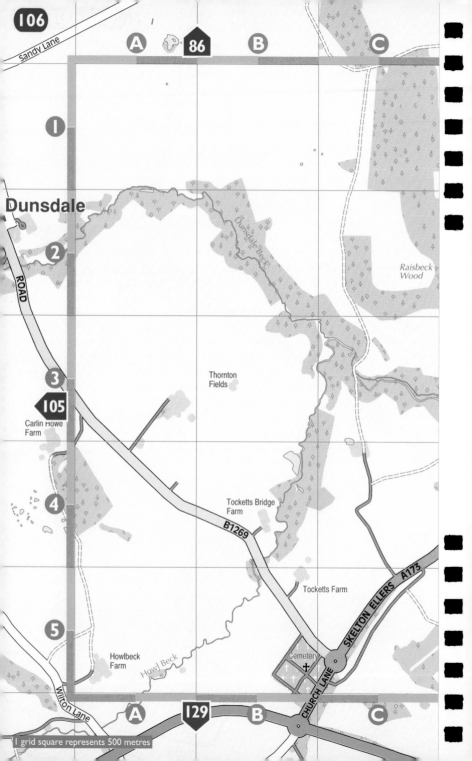

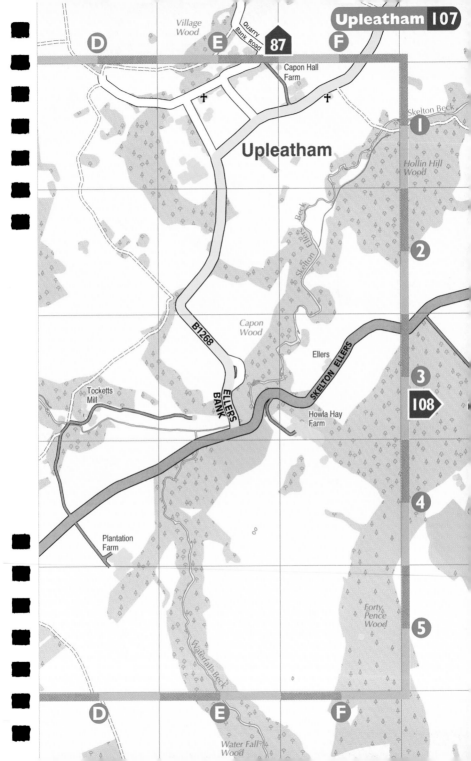

D

Village
Wood

E

Quarry
Bank Road

87

F

Capon Hall
Farm

✝

✝

1

Skelton Beck

Upleatham

Hollin Hill
Wood

2

Skelton Ellers Beck

Capon
Wood

Ellers

SKELTON ELLERS

3

108

Tocketts
Mill

B1268

ELLERS
BANK

Howla Hay
Farm

4

Plantation
Farm

Forty
Pence
Wood

5

D

E

F

Waterfall Beck

Water Fall
Wood

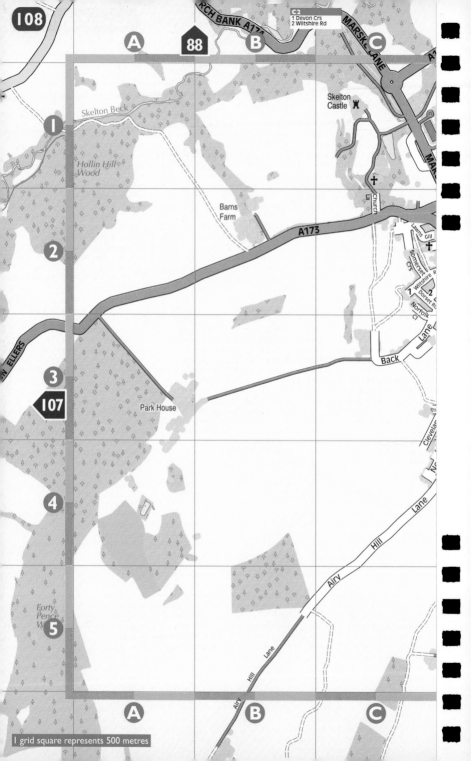

108

A

88

RCH BANK A173

B

C2
1 Devon Crs
2 Wiltshire Rd

MARSK LANE

C

Skelton Beck

1

Hollin Hill
Wood

Skelton
Castle

Barns
Farm

A173

Church La

Lawns Gill

Somerset Crs

Wiltshire Rd

Dorset Rd

7

2

Norfolk
Cl

Back

Lane

Cleveland

N ELLERS

2

3

107

Park House

4

Hill

Lane

Airy

5

Forty
Pence
W

Airy

Hill

Lane

A

B

C

I grid square represents 500 metres

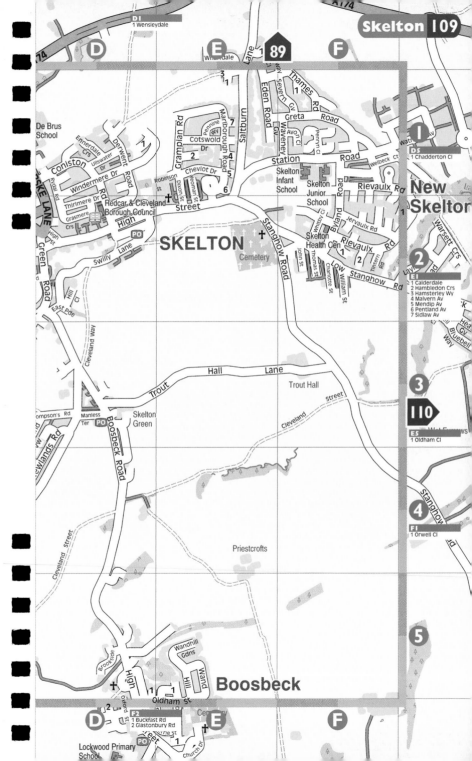

D1
1 Wensleydale

D

E
Wharfdale

89

F

1 74

De Brus
School

Ennerdale
Crs
Coniston
Ullswater
Dr
Windermere Dr
Derwent Road
Thirlmere Dr
Grasmere
Crs
Rydal Rd
High St
Green Road
East Pde

Robinson
St
Street
High Street
Redcar & Cleveland
Borough Council
PO
Swilly Lane

SKELTON

Grampian Rd
Pennine
Cotswold
Dr
Cheviot Dr
Dixon St
Yeoman St
Marlborough Road
7
2
4
5
6

Saltburn

Eden Road

Cemetery

Stanghow Road

Severn Gv
Wav
Greta
Thames Rd
Waveney
Gv
Avon Cl
Penryn Cl
Station
Skelton
Infant
School
Skelton
Junior
School
Skelton
Health Cen
1
Granam Cl
Byland Road
Welbeck Rd
Rievaulx Rd
Jervaulx Rd
Rievaulx Rd
Tintern Rd
2
John St
Thomas St
Charlotte St
Low William St
Low Stanghow Road

I
D5
1 Chadderton Cl

New
Skelton

Warsett Crs
Lav
Bluebell Way

2
E1
1 Calderdale
2 Hambledon Crs
3 Hamsterley Wy
4 Malvern Av
5 Mendip Av
6 Pentland Av
7 Sidlaw Av

Cleveland Way

Trout   Hall   Lane

Trout Hall

Cleveland Street

3
E5
110
1 Oldham Cl

ompson's Rd
Manless
Ter
PO
Boosbeck Road
Skelton
Green

ewlands Rd

Cleveland Street

Stanghow

4
F1
1 Orwell Cl

Priestcrofts

5

Brookside
High Street
Wandhill
Gdns
Wand Hill
Oxford St

Boosbeck

D
2
F2
1 Buckfast Rd
2 Glastonbury Rd

Oldham St
Glenrydale St
Cem Way
Church Dr

E

F

PO

Lockwood Primary
School

110

A

90

B

C

Hagg
Farm

School

A2
1 Fountains Ct

Laburnum
Linden
Lilac
Laurel
Maple Gv

Chestnut
Hawthorn

Woodside
Willow Dr

Dr
7

Skelto

Millholme Dr
7

Skelton Rd

Spri
Millholme Ter

2
Fo

I

Watness Av

Wandhills Av
7

Millholme
Farm

Glads

1 Brankin Ct
B I

Rievaulx

Byland
Road

Jervaulx Rd

New
Skelton

Layland Beck

Skelton Rd

Rievaulx
Rd

Warsett Crs

2

Low
St

Richards St

North
Skelton

Cleveland Street

1
2

1 Millholme Cl
2 Park Rd

C I

Layland
Road

Rd

Holmebeck
Road

Vaughan St

PO

Williams St

Wharton St

Harebell
Ct

Heather
Gv

Bluebell
Way

Bolckow
Street

3

109

street

Wet Furrows
Farm

East
Pastures

4

Stanghow Road

5

Greenhills
Farm

A

B

C

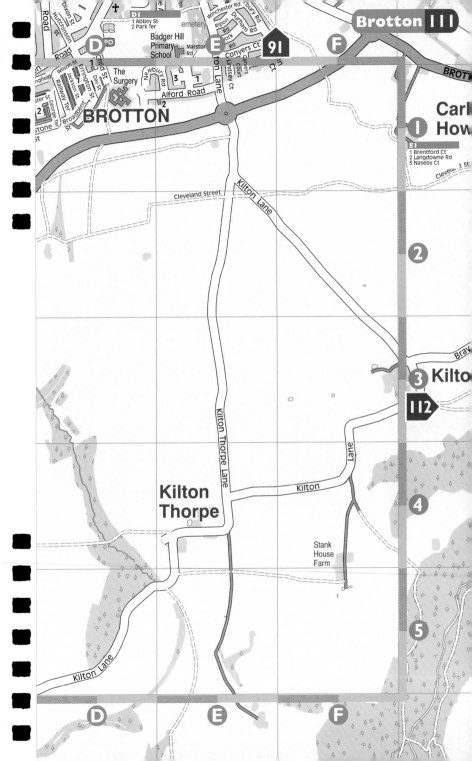

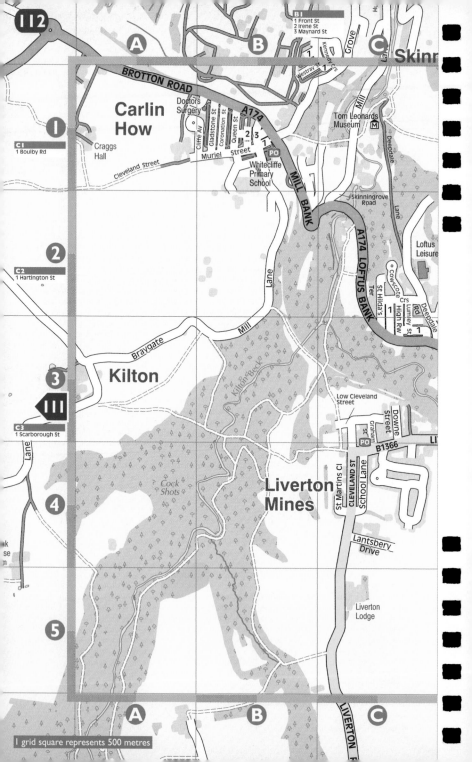

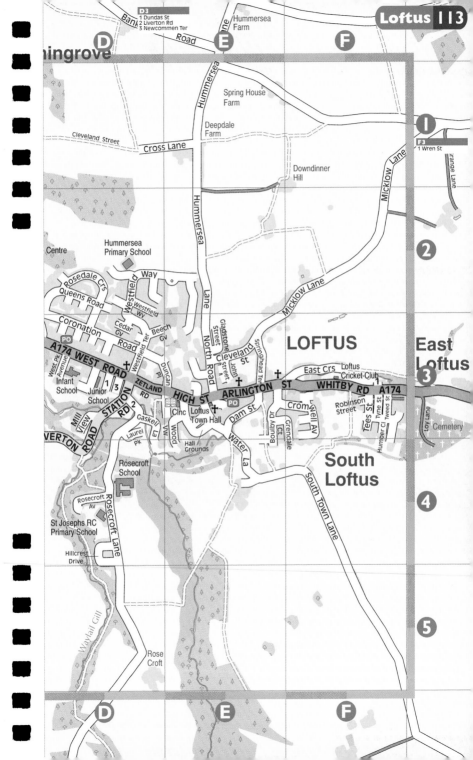

A

B

A3
1 Sawley Cl
2 Woburn Av

C

Bottom House
Farm

B3
1 Atherstone Wy
2 Branksome Hall
Dr

1

B4
1 Coppice Wk

A-1(M)

Newton Lane

A68

Abbots

2

B5
1 Mowden Wk

Stag
House

Mount
Pleasant

Wentworth
Way

3

C1
1 Abercorn Ct
2 Amberley Gv

Jedburgh
Av
Tintern
Av
Marrick

Drive
Ellerton
Cl
Hexham
Cl
Wimborne

Minors Crs
Arundel
Dr
Rotbury
Dr
Kenilworth

Witton Crs

Meadowfield Rd

Highfield Road

Malvern

PO

Primary
School

Newton

Berwick
Rd

Nickstream
Lane

Bates

Whitby

Selby Crs

Way

Lane

Elver Pl

Cottl

Gham

Crs

Dumster

1

Ambleforth
Vw

Bylands Wy

Rosedale
Crs

Easby
Pl

Bolton
Cl

3

Hunstanworth

Sherborne
Cl

Branksome
Comprehensive
School

Finchale Crescent

Wartham

Kirkstall
Crs

1

4

Archde

4

C3
1 Richmond Cl
2 Warwick Sq

Cocker Beck

Eggleston

Dryburgh
Vw

View

Fountains
Vw

Branksome

Cockerton C of E
Primary School

B6279

STAINDROP

Cockerto

Coniscliffe
Grange

1

Chap

Edgecombe Gv

ROAD

Hall
Vw

Mowden
Hall Dr

Edgecombe
Gv

Mowden

Lunedale

5

C4
1 Berrybank Crest
2 Cleasby Vw
3 Denton Cl
4 Redworth Rd

Parkland
Drive

Barnes

1

Road

4

3

Claxton Avenue

Kew Rd

Laz

enby Crs

5

Road

Conyers Avenue
Junior Sch
Bushel Hl Ct

Lazenby Gv

2

Chester

Mowden

Parkland Gv

Fulthorpe

2

3

Villiers

eton Dr

4

Nunn

A

B

C5
1 Barnes Cl
2 Birkdale Rd
3 Conyers Cl
4 Conyers Gv
5 Lazenby Gv

C

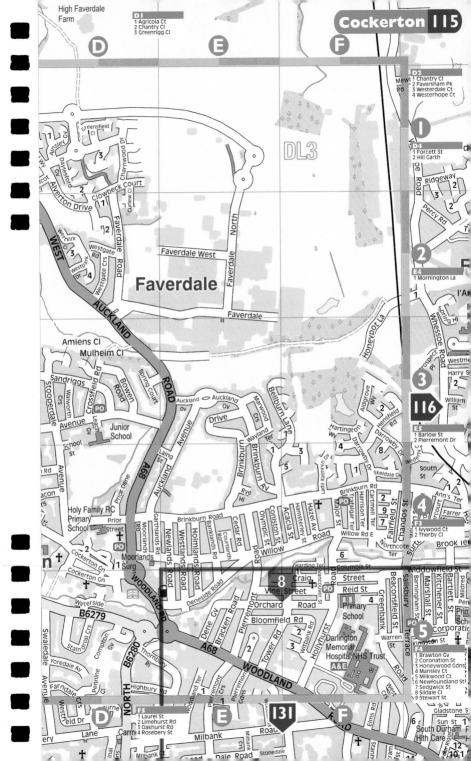

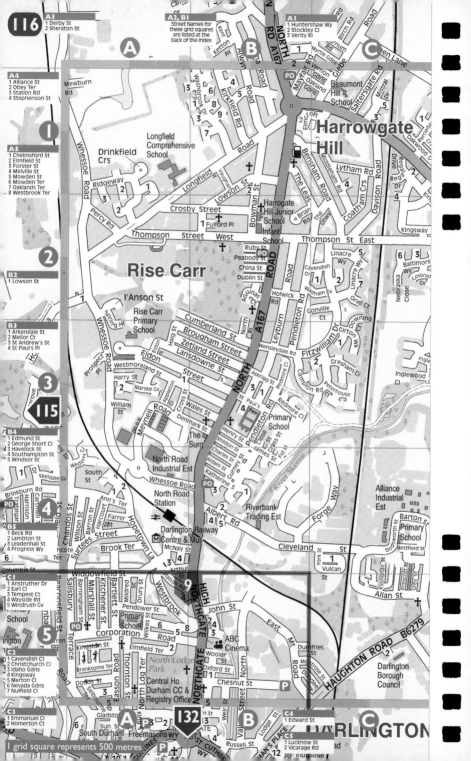

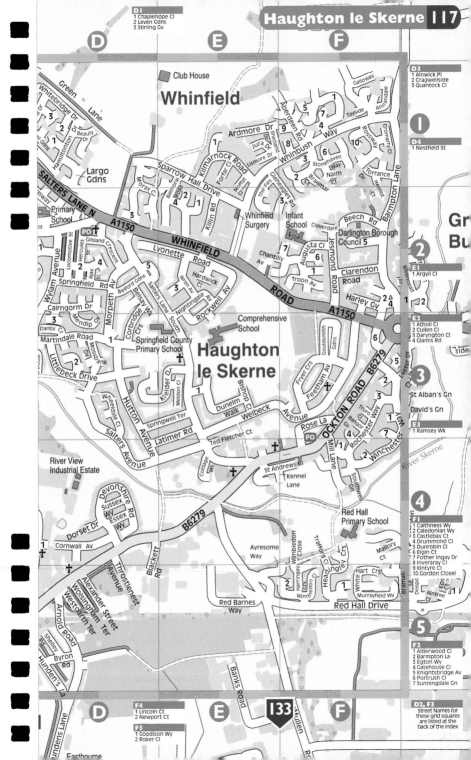

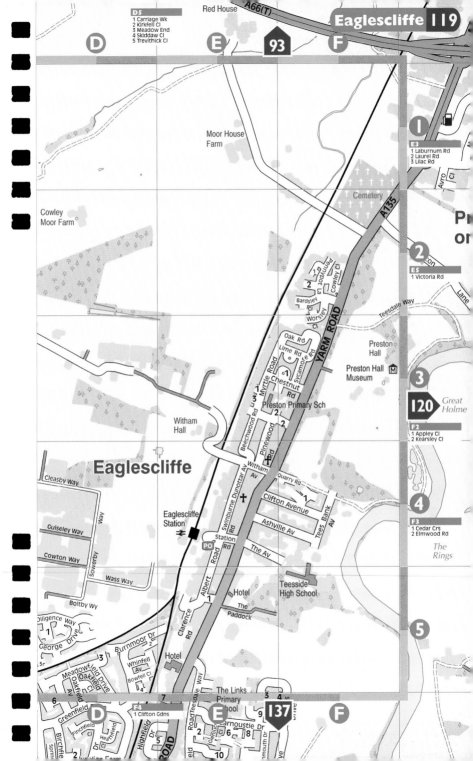

120

A135

A **94** **B** Sowith Way **C**

J. Westland

Adam St.

Boeing Wy.

Boeing Way Short Cl.

Bowesfield-Lane

Bowesfield Industrial Estate

Vickers Cl.

Douglas Close

Diamond Ct

Moss Way

Concorde Way

1

Avro Cl.

Handley Close

Lockheed Close

Cemetery

A135

Preston-on-Tees

Preston Farm Industrial Estate

The Holmes

Preston Lane

2

Teesdale Way

Cowley Cl.

Pen...

M... ROAD

Preston Hall

Preston Hall Museum M

3

119

Great Holme

Bassleton Wood

Bassleton Beck

4

Av..

The Rings

Quarry Farm

5

Barwick

A **138** **B** Barwick Lane **C**

Barwick

Bar...

Bar...

Warble...

Pi...

I grid square represents 500 metres

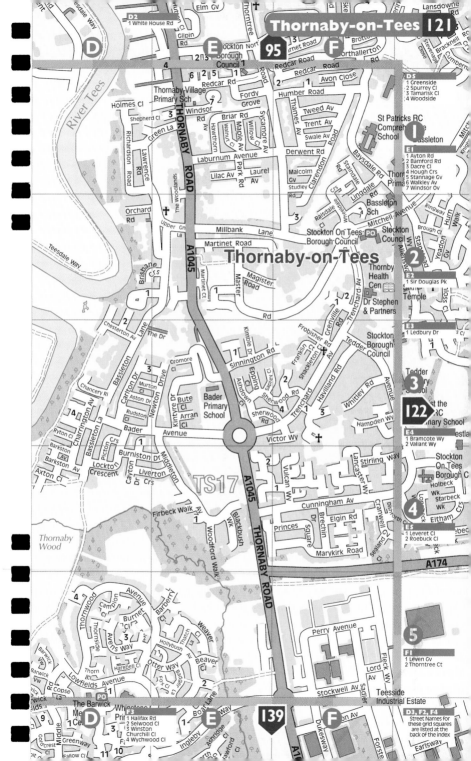

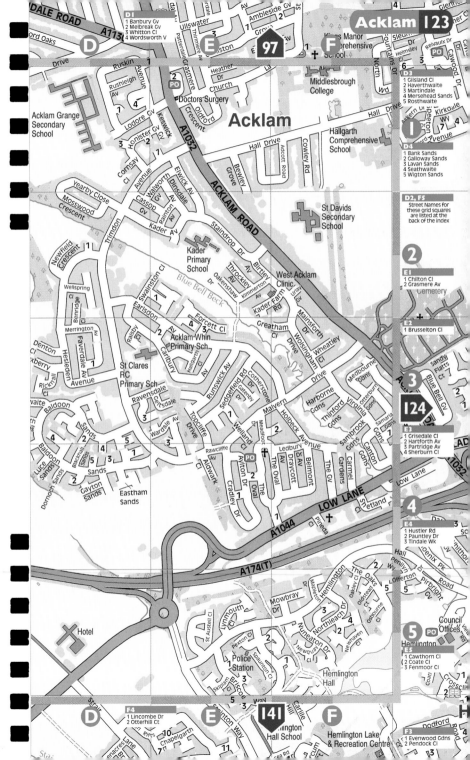

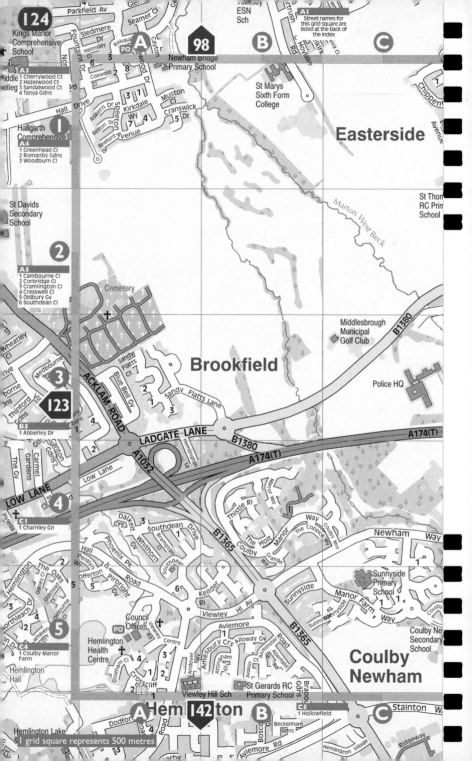

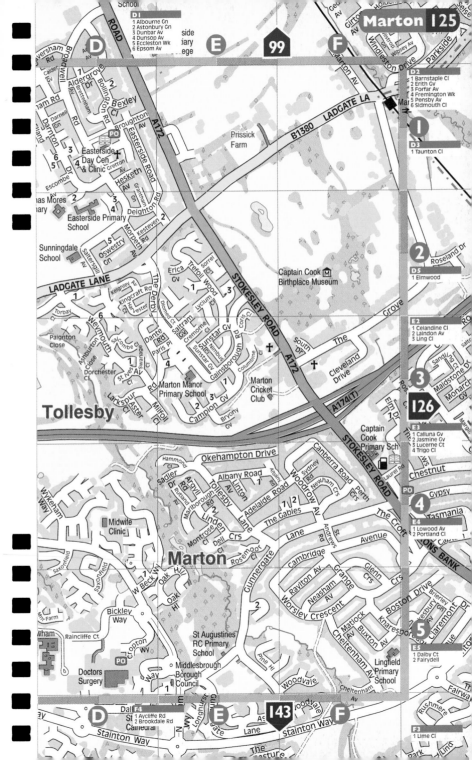

105 th Cote m

A3
1 Gold Crest
2 Kestrel Hide
3 Merlin Cl
4 Middlesbrough Rd
5 Redwing Rising
6 Ruff Tail

A

B

C

Wilton L

Park Wo

Avron Ct

Maltby

Pine Ro

I

A4
1 Rosebay Ct
2 Sorrell Gv

Lime Road

2

C1
1 Brockrigg Ct

A171

Woodhouse

A171

Howlbeck Road

Venables Rd

Infant School

Clevelan

Grosvenor Pl

Park

Allison St

Cobble Carr

TS14

Poplar Pl

Barnaby Pl

Woodhouse Road

Park Lane

South St

St

Thomson St

3

C2
1 Cauley Cl
2 Borrowby Ct
3 Larch Rd
4 Newholme Ct
5 Scaling Ct

Ltl Grebe

Montagu's Harrier

Fulmar Head

Whinchat Tail

Great Auk

Peregrine Ct

Whinchat Tail

Middlesbrough Road

West End

Rectory Av

Rectory Cl

Kingfisher

Montagu's

Heron Ga

Ltl Crake

Stokesley Road

Way

Stokesley Rd

Galley Hill Primary Sch

Primrose Cl

Primrose

Hawthorne Dr

Campion Drive

Thames Avenue

Avon Dr

Hutton Lane

Lincoln

PO

Stafford

Derby Rd

Enfiel

4

C3
1 Chapelbeck Bungalows
2 Danesfort Av

Landsdale

Staindale

St Paulinas RC Primary Sch

Bracken

Lucerne

Rowan Cl

Trefoil Cl

Sorrell

The

Rosedale

Crs

Tidkin Lane

Neville Gv

Lucia Lane

St Leonards Road

Bernaldby Av

Severn Av

Derwent Av

Leven

Dorset

Devon Rd

Cornwall Rd

Hereford

Warwick Rd

Meath Way

Ledburn Way

Bosworth

Sorteene

Blakmr

Evendale

Overdale

Farndale

Weardale

Glendale

Askew Dr

Tindale

Mossdale

Pyg Dr

Avenue

Meynell Av

Rowland

Keld

The Gv

Thweng Wy

Morton

Fanacurt Rd

Latimer Lane

Lowcross Av

Newstead Primary School

Hutton Lane

Avenue

Gloucester Rd

Crescent

Fryup

Primary School

Ashford Cl

Badsworth Cl

Roxby

Lealholm Wy

5

C4
1 Kent Rd
2 Meath Wy
3 Somerset Rd

Hutton La

Sandwood Pk

n Gate

Hutton Hall

Aldenham Road

Goathland Grove

Ilkley G

Wyckham

Road

Link

A

B

C

C5
1 Arden Cl
2 Beaufort Cl
3 Cleator Dr
4 Crowhurst Cl
5 Linlithgow Cl
6 Whorlton Cl

Tees Link

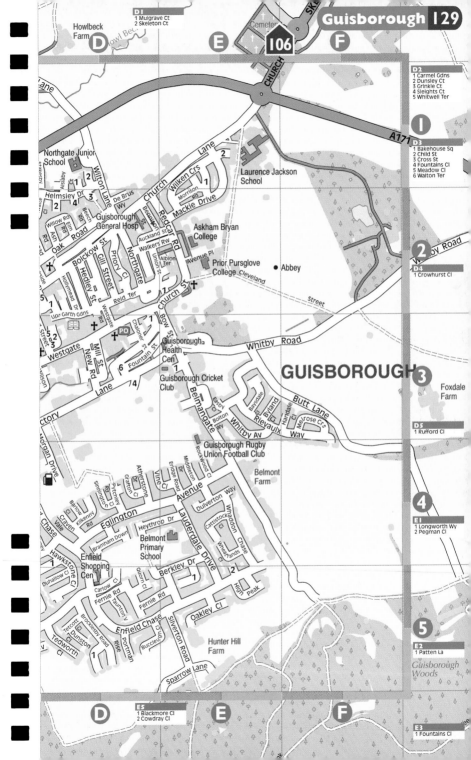

114

A   B   C

I

2

3

4

5

A   B   C

Baydale Beck

1 Arncliffe Gv
2 Shawbrow Vw

Conyers Avenue

Junior Sch

Chester Gv

Mowden
Infant Sch

Fulthorpe
Avenue

Carleton Dr

Wilton
Drive

Broadmeado

Halnaby Av

Bigburn Dr

Garthorne Av

Tees Grange Av

Greyfriars Close

Leith

Road

Hummersk

Barrett Road

Hummerskn

Hummersknott
Comprehensive
School

Wycliffe
Wy

CONISCLIFFE ROAD

Picnic
Site

Teesdale Av

Baydale
Road

Salutation

The
Holmes

Baydale
Farm

Darlington
North Yorkshire County

River Tees

1 grid square represents 500 metres

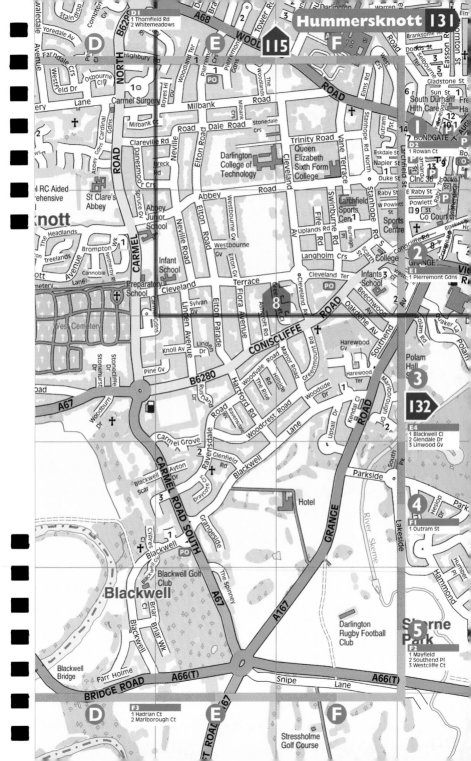

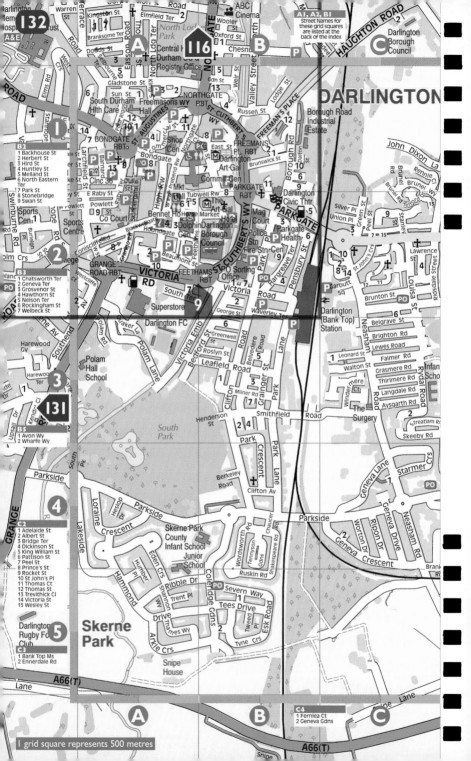

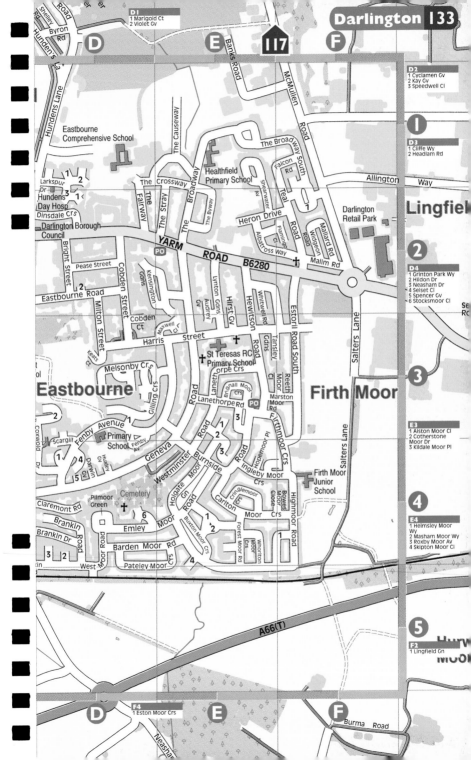

117

D1
1 Marigold Ct
2 Violet Gv

D2
1 Cyclamen Gv
2 Kay Gv
3 Speedwell Cl

D3
1 Cliffe Wy
2 Headlam Rd

D4
1 Grinton Park Wy
2 Hildon Dr
3 Neasham Dr
4 Selset Cl
5 Spencer Gv
6 Stocksmoor Cl

E3
1 Alston Moor Cl
2 Cotherstone Moor Dr
3 Kildale Moor Pl

E4
1 Helmsley Moor Wy
2 Masham Moor Wy
3 Roxby Moor Av
4 Skipton Moor Cl

F2
1 Lingfield Gn

F4
1 Eston Moor Crs

Lingfiel

Se
RC

Hurw
Moo

Burma Road

A

B

C

1

Long Plantation

Westgate Farm

A67

Low Goosepool Farm

A67

2

Teesside Airport Station

Darlington

Stockton-on-Tees

3

Teesside International Airport

tel

4

5

Featherstone House

A

B

C

1 grid square represents 500 metres

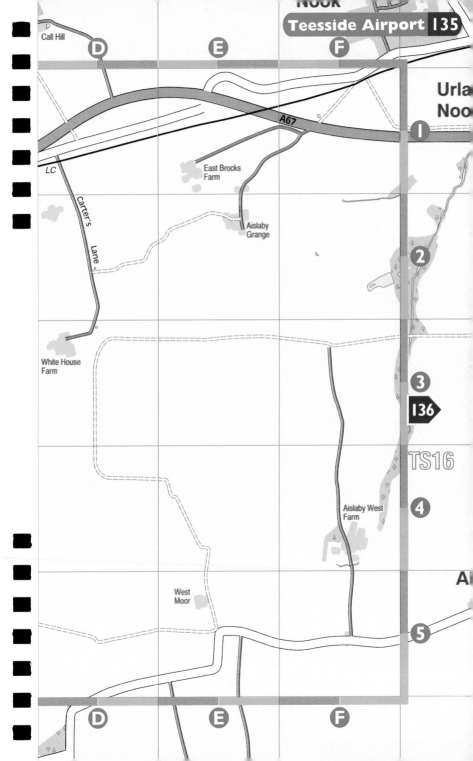

Nook

D

Call Hill

E

F

Urla
Noo

I

A67

LC

Carter's
Lane

East Brocks
Farm

Aislaby
Grange

2

White House
Farm

3

136

TS16

Aislaby West
Farm

4

West
Moor

Ai

5

D

E

F

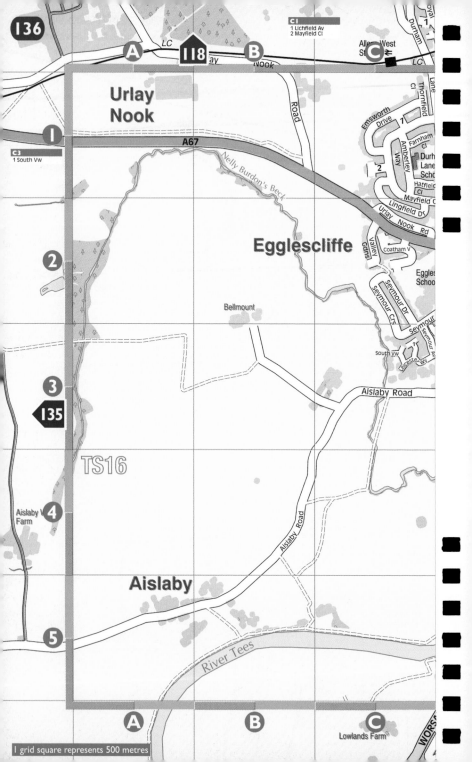

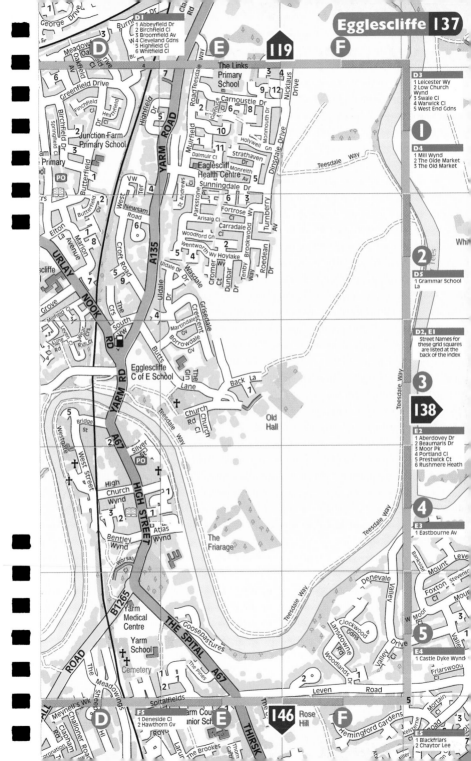

D1
1 Abbeyfield Dr
2 Birchfield Cl
3 Broomfield Av
4 Cleveland Gdns
5 Highfield Cl
6 Whitfield Cl

119

D3
1 Leicester Wy
2 Low Church Wynd
3 Swale Cl
4 Warwick Cl
5 West End Gdns

D4
1 Mill Wynd
2 The Olde Market
3 The Old Market

D5
1 Grammar School La

D2, E1
Street Names for these grid squares are listed at the back of the index

138

E2
1 Aberdovey Dr
2 Beaumaris Dr
3 Moor Pk
4 Portland Cl
5 Prestwick Ct
6 Rushmere Heath

E3
1 Eastbourne Av

E4
1 Castle Dyke Wynd

146

F5
1 Deneside Cl
2 Hawthorn Gv

E5
1 Blackfriars
2 Chaytor Lee

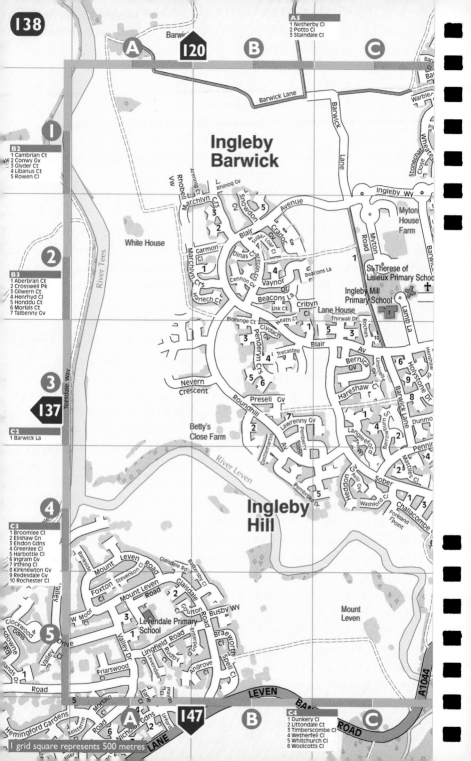

The Barwick Medical Cen

Whinstone Primary School

Beckfield Medical Centre

Teesside Industrial Estate

White House Farm

High Leven

Leven Bridge

140

Fleck Wy
Lord
Av
Sadler
ockwell Av

Robson Av

Teesside
Industrial Estate

A 122

Earlsway

Earlsway

I

Hailsham Av

Fleck
Way

Forsw

William
Crossthwaite
Av
Allison
Avenue

2

Avenue

LOW LANE

A1044

A19(T)

LOW

LANE

A1044

Maltby

Willows
Av

Beech
Grove

Dunsmore
Cl

Lane

High

T

Bridge

A1044

3

139

High Lane

Roger

Lane

4

Maltby
Grange

A19(T)

White
House Farm

5

Roger

Stainton Vale
Farm

Maltby

T

A

B

C

A

B

C

Lane

1 grid square represents 500 metres

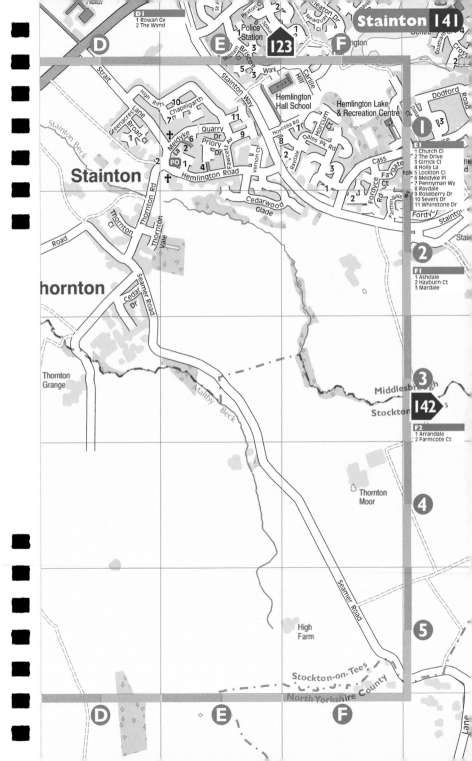

142

Hemlington
Health
Centre

Hemlington
Hall

A

124

Viewley Hill Sch

Hemlington

Dodford Road

Hemlington Lake
& Recreation Centre

I

1 Swallowfields

House
Fonteyn Ct
Earls Ct
Enderby Gdns
Ellis Gdns
Folkstone Cl

Cass

Faygate Ct

Fordyce Rd

Farthingale Wy

Fordyce Rd

Stainton Way

Stainton Grange

2

Coatham Cl
Scliff

Aylesbury Crs
Alloway Gv
Attingham
Axminster Road
Avalon

B

1 Caldwell Cl
2 Crimdon Cl
3 Dalcross Ct
4 Darwen Ct
5 Freshingham Cl

St Gerards RC
Primary School

Boscombe Gdns
Beckenham Gdns
Aberfelis
Brabourn Gdns

Avlemore Rd

Hemlington Village Rd

Coulby
Secondary
School

Coulby
Newham

Stainton Wa

Ridgeway

The B

C

B1365

1

TS8

Larchfield
Farm

3

141

Middlesbrough

on-Tees

Fox
Covert

Thornton
Moor

4

Thornton
Low
Moor

Seamer Road

5

on-Tees
shire County

La

Muff Lane

A

B

Antelope
Lodge

C

I grid square represents 500 metres

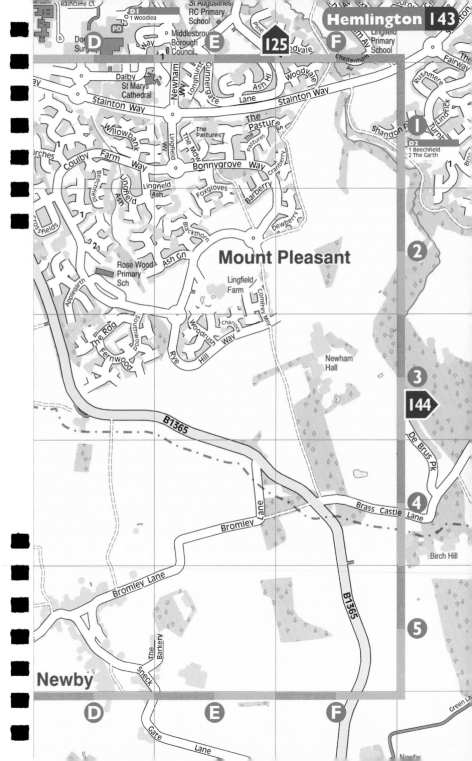

Lingfield Primary School

Cheltenham Av

Stainton

Sudbury

The Camaustie

1 Hawkstone

DIXONS

BANK

Fairway

Rushmere

Lindrick

Turnberry

Westray

Broadstone Way

Astbury

Fairwood Park

Kedlestone Park

Eagle Park

Eagle Park

Fulford Way

Fearnhead

Brass Castle Lane

Bonny Gv

West Moor Farm

Ryehill Cl

Crookers

Towers

2

Bonny Grove Farm

1
B1
1 Brass Wynd

Undon Park

2
C1
1 Brackenhill Cl
2 Bromley Hill Cl

Newham Hall

3
143

De Brus Pk

Brass Castle Lane

Ryehill Farm

4

Brass Castle Lane

Middlesbrough
North Yorkshire County

Birch Hill

High Tunstall Farm

B1365

5

Tunstall

Green Lane

Lane

Newby

1 grid square represents 500 metres

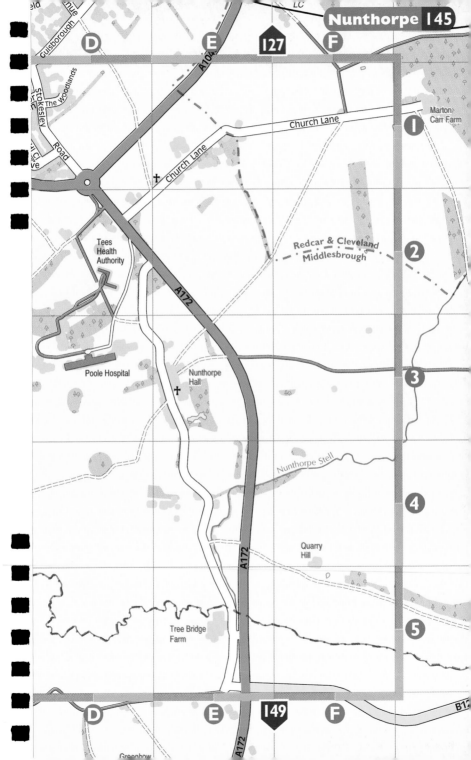

Guisborough

D

E

127

F

Stokesley Road

The Woodlands

A104

Church Lane

Church Lane

LC

Marton Carr Farm

I

†

Tees Health Authority

Redcar & Cleveland

Middlesbrough

A172

2

Poole Hospital

Nunthorpe Hall

†

3

Nunthorpe Stell

4

Quarry Hill

A172

Tree Bridge Farm

5

D

E

149

F

A172

B12

Greenhow

D

E

138

F

1 Carpenter Cl
2 Caterton Cl
3 Daltry Cl
4 Fowler Cl
5 Westworth Cl
6 Wharton Cl
7 Winpenny Cl

Lingfield Road

Valley Dr

Friarswood

Levendale Cl

Braeworth

Spell Cl

LEVEN

BANK

ROAD

A1044

Bridge

Kelsterne

Kirk Road

Mortain Cl

St Nicholas Gdns

Earle Cl

Taylin Cl

Urford Cl

Fewston Cl

GREEN

LANE

I

Holdenfields

Red Hall Wood

2

A67

Spell
Close Farm

Red
Hall Farm

3

Red Hall Lane

Re...
W

4

Springfield Gv

Penders Cl

St Lane

PUMP

La

Kirklevington Co
Primary Sch

5

A19(T)

D

E

F

on-Tees

County

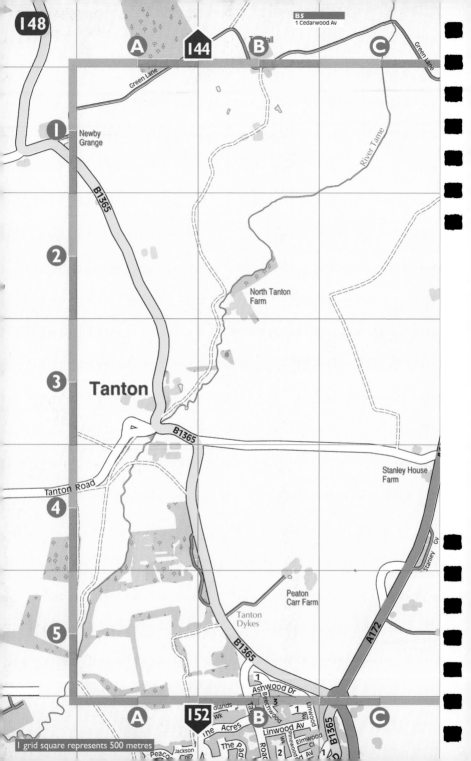

D
E
145
F

B1

I

Greenhow
Moor

A172

2

Stanley
Grange

Greenhow
Hill

PANNIERMAN LANE

Angrove North
Farm

3

150

Yarm Lane

Yarm Lane

Yarm Lane

A172

The
Gra

4

East
Angrove

Quakers Grove
Farm

5

A173

Winley Hill
Farm

D
E
153
F

e West

Leven

Applebridge

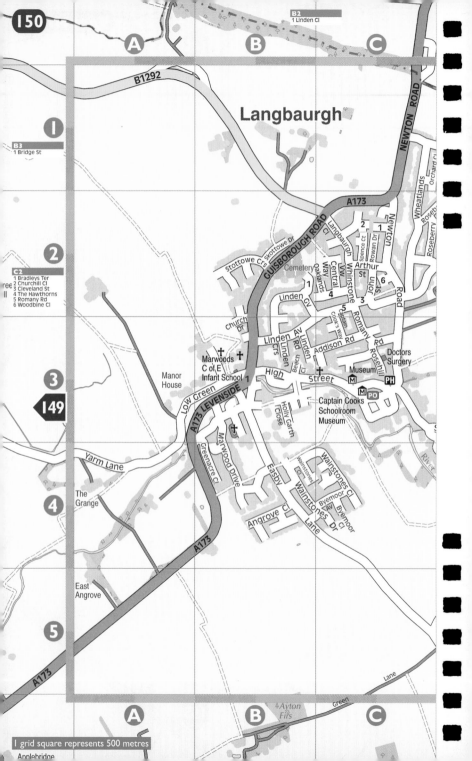

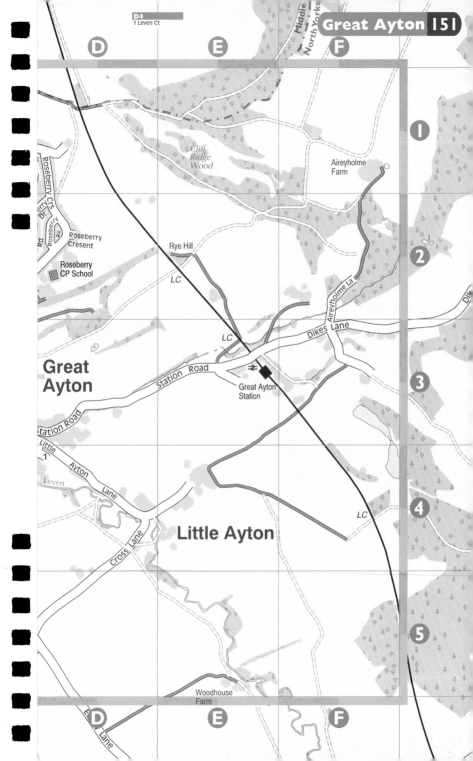

D4
1 Leven Ct

D

E

F

I

Middle North Yorks

Cliff Ridge Wood

Aireyholme Farm

Roseberry Crs

Roseberry Dr

Roseberry Av

Roseberry Cresent

Roseberry CP School

Rye Hill

LC

LC

Aireyholme La

Dikes Lane

Dik

Great Ayton

Station Road

Station Road

Great Ayton Station

Little

Ayton Lane

Leven

Little Ayton

Cross Lane

LC

Woodhouse Farm

E Lane

D

E

F

2

3

4

5

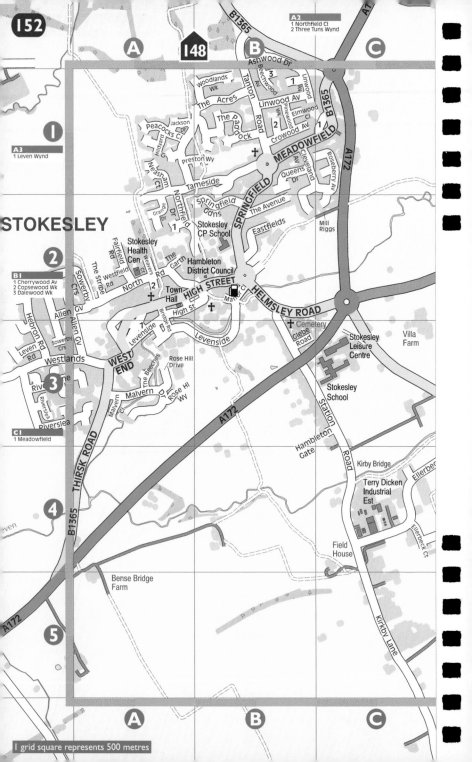

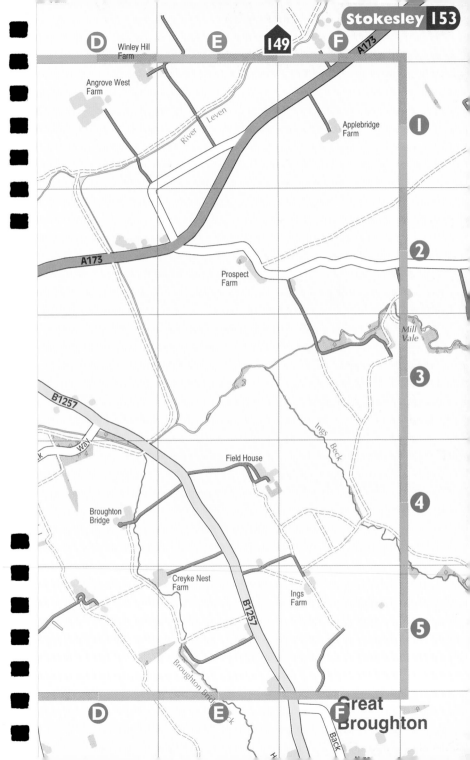

Acklam	123 E1	Haughton Le Skerne 117 E3
Aislaby	136 A5	Haverton Hill 60 C4
Berwick Hills	99 D3	The Headland 19 F2
Billingham	60 A3	Hemlington 142 A1
Bishop Auckland	26 C1	High Leven 139 E5
Bishopsgarth	72 B3	High Throston 16 A3
Blackwell	131 D5	Hummersknott 130 C2
Boosbeck	109 E5	Ingleby Barwick 138 B1
Brambles Farm	80 A5	Ingleby Hill 138 B4
Branksome	114 B4	Kilton 112 A3
Brookfield	124 A3	Kilton Thorpe 111 E4
Brotton	111 D1	Kirkleatham 84 B1
Cargo Fleet	79 F4	Lackenby 102 C1
Carlin How	112 A1	Langbaurgh 150 B1
Chilton Lane	21 F4	Lazenby 83 F5
Coatham	50 C4	Linthorpe 97 E4
Cockerton	114 C4	Little Ayton 151 E4
Coulby Newham	124 C5	Liverton Mines 112 B4
Cowpen Bewley	43 F5	Loftus 113 F3
Dean Bank	20 B2	Maltby 140 B3
Dormanstown	67 E2	Marske-by-the-Sea 70 A4
Dunsdale	105 F2	Marton 125 E4
Eaglescliffe	119 D4	Marton Grove 98 C2
Eastbourne	133 D3	Middlesbrough 99 D1
Easterside	124 C1	Middlestone Moor 14 A5
Egglescliffe	136 B2	Middleton 18 C2
Elton	92 A5	Middridge 36 C3
Eston	101 F2	Mount Pleasant 75 E3
Fairfield	73 D5	Mount Pleasant 143 E2
Faverdale	115 D2	Mowden 114 B5
Ferryhill	21 D1	New Brotton 91 D4
Firth Moor	133 F3	Newby 143 D5
Grangetown	82 B4	New Marske 87 D3
Graythorp	32 C4	New Skelton 110 A1
Great Ayton	151 D3	Newton Aycliffe 53 F2
Greatham	31 E4	Newton Bewley 42 B1
Guisborough	129 E3	Normanby 101 E4
Hardwick	73 D2	North Ormesby 79 F5
Harrowgate Hill	116 C1	North Skelton 110 B2
Hart	10 B4	Norton 74 B1
Hartburn	93 E3	Nunthorpe 126 C5
Hartlepool	3 C2	Ormesby 100 C5
Hart Station	11 D3	Owton Manor 23 D5
Pallister	99 F1	
Park End	99 F4	
Port Clarence	78 C1	
Portrack	96 A1	
Preston-on-Tees	120 A2	
Redcar	68 C2	
Redworth	52 B4	
Rift House	23 D4	
Rise Carr	116 A2	
Roseworth	73 F1	
Saltburn-by-the-Sea	89 F1	
School Aycliffe	53 E4	
Seal Sands	46 C5	
Seaton Carew	33 E1	
Sedgefield	29 F4	
Shildon	35 F4	
Skelton	109 E2	
Skerne Park	132 A5	
South Bank	80 C4	
South Loftus	113 F4	
Spennymoor	14 B3	
Stainton	141 D1	
Stockton-on-Tees	74 C4	
Tanton	148 A3	
Teesport	64 B3	
Teesville	101 D1	
Thornaby-on-Tees	121 E2	
Thornton	140 C2	
Tollesby	125 D3	
Tudhoe Grange	15 E1	
Upleatham	107 E1	
Urlay Nook	136 A1	
Warrenby	50 A4	
Westfield	68 A1	
West Park	16 B4	
West View	12 A4	
Whinfield	117 E1	
Wilton	84 B5	
Wolviston	41 D3	
Woodham	39 D2	
Yarm	146 A1	
Yearby	85 E2	

USING THE STREET INDEX

Street names are listed alphabetically. Each street name is followed by its postal town or area locality, the Postcode District, the page number, and the reference to the square in which the name is found.

Example: **Abberley Dr** *CNHM/HEM* TS8 .... **124** B5 ▣

Some entries are followed by a number in a blue box. This number indicates the location of the street within the referenced grid square. The full street name is listed at the side of the map page.

GENERAL ABBREVIATIONS

ACC	ACCESS	CON	CONVENT	FK	FORK
ALY	ALLEY	COT	COTTAGE	FLD	FIELD
AP	APPROACH	COTS	COTTAGES	FLDS	FIELDS
AR	ARCADE	CP	CAPE	FLS	FALLS
ASS	ASSOCIATION	CPS	COPSE	FLS	FLATS
AV	AVENUE	CR	CREEK	FM	FARM
BCH	BEACH	CREM	CREMATORIUM	FT	FORT
BLDS	BUILDINGS	CRS	CRESCENT	FWY	FREEWAY
BND	BEND	CSWY	CAUSEWAY	FY	FERRY
BNK	BANK	CT	COURT	GA	GATE
BR	BRIDGE	CTRL	CENTRAL	GAL	GALLERY
BRK	BROOK	CTS	COURTS	GDN	GARDEN
BTM	BOTTOM	CTYD	COURTYARD	GDNS	GARDENS
BUS	BUSINESS	CUTT	CUTTINGS	GLD	GLADE
BVD	BOULEVARD	CV	COVE	GLN	GLEN
BY	BYPASS	CYN	CANYON	GN	GREEN
CATH	CATHEDRAL	DEPT	DEPARTMENT	GND	GROUND
CEM	CEMETERY	DL	DALE	GRA	GRANGE
CEN	CENTRE	DM	DAM	GRG	GARAGE
CFT	CROFT	DR	DRIVE	GT	GREAT
CH	CHURCH	DRO	DROVE	GTWY	GATEWAY
CHA	CHASE	DRY	DRIVEWAY	GV	GROVE
CHYD	CHURCHYARD	DWGS	DWELLINGS	HGR	HIGHER
CIR	CIRCLE	E	EAST	HL	HILL
CIRC	CIRCUS	EMB	EMBANKMENT	HLS	HILLS
CL	CLOSE	EMBY	EMBASSY	HO	HOUSE
CLFS	CLIFFS	ESP	ESPLANADE	HOL	HOLLOW
CMP	CAMP	EST	ESTATE	HOSP	HOSPITAL
CNR	CORNER	EX	EXCHANGE	HRB	HARBOUR
CO	COUNTY	EXPY	EXPRESSWAY	HTH	HEATH
COLL	COLLEGE	EXT	EXTENSION	HTS	HEIGHTS
COM	COMMON	F/O	FLYOVER	HVN	HAVEN
COMM	COMMISSION	FC	FOOTBALL CLUB	HWY	HIGHWAY

IMP	IMPERIAL
IN	INLET
IND EST	INDUSTRIAL ESTATE
INF	INFIRMARY
INFO	INFORMATION
INT	INTERCHANGE
IS	ISLAND
JCT	JUNCTION
JTY	JETTY
KG	KING
KNL	KNOLL
L	LAKE
LA	LANE
LDG	LODGE
LGT	LIGHT
LK	LOCK
LKS	LAKES
LNDG	LANDING
LTL	LITTLE
LWR	LOWER
MAG	MAGISTRATE
MAN	MANSIONS
MD	MEAD
MDW	MEADOWS
MEM	MEMORIAL
MKT	MARKET
MKTS	MARKETS
ML	MALL
ML	MILL
MNR	MANOR
MS	MEWS
MSN	MISSION
MT	MOUNT
MTN	MOUNTAIN
MTS	MOUNTAINS
MUS	MUSEUM
MWY	MOTORWAY
N	NORTH
NE	NORTH EAST
NW	NORTH WEST
O/P	OVERPASS
OFF	OFFICE

ORCH	ORCHARD
OV	OVAL
PAL	PALACE
PAS	PASSAGE
PAV	PAVILION
PDE	PARADE
PH	PUBLIC HOUSE
PK	PARK
PKWY	PARKWAY
PL	PLACE
PLN	PLAIN
PLNS	PLAINS
PLZ	PLAZA
POL	POLICE STATION
PR	PRINCE
PREC	PRECINCT
PREP	PREPARATORY
PRIM	PRIMARY
PROM	PROMENADE
PRS	PRINCESS
PRT	PORT
PT	POINT
PTH	PATH
PZ	PIAZZA
QD	QUADRANT
QU	QUEEN
QY	QUAY
R	RIVER
RBT	ROUNDABOUT
RD	ROAD
RDG	RIDGE
REP	REPUBLIC
RES	RESERVOIR
RFC	RUGBY FOOTBALL CLUB
RI	RISE
RP	RAMP
RW	ROW
S	SOUTH
SCH	SCHOOL
SE	SOUTH EAST
SER	SERVICE AREA
SH	SHORE

SHOP	SHOPPING
SKWY	SKYWAY
SMT	SUMMIT
SOC	SOCIETY
SP	SPUR
SPR	SPRING
SQ	SQUARE
ST	STREET
STN	STATION
STR	STREAM
STRD	STRAND
SW	SOUTH WEST
TDG	TRADING
TER	TERRACE
THWY	THROUGHWAY
TNL	TUNNEL
TOLL	TOLLWAY
TPK	TURNPIKE
TR	TRACK
TRL	TRAIL
TWR	TOWER
U/P	UNDERPASS
UNI	UNIVERSITY
UPR	UPPER
V	VALE
VA	VALLEY
VIAD	VIADUCT
VIL	VILLA
VIS	VISTA
VLG	VILLAGE
VLS	VILLAS
VW	VIEW
W	WEST
WD	WOOD
WHF	WHARF
WK	WALK
WKS	WALKS
WLS	WELLS
WY	WAY
YD	YARD
YHA	YOUTH HOSTEL

POSTCODE TOWNS AND AREA ABBREVIATIONS

ACK/BRKF	Acklam/Brookfield
BAUK	Bishop Auckland
BLGHM	Billingham
BLGHMW/WYN	Billingham west/Wynyard
CNHM/HEM	Coulby Newham/Hemlington
DARLE	Darlington east
DARLW	Darlington west
EGG/EAG	Egglescliffe/Eaglescliffe
ESTON	Eston
FYHL	Ferryhill
GTAY/STK	Great Ayton/Stokesley
GUIS	Guisborough

HTLP	Hartlepool
HTLPS	Hartlepool south
HTLPW	Hartlepool west
LOFT/ST	Loftus/Staithes
MARSKE	Marske-by-the-Sea/New Marske
MBORO	Middlesbrough
MGRV/ESTR	Marton Grove/Easterside
MTN/NUN	Marton/Nunthorpe
NACLF	Newton Aycliffe
NORM/PKE	North Ormesby/Park End
NORTON	Norton
RDARL	Rural Darlington

REDCAR	Redcar
RHTLP	Rural Hartlepool
SALT/BTN/SK	Saltburn-by-the-Sea/Brotton/Skelton
SEDG	Sedgefield
SHIL	Shildon
SPEN	Spennymoor
STOCN	Stockton-on-Tees north
STOCS	Stockton-on-Tees south
TEESM	Tees Mouth
THNBY	Thornaby-on-Tees
YARM	Yarm

Abb - Alb

Index - streets

A

Abberley Dr *CNHM/HEM* TS8 ...... 124 B5 🗓
Abbey Cl *STOCN* TS19 .... 72 B5 🗓
Abbey Ct *ESTON* TS6 .... 101 F2
Abbeyfield Dr *EGG/EAG* TS16 .... 137 D1 🗓
Abbey Gdns *DARLW* DL3 .... 131 D1
Abbey Rd *BAUK* DL14 .... 27 D4
   DARLW DL3 .... 8 A5
Abbey St *HTLP* TS24 .... 19 E2 🗓
   SALT/BTN/SK TS12 .... 111 D1 🗓
Abbotsfield Wy *DARLW* DL3 ...... 114 C1
Abbotsford Rd *ACK/BRKF* TS5 .... 97 D4 🗓
Abbots Wy *STOCN* TS19 .... 72 B5
Abdale Av *ACK/BRKF* TS5 .... 97 D4
Aberbran Ct *THNBY* TS17 .... 138 B3 🗓
Abercorn Ct *DARLW* DL3 .... 114 C1 🗓
Abercrombie Rd *REDCAR* TS10 ... 67 E1
Aberdare Rd *ESTON* TS6 .... 82 A4
Aberdeen Rd *DARLE* DL1 .... 117 F1
   HTLPS TS25 .... 23 F4
Aberdovey Dr *EGG/EAG* TS16 ... 137 D2 🗓
Aberfalls Rd *CNHM/HEM* TS8 .... 124 B5 🗓
Abingdon Rd *MBORO* TS1 .... 5 H6
Abridge Cl *MARSKE* TS11 .... 86 B3 🗓
Acacia Rd *BAUK* DL14 .... 27 D2
   STOCN TS19 .... 74 B4
Acacia St *DARLW* DL3 .... 115 F4
Acclom St *HTLP* TS24 .... 17 F2
Achilles Cl *ESTON* TS6 .... 81 D5 🗓
Acklam Rd *ACK/BRKF* TS5 .... 97 D3
   THNBY TS17 .... 95 F4

Acklam St North *TEESM* TS2 .... 78 A2
Acklam St South *TEESM* TS2 .... 5 E1
Acle Burn *FYHL* DL17 .... 38 B1
Acle Mdw *FYHL* DL17 .... 38 B1
Aclet Cl *BAUK* DL14 .... 27 D5
Acorn Bank *THNBY* TS17 .... 139 D3
The Acres *GTAY/STK* TS9 .... 152 B1
Adam Cl *REDCAR* TS10 .... 68 A4
Adam St *STOCS* TS18 .... 94 C5
Adcott Rd *ACK/BRKF* TS5 .... 123 F1
Adderley St *STOCS* TS18 .... 94 C3 🗓
Addington Dr *NORM/PKE* TS3 ..... 99 F1
Addison Rd *ACK/BRKF* TS5 .... 97 F2
   GTAY/STK TS9 .... 150 B3
   HTLP TS24 .... 18 A3 🗓
Adelaide Gv *STOCS* TS18 .... 93 F3
Adelaide Pl *MARSKE* TS11 .... 70 C5 🗓
Adelaide Rd *MTN/NUN* TS7 .... 125 E4
Adelaide St *BAUK* DL14 .... 27 D1 🗓
   DARLE DL1 .... 132 C2 🗓
Aden St *ACK/BRKF* TS5 .... 97 E1 🗓
Admirals Av *NORM/PKE* TS3 .... 79 F5
Admiral Wy *HTLP* TS24 .... 3 F1
Adshead Rd *REDCAR* TS10 .... 67 E2
Adstock Av *MGRV/ESTR* TS4 .... 99 D5
Agecroft Gdns *ACK/BRKF* TS5 ..... 97 D3 🗓
Agnew Wy *NACLF* DL5 .... 38 B3
Agricola Ct *DARLW* DL3 .... 115 D1 🗓
Ainderby Gv *STOCS* TS18 .... 92 C3
Ainderby Wy *MGRV/ESTR* TS4 ..... 98 C4 🗓
Ainsdale Cl *MARSKE* TS11 .... 86 B3 🗓
Ainsford Wy *MTN/NUN* TS7 .... 101 D4

Ainsley Gv *DARLW* DL3 .... 115 D1
Ainsley St *HTLPS* TS25 .... 3 F6
Ainstable Rd *MTN/NUN* TS7 ...... 101 D4
Ainsty Hunt *NACLF* DL5 .... 37 E4
Ainsworth Wy *MTN/NUN* TS7 .... 101 D4
Ainthorpe Rd *ESTON* TS6 .... 102 B1
Aintree Gv *THNBY* TS17 .... 96 B3
Aintree Rd *REDCAR* TS10 .... 68 C2
   STOCS TS18 .... 76 B4 🗓
Airdrie Gv *HTLPS* TS25 .... 23 E4
Aireborough Cl *STOCN* TS19 .... 73 F4 🗓
Aire St *ESTON* TS6 .... 80 B3
   MBORO TS1 .... 97 F1
Aireyholme La *GTAY/STK* TS9 .... 151 F3
Airy Hill La *SALT/BTN/SK* TS12 .. 108 C5
Aiskew Gv *STOCN* TS19 .... 92 C1
Aislaby Ct *GUIS* TS14 .... 129 D1
Aislaby Gv *BLGHM* TS23 .... 42 A4 🗓
Aislaby Rd *EGG/EAG* TS16 .... 136 B4
Ajax St *DARLE* DL1 .... 117 D2
Ajax Wy *ESTON* TS6 .... 80 C4 🗓
Alan St *ESTON* TS6 .... 80 C5 🗓
Albany Rd *MTN/NUN* TS7 .... 125 E4
   NORTON TS20 .... 75 D2
Albatross St *MBORO* TS1 .... 5 E6
Albatross Wy *DARLE* DL1 .... 133 E2
Albert Ms *MBORO* TS1 .... 5 C3
Alberto St *STOCS* TS18 .... 7 F1
Albert Rd *DARLE* DL1 .... 116 B4
   EGG/EAG TS16 .... 119 E5
   ESTON TS6 .... 101 F2
   MBORO TS1 .... 5 G2 🗓
   STOCN TS19 .... 93 D1

STOCS TS18 .... 7 F4
Albert St DARLE DL1 .... 132 C2 🄷
  HTLP TS24 .... 2 C3
  REDCAR TS10 .... 51 E4
  SHIL DL4 .... 35 F2
  TEESM TS2 .... 5 G1
Albert Ter MBORO TS1 .... 98 A1
Albion Av SHIL DL4 .... 35 E2
Albion St SPEN DL16 .... 14 A5
  STOCS TS18 .... 7 F5
Albion Ter BAUK DL14 .... 27 D2
  GUIS TS14 .... 129 E2
  HTLP TS24 .... 19 E3
  SALT/BTN/SK TS12 .... 89 C3
Albourne Gn MGRV/ESTR TS4 .... 125 D1 🄷
Alconbury Wy NORM/PKE TS3 .... 100 B2 🄷
Aldam St DARLI DL1 .... 116 B4
Aldbrough Cl STOCN TS19 ...... 93 D1 🄷
Aldeburgh Cl HTLPS TS25 ...... 31 D2
Aldenham Rd GUIS TS14 .... 128 C5
Aldergrove Dr MGRV/ESTR TS4.. 125 D1 🄷
Alderlea MTN/NUN TS7 .... 126 A3
Alder Rd STOCN TS19 .... 74 B4
Alderson St BAUK DL14 .... 27 D3
  HTLPW TS26 .... 2 A3
Alderwood Cl DARLE DL1 .... 117 F2 🄷
  MTN/NUN TS7 .... 101 D4
  RHTLP TS27 .... 11 E3
Aldgrove Wy DARLW DL3 .... 115 F3
Aldhun Cl BAUK DL14 .... 27 D5
Aldridge Rd NORM/PKE TS3 ..... 99 E3
Aldwark Cl ACK/BRKF TS5 ...... 123 E4
Aldwych Cl ESTON TS6 .... 101 E4
Alexander St DARLI DL1 .... 117 D5
Alexandra Rd ESTON TS6 .... 81 F4
Alexandra St SHIL DL4 .... 35 F2 🄷
Alford Ct HTLPS TS25 .... 23 F4 🄷
Alford La STOCN TS19 .... 73 F4
Alford Rd SALT/BTN/SK TS12 ... 111 E1
Alfred St HTLP TS24 .... 19 E1 🄷
  REDCAR TS10 .... 51 F4
Alfriston Cl THNBY TS17 ...... 139 D2 🄷
Alice Rw STOCS TS18 .... 6 D5
Alington Rd NACLF DL5 .... 38 E5
Allan St DARLE DL1 .... 116 C5
Allendale Rd BLGHM TS23 ...... 58 B3
  MTN/NUN TS7 .... 100 C4
  STOCS TS18 .... 6 A2
Allendale St HTLPS TS25 ...... 25 D5
Allendale Tee MARSKE TS11 .... 86 B3
Allensway THNBY TS17 .... 122 B2
Allerford Cl THNBY TS17 ...... 139 D4 🄷
Allerton Cl HTLP TS24 .... 18 A2
Allerton Pk MTN/NUN TS7 ...... 126 C5
Alliance St DARLW DL3 .... 116 A4 🄷
  HTLP TS24 .... 19 E1
  STOCS TS18 .... 94 B3
Allington Dr BLGHM TS23 ...... 41 F5
Allington Wy DARLE DL1 .... 133 F1
Allison Av THNBY TS17 .... 139 F2
Allison St GUIS TS14 .... 128 C3
  STOCS TS18 .... 7 F5
Alloa Gv HTLPS TS25 .... 23 F4
Alloway Gv CNHM/HEM TS8 ...... 124 B5
All Saints' Rd SHIL DL4 ...... 35 F5 🄷
Alma Pde REDCAR TS10 .... 51 E4
Alma Rd SHIL DL4 .... 35 F4
Alma St HTLPW TS26 .... 2 B2 🄷
  HTLPW TS26 .... 17 E4
  STOCS TS18 .... 7 F3
Almond Ct MGRV/ESTR TS4 ...... 98 B4 🄷
  STOCN TS19 .... 93 D1
Alnport Rd STOCS TS18 .... 75 E5
Alnwick Cl BAUK DL14 .... 26 C3
  FYHL DL17 .... 21 E2
  REDCAR TS10 .... 69 E2 🄷
  RHTLP TS27 .... 11 E4
Alnwick Cr MGRV/ESTR TS4 ..... 98 C3
Alnwick Gv NACLF DL5 .... 39 D3 🄷
  NORTON TS20 .... 57 F5
Alnwick Pl DARLE DL1 .... 117 D3 🄷
Alpha Gv NORTON TS20 .... 75 D3 🄷
Alphonsus St NORM/PKE TS3 .... 79 D5
Alston Crs NACLF DL5 .... 37 E5
Alston Moor Cl DARLI DL1 ..... 133 E2 🄷
Alston St HTLPW TS26 .... 2 B5
Althorpe Cl NORM/PKE TS3 ..... 100 B3
Althorpe Cl REDCAR TS10 ...... 51 E5 🄷
Alton Rd ACK/BRKF TS5 .... 97 D2
Alva Gv HTLPS TS25 .... 23 F5
Alverstone Av HTLPS TS25 ..... 24 A2
Alverton Cl NORM/PKE TS3 ..... 100 B2 🄷
Alverton Ct NACLF DL5 .... 38 A4
Alverton Dr DARLW DL3 .... 115 D1
Alvis Cl BLGHM TS23 .... 60 A2
Alvis Ct BLGHM TS23 .... 60 A2
Alwent Cl DARLW DL3 .... 130 A1
Alwent Rd MBORO TS1 .... 5 E5
Alwin Cl THNBY TS17 .... 139 D3
Alwinton Ct MTN/NUN TS7 ...... 100 C5 🄷
Amberley Cl STOCS TS18 .... 93 E3 🄷
Amberley Gv DARLW DL3 .... 114 C1 🄷

Amberley Wy EGG/EAG TS16 ..... 136 C1
Amber St MBORO TS1 .... 5 F5
  SALT/BTN/SK TS12 .... 89 F1
Amberton Rd HTLP TS24 .... 18 A2
Amberwood Cl RHTLP TS27 ...... 11 E3 🄷
Amble Cl HTLPW TS26 .... 16 C4
Ambleside Av REDCAR TS10 ..... 68 B2
Ambleside Gv ACK/BRKF TS5 .... 97 E5
Ambleside Rd BLGHM TS23 ...... 59 D5 🄷
  ESTON TS6 .... 101 E3
Ambrose Rd ESTON TS6 .... 102 A3
Amersham Rd NORM/PKE TS3 ..... 99 F4
Amesbury Crs CNHM/HEM TS8 .... 124 B5
Amiens Cl DARLW DL3 .... 115 D3
Ammerston Rd MBORO TS1 .... 4 D4
Ampleforth Av ESTON TS6 ...... 101 F2
Ampleforth Rd BLGHM TS23 ..... 59 E1 🄷
  NORM/PKE TS3 .... 99 E3
Ampleforth Wy DARLW DL3 ...... 114 B4
Anchorage Ms THNBY TS17 ...... 95 E2 🄷
Ancroft Dr MTN/NUN TS7 .... 100 C5
Ancroft Gdns NORTON TS20 ..... 75 D2
Anderson Rd THNBY TS17 .... 95 F3 🄷
Andover Wy CNHM/HEM TS8 ...... 124 A5
Andrew St HTLP TS24 .... 2 C4
Anglesey Gv HTLPW TS26 .... 17 D1
Angle St MGRV/ESTR TS4 .... 78 C5
Angrove Cl GTAY/STK TS9 ...... 150 B4
  YARM TS15 .... 138 D5
Angus St HTLPW TS26 .... 17 F4
Anlaby Cl BLGHM TS23 .... 42 A3
Annandale DARLE DL1 .... 117 F1
Annandale Crs HTLP TS24 ...... 12 B5
Annan Rd BLGHM TS23 .... 42 A5
Anne Swyft Rd NACLF DL5 ...... 55 D2
Annfield Cl BLGHM TS23 .... 41 F5 🄷
Annie St MBORO TS1 .... 4 B5
Ann's Ter DARLW DL3 .... 116 A4
Ann St ESTON TS6 .... 80 C4
Ansdale Rd NORM/PKE TS3 ...... 100 C1 🄷
Anstruther Dr DARLE DL1 ...... 116 C1 🄷
Antrim Av STOCN TS19 .... 72 C5
Appleby Av NORM/PKE TS3 ...... 99 F1
Appleby Cl MARSKE TS11 .... 86 B3 🄷
Appleby Gv HTLP TS24 .... 18 A2
Appleby Rd BLGHM TS23 .... 59 D1
Applegarth CNHM/HEM TS8 ...... 143 D2
Apple Orchard Bank MARSKE TS11 . 88 A5
Appleton Cl DARLI DL1 .... 116 A3
Appleton Rd ACK/BRKF TS5 ..... 97 D3
  STOCN TS19 .... 74 B4
Appletree Gdns MTN/NUN TS7 ... 101 D5 🄷
Applewood Cl RHTLP TS27 ...... 11 E3
Apsley Cl EGG/EAG TS16 .... 119 F2 🄷
Apsley St MBORO TS1 .... 98 B1
Aquinas Cl DARLW DL3 .... 116 B2
Arabella Cl HTLP TS24 .... 19 D1 🄷
Arabella St HTLP TS24 .... 19 D1
Arbroath Gv HTLPS TS25 .... 23 E4
Arch Ct HTLP TS24 .... 18 B1
Archdeacon Crs DARLW DL3 ..... 114 C4
Archer Av BAUK DL14 .... 26 C5
Archer St DARLW DL3 .... 9 E4
  THNBY TS17 .... 95 E5
Archibald St ACK/BRKF TS5 .... 97 E1 🄷
Arden Cl GUIS TS14 .... 128 C5
Arden Gv STOCN TS19 .... 93 D2
Ardmore Dr DARLE DL1 .... 117 E1
Ardrossan Cl HTLPS TS25 ...... 23 F4 🄷
Ardrossan Rd HTLPS TS25 ...... 23 F4 🄷
Arennig Ct THNBY TS17 .... 138 A1
The Argory THNBY TS17 .... 139 D2
Argyle Rd ESTON TS6 .... 81 F3
Argyll Cl DARLE DL1 .... 117 E1 🄷
Argyll Rd HTLPS TS25 .... 23 F4
  MTN/NUN TS7 .... 125 E4
  NORTON TS20 .... 74 B2
Arisaig Cl EGG/EAG TS16 ...... 137 E2
Arkendale St DARLE DL1 .... 116 B3 🄷
Arken Ter NORTON TS20 .... 75 D3
Arkle Crs DARLE DL1 .... 132 A5
Arkley Crs HTLP TS24 .... 12 C5
Ark Royal Cl HTLPS TS25 ...... 24 C4
Arlington Rd ACK/BRKF TS5 .... 98 A2
Arlington St LOFT/ST TS13 .... 113 A3
  STOCS TS18 .... 94 B3 🄷
  STOCS TS18 .... 94 C3 🄷
Armadale Cl STOCN TS19 .... 72 B5
Armadale Gv HTLPS TS25 .... 23 E4
Armitage Rd REDCAR TS10 ...... 67 D2
Armoury St SPEN DL16 .... 15 D2 🄷
Armstrong Cl NACLF DL5 .... 39 E4 🄷
Arncliffe Av STOCS TS18 ...... 94 B4 🄷
Arncliffe Gdns HTLPW TS26 .... 17 F5
Arncliffe Gv DARLW DL3 .... 130 A1 🄷
Arncliffe Rd ACK/BRKF TS5 .... 97 D1
Arnold Gv HTLPS TS25 .... 23 D3 🄷
Arnold Rd DARLI DL1 .... 117 D5
Arnside Av NORM/PKE TS3 ...... 99 F1 🄷
Arran Cl THNBY TS17 .... 121 E3
Arrandale CNHM/HEM TS8 .... 141 F2 🄷
Arran Gv HTLPS TS25 .... 23 F4
Arrathorne Rd STOCS TS18 ..... 92 C4
Arthur St GTAY/STK TS9 .... 150 C2
  REDCAR TS10 .... 51 D4

Arthur Ter BAUK DL14 .... 27 D4
Arundel Cl BAUK DL14 .... 26 C3
Arundel Dr DARLW DL3 .... 114 C3
Arundel Rd BLGHM TS23 .... 58 C1
  ESTON TS6 .... 82 A5
Ascot Av ACK/BRKF TS5 .... 97 D3 🄷
Ascot Dr STOCS TS18 .... 76 B4
Ascot Rd REDCAR TS10 .... 68 C2
Ashbourne Cl ESTON TS6 .... 102 B2
Ashbourne Rd STOCN TS19 ...... 74 C4
Ashburn St HTLPS TS25 .... 25 D5 🄷
Ashburton Cl CNHM/HEM TS8 .... 125 D3
Ashby Gv HTLPS TS25 .... 31 D2
Ashby Rd BLGHM TS23 .... 58 C1 🄷
Ashcombe Cl
  BLGHMW/WYN TS22 .... 40 C5 🄷
Ashcroft Gdns BAUK DL14 ...... 27 E3
Ashcroft Rd DARLW DL3 .... 8 B6
Ashdale CNHM/HEM TS8 .... 141 F1 🄷
Ashdown Cl THNBY TS17 .... 121 D3
Ashdown Wy BLGHM TS23 .... 42 C5
Ashfield NACLF DL5 .... 54 A1
Ashfield Av MGRV/ESTR TS4 .... 98 B3
Ashfield Cl HTLPS TS25 .... 31 D4
Ashford Av ACK/BRKF TS5 ...... 96 C4
Ashford Cl GUIS TS14 .... 128 C5
Ash Gn CNHM/HEM TS8 .... 143 E2
Ash Gv ESTON TS6 .... 81 D4
  SHIL DL4 .... 35 F5
  SPEN DL16 .... 14 C4
  YARM TS15 .... 146 B5
Ashgrove Av HTLPS TS25 .... 24 A2
Ash Hl CNHM/HEM TS8 .... 143 E1
Ashkirk Rd ESTON TS6 .... 101 E2
Ashley Gdns HTLP TS24 .... 17 E3
Ashling Wy ACK/BRKF TS5 ...... 97 E2
Ashridge Cl MARSKE TS11 ...... 86 B3
  THNBY TS17 .... 139 E1
Ash Rd GUIS TS14 .... 129 D2
Ash St BLGHM TS23 .... 61 D4
Ashton Rd NORTON TS20 .... 74 A1
Ash Tree Cl DARLE DL1 .... 130 C1
Ashville Av EGG/EAG TS16 ..... 119 E4
  NORTON TS20 .... 57 F5
Ashwood Cl MTN/NUN TS7 .... 101 D5 🄷
  RHTLP TS27 .... 11 E3
Ashwood Dr GTAY/STK TS9 ...... 148 B5
Askern Dr ACK/BRKF TS5 .... 124 A1
Aske Rd MBORO TS1 .... 5 E6
  REDCAR TS10 .... 51 F5
Askrigg Cl NACLF DL5 .... 38 B5
Askrigg St DARLE DL1 .... 116 B3
Askwith Rd ACK/BRKF TS5 ...... 97 F3 🄷
Aspen Dr ACK/BRKF TS5 .... 98 B3
Aspen Rd EGG/EAG TS16 .... 137 D2 🄷
Association St SHIL DL4 ...... 35 E2 🄷
Astbury CNHM/HEM TS8 .... 144 A2
Aster Cl MTN/NUN TS7 .... 125 D3
Asterley Dr ACK/BRKF TS5 ..... 96 C5
Astley Cl STOCN TS19 .... 93 D1 🄷
Astonbury Gn MGRV/ESTR TS4 ... 125 D1 🄷
Aston Dr THNBY TS17 .... 121 D3
Aston Rd BLGHMW/WYN TS22 ..... 58 A1
Atherstone Dr GUIS TS14 ...... 129 D4
Atherstone Wy DARLW DL3 ...... 114 B3 🄷
Atherton Cl SPEN DL16 .... 15 D4
Atholl Cl DARLE DL1 .... 117 E2 🄷
Atholl Gv HTLPS TS25 .... 23 F4 🄷
  REDCAR TS10 .... 67 F1
Athol St MBORO TS1 .... 98 A1
Atkinson Gdns NACLF DL5 ...... 55 D5
Atlas Wynd YARM TS15 .... 137 D4
Attingham Cl CNHM/HEM TS8 .... 124 B5
Attlee Rd ESTON TS6 .... 82 A5
Atwater Cl YARM TS15 .... 146 C1
Atwick Cl BLGHM TS23 .... 42 A3 🄷
Auckland Av DARLW DL3 .... 115 D4
  MTN/NUN TS7 .... 126 A4
Auckland Ms NACLF DL5 .... 39 D5 🄷
Auckland Ov DARLW DL3 .... 115 E3
Auckland Rd BLGHM TS23 .... 42 C4
  FYHL DL17 .... 21 E1
Auckland St GUIS TS14 .... 129 D2
Auckland Ter SHIL DL4 .... 35 D2
Auckland Wy HTLPW TS26 .... 2 B2
  STOCS TS18 .... 93 D3
Auckland Wynd SHIL DL4 .... 35 D2 🄷
Audrey Gv DARLW DL3 .... 133 E2
  STOCS TS18 .... 93 E3 🄷
Augusta Cl DARLE DL1 .... 117 E2
Austin Av STOCS TS18 .... 94 B4
Autumn Gv STOCN TS19 .... 93 E2
Avalon Ct CNHM/HEM TS8 .... 124 B5
Avebury Cl THNBY TS17 .... 139 E2 🄷
Avens Wy THNBY TS17 .... 121 D5
Avenue Crs BLGHM TS23 .... 59 D5
Avenue Rd HTLP TS24 .... 2 B2 🄷
  HTLPW TS26 .... 2 B2
The Avenue ACK/BRKF TS5 ...... 98 A3
  EGG/EAG TS16 .... 119 E4
  ESTON TS6 .... 101 E1
  GTAY/STK TS9 .... 152 B2
  GUIS TS14 .... 128 A4
  MTN/NUN TS7 .... 126 C5
  REDCAR TS10 .... 51 F5

SALT/BTN/SK TS12 .... 91 E5
STOCN TS19 .... 93 D1
THNBY TS17 .... 95 F4
Aviemore Rd CNHM/HEM TS8 .... 124 B5
Avill Gv THNBY TS17 .... 138 C4
Avon Cl SALT/BTN/SK TS12 .... 109 F1
THNBY TS17 .... 121 F1
Avondale Cl ESTON TS6 .... 82 A5
Avondale Gdns HTLP TS24 .... 17 F2
Avon Dr GUIS TS14 .... 128 D4
Avon Gv BLGHMW/WYN TS22 .... 40 C5
Avon Rd NORTON TS20 .... 75 E2
REDCAR TS10 .... 67 F2
Avon St SALT/BTN/SK TS12 .... 89 E3
Avon Wy DARLE DL1 .... 132 B5
Avro Cl STOCS TS18 .... 120 A1
Axminster Rd CNHM/HEM TS8 .... 124 B5
Axton Cl THNBY TS17 .... 121 D4
Aycliffe Cl STOCN TS19 .... 92 C1
Aycliffe Rd MTN/NUN TS7 .... 125 F4
Aylmer Gv NACLF DL5 .... 38 B5
Aylsham Cl THNBY TS17 .... 139 E1
Aylton Dr ACK/BRKF TS5 .... 123 E4
Ayresome Grange Rd
ACK/BRKF TS5 .... 97 E1
Ayresome Green La
ACK/BRKF TS5 .... 97 E1
Ayresome Park Rd ACK/BRKF TS5 ... 97 F1
Ayresome Rd ACK/BRKF TS5 .... 77 D5
Ayresome St MBORO TS1 .... 97 E1
Ayresome Wy DARLE DL1 .... 117 E4
Ayr Gv HTLPS TS25 .... 23 F4
Aysgarth Cl NACLF DL5 .... 38 A5
Aysgarth Rd ACK/BRKF TS5 .... 97 E3
DARLE DL1 .... 132 C3
STOCS TS18 .... 93 F2
Ayton Ct GUIS TS14 .... 128 C1
Ayton Crs ESTON TS6 .... 102 A3
Ayton Dr DARLW DL3 .... 131 E4
REDCAR TS10 .... 68 A3
Ayton Pl NORTON TS20 .... 75 D4
Ayton Rd THNBY TS17 .... 121 E1
Azalia Cl STOCN TS19 .... 74 C4

B

Babbacombe Dr FYHL DL17 .... 21 F2
Back Child St SALT/BTN/SK TS12 ...... 91 D5
Backhouse St DARLE DL1 .... 9 G6
Back La EGG/EAG TS16 .... 137 E3
SALT/BTN/SK TS12 .... 108 C3
Back Throston St HTLP TS24 .... 19 E2
Baden St HTLPW TS26 .... 23 F1
Bader Av THNBY TS17 .... 124 B5
Badger La THNBY TS17 .... 121 E5
Badminton Gv NACLF DL5 .... 39 D3
Badsworth Cl GUIS TS14 .... 128 C5
Baff St SPEN DL16 .... 15 D4
Bailey Gv NORM/PKE TS3 .... 99 E1
Bailey St HTLP TS24 .... 2 B1
Bainton Cl BLGHM TS23 .... 42 A3
Bakehouse Hl DARLE DL1 .... 9 F5
Bakehouse Sq GUIS TS14 .... 129 D3
Baker St MBORO TS1 .... 5 F4
Bakery Dr STOCN TS19 .... 73 F4
Bakery St STOCS TS18 .... 7 E4
Balaclava St STOCS TS18 .... 7 F3
Balcary Ct HTLPS TS25 .... 23 E5
Balder Rd NORTON TS20 .... 74 C1
Baldoon Sands ACK/BRKF TS5 .... 123 D3
Balfour St ACK/BRKF TS5 .... 97 D3
Baliol Gn NACLF DL5 .... 55 D2
Baliol Rd NACLF DL5 .... 55 D1
Ballater Gv HTLPS TS25 .... 23 F5
Balmoral Av BLGHM TS23 .... 59 D1
THNBY TS17 .... 95 F4
Balmoral Ct HTLPS TS25 .... 23 F5
Balmoral Dr MGRV/ESTR TS4 .... 98 C3
Balmoral Gv BAUK DL14 .... 26 C3
Balmoral Rd DARLE DL1 .... 117 E3
HTLPS TS25 .... 23 E5
NORM/PKE TS3 .... 100 A4
Balmoral Ter STOCS TS18 .... 93 D3
Balmor Rd ESTON TS6 .... 101 E3
Baltic Cl STOCS TS18 .... 7 H2
Baltic Rd STOCS TS18 .... 7 H2
Baltimore Wy DARLE DL1 .... 116 C2
Bamburgh Av BAUK DL14 .... 26 B3
Bamburgh Cl REDCAR TS10 .... 69 D2
Bamburgh Ct RHTLP TS27 .... 11 F4
Bamburgh Crs NACLF DL5 .... 39 D3
Bamburgh Dr MTN/NUN TS7 .... 100 C5
Bamburgh Pde SPEN DL16 .... 15 E3
Bamburgh Rd RHTLP TS27 .... 11 E4
Bamford Cl THNBY TS17 .... 121 E2
Banbury Gv ACK/BRKF TS5 .... 123 D1
Banff Gv HTLPS TS25 .... 23 F5
Bangor Cl ESTON TS6 .... 82 A5
Bangor Gv DARLE DL1 .... 117 F3
Bangor St HTLPW TS26 .... 23 F1
Bankfields Ct ESTON TS6 .... 101 F4
Bankfields Rd ESTON TS6 .... 101 F4

Banklands Rd DARLW DL3 .... 115 E4
Bank Rd BLGHM TS23 .... 58 C5
Bank Sands ACK/BRKF TS5 .... 123 D4
Bankside YARM TS15 .... 138 A4
Banks Rd DARLE DL1.......................... 117 E5
Bankston Cl HTLPW TS26 .... 16 B3
Bank St REDCAR TS10 .... 51 E4
Bank Top Ms DARLE DL1 .... 132 C5
Bannockburn Wy BLGHM TS23 .... 42 B4
Baptist St HTLP TS24 .... 19 E2
Barbara Mann Ct HTLPW TS26 .... 2 A2
Barberry CNHM/HEM TS8 .... 143 E2
Barberry Cl THNBY TS17 .... 121 E5
Barden Moor Rd DARLE DL1 .... 133 D4
Barden Rd NORM/PKE TS3 .... 99 E2
Bardsley St EGG/EAG TS16 .... 119 F2
Barford Cl HTLPS TS25 .... 31 D3
NORTON TS20 .... 57 D5
REDCAR TS10 .... 68 A3
Barholm Cl NORM/PKE TS3 .... 100 B3
Barker Rd ACK/BRKF TS5 .... 97 E4
THNBY TS17 .... 95 F4
The Barkery CNHM/HEM TS8 .... 143 D5
Barkston Av THNBY TS17 .... 121 D4
Barkston Cl BLGHMW/WYN TS22 ...... 41 D5
Barlborough Av STOCN TS19 .... 73 F5
Barle Cl THNBY TS17 .... 139 D4
Barley Hill Cl ESTON TS6 .... 102 A4
Barlow Cl GUIS TS14 .... 129 D4
Barlow Ct BLGHM TS23 .... 42 A4
Barlow St DARLW DL3 .... 8 A2
Barmoor Gv NORTON TS20 .... 57 F4
Barmouth Rd ESTON TS6 .... 101 F1
Brampton La DARLE DL1 .... 117 F2
Barmton Rd BLGHM TS23 .... 42 A4
Barnaby Av ACK/BRKF TS5................. 97 E1
Barnaby Crs ESTON TS6 .... 102 A3
Barnaby Pl GUIS TS14 .... 128 B3
Barnaby Rd MTN/NUN TS7 .... 127 D4
Barnack Av MTN/NUN TS7 .... 126 A4
Barnard Av BAUK DL14 .... 27 D3
STOCN TS19 .... 93 E2
Barnard Cl NACLF DL5 .... 39 D3
SPEN DL16 .... 15 E1
THNBY TS17 .... 95 E3
Barnard Gv MGRV/ESTR TS4 .... 98 C3
HTLP TS24 .... 11 F2
REDCAR TS10 .... 69 D1
Barnard Rd BLGHM TS23 .... 59 D2
Barnard St DARLW DL3 .... 9 E4
Barnes Cl DARLW DL3 .... 114 C5
Barnes Rd DARLW DL3 .... 114 B5
Barnes Wallis Wy MARSKE TS11 ...... 70 A5
Barnet Wy BLGHM TS23 .... 42 C4
Barnfield Rd SPEN DL16 .... 15 E2
Barningham St DARLW DL3 .... 9 E1
Barnstaple Cl CNHM/HEM TS8 .... 125 D2
Barra Gv HTLPS TS25 .... 23 F5
Barras Gv NORM/PKE TS3 .... 100 B1
Barras Wy STOCN TS19 .... 72 C3
Barrett Rd DARLW DL3 .... 130 C2
Barrhead Cl STOCN TS19 .... 72 B5
Barrington Av STOCN TS19 .... 72 B5
Barrington Crs NORM/PKE TS3 .... 100 B2
Barrington Rd NACLF DL5 .... 54 B1
Barritt St MBORO TS1 .... 5 F6
Barron St DARLW DL3 .... 116 A4
Barrowburn Gn THNBY TS17 .... 138 B2
Barsford Rd NORM/PKE TS3 .... 100 B1
Barton Av HTLPS TS25 .... 23 F2
Barton Cl NACLF DL5 .... 38 A4
THNBY TS17 .... 121 D3
Barton Crs BLGHMW/WYN TS22 .... 58 A1
Barton Rd TEESM TS2 .... 77 E2
Barton St DARLE DL1 .... 116 C4
Barwick Cl THNBY TS17 .... 120 C5
Barwick Flds THNBY TS17 .... 138 C1
Barwick La THNBY TS17 .... 138 C2
Barwick Vw THNBY TS17 .... 120 C5
Barwick Wy THNBY TS17 .... 138 C2
Basil St NORM/PKE TS3 .... 79 D5
Bassleton La THNBY TS17 .... 121 D3
Bates Av DARLW DL3 .... 114 C3
Bath La STOCS TS18 .... 7 C3
Bath Pl STOCS TS18 .... 7 C3
Bath Rd ESTON TS6 .... 102 A2
Bath St REDCAR TS10 .... 51 E4
SALT/BTN/SK TS12 .... 89 E2
Bath Ter HTLP TS24 .... 19 F2
Battersby Cl YARM TS15 .... 138 A4
Baydale Rd DARLW DL3 .... 130 C3
Baysdale Cl GUIS TS14 .... 129 E3
Baysdale Gdns SHIL DL4 .... 36 B3
Baysdale Gv REDCAR TS10 .... 67 E2
Baysdale Rd THNBY TS17 .... 121 F1
Beachfield Dr HTLPS TS25 .... 23 F2
Beacon Av SEDG TS21 .... 29 F4
Beacon Dr MARSKE TS11 .... 86 C3
Beacon La SEDG TS21 .... 29 F4
Beaconsfield Rd NORTON TS20 .... 58 A5
Beaconsfield Sq HTLP TS24 .... 19 E2
Beaconsfield St DARLW DL3 .... 8 D1
HTLP TS24 .... 19 E2
Beacons La THNBY TS17 .... 138 B2
Beacon St HTLP TS24 .... 19 E1

Beadlam Av MTN/NUN TS7 .... 127 D4
Beadnell Cl THNBY TS17 .... 139 E1
Beadnell Wy REDCAR TS10 .... 69 E3
Beadon Gv ACK/BRKF TS5 .... 97 D2
Beale Cl THNBY TS17 .... 139 E1
Beamish Rd BLGHM TS23 .... 59 E1
Beardmore Av MARSKE TS11 .... 70 A4
Beaufort Cl GUIS TS14 .... 128 C5
Beaufort St MBORO TS1 .... 5 E4
Beauly Dr DARLE DL1 .... 117 D1
Beauly Gv HTLPS TS25 .... 23 F5
Beaumaris Dr EGG/EAG TS16 .... 137 E2
Beaumont Cl NACLF DL5 .... 38 C3
Beaumont Rd NORM/PKE TS3 .... 79 E5
Beaumont St BAUK DL14 .... 27 D3
DARLE DL1 .... 9 F6
FYHL DL17 .... 20 B1
Beaumont St West DARLE DL1 .... 9 E5
Beaumont Vw NORTON TS20 .... 75 E2
Beaumont Wy NACLF DL5 .... 54 C4
Beaver Cl THNBY TS17 .... 121 E5
Beccles Cl STOCN TS19 .... 73 D4
Beckenham Gdns CNHM/HEM TS8 .. 142 B2
Beckfields Av THNBY TS17 .... 139 D3
Beck Rd DARLE DL1 .... 9 G2
Beckston Cl HTLPW TS26 .... 16 B4
Bedale Av BLGHM TS23 .... 58 C4
Bedale Gv STOCN TS19 .... 93 C2
Bedale Hunt NACLF DL5 .... 37 E4
Bedburn Dr DARLW DL3 .... 130 A1
Bede Cl STOCN TS19 .... 73 F3
Bede Crs NACLF DL5 .... 54 C2
Bede Gv HTLPS TS25 .... 23 E2
Bede Rd DARLW DL3 .... 130 C2
Bedford Rd MTN/NUN TS7 .... 126 C4
Bedford St DARLE DL1 .... 132 A3
HTLP TS24 .... 19 E2
MBORO TS1 .... 5 D1
STOCS TS19 .... 6 D1
Bedford Ter BLGHM TS23 .... 59 D3
Beech Av SPEN DL16 .... 14 C4
Beech Cl GTAY/STK TS9 .... 150 B3
Beech Crs FYHL DL17 .... 21 D2
Beechers Gv FYHL DL17 .... 39 D2
Beeches Ri MTN/NUN TS7 .... 126 A5
The Beeches ESTON TS6 .... 101 E2
GTAY/STK TS9 .... 152 A3
Beechfield CNHM/HEM TS8 .... 143 E2
NACLF DL5 .... 54 A1
Beech Gv CNHM/HEM TS8 .... 140 B2
ESTON TS6 .... 81 D5
FYHL DL17 .... 21 D2
LOFT/ST TS13 .... 113 D3
SALT/BTN/SK TS12 .... 90 C4
Beech Grove Rd ACK/BRKF TS5 .... 98 A4
Beech Rd BAUK DL14 .... 27 E4
DARLE DL1 .... 117 F2
GUIS TS14 .... 129 D2
Beech St MBORO TS1 .... 5 H3
Beech Ter TEESM TS2 .... 61 D5
Beechwood Av DARLW DL3 .... 8 D6
GTAY/STK TS9 .... 148 B5
MGRV/ESTR TS4 .... 98 C3
SALT/BTN/SK TS12 .... 89 E3
Beechwood Dr BAUK DL14 .... 27 E4
Beechwood Rd EGG/EAG TS16 .... 119 E4
THNBY TS17 .... 95 E5
Beeford Cl BLGHM TS23 .... 42 A2
Beeford Dr ACK/BRKF TS5 .... 124 A1
Bek Rd NACLF DL5 .... 55 D1
Belasis Av BLGHM TS23 .... 59 D5
Belasis Ct BLGHM TS23 .... 59 F3
Belford Cl STOCN TS19 .... 73 E5
Belford Gdns DARLE DL1 .... 117 D2
Belford Wy NACLF DL5 .... 37 E5
Belgrave Ct HTLPS TS25 .... 25 D5
Belgrave Dr ESTON TS6 .... 101 E5
Belgrave St DARLE DL1 .... 132 C3
Belk Cl ESTON TS6 .... 81 F4
Belk St MBORO TS1 .... 98 A1
Bellamy Ct NORM/PKE TS3 .... 99 F1
Bellasis Cl NACLF DL5 .... 39 D5
Bellburn La DARLW DL3 .... 115 E3
Bell Cl STOCS TS18 .... 6 D5
Bellerby Rd STOCS TS18 .... 93 D3
Belle Vue Ct NORTON TS20 .... 75 E3
Belle Vue Gv MGRV/ESTR TS4 .... 98 C3
Belle Vue Rd ACK/BRKF TS5 .... 97 F2
Belle Vue St SPEN DL16 .... 14 C4
Belle Vue Wy HTLPS TS25 .... 2 C6
Bell's Pl DARLW DL3 .... 9 F4
Bell St ACK/BRKF TS5 .... 97 E1
BAUK DL14 .... 27 D3
NORTON TS20 .... 75 D3
Belmangate GUIS TS14 .... 129 E3
Belmont Av ACK/BRKF TS5 .... 123 F4
BLGHMW/WYN TS22 .... 58 B1
ESTON TS6 .... 101 D5
STOCN TS19 .... 74 B4
Belmont Gdns HTLPW TS26 .... 17 F5
Belmont St ESTON TS6 .... 102 B2
Belsay Cl FYHL DL17 .... 21 E1
STOCN TS19 .... 73 E5
Belsay Ct SEDG TS21 .... 29 D3
Belsay Wk DARLE DL1........................ 117 D2

Belton Dr *ACK/BRKF* TS5 ...... 124 A1
Belvedere Rd *DARLE* DL1 ...... 132 B3
  MGRV/ESTR TS4 ...... 98 C3
  THNBY TS17 ...... 95 F4 □
Belvoir Gv *BAUK* DL14 ...... 26 C3 □
Benedict St *NORM/PKE* TS3 ...... 79 D5 □
Beningborough Gdns
  THNBY TS17 ...... 139 D1
Benmore Rd *HTLPS* TS25 ...... 23 E5
Bennett Rd *HTLPS* TS25 ...... 22 C2
Bennison Crs *REDCAR* TS10 ...... 67 E2
Bennison St *GUIS* TS14 ...... 129 D2
Benridge Cl *ACK/BRKF* TS5 ...... 123 D3
Bensham Rd *DARLE* DL1... ...... 116 B1
Benson St *ACK/BRKF* TS5 ...... 97 F2 □
  HTLPW TS26 ...... 2 A4 □
  NORTON TS20 ...... 75 D1
Bentick St *HTLPW* TS26 ...... 2 A2
Bentinck Av *ACK/BRKF* TS5 ...... 98 A4
Bentinck Rd *STOCN* TS19 ...... 93 D2
Bentley Av *BLGHM* TS23 ...... 60 A1
Bentley St *HTLPW* TS26 ...... 2 A4 □
Bentley Wynd *YARM* TS15 ...... 137 D4
Benton Rd *BLGHM* TS23 ...... 41 F3
Benton Rd *ACK/BRKF* TS5 ...... 98 A5
Benwell Cl *STOCN* TS19 ...... 73 E5 □
Berberis Gv *STOCN* TS19 ...... 93 E1 □
Beresford Crs *NORM/PKE* TS3 ...... 100 B1
Beresford St *SHIL* DL4 ...... 35 F5
Berkeley Av *HTLPS* TS25 ...... 31 F1
Berkeley Cl *BLGHM* TS23 ...... 58 C2 □
Berkeley Dr *REDCAR* TS10 ...... 69 D3 □
Berkeley Gv *BAUK* DL14 ...... 26 C3
Berkeley Rd *DARLE* DL1 ...... 132 B4
Berkley Dr *GUIS* TS14 ...... 129 D5
Berkshire Rd *NORTON* TS20 ...... 75 F2
Bernaldby Av *GUIS* TS14 ...... 128 B4
Berner St *ACK/BRKF* TS5 ...... 97 F2
Bernica Gv *THNBY* TS17 ...... 138 C3
Berriedale Dr *DARLE* DL1 ...... 116 C1
Berrington Gdns *THNBY* TS17 ...... 139 D2
Berrybank Crest *DARLW* DL3 ...... 114 C4 □
Bertha St *FYHL* DL17 ...... 21 D2
  HTLP TS24 ...... 3 E5
Bertie Rd *NACLF* DL5 ...... 38 B5
Berwick Gv *NORTON* TS20 ...... 57 F5
Berwick Hills Av *NORM/PKE* TS3 ...... 100 A1
Berwick Rd *DARLW* DL3 ...... 114 C3
Berwick St *HTLPS* TS25 ...... 25 D5
Bessemer St *FYHL* DL17 ...... 20 B2
Bethune Rd *ACK/BRKF* TS5 ...... 97 D2
Betjeman Cl *BLGHM* TS23 ...... 42 A3 □
Bevanlee Rd *ESTON* TS6 ...... 81 D4
Beverley Rd *BLGHM* TS23 ...... 42 B3
  MGRV/ESTR TS4 ...... 98 B5
  MTN/NUN TS7 ...... 127 D4
  REDCAR TS10 ...... 69 E2
Bewholme Cl *BLGHM* TS23 ...... 42 A2 □
Bewick Crs *NACLF* DL5 ...... 54 C1
Bewley Av *ACK/BRKF* TS5 ...... 123 E1
Bexley Cl *MGRV/ESTR* TS4 ...... 125 D1
Bexley Dr *ESTON* TS6 ...... 101 E5
  HTLPS TS25 ...... 23 F3
Bickersteth Cl *STOCS* TS18 ...... 94 C3
Bickford Ter *NACLF* DL5 ...... 54 C5
Bickley Cl *BLGHMW/WYN* TS22 ...... 57 F1 □
Bickley Wy *CNHM/HEM* TS8 ...... 125 D5
Biddick Cl *STOCN* TS19 ...... 73 E5
Bielby Av *BLGHM* TS23 ...... 42 A3
Biggin Cl *ACK/BRKF* TS5 ...... 124 A1 □
Billingham Bank *BLGHM* TS23 ...... 58 C5
Billingham Rd *NORTON* TS20 ...... 75 D1
Bilsdale Av *REDCAR* TS10 ...... 67 F2
Bilsdale Rd *HTLPS* TS25 ...... 32 C1
  MGRV/ESTR TS4 ...... 98 C1
  STOCN TS19 ...... 6 A1
Binchestre Ctt *NACLF* DL5 ...... 53 E3 □
Bingfield Ct *BLGHM* TS23 ...... 42 A3
Binks St *ACK/BRKF* TS5 ...... 98 A2 □
Birch Av *BAUK* DL14 ...... 27 D4
  SHIL DL4 ...... 35 F3
Birch Cl *YARM* TS15 ...... 146 C5
The Birches *CNHM/HEM* TS8 ...... 142 C1
Birchfield Cl *EGG/EAG* TS16 ...... 137 D1 □
Birchfield Dr *EGG/EAG* TS16 ...... 137 D1
Birchgate Rd *ACK/BRKF* TS5 ...... 97 F4
Birch Gv *STOCN* TS19 ...... 74 A2
Birchill Gdns *HTLPW* TS26 ...... 17 D5
Birchington Av *ESTON* TS6 ...... 82 A3
  ESTON TS6 ...... 102 B1
Birchmere *SPEN* DL16 ...... 14 C1
Birch Tree Cl *MTN/NUN* TS7 ...... 101 D5 □
Birchwood Av *MGRV/ESTR* TS4 ...... 98 C3
Birchwood Rd *MTN/NUN* TS7 ...... 126 B3
Birdsall Brow *NORTON* TS20 ...... 57 E5 □
Birdsall Rd *REDCAR* TS10 ...... 51 F5
Biretta Cl *STOCN* TS19 ...... 72 C5
Birkdale Cl *RHTLP* TS27 ...... 11 E3 □
Birkdale Dr *ESTON* TS6 ...... 102 C3
Birkdale Rd *DARLW* DL3 ...... 114 C5 □
  MARSKE TS11 ...... 86 B2
  STOCS TS18 ...... 93 D3
Birkhall Rd *NORM/PKE* TS3 ...... 100 B1
Birkley Rd *NORTON* TS20 ...... 75 D3
Birtley Av *ACK/BRKF* TS5 ...... 123 E2

Biscop Crs *NACLF* DL5 ...... 39 D5
Bisham Av *ACK/BRKF* TS5 ...... 97 E3 □
Bishop Cl *DARLE* DL1 ...... 117 E3
Bishop's Cl *SPEN* DL16 ...... 15 E3 □
Bishop St *ACK/BRKF* TS5 ...... 97 D1
  BAUK DL14 ...... 27 D1 □
  STOCS TS18 ...... 7 C4
Bishops Wy *STOCN* TS19 ...... 72 C4
Bishopton Av *STOCN* TS19 ...... 73 F5
Bishopton Ct *STOCN* TS19 ...... 93 D1
Bishopton La *STOCS* TS18 ...... 7 E2
Bishopton Rd *MGRV/ESTR* TS4 ...... 98 B3
  STOCN TS19 ...... 6 D2
  STOCS TS18 ...... 6 A2
Bishopton Rd West *STOCN* TS19 ...... 72 C5
Blackburn Cl *STOCN* TS19 ...... 93 E1 □
Blackburn Gv *MARSKE* TS11 ...... 69 F4
Blackbush Wk *THNBY* TS17 ...... 121 E4
Blackett Av *NORTON* TS20 ...... 75 D3
Blackett Rd *DARLE* DL1 ...... 117 D5
Blackett St *BAUK* DL14 ...... 27 E2
Blackfriars *YARM* TS15 ...... 137 E5 □
Blackhall Sands *ACK/BRKF* TS5 ...... 123 D4
Blackmore Cl *GUIS* TS14 ...... 129 E5 □
The Black Pth *NORTON* TS20 ...... 7 H1
Blacksail Cl *STOCN* TS19 ...... 6 C3
Blackthorn *CNHM/HEM* TS8 ...... 143 E2
Blackthorn Gv *STOCN* TS19 ...... 93 E1
Blackwell *DARLW* DL3 ...... 131 D4
Blackwell Br *DARLW* DL3 ...... 131 D5
Blackwell Cl *BLGHM* TS23 ...... 42 C5 □
  DARLW DL3 ...... 131 E4 □
Blackwellgate *DARLE* DL1 ...... 9 F5
Blackwell Gv *DARLW* DL3 ...... 131 D5
Blackwell La *DARLW* DL3 ...... 131 E4
Blackwell Scar *DARLW* DL3 ...... 131 D4
Blackwood Cl *RHTLP* TS27 ...... 11 F3 □
Bladon Dr *MARSKE* TS11 ...... 70 B4
Blair Av *SPEN* DL16 ...... 15 E3
  THNBY TS17 ...... 138 B2
Blairgowrie Gv *HTLPS* TS25 ...... 23 E5 □
Blair Gv *BAUK* DL14 ...... 26 C3
Blairmore Gdns *EGG/EAG* TS16 ...... 137 E1 □
Blake Cl *BLGHM* TS23 ...... 41 F3
Blakelock Gdns *HTLPS* TS25 ...... 23 F1
Blakelock Rd *HTLPS* TS25 ...... 23 F1
Blakeston Ct *STOCN* TS19 ...... 56 C5
Blakeston La *SEDG* TS21 ...... 56 B4
Blakeston Rd *BLGHM* TS23 ...... 42 B5
Blake St *HTLPW* TS26 ...... 17 F3
  SHIL DL4 ...... 35 F4 □
Blakey Cl *REDCAR* TS10 ...... 68 B4
Blakiston Ct *FYHL* DL17 ...... 38 B2
Blanchland Rd *NORM/PKE* TS3 ...... 100 A4
Blandford St *FYHL* DL17 ...... 20 B2 □
Blankney Cl *GUIS* TS14 ...... 128 C4
Blantyre Rd *ESTON* TS6 ...... 101 E2
Blatchford Rd *ESTON* TS6 ...... 80 B4
Blayberry Cl *REDCAR* TS10 ...... 68 B4
Blenheim Cl *MARSKE* TS11 ...... 70 B4
Blenheim Rd *MGRV/ESTR* TS4 ...... 78 C5 □
Blenheim Rd South
  MGRV/ESTR TS4 ...... 98 C1 □
Blenheim Ter *REDCAR* TS10 ...... 51 D5
Bletchley Cl *STOCN* TS19 ...... 73 E5 □
Bloomesley Cl *NACLF* DL5 ...... 38 B2
Bloomfield Rd *DARLW* DL3 ...... 8 B1
Blorenge Ct *THNBY* TS17 ...... 138 B3
Bluebell Cl *NACLF* DL5 ...... 38 A4
Bluebell Dr *SPEN* DL16 ...... 14 B4
Blue Bell Gv *ACK/BRKF* TS5 ...... 124 A3 □
  STOCN TS19 ...... 93 E1 □
Bluebell Meadow *NACLF* DL5 ...... 38 A4 □
Bluebell Wy *NACLF* DL5 ...... 38 A4
  SALT/BTN/SK TS12 ...... 110 A3
Blue House Point Rd *STOCS* TS18 ...... 76 A5
Blue Post Yd *STOCS* TS18 ...... 7 F5 □
Blythport Cl *STOCS* TS18 ...... 95 D3 □
Boar La *THNBY* TS17 ...... 139 E1
Boathouse La *STOCS* TS18 ...... 95 D3
Bob Hardisty Dr *BAUK* DL14 ...... 27 D2
Bodiam Dr *REDCAR* TS10 ...... 69 E3
Bodmin Gv *HTLPW* TS26 ...... 16 C2
Boeing Wy *STOCS* TS18 ...... 120 B1
Bolam Gv *BLGHM* TS23 ...... 42 A4
Bolckow Rd *ESTON* TS6 ...... 81 F3
Bolckow St *ESTON* TS6 ...... 102 B3
  GUIS TS14 ...... 129 D2
  MBORO TS1 ...... 5 F2
  SALT/BTN/SK TS12 ...... 110 A3
Boldron Cl *STOCS* TS18 ...... 92 C4 □
Bollington Rd *MGRV/ESTR* TS4 ...... 125 D1
Bolsover Rd *NORTON* TS20 ...... 75 D3
Boltby Cl *ACK/BRKF* TS5 ...... 124 A1 □
Bolton Cl *DARLW* DL3 ...... 114 C4
Bolton Gv *GUIS* TS14 ...... 69 D2 □
Bolton Ct *MGRV/ESTR* TS4 ...... 98 B3 □
Bolton Gv *BAUK* DL14 ...... 26 C3
  HTLPS TS25 ...... 23 D4
Bolton Wy *GUIS* TS14 ...... 129 E3
Bondene Gv *STOCN* TS19 ...... 72 C4 □
Bondfield Rd *ESTON* TS6 ...... 101 F1
Bondgate *DARLW* DL3 ...... 9 F4
Bondgate Rbt. *DARLW* DL3 ...... 9 E4
Bond St *HTLP* TS24 ...... 19 E2

Bone St *STOCS* TS18 ...... 7 G2
Bonington Crs *BLGHM* TS23 ...... 41 F3
Bonny Gv *CNHM/HEM* TS8 ...... 144 B1
Bonnygrove Wy *CNHM/HEM* TS8 ...... 143 E1
Bonnyrigg Cl *THNBY* TS17 ...... 139 D3
Boosbeck Rd *SALT/BTN/SK* TS12 ...... 109 D3
Borough Rd *DARLE* DL1 ...... 9 H4
  MBORO TS1 ...... 5 E4
  MGRV/ESTR TS4 ...... 78 C5
  REDCAR TS10 ...... 68 C1
Borrowby Ct *GUIS* TS14 ...... 128 C2 □
Borrowdale Gv *ACK/BRKF* TS5 ...... 97 E5 □
  EGG/EAG TS16 ...... 137 E3
Borrowdale Rd *ESTON* TS6 ...... 82 B5
Borrowdale St *HTLPS* TS25 ...... 24 A2
Boscombe Gdns *CNHM/HEM* TS8 ...... 142 B1
Boston Cl *DARLE* DL1 ...... 117 D2 □
  HTLPS TS25 ...... 31 E1
Boston Dr *MTN/NUN* TS7 ...... 125 F5
Boswell St *MBORO* TS1 ...... 5 G4
Bosworth Wy *BLGHM* TS23 ...... 42 B5
Botany Wy *MTN/NUN* TS7 ...... 126 C5
Bothal Dr *STOCN* TS19 ...... 72 C4 □
Botham Gv *DARLW* DL3 ...... 116 B1 □
Bouch St *SHIL* DL4 ...... 35 F5
Boulby Dr *LOFT/ST* TS13 ...... 113 E4
Boulby Rd *LOFT/ST* TS13 ...... 112 C1 □
  REDCAR TS10 ...... 67 E2
Boundary Rd *ESTON* TS6 ...... 101 E4 □
  MBORO TS1 ...... 5 E2
Bournemouth Av *NORM/PKE* TS3 ...... 100 B4
Bournemouth Dr *HTLP* TS24 ...... 11 F2
Bournemouth Rd *NORM/PKE* TS3 ...... 100 B4
Bousfield Crs *NACLF* DL5 ...... 38 C4
Bowen Rd *DARLW* DL3 ...... 115 D3
Bowes Cl *FYHL* DL17 ...... 21 D5
Bowesfield Crs *STOCS* TS18 ...... 95 D5
Bowesfield La *STOCS* TS18 ...... 94 C3
Bowes Gv *BAUK* DL14 ...... 26 C3 □
  SPEN DL16 ...... 15 D1
Bowes Moor Cl *DARLE* DL1 ...... 133 F4
Bowes Rd *BLGHM* TS23 ...... 41 E5
  NACLF DL5 ...... 54 C1
  TEESM TS2 ...... 77 F2
Bowfell Cl *EGG/EAG* TS16 ...... 119 D5
Bowfell Rd *NORM/PKE* TS3 ...... 99 E2 □
Bowhill Wy *BLGHM* TS23 ...... 42 C4
Bowland Cl *MTN/NUN* TS7 ...... 126 B5
Bowley Cl *ESTON* TS6 ...... 101 D3 □
Bowley Wk *MBORO* TS1 ...... 4 C4
Bowman St *DARLW* DL3 ...... 116 B2
Bowness Cl *HTLPS* TS25 ...... 24 A3 □
Bowness Gv *FYHL* DL17 ...... 20 C1 □
  REDCAR TS10 ...... 68 B1 □
Bowron St *NORTON* TS20 ...... 75 D4
Bowser St *HTLP* TS24 ...... 3 E5
Bow St *GUIS* TS14 ...... 129 D3 □
  MBORO TS1 ...... 4 D6
Boxer Ct *ESTON* TS6 ...... 80 C4
Boyes Hill Gv *DARLW* DL3 ...... 8 A3
Boyne Ct *SEDG* TS21 ...... 29 D3 □
Boynston Gv *SEDG* TS21 ...... 29 E4
Boynton Rd *MGRV/ESTR* TS4 ...... 98 C2
Brabazon Dr *MARSKE* TS11 ...... 70 A5
Brabourn Gdns *CNHM/HEM* TS8 ...... 124 B5
Brackenberry Crs *REDCAR* TS10 ...... 69 D3
Bracken Crs *GUIS* TS14 ...... 128 A4
Brackenfield Ct *ESTON* TS6 ...... 102 A4 □
Brackenhill Cl *MTN/NUN* TS7 ...... 144 C1 □
Bracken Rd *DARLW* DL3 ...... 8 B2
  STOCN TS19 ...... 74 A2
Bracknell Rd *THNBY* TS17 ...... 96 A5
Bradbury Rd *NACLF* DL5 ...... 54 B3
  NORTON TS20 ...... 57 F5
Bradford Cl *NACLF* DL5 ...... 54 C2
Bradhope Rd *NORM/PKE* TS3 ...... 99 D2
Bradley Cl *BLGHM* TS23 ...... 42 B5 □
Bradleys Ter *GTAY/STK* TS9 ...... 150 C2 □
Bradshaw Ct *HTLP* TS24 ...... 12 B5 □
Brae Head *EGG/EAG* TS16 ...... 137 E1 □
Braemar Cl *DARLE* DL1 ...... 117 F1
Braemar Gv *ESTON* TS6 ...... 101 D1
Braemar Rd *ACK/BRKF* TS5 ...... 97 D4 □
  BLGHM TS23 ...... 41 E5
  HTLPS TS25 ...... 23 E5
Braeside *YARM* TS15 ...... 146 C5
Braeworth Cl *YARM* TS15 ...... 138 B5
Brafferton Cl *NACLF* DL5 ...... 38 C3
Brafferton Dr *BLGHM* TS23 ...... 42 B3 □
Brafferton St *HTLPW* TS26 ...... 17 E4
Braid Crs *BLGHM* TS23 ...... 58 C3
Braidwood Rd *ESTON* TS6 ...... 101 E3 □
Braithwaite St *BAUK* DL14 ...... 26 C1 □
  SHIL DL4 ...... 35 D3 □
Bramble Rd *STOCN* TS19 ...... 74 A2
Brambling Cl *NORTON* TS20 ...... 57 E5
Bramcote Wy *THNBY* TS17 ...... 121 E4 □
Bramham Cha *NACLF* DL5 ...... 53 E5
Bramham Down *GUIS* TS14 ...... 129 D4
Bramley Gv *MTN/NUN* TS7 ...... 126 A3
Brampton Cl *CNHM/HEM* TS8 ...... 124 A4
Bramwith Av *NORM/PKE* TS3 ...... 99 F4
Brancepeth Av *NORM/PKE* TS3 ...... 99 E4
Brancepeth Cl *MARSKE* TS11 ...... 86 C3
  NACLF DL5 ...... 39 D3 □

Brancepeth Ct *BLGHM* TS23 ...... 41 E5 ⬛
Brancepeth Gv *BAUK* DL14 ...... 26 C3 ⬛
Brancepeth Rd *FYHL* DL17 ...... 21 D1
Brandon Cl *BLGHM* TS23 ...... 41 F4
  HTLPS TS25 ...... 30 C3
Brandon Rd *NORM/PKE* TS3 ...... 100 B2 ⬛
Brankin Ct *SALT/BTN/SK* TS12 ...... 110 B1 ⬛
Brankin Dr *DARLE* DL1 ...... 133 D4
Brankin Rd *DARLE* DL1 ...... 132 C4
Brankyn Gdns *THNBY* TS17 ...... 138 C2
Bransome Av *ACK/BRKF* TS5 ...... 98 A5 ⬛
Bransome Hall Dr *DARLW* DL3 .. 114 B3 ⬛
Bransome Gv *STOCS* TS18 ...... 93 D4
Bransome Ter *DARLW* DL3 ...... 9 E2
Bransdale *SPEN* DL16 ...... 14 C2
Bransdale Cl *STOCN* TS19 ...... 6 B2
Bransdale Gv *REDCAR* TS10 ...... 67 E2
Bransdale Rd *NORM/PKE* TS3 ...... 99 E2
Brantwood Cl *THNBY* TS17 ...... 139 E2
Brass Castle La *CNHM/HEM* TS8 .. 143 F4
Brass Wynd *MTN/NUN* TS7 ...... 144 B1 ⬛
Brawton Gv *DARLW* DL3 ...... 115 F4 ⬛
Braygate *LOFT/ST* TS13 ...... 112 A3
Brechin Dr *THNBY* TS17 ...... 121 F4
Brechin Gv *HTLPS* TS25 ...... 23 F5 ⬛
Breckon Hill Rd *MGRV/ESTR* TS4 .. 78 C5
Breck Rd *DARLW* DL3 ...... 131 D1
Brecon Crs *THNBY* TS17 ...... 138 B2
Brecon Dr *REDCAR* TS10 ...... 67 F3
Brecongill Cl *HTLP* TS24 ...... 18 A2
Brecon Side *DARLE* DL1 ...... 117 F3 ⬛
Breen Cl *NORM/PKE* TS3 ...... 79 D3 ⬛
Brenda Rd *HTLPS* TS25 ...... 24 A2
Brendon Crs *BLGHM* TS23 ...... 59 D2
Brendon Gv *THNBY* TS17 ...... 139 D4
Brenkley Cl *NORTON* TS20 ...... 57 D5 ⬛
Brent Ct *BLGHM* TS23 ...... 58 B3
Brentford St *SALT/BTN/SK* TS12 .. 111 E1 ⬛
Brentford Rd *NORTON* TS20 ...... 74 C3
Brentnall St *MBORO* TS1 ...... 5 E4
Brereton Rd *MGRV/ESTR* TS4 ...... 98 C5
Bretby Cl *MGRV/ESTR* TS4 ...... 98 C4 ⬛
Brettenham Av *MGRV/ESTR* TS4 .. 125 D1
Brewer St *BAUK* DL14 ...... 27 D3 ⬛
Brewery St *HTLP* TS24 ...... 2 C4
Brewsdale Rd *NORM/PKE* TS3 ...... 79 E4
Brian Rd *DARLE* DL1 ...... 116 B2
Briar Cl *DARLW* DL3 ...... 131 D5
  SPEN DL16 ...... 14 B5
Briardene Av *ACK/BRKF* TS5 ...... 98 A4
Briardene Ct *STOCN* TS19 ...... 72 C2
Briar Hill Gdns *HTLPW* TS26 ...... 17 D5 ⬛
Briar Rd *THNBY* TS17 ...... 121 E1
Briarvale Av *ACK/BRKF* TS5 ...... 97 F4
Briar Wk *DARLW* DL3 ...... 131 D5
  HTLPW TS26 ...... 17 F4 ⬛
Brickton Rd *ACK/BRKF* TS5 ...... 97 D2
Bridge Ct *ESTON* TS6 ...... 101 E3
Bridgend Cl *ESTON* TS6 ...... 82 A4
Bridge Rd *BAUK* DL14 ...... 26 C1
  GTAY/STK TS9 ...... 152 A2
  REDCAR TS10 ...... 50 C4
  STOCS TS9 ...... 7 C6
  STOCS TS18 ...... 95 D3
Bridge St *GTAY/STK* TS9 ...... 150 B3 ⬛
  HTLP TS24 ...... 3 F3 ⬛
  NORTON TS20 ...... 75 D4 ⬛
  THNBY TS17 ...... 95 E5 ⬛
  YARM TS15 ...... 137 D3
Bridge St East *TEESM* TS2 ...... 5 C2
Bridge St West *TEESM* TS2 ...... 5 E2
Bridge Ter *DARLE* DL1 ...... 132 C2 ⬛
The Bridle *FYHL* DL17 ...... 38 C2
Bridnor Rd *NORM/PKE* TS3 ...... 99 E4 ⬛
Bridport Cl *STOCS* TS18 ...... 75 F5 ⬛
Brierley Gn *MTN/NUN* TS7 ...... 126 A5 ⬛
Brierton La *HTLPS* TS25 ...... 22 B4
Brierville Rd *STOCN* TS19 ...... 74 B4 ⬛
Brigandine Cl *HTLPS* TS25 ...... 24 C5
Briggs Av *ESTON* TS6 ...... 80 C5
Brigham Rd *NORM/PKE* TS3 ...... 99 D3
Brighton Cl *THNBY* TS17 ...... 121 D3 ⬛
Brighton Rd *DARLE* DL1 ...... 132 C4
Bright St *DARLE* DL1 ...... 133 D2 ⬛
  HTLPW TS26 ...... 17 E4
  MBORO TS1 ...... 5 H4
  STOCS TS18 ...... 7 F4
Brignall Moor Crs *DARLE* DL1 .. 133 E3 ⬛
Brignall Rd *STOCS* TS18 ...... 94 B4
Brignell Rd *TEESM* TS2 ...... 77 F2
Brig Open *HTLP* TS24 ...... 19 E2 ⬛
Brimham Ct *THNBY* TS17 ...... 139 E1
Brimham Ct *REDCAR* TS10 ...... 68 A2
Brimston Cl *HTLPW* TS26 ...... 16 C4
Brindle Cl *MTN/NUN* TS7 ...... 126 A5
Brine St *MGRV/ESTR* TS4 ...... 78 C5 ⬛
Brinewells Gn *MGRV/ESTR* TS4 .. 99 D1 ⬛
Brinkburn Av *DARLW* DL3 ...... 115 E4
Brinkburn Dr *DARLW* DL3 ...... 115 E4
Brinkburn Rd *DARLW* DL3 ...... 115 E4
  HTLPS TS25 ...... 23 F1
  NORTON TS20 ...... 74 C3
Brisbane Crs *THNBY* TS17 ...... 121 D2
Brisbane Gv *STOCS* TS18 ...... 93 F3
Briscoe Wy *CNHM/HEM* TS8 ...... 123 E5

Bristol Av *SALT/BTN/SK* TS12 ...... 89 E2
Bristow St *NORM/PKE* TS3 ...... 79 E5 ⬛
Britain Av *ACK/BRKF* TS5 ...... 97 E5 ⬛
Britannia Cl *HTLP* TS24 ...... 3 E1 ⬛
Britannia Pl *REDCAR* TS10 ...... 67 D2
Britannia Rd *STOCN* TS19 ...... 6 D2
Broadbent St *SALT/BTN/SK* TS12 .. 111 D1
Broad Cl *CNHM/HEM* TS8 ...... 141 D1
Broad Field Rd *HTLP* TS24 ...... 19 E1
Broadgate Rd *ACK/BRKF* TS5 ...... 97 E4
Broadhaven Cl *ESTON* TS6 ...... 102 A1
Broadmeadows *DARLW* DL3 ...... 130 C1
Broadstone *CNHM/HEM* TS8 ...... 144 A1
Broadway *ESTON* TS6 ...... 82 A3
Broadway East *REDCAR* TS10 ...... 67 D2
The Broadway *DARLE* DL1 ...... 133 E2
Broadway West *REDCAR* TS10 ...... 66 C3
Broadwell Rd *MGRV/ESTR* TS4 ...... 99 D5
Brocklesby Rd *GUIS* TS14 ...... 129 D5
Brockrigg Ct *GUIS* TS14 ...... 128 C1 ⬛
Brogden Gn *NORM/PKE* TS3 ...... 99 E3
Broken Banks *BAUK* DL14 ...... 26 C1
Bromley Hill Cl *MTN/NUN* TS7 .. 144 C1 ⬛
Bromley La *CNHM/HEM* TS8 ...... 143 D5
Bromley Rd *STOCS* TS18 ...... 93 F5
Brompton Gv *STOCS* TS18 ...... 93 E4 ⬛
Brompton Rd *ACK/BRKF* TS5 ...... 97 F4
Brompton St *ACK/BRKF* TS5 ...... 97 F1
Brompton Wk *DARLW* DL3 ...... 131 D2
Brook Cl *NACLF* DL5 ...... 39 D3
Brookdale Rd *MTN/NUN* TS7 ...... 125 F4 ⬛
The Brookes *YARM* TS15 ...... 146 B1
Brookfield Cl *STOCN* TS19 ...... 92 C1
Brooklands *BAUK* DL14 ...... 27 D5
Brooksbank Av *REDCAR* TS10 ...... 68 B1
Brooksbank Cl *MTN/NUN* TS7 ...... 127 D2
Brooksbank Rd *MTN/NUN* TS7 ...... 127 D2
Brookside *SALT/BTN/SK* TS12 ...... 109 D5
Brookside Av *MGRV/ESTR* TS4 ...... 98 B4 ⬛
Brook St *HTLPW* TS26 ...... 17 F4
  SPEN DL16 ...... 15 D2 ⬛
  TEESM TS2 ...... 5 C1 ⬛
Brook Ter *DARLW* DL3 ...... 116 A4
Brookwood Wy *EGG/EAG* TS16 ...... 137 E2
Broomfield Av *EGG/EAG* TS16 ...... 137 D1 ⬛
Broomhill Gdns *HTLPW* TS26 ...... 17 D5
Broomlee Cl *THNBY* TS17 ...... 138 C3 ⬛
Broom Rd *FYHL* DL17 ...... 21 D1
Broomside *FYHL* DL17 ...... 21 D1
Broom St *SPEN* DL16 ...... 15 F2
Brotton Rd *LOFT/ST* TS13 ...... 112 A1
  THNBY TS17 ...... 95 F5
Brougham Cl *DARLW* DL3 ...... 116 A3
  TEESM TS2 ...... 5 E1
Brougham Ter *HTLP* TS24 ...... 18 A3
Brough Cl *NACLF* DL5 ...... 39 F5
  THNBY TS17 ...... 122 A2
Brough Cl *RHTLP* TS27 ...... 11 F4
Brough Gv *BAUK* DL14 ...... 26 C3 ⬛
Brough Rd *BLGHM* TS23 ...... 59 D1 ⬛
Broughton Av *MGRV/ESTR* TS4 ...... 125 D1
Broughton Rd *BLGHMW/WYN* TS22.. 58 A1
Browning Av *HTLPS* TS25 ...... 23 D2
Brownsea Ct *THNBY* TS17 ...... 139 D2 ⬛
Brown St *SHIL* DL4 ...... 35 E2
Broxa Cl *REDCAR* TS10 ...... 68 A4
Bruce Av *ACK/BRKF* TS5 ...... 97 D3
Bruce Crs *HTLP* TS24 ...... 12 C4
Bruce Rd *NACLF* DL5 ...... 54 B1
Brundall Cl *STOCN* TS19 ...... 73 D4 ⬛
Brunel Cl *HTLP* TS24 ...... 18 B1
Brunel Rd *DARLE* DL1 ...... 132 C1
  ESTON TS6 ...... 80 B4
Brunel St *FYHL* DL17 ...... 20 A1
Brunel Wy *DARLE* DL1 ...... 132 C1
Brunner Rd *BLGHM* TS23 ...... 76 A1
Brunswick Av *ESTON* TS6 ...... 81 D5
Brunswick St *DARLE* DL1 ...... 9 G4
  HTLP TS24 ...... 2 D3 ⬛
  MBORO TS1 ...... 5 F2
  STOCS TS18 ...... 7 F5
Brunswick St North *DARLE* DL1 ...... 9 H4 ⬛
Bruntoft Av *HTLP* TS24 ...... 12 B4
Bruntons Manor Ct
  NORM/PKE TS3 ...... 100 A2 ⬛
Brunton St *DARLE* DL1 ...... 132 C2
Brusselton Cl *ACK/BRKF* TS5 ...... 123 E2 ⬛
Brusselton Vw *BAUK* DL14 ...... 26 C5
Bryan St *SPEN* DL16 ...... 15 E2
Brylston Rd *NORM/PKE* TS3 ...... 100 B1 ⬛
Bryony Ct *GUIS* TS14 ...... 128 A4
Bryony Gv *MTN/NUN* TS7 ...... 125 E3
Buccleugh Cl *GUIS* TS14 ...... 129 D5
Buchanan St *STOCS* TS18 ...... 7 E5
Buckfast Rd *SALT/BTN/SK* TS12 .. 109 F2 ⬛
Buckie Gv *HTLPS* TS25 ...... 23 F5 ⬛
Buckingham Av *RHTLP* TS27 ...... 10 B5
Buckingham Dr *ESTON* TS6 ...... 101 E5
Buckingham Rd *REDCAR* TS10 ...... 51 E5
  STOCS TS18 ...... 6 C6
Buckland Cl *THNBY* TS17 ...... 139 E2
Buck St *TEESM* TS2 ...... 78 A2
Budworth Cl *BLGHM* TS23 ...... 42 A3 ⬛
Bull Wynd *DARLE* DL1 ...... 9 F5 ⬛
Bulmer Cl *NACLF* DL5 ...... 39 E5

Bulmer Pl *HTLP* TS24 ...... 12 B5 ⬛
Bulmer Wy *MBORO* TS1 ...... 4 C3
Bunting Cl *HTLPW* TS26 ...... 17 D1
  THNBY TS17 ...... 139 D1
Burbank St *HTLP* TS24 ...... 2 D4
Burdale Cl *EGG/EAG* TS16 ...... 118 C5 ⬛
Burdon Cl *NACLF* DL5 ...... 38 B5
  STOCN TS19 ...... 73 E5 ⬛
Burford Av *STOCS* TS18 ...... 94 A4
Burgess St *STOCS* TS18 ...... 7 E3 ⬛
Burghley Ms *NACLF* DL5 ...... 39 D3
Burke Pl *HTLP* TS24 ...... 19 D1
Burke St *SHIL* DL4 ...... 35 E3
Burlam Rd *ACK/BRKF* TS5 ...... 97 E2
Burleigh Pl *DARLW* DL3 ...... 8 D5
Burnaby Cl *HTLPS* TS25 ...... 24 A3
Burneston Ct *DARLW* DL3 ...... 130 A2 ⬛
Burneston Gv *STOCS* TS18 ...... 92 C3 ⬛
Burnet Cl *THNBY* TS17 ...... 121 D5
Burnhill Wy *FYHL* DL17 ...... 38 B1
  NACLF DL5 ...... 37 F5
Burnholme Av *NORM/PKE* TS3 .. 100 A1 ⬛
Burniston Dr *BLGHMW/WYN* TS22 ... 57 F1
  THNBY TS17 ...... 121 D4
Burn La *NACLF* DL5 ...... 38 A3
Burnmere *SPEN* DL16 ...... 14 C1 ⬛
Burnmoor Cl *REDCAR* TS10 ...... 68 B4
Burnmoor Dr *EGG/EAG* TS16 ...... 119 D5
Burn Rd *HTLPS* TS25 ...... 2 C5
Burnsall Rd *NORM/PKE* TS3 ...... 99 D2
Burns Av *HTLPS* TS25 ...... 23 D2
Burn's Cl *RHTLP* TS27 ...... 10 B4
Burnside Ct *STOCS* TS18 ...... 6 A6
Burnside Gv *STOCS* TS18 ...... 6 A6
Burnside Rd *DARLE* DL1 ...... 133 E4
Burns Rd *ESTON* TS6 ...... 101 E1
Burnston Cl *HTLPW* TS26 ...... 16 C3
Burnsville Rd *ESTON* TS6 ...... 81 F4
Burn Ter *SPEN* DL16 ...... 15 D2
Burn Valley Gv *HTLPS* TS25 ...... 2 A6
Burn Valley Rd *HTLPW* TS26 ...... 23 F1
Burnynghill Cl *NACLF* DL5 ...... 53 E2
Burringham Rd *NORTON* TS20 ...... 74 B1
Burtree Rd *NACLF* DL5 ...... 54 C4
Burtur Dr *STOCN* TS19 ...... 72 C5
Burwell Rd *NORM/PKE* TS3 ...... 100 B3
Burwell Wk *HTLPS* TS25 ...... 31 D2
Bury Rd *NACLF* DL5 ...... 55 D1
Burythorpe Cl *MGRV/ESTR* TS4 ...... 98 C2 ⬛
Busby Wy *YARM* TS15 ...... 138 B5
Bushel Hill Ct *DARLW* DL3 ...... 114 C5
Bushel Hill Dr *DARLW* DL3 ...... 114 C5
Bushston Cl *HTLPW* TS26 ...... 16 C3 ⬛
Bush St *ACK/BRKF* TS5 ...... 97 F1
Busty Ter *SHIL* DL4 ...... 35 D1
Bute Av *HTLPS* TS25 ...... 23 F2 ⬛
Bute Cl *THNBY* TS17 ...... 121 E3
Bute St *STOCS* TS18 ...... 7 E4
Butler Rd *NACLF* DL5 ...... 54 B1
Butler St *NORTON* TS20 ...... 75 D3 ⬛
Butsfield Av *BLGHM* TS23 ...... 42 A3 ⬛
Buttercup Cl *STOCN* TS19 ...... 73 E3
Butterfield Cl *EGG/EAG* TS16 ...... 137 D2 ⬛
Butterfield Dr *EGG/EAG* TS16 ...... 137 D2
Butterfield Gv *EGG/EAG* TS16 ...... 137 D2
Buttermere *SPEN* DL16 ...... 14 C1
Buttermere Av *ACK/BRKF* TS5 ...... 97 D5
Buttermere Rd *ESTON* TS6 ...... 82 B5
  REDCAR TS10 ...... 68 A4
  STOCS TS18 ...... 6 A3
Butterwick Ct *NACLF* DL5 ...... 38 C4
Butterwick Rd *HTLP* TS24 ...... 12 A4 ⬛
  SEDG TS21 ...... 29 E3
Butt La *GUIS* TS14 ...... 129 F3
Butts La *EGG/EAG* TS16 ...... 137 D3
  RHTLP TS27 ...... 10 A4
Buxton Av *MTN/NUN* TS7 ...... 125 F5
Buxton Gdns *BLGHMW/WYN* TS22 ... 58 A1
Buxton Moor Crs *DARLE* DL1...... 133 E4
Buxton Rd *STOCS* TS18 ...... 7 H2
Bydales Dr *MARSKE* TS11 ...... 71 D5
Byelands St *MBORO* TS1 ...... 98 C1
Byemoor Av *GTAY/STK* TS9 ...... 150 C4
Byemoor Cl *GTAY/STK* TS9 ...... 150 C4
Byerley Rd *SHIL* DL4 ...... 35 C3
Byfleet Av *NORM/PKE* TS3 ...... 99 F1 ⬛
Byland Cl *GUIS* TS14 ...... 129 E3
  REDCAR TS10 ...... 68 A3
Byland Gv *HTLPS* TS25 ...... 25 D5
Byland Rd *MTN/NUN* TS7 ...... 127 D4
  SALT/BTN/SK TS12 ...... 109 F2
Bylands Gv *STOCN* TS19 ...... 93 D2
Bylands Rd *ESTON* TS6 ...... 101 E2
Bylands Wy *DARLW* DL3 ...... 114 B4
Byland Wy *BLGHM* TS23 ...... 59 F3
By Pass Rd *BLGHM* TS23 ...... 58 B4
Byrnelside Av *MGRV/ESTR* TS4 ...... 98 B3 ⬛
Byron Av *BAUK* DL14 ...... 27 D3 ⬛
Byron Cl *BLGHM* TS23 ...... 42 A3 ⬛
Byron Crt *SALT/BTN/SK* TS12 ...... 91 D4
Byron Rd *DARLE* DL1 ...... 117 D5
Byron St *HTLPW* TS26 ...... 17 E4
The Byway *DARLE* DL1 ...... 133 C2
Bywell Gv *MTN/NUN* TS7 ...... 100 C5

C

Cadogan St *MBORO* TS1...................... 97 F1
  NORM/PKE TS3............................. 79 E5 ⓔ
Cadwell Cl *NORM/PKE* TS3.............. 100 C3
Caedmon Crs *DARLW* DL3................ 130 C2
Caernarvon Cl *ESTON* TS6................ 82 A5
Caernarvon Gv *HTLPW* TS26........... 16 C2
Cairngorm Dr *DARLE* DL1............... 117 D2
Cairn Rd *HTLPS* TS25...................... 31 E1
Cairnston Rd *HTLPW* TS26.............. 16 B3
Caistor Dr *HTLPS* TS25.................... 31 E2
Caithness Rd *ESTON* TS6................ 101 D1
  HTLPS TS25............................... 31 E1
Caithness Wy *DARLE* DL1.............. 117 F1 ⓔ
Calcott Cl *STOCN* TS19.................... 73 E5
Calder Cl *BLGHMW/WYN* TS22...... 40 C5 ⓔ
Calderdale *SALT/BTN/SK* TS12....... 109 E1 ⓔ
Calder Gv *HTLPS* TS25.................... 23 E5 ⓔ
  MGRV/ESTR TS4.......................... 125 D1
  REDCAR TS10............................. 68 A2 ⓔ
Caldermere *SPEN* DL16.................... 14 C1 ⓔ
Caldicot Cl *STON* TS19.................... 82 A5
Caldwell Cl *CNHM/HEM* TS8......... 142 A1 ⓔ
Caledonian Rd *HTLPS* TS25............ 23 F2
Caledonian Wy *DARLE* DL1............ 117 E2 ⓔ
Calf Fallow La *NORTON* TS20......... 57 E4 ⓔ
California Cl *STOCS* TS18................. 7 E4
California Rd *ESTON* TS6................ 102 B2
California St *STOCS* TS18................. 7 E4 ⓔ
Callander Rd *HTLPS* TS25............... 23 E5
Calluna Gv *MTN/NUN* TS7............ 125 E5 ⓔ
Calthorpe Ct *MBORO* TS1............... 4 D4 ⓔ
Calverley Rd *NORM/PKE* TS3......... 100 B2
Calvert Cl *NORM/PKE* TS3.............. 79 E5 ⓔ
Calvert's La *STOCS* TS18................. 7 C4 ⓔ
Cambourne Cl *CNHM/HEM* TS8..... 124 A5 ⓔ
Cambrian Av *REDCAR* TS10............ 67 F3
Cambrian Ct *THNBY* TS17............. 138 B2 ⓔ
Cambrian Rd *BLGHM* TS23............. 58 B1
Cambridge Av *ACK/BRKF* TS5........ 97 E4 ⓔ
  MTN/NUN TS7............................. 125 F5
Cambridge Rd *ACK/BRKF* TS5........ 97 E4
  NORM/PKE TS3........................... 79 E4
  THNBY TS17.............................. 95 E4
Cambridge St *SALT/BTN/SK* TS12.. 89 E2 ⓔ
  SPEN DL16................................. 15 D3 ⓔ
Cambridge Ter *TEESM* TS2............. 61 D5
Camden St *MBORO* TS1.................. 78 C5
  STOCS TS18............................... 94 B3 ⓔ
Camellia Crs *NORTON* TS20........... 74 B3 ⓔ
Camelon St *HTLPS* TS25................. 95 F4 ⓔ
Cameron Rd *HTLP* TS24................. 18 A3
Cameron St *NORTON* TS20............ 74 C1 ⓔ
Campbell Rd *HTLPS* TS25............... 23 E5
Campion Ct *NACLF* DL5................. 39 D2 ⓔ
Campion Dr *GUIS* TS14.................. 128 A4
Campion Gv *MTN/NUN* TS7........... 125 E3
Campion Rd *DARLE* DL1................ 116 B3
Campion St *HTLPW* TS26............... 2 A4 ⓔ
Canberra Gv *STOCS* TS18................ 93 F3
Canberra Rd *MTN/NUN* TS7.......... 125 F5
Canewood *NORM/PKE* TS3............ 100 B2 ⓔ
Cannobie Cl *DARLW* DL3............... 131 D2
Cannock Rd *NORM/PKE* TS3.......... 99 D5
Cannon Park Rd *MBORO* TS1.......... 4 C4
Cannon Park Wy *MBORO* TS1......... 4 C3
Cannon St *MBORO* TS1.................... 4 A5
Canon Gv *YARM* TS15................... 146 C5
Canterbury Gv *ACK/BRKF* TS5....... 98 A2
  DARLE DL1................................ 117 F3 ⓔ
Canterbury Rd *REDCAR* TS10......... 69 E2
  SALT/BTN/SK TS12...................... 90 D5
Canton Gdns *ACK/BRKF* TS5......... 123 F4
Captain Cook's Crs *MTN/NUN* TS7.. 126 A4
Captain Cook's Wy *GTAY/STK* TS9. 150 C2
Carburt Rd *STOCN* TS19................ 72 C2
Carcut Rd *NORM/PKE* TS3............ 79 E4
Cardigan Cl *ESTON* TS6................. 82 A5
Cardigan Gv *HTLPW* TS26.............. 17 D1
Cardinal Gdns *DARLW* DL3........... 131 D1
Cardinal Gv *STOCN* TS19.............. 72 B5
Carey Cl *MBORO* TS1..................... 4 C5 ⓔ
Cargo Fleet La *NORM/PKE* TS3...... 79 F4
Cargo Fleet Rd *MBORO* TS1........... 78 C4
  NORM/PKE TS3........................... 78 C4
Carileph Cl *NACLF* DL5................. 54 B1
Carisbrooke Av *NORM/PKE* TS3.... 100 B3
Carisbrooke Rd *HTLPW* TS26......... 16 C5
Carisbrooke Wk *DARLW* DL3......... 130 D3
Carisbrooke Wy *REDCAR* TS10...... 69 D2
Carlbury Av *ACK/BRKF* TS5.......... 98 A5
Carlbury Crs *DARLW* DL3.............. 130 B1
Carlbury Rd *NACLF* DL5................ 55 D5
Carleton Dr *DARLW* DL3............... 130 C1
Carleton Gv *DARLW* DL3............... 130 C1 ⓔ
Carlile Hl *CNHM/HEM* TS8........... 141 F1
Carlisle Gv *BAUK* DL14................. 26 C3 ⓔ
Carlisle St *HTLPS* TS25.................. 25 D5
Carlow Cl *GUIS* TS14.................... 129 D5
Carlow St *MBORO* TS1................... 97 E1
Carlton Av *BLGHMW/WYN* TS22... 58 A1

Carlton Cl *STOCS* TS18..................... 7 E3
Carlton Dr *THNBY* TS17............... 121 D3
Carlton Moor Crs *DARLE* DL1........ 133 E4
Carlton St *FYHL* DL17.................... 21 F4
  HTLPW TS26.............................. 2 A3
Carlyle Rd *ESTON* TS6................. 101 F1
Carmarthen Rd *NORM/PKE* TS3..... 100 A4 ⓔ
Carmel Gdns *ACK/BRKF* TS5.......... 123 F4
  DARLW DL3............................. 131 D2
  GUIS TS14.............................. 129 D2 ⓔ
  MTN/NUN TS7.......................... 127 D4 ⓔ
  NORTON TS20.......................... 75 E2 ⓔ
Carmel Gv *DARLW* DL3................ 131 E3
Carmel Rd North *DARLW* DL3........ 131 D2
Carmel Rd South *DARLW* DL3........ 131 E4
Carnoustie Dr *EGG/EAG* TS16....... 137 E1
Carnoustie Gv *RHTLP* TS27............ 11 E3 ⓔ
Carnoustie Rd *MARSKE* TS11.......... 86 C3
Carnoustie Wy *CNHM/HEM* TS8.... 144 A1
Caroline St *BAUK* DL14.................. 27 D3 ⓔ
  NORM/PKE TS3.......................... 2 B4
Carpenter Cl *YARM* TS15.............. 147 D1 ⓔ
Carradale Cl *EGG/EAG* TS16.......... 137 E2
Carriage Wk *EGG/EAG* TS16......... 119 D3 ⓔ
Carrick St *HTLP* TS24.................... 12 B5
Carroll Rd *DARLW* DL3................ 130 C2
Carrol St *STOCS* TS18.................... 7 H3
Carron Gv *ESTON* TS6.................. 101 E3
Carr St *HTLPW* TS26..................... 17 F3
  SPEN DL16............................... 14 C2
  STOCS TS18.............................. 6 C5
Carter's La *EGG/EAG* TS16........... 135 D2
Carthorpe Dr *BLGHM* TS23............ 42 A5
Cartmell Ter *DARLW* DL3............. 115 F4
Cartmel Rd *REDCAR* TS10............. 68 B2
Carvers Ct *SALT/BTN/SK* TS12...... 91 E5
Carwardine Cl *NACLF* DL5............. 38 B2
Casebourne Rd *HTLPS* TS25........... 24 B2
Casper Ct *EGG/EAG* TS16............ 137 E1 ⓔ
Cass House Rd *CNHM/HEM* TS8.... 141 F1
Casson Wy *BLGHM* TS23................ 41 F5
Cassop Gv *ACK/BRKF* TS5........... 123 D2
Castlebay Ct *DARLE* DL1.............. 117 F1 ⓔ
Castle Chare *BAUK* DL14............... 27 E1 ⓔ
Castle Cl *STOCN* TS19................... 73 E5
Castle Dyke Wynd *YARM* TS15...... 137 D4 ⓔ
Castle Howard Cl *RHTLP* TS27....... 11 F4
Castlemartin *YARM* TS15.............. 138 B4
Castlereagh *NACLF* DL5................. 54 B1
Castlereagh Rd *STOCN* TS19.......... 6 C1
Castle Rd *REDCAR* TS10................ 69 D2
Castleton Av *ACK/BRKF* TS5.......... 97 D4
Castleton Dr *BLGHMW/WYN* TS22.. 58 A1
Castleton Rd *ESTON* TS6............... 102 B1
  HTLPS TS25.............................. 33 D1 ⓔ
  STOCS TS18.............................. 94 B3
Castle Wy *MGRV/ESTR* TS4.......... 98 C3
Castlewood *NORM/PKE* TS3.......... 100 B3
Castle Wynd *MTN/NUN* TS7.......... 144 C1
Catcote Rd *HTLPS* TS25................ 23 D2
Caterton Cl *YARM* TS15............... 147 D1 ⓔ
Cat Flatt La *MARSKE* TS11............. 69 F5
Cathedral Dr *STOCN* TS19............. 72 C5
Cathedral Gdns *TEESM* TS2............ 5 F1
Catherine Cl *SPEN* DL16............... 15 E3 ⓔ
Catherine Rd *HTLP* TS24................ 3 E3
Catherine St *HTLP* TS24................ 19 F2
Cattersty Wy *SALT/BTN/SK* TS12.... 91 D4
Cattistock Cl *GUIS* TS14................ 129 E4
Caudwell Cl *STOCN* TS19.............. 72 C2 ⓔ
The Causeway *BLGHM* TS23........... 58 C2
  DARLE DL1.............................. 133 E1
Cavendish Cl *DARLE* DL1.............. 116 C2 ⓔ
  FYHL DL17.............................. 20 B2 ⓔ
Cavendish Dr *DARLE* DL1............. 116 B2
Cavendish Rd *MGRV/ESTR* TS4..... 98 C4
Caversham Rd *MGRV/ESTR* TS4..... 99 D5
Cawdor Cl *MARSKE* TS11............... 86 C3
Cawood Dr *ACK/BRKF* TS5........... 98 A4
Cawthorn Cl *CNHM/HEM* TS8....... 123 E5 ⓔ
Caxton Gv *HTLPS* TS25.................. 23 D2 ⓔ
Caxton St *ACK/BRKF* TS5.............. 98 A1
Cayton Cl *REDCAR* TS10............... 68 A4
Cayton Dr *ACK/BRKF* TS5............. 98 A5
  BLGHMW/WYN TS22................... 41 D5
  THNBY TS17............................ 121 D3
Cecil St *MBORO* TS1...................... 4 C4
  STOCS TS18.............................. 94 C3
Cedar Cl *ESTON* TS6.................... 101 E2
  FYHL DL17.............................. 21 D3 ⓔ
Cedar Ct *SPEN* DL16..................... 15 E3 ⓔ
Cedar Crs *EGG/EAG* TS16............. 119 F3 ⓔ
Cedar Dr *CNHM/HEM* TS8............ 141 D2
Cedar Gv *LOFT/ST* TS13............... 113 D5
  SALT/BTN/SK TS12.................... 90 C5
  SHIL DL4................................. 35 E4
  THNBY TS17............................ 95 E5
Cedar Rd *BAUK* DL14.................... 27 E2
  DARLW DL3............................. 115 E4
  MTN/NUN TS7.......................... 126 B3
  MTN/NUN TS7.......................... 127 D1
Cedar St *STOCS* TS18..................... 7 H3
Cedarwood Av *GTAY/STK* TS9....... 148 B5 ⓔ
Cedarwood Gld *CNHM/HEM* TS8... 141 E2
Celandine Cl *MTN/NUN* TS7......... 125 E2 ⓔ

Celandine Wy *STOCN* TS19............ 73 D4
Cemetery La *DARLW* DL3............. 130 C2
Cennon Gv *THNBY* TS17............... 138 B2
Centenary Crs *NORTON* TS20.......... 74 C2
Central Av *ACK/BRKF* TS5............. 97 D2 ⓔ
  BLGHM TS23............................ 58 C4
  NACLF DL5.............................. 38 C5
Central Dr *SPEN* DL16................... 14 B5
Central Pde *SHIL* DL4................... 35 E3
Central Rd *HTLP* TS24.................. 18 C2
Central Ter *REDCAR* TS10.............. 51 E4 ⓔ
Central Wy *GTAY/STK* TS9............ 150 C2
Cestria Wy *NACLF* DL5................. 37 F4
Chadburn Cn *ACK/BRKF* TS5.......... 98 B5
Chadburn Rd *NORTON* TS20........... 74 C3
Chadderton Cl
  SALT/BTN/SK TS12.................... 109 D5 ⓔ
Chadderton Dr *THNBY* TS17.......... 122 A1
Chadwell Av *NORM/PKE* TS3......... 99 F4 ⓔ
Chaffinch Cl *HTLPW* TS26............. 17 D1
Chalfield Cl *THNBY* TS17.............. 139 E2
Chalford Oaks *ACK/BRKF* TS5........ 96 C5
Chalk Cl *STOCS* TS18.................... 94 C3 ⓔ
Challacombe Crs *THNBY* TS17........ 138 C4
Challoner Rd *HTLP* TS24................ 17 F2
  YARM TS15.............................. 146 A1
Chaloner St *GUIS* TS14................. 129 D3
Chancel Wy *ESTON* TS6................ 102 A2
Chancery La *DARLE* DL1................. 9 F5 ⓔ
Chancery Ri *THNBY* TS17............. 121 D3
Chandlers Cl *HTLP* TS24................. 3 F2 ⓔ
Chandlers Rdg *MTN/NUN* TS7....... 126 C5
Chandos St *DARLW* DL3............... 116 A4
Chantilly Av *DARLE* DL1.............. 117 E2
Chantry Cl *DARLW* DL3............... 115 D5 ⓔ
  DARLW DL3............................. 115 D2 ⓔ
  NORM/PKE TS3......................... 99 E4
  NORTON TS20.......................... 74 C1 ⓔ
Chapelbeck Bungalows
  GUIS TS14.............................. 128 C3 ⓔ
Chapel Cl *MARSKE* TS11............... 70 B5
Chapelgarth *CNHM/HEM* TS8........ 141 E1
Chapel Rd *BLGHM* TS23................. 58 C5
Chapel St *ESTON* TS6................... 83 E5 ⓔ
  MARSKE TS11........................... 70 B5
  SHIL DL4................................. 35 E4
  THNBY TS17............................ 95 E3
Chaplehope Cl *DARLE* DL1........... 117 D1 ⓔ
Chapman Cl *NACLF* DL5............... 39 D5 ⓔ
Chapman Ct *NORM/PKE* TS3......... 100 A2
Chapman St *NORTON* TS20............ 75 D2 ⓔ
Charlbury Rd *NORM/PKE* TS3......... 99 F1
Charles St *DARLE* DL1................. 116 B4
  HTLP TS24.............................. 3 E5
  REDCAR TS10.......................... 51 F4
  SHIL DL4................................. 35 E5
  SPEN DL16............................... 14 C3
  THNBY TS17............................ 95 E4
Charlock *CNHM/HEM* TS8............ 143 E3
Charlotte St *HTLPW* TS26.............. 2 A5
  REDCAR TS10.......................... 51 F4
  SALT/BTN/SK TS12.................... 109 F2
  TEESM TS2.............................. 4 D1
Charlton Rd *REDCAR* TS10............ 67 E1
Charnley Gn *MGRV/ESTR* TS4....... 124 C1 ⓔ
Charnwood Cl *MARSKE* TS11......... 87 E1 ⓔ
Charnwood Dr *DARLW* DL3........... 115 D1
  MTN/NUN TS7.......................... 127 D3
Charrington Av *THNBY* TS17......... 121 D4
Charterhouse St *HTLPS* TS25.......... 23 F2 ⓔ
Chartwell Cl *MARSKE* TS11........... 70 A4
  THNBY TS17............................ 139 E2 ⓔ
Charwood *NORM/PKE* TS3............ 100 B2 ⓔ
Chase Cl *DARLW* DL3................... 114 D4
The Chase *STOCN* TS19................. 93 D1 ⓔ
Chatham Gdns *HTLP* TS24.............. 17 F2
Chatham Rd *HTLP* TS24................. 17 F2
Chatsworth Av *BAUK* DL14............ 27 D3 ⓔ
Chatsworth Cl *STOCS* TS19............ 73 F4 ⓔ
Chatsworth Gdns
  BLGHMW/WYN TS22................... 58 B1
Chatsworth Ter *DARLE* DL1.......... 132 B3 ⓔ
Chaucer Av *HTLPS* TS25................ 23 D2
Chaucer Rd *DARLE* DL1................ 132 B4
Chaytor Lee *YARM* TS15.............. 137 E5 ⓔ
Cheam Av *NORM/PKE* TS3............ 99 F1
Cheapside *SHIL* DL4..................... 35 F2 ⓔ
  SPEN DL16............................... 15 D3
Cheddar Cl *ESTON* TS6................. 82 A5
Chelmsford Av *STOCS* TS18............ 93 E2
Chelmsford Cl *ACK/BRKF* TS5........ 98 A3
Chelmsford St *DARLW* DL3............. 9 E2 ⓔ
  THNBY TS17............................ 95 E3
Chelmsford Wk *ACK/BRKF* TS5..... 98 A3 ⓔ
Chelsea Gdns *NORTON* TS20.......... 57 D5
Chelston Cl *HTLPW* TS26.............. 16 B5 ⓔ
Cheltenham Av *CNHM/HEM* TS8.... 125 F5
  MTN/NUN TS7.......................... 125 F5
  THNBY TS17............................ 95 F4 ⓔ
Cheltenham Cl *ACK/BRKF* TS5....... 98 A3 ⓔ
Cheltenham Rd *STOCS* TS18........... 76 A4
Cheltenham Wy *FYHL* DL17........... 39 D2
Chepstow Cl *BLGHM* TS23.............. 58 A5
Cherry Ct *STOCN* TS19.................. 74 C2 ⓔ
Cherry Tree Cl *MTN/NUN* TS7....... 101 D5 ⓔ

Cherry Tree Gdns *NORTON* TS20 ..... 75 E2 ◨
Cherrywood Av *GTAY/STK* TS9 ..... 152 B1 ◨
Cherrywood Ct *ACK/BRKF* TS5 ..... 124 A3 ◨
Chertsey Av *NORM/PKE* TS3 .... 99 F1
Chesham Cl *NORTON* TS20 .... 75 E1 ◨
Chesham Gv *NORTON* TS20 .... 75 E1
Chesham Rd *NORTON* TS20 .... 75 E1 ◨
Chesham St *ACK/BRKF* TS5 .... 98 A2 ◨
Cheshire Rd *NORTON* TS20 .... 75 E2
Chesneywood *NORM/PKE* TS3 ...... 100 B2 ◨
Chesnut St *DARLE* DL1 .... 9 G2
Chester Gv *DARLW* DL3 .... 130 B1
Chester Rd *HTLP* TS24 .... 17 F5
   REDCAR TS10 .... 69 E2
Chester St *BAUK* DL14 .... 27 E2
   MBORO TS1 .... 97 F1
Chesterton Av *THNBY* TS17 .... 121 D3
Chesterton Cl *NORTON* TS20 .... 75 D2 ◨
Chesterton Rd *HTLPS* TS25 .... 23 D2 ◨
Chesterwood *NORM/PKE* TS3 ..... 100 B2 ◨
Chestnut Av *FYHL* DL17 .... 20 C1
   REDCAR TS10 .... 69 D1
   SPEN DL16 .... 14 C4
Chestnut Cl *ESTON* TS6 .... 83 E5
   SALT/BTN/SK TS12 .... 88 C3
   SHIL DL4 .... 35 F3
Chestnut Dr *MTN/NUN* TS7 .... 126 A4
Chestnut Gv *SALT/BTN/SK* TS12 .... 90 C5
Chestnut Rd *EGG/EAG* TS16 .... 119 E5
   SEDG TS21 .... 29 E3
Chestnut Sq *STOCN* TS19 .... 74 B4 ◨
Chesworth Cl *NORM/PKE* TS3 ..... 100 B2 ◨
Cheviot Crs *BLGHM* TS23 .... 58 C3
Cheviot Dr *SALT/BTN/SK* TS12 ... 109 E1
Chez Nous Av *HTLPS* TS25 .... 24 A2 ◨
Chichester Gv *HTLPS* TS25 .... 31 E2
Chilcroft Cl *BLGHMW/WYN* TS22 ... 57 F1 ◨
Childeray St *STOCS* TS18 .... 6 C6
Child St *GUIS* TS14 .... 129 D3 ◨
   SALT/BTN/SK TS12 .... 91 D5
Chillingham Ct *BLGHM* TS23 .... 42 A4
Chillingham Gv *NACLF* DL5 .... 39 D3 ◨
Chiltern Av *REDCAR* TS10 .... 67 F2
Chilton Cl *ACK/BRKF* TS5 .... 123 E1 ◨
   DARLW DL3 .... 130 C2
   STOCN TS19 .... 72 C2
Chilton Ct *NACLF* DL5 .... 39 D3
Chilton La *FYHL* DL17 .... 21 F5
Chiltons Av *BLGHM* TS23 .... 59 D5
China St *DARLW* DL3 .... 116 B2
The Chine *SALT/BTN/SK* TS12....... 89 D2
Chingford Av *NORM/PKE* TS3 ..... 100 B3
Chingford Gv *STOCN* TS19 .... 73 E5
Chipchase Rd *ACK/BRKF* TS5 .... 97 F2
Chippenham Rd *MGRV/ESTR* TS4 ... 124 C1
Chopwell Cl *STOCN* TS19 .... 73 D2 ◨
Christchurch Cl *DARLE* DL1 .... 116 C2 ◨
Christchurch Dr *STOCS* TS18 .... 93 D3
Christopher St *HTLPW* TS26 .... 2 A1 ◨
   NORTON TS20 .... 75 D4 ◨
Church Cl *CNHM/HEM* TS8 .... 141 E1 ◨
   EGG/EAG TS16 .... 137 E3
   HTLP TS24 .... 19 E2
   MARSKE TS11 .... 70 C5
   MTN/NUN TS7 .... 100 C5 ◨
   NACLF DL5 .... 54 C1 ◨
   THNBY TS17 .... 95 D4
Church Dr *BAUK* DL14 .... 27 F4
   GTAY/STK TS9 .... 150 B3
Churchend Cl *BLGHM* TS23 .... 58 C5 ◨
Church Howle Crs *MARSKE* TS11 ... 71 D5
Churchill Cl *ESTON* TS6 .... 102 A1 ◨
   GTAY/STK TS9 .... 150 C2 ◨
Church La *ACK/BRKF* TS5 .... 97 F5 ◨
   ACK/BRKF TS5 .... 123 E1
   ESTON TS6 .... 81 F4 ◨
   FYHL DL17 .... 20 C1
   GUIS TS14 .... 129 D2 ◨
   MARSKE TS11 .... 70 C4
   MTN/NUN TS7 .... 100 C5 ◨
   MTN/NUN TS7 .... 145 E1
   SALT/BTN/SK TS12 .... 108 C2
Church Mt *ESTON* TS6 .... 102 A2 ◨
Church Rd *BLGHM* TS23 .... 58 C5 ◨
   EGG/EAG TS16 .... 137 E3
   FYHL DL17 .... 20 C1
   STOCS TS18 .... 7 G3
Church Rw *BLGHMW/WYN* TS22 .... 41 E5 ◨
   DARLE DL1 .... 9 E5 ◨
   HTLP TS24 .... 2 C4
Church St *FYHL* DL17 .... 21 F4
   GUIS TS14 .... 129 E2 ◨
   HTLP TS24 .... 2 D2
   HTLPS TS25 .... 25 D5
   MARSKE TS11 .... 70 C4 ◨
   REDCAR TS10 .... 50 C4
   SHIL DL4 .... 35 E2
   SPEN DL16 .... 15 D3 ◨
Church St South *MARSKE* TS11 ...... 70 B4
Church Wk *HTLP* TS24 .... 19 E2
Cinderwood *NORM/PKE* TS3 ...... 100 B2
Clairville Rd *MGRV/ESTR* TS4....... 98 C1
Clanny Rd *NACLF* DL5 .... 55 D2

Clapham Gn *NORM/PKE* TS3 .... 99 D2 ◨
Clapham Rd *YARM* TS15 .... 146 A1
Clare Av *DARLW* DL3 .... 130 C1
Claremont Dr *HTLPW* TS26 .... 17 E5
   MTN/NUN TS7 .... 126 A5
Claremont Gdns *STOCN* TS19 .... 93 D1
Claremont Gv *SEDG* TS21 .... 29 D5 ◨
Claremont Rd *NACLF* DL5 .... 133 D4
Clarence Chare *NACLF* DL5 .... 54 C2
Clarence Cl *NACLF* DL5 .... 55 D2 ◨
Clarence Gdns *BAUK* DL14 .... 27 D1
Clarence Gn *NACLF* DL5 .... 55 D2
Clarence Rd *EGG/EAG* TS16 .... 119 E5
   HTLP TS24 .... 18 A3
   MTN/NUN TS7 .... 127 D5
Clarence Rw *STOCS* TS18 .... 7 H2
Clarence St *BAUK* DL14 .... 26 C1
   BLGHM TS23 .... 60 C4 ◨
   HTLP TS24 .... 19 E1 ◨
   SPEN DL16 .... 15 D3
   STOCS TS18 .... 7 C1
The Clarence *BAUK* DL14 .... 27 D1 ◨
Clarendon Rd *DARLE* DL1 .... 117 F2
   MBORO TS1 .... 5 F5
   NORTON TS20 .... 74 C3
   THNBY TS17 .... 121 F1
Clarendon St *REDCAR* TS10 .... 51 F4
Clareville Rd *DARLW* DL3 .... 131 D1
Clarkson Ct *HTLPS* TS25 .... 23 E4 ◨
Clark St *HTLP* TS24 .... 2 D4
Claude Av *ACK/BRKF* TS5 .... 97 F4
Clavering Rd *RHTLP* TS27 .... 11 F3 ◨
Claxton Av *DARLW* DL3 .... 114 C5
Claxton Cl *STOCN* TS19 .... 72 C2 ◨
Claydon Gv *THNBY* TS17 .... 139 D3 ◨
Claygate *BLGHM* TS23 .... 41 F4 ◨
Claymore Rd *HTLPS* TS25 .... 31 E1
Clayton St *BAUK* DL14 .... 27 D1
Cleadon Av *BLGHM* TS23 .... 42 A4
Clearpool Cl *HTLP* TS24 .... 18 B1 ◨
Cleasby Vw *DARLW* DL3 .... 114 C4 ◨
Cleatlam Cl *STOCN* TS19 .... 73 D3
Cleator Dr *GUIS* TS14 .... 128 C5 ◨
Clee Ter *BLGHM* TS23 .... 59 D2 ◨
Clements Ri *NORTON* TS20 .... 74 B1 ◨
Clepstone Av *ACK/BRKF* TS5 .... 97 E4
Clevecoat Wk *RHTLP* TS27 .... 10 B5
Clevegate *MTN/NUN* TS7 .... 126 B5
Cleveland Av *ACK/BRKF* TS5 .... 97 F4 ◨
   BAUK DL14 .... 27 D3
   DARLW DL3 .... 8 C4
   DARLW DL3 .... 8 C6
   GTAY/STK TS9 .... 152 B1 ◨
   NORTON TS20 .... 75 D2
   SHIL DL4 .... 36 A3
Cleveland Cl *MTN/NUN* TS7 .... 126 C1
Cleveland Ct *ESTON* TS6 .... 81 D3 ◨
   FYHL DL17 .... 21 F2 ◨
Cleveland Dr *MTN/NUN* TS7 .... 125 F3
Cleveland Gdns *EGG/EAG* TS16 ..... 137 D3 ◨
Cleveland Rd *HTLP* TS24................ 18 A1
Cleveland St *DARLE* DL1 .... 116 B4
   ESTON TS6 .... 101 F3
   ESTON TS6 .... 102 B2 ◨
   GTAY/STK TS9 .... 150 C2 ◨
   GUIS TS14 .... 128 C2
   GUIS TS14 .... 129 E2
   HTLP TS24 .... 19 E1 ◨
   LOFT/ST TS13 .... 112 A1
   LOFT/ST TS13 .... 112 C4
   LOFT/ST TS13 .... 113 E3
   REDCAR TS10 .... 51 E4 ◨
   SALT/BTN/SK TS12 .... 89 F2 ◨
   SALT/BTN/SK TS12 .... 109 D5
   SALT/BTN/SK TS12 .... 110 C2
   TEESM TS2 .... 5 C1
Cleveland Ter *DARLW* DL3 .... 8 A6
Cleveland Vw *FYHL* DL17 .... 21 E2 ◨
   MARSKE TS11 .... 69 F5
   NORM/PKE TS3 .... 100 A2
   SALT/BTN/SK TS12 .... 108 C4
Cleveland Wy *LOFT/ST* TS13 .... 91 F2 ◨
   SALT/BTN/SK TS12 .... 89 D4
Cleves Cl *FYHL* DL17 .... 21 E1 ◨
Cliffe Av *LOFT/ST* TS13 .... 112 B1
Cliffe Ct *HTLPS* TS25 .... 25 D4
Cliffe St *SALT/BTN/SK* TS12 .... 91 E5
Cliffe Wy *DARLE* DL1 .... 133 D3 ◨
Clifford Av *BAUK* DL14 .... 27 D3
Clifford Cl *HTLP* TS24 .... 12 B5 ◨
Clifford St *REDCAR* TS10 .... 51 E4 ◨
Cliff Ter *HTLP* TS24 .... 19 F2
The Cliff *HTLPS* TS25 .... 25 D4
Cliffwood Cl *ESTON* TS6 .... 102 B3 ◨
Clifton Av *BLGHMW/WYN* TS22 ..... 58 A1
   DARLE DL1 .... 132 B4
   HTLPW TS26 .... 17 F5
   STOCS TS18 .... 94 B4
   STOCS TS18 .... 119 E4
Clifton Gdns *STOCS* TS18 .... 119 F4 ◨
Clifton Pl *ESTON* TS6 .... 101 F3 ◨
Clifton Rd *DARLE* DL1 .... 132 B3
Clifton St *MBORO* TS1 .... 5 E6
Clive Crs *NORTON* TS20................. 74 C2
Clive Rd *ACK/BRKF* TS5 .... 97 F2

ESTON TS6 .... 101 F3
Clive St *FYHL* DL17 .... 21 F3
Clockwood Gdns *YARM* TS15 ...... 137 F5 ◨
The Cloisters *STOCN* TS19 .... 72 C5
Close St *DARLE* DL1 .... 116 B3
The Close *SPEN* DL16 .... 15 E1
Clover Ct *NACLF* DL5 .... 38 C2
Cloverdale *DARLE* DL1 .... 117 F2
Clover Wood Cl *MTN/NUN* TS7 ... 126 B4 ◨
Clowbeck Ct *DARLW* DL3 .... 115 D2
Clydach Gv *THNBY* TS17 .... 138 B3
Clyde Gdns *BLGHMW/WYN* TS22 .... 40 C5
Clyde Pl *HTLP* TS24 .... 18 C1
Clynes Rd *ESTON* TS6 .... 82 A5
Coach House Ms *ESTON* TS6 ...... 101 E4
Coach Rd *SALT/BTN/SK* TS12 .... 90 C4
Coal La *BLGHMW/WYN* TS22 .... 40 A1
   BLGHMW/WYN TS22 .... 41 E3
Coast Rd *REDCAR* TS10 .... 69 E1
Coate Cl *CNHM/HEM* TS8 .... 123 E5 ◨
Coatham Av *NACLF* DL5 .... 54 B3
Coatham Cl *CNHM/HEM* TS8 ...... 124 A5
Coatham Crs *DARLE* DL1 .... 116 C2
Coatham Dr *HTLPW* TS26 .... 16 B5
Coatham Gv *BLGHM* TS23 .... 42 A4
Coatham Rd *REDCAR* TS10 .... 51 D4
   STOCN TS19 .... 73 D2
Coatham v *EGG/EAG* TS16 .... 136 C2
Coatsay Cl *STOCN* TS19 .... 73 D3 ◨
Cobble Carr *GUIS* TS14 .... 128 C3
Cobblewood *NORM/PKE* TS3 ...... 100 A2
Cobden Ct *DARLE* DL1 .... 133 D3
Cobden St *DARLE* DL1 .... 133 D2
   HTLPW TS26 .... 17 E4
   STOCS TS18 .... 7 F4 ◨
   THNBY TS17 .... 95 F4
Cobham St *MBORO* TS1 .... 98 A1
Coburg St *DARLE* DL1 .... 9 G4
Cobwood *NORM/PKE* TS3 .... 100 B2 ◨
Cocken Rd *STOCN* TS19 .... 73 D3
Cockerton Gn *DARLW* DL3 .... 115 D5
Cockfield Av *BLGHM* TS23 .... 42 B4
Cockton Hill Rd *BAUK* DL14 .... 27 D3
Colburn Av *NACLF* DL5 .... 37 F4
Colchester Rd *NORTON* TS20......... 75 D1
Coledale Rd *NORM/PKE* TS3 .... 99 E3
Colenso St *HTLPW* TS26 .... 23 F1
Coleridge Av *HTLPS* TS25 .... 24 A2
Coleridge Gdns *DARLE* DL1 .... 132 B5
Coleridge Rd *BLGHM* TS23 .... 42 A3
Coleshill Cl *BLGHM* TS23 .... 59 D1 ◨
Coleton Gdns *THNBY* TS17 .... 139 D2
College Rd *NORM/PKE* TS3 .... 100 A1
College St *SHIL* DL4 .... 35 D2
Colliers Gn *MGRV/ESTR* TS4 .... 79 D5 ◨
Collin Av *MGRV/ESTR* TS4............. 98 B4
Collingwood Cha
   SALT/BTN/SK TS12 .... 91 D4
Collingwood Rd *BLGHM* TS23 ...... 75 F1
   HTLPW TS26 .... 17 F4
Collins Av *NORTON* TS20............... 75 E2
Collinson Av *ACK/BRKF* TS5 .... 96 C4
Colmore Av *NORM/PKE* TS3 .... 80 B5
Colorado Gv *DARLE* DL1 .... 116 C2
Colpitt Cl *NORTON* TS20................ 74 C1 ◨
Colsterdale Cl *BLGHM* TS23 .... 42 A5
Coltman St *NORM/PKE* TS3 .... 79 E5 ◨
Columbia Dr *THNBY* TS17.............. 7 H5
Columbine Cl *MTN/NUN* TS7 ..... 125 D3
Colville St *MBORO* TS1 .... 4 D6
Colwell Ct *NACLF* DL5 .... 37 E5
Colwyn Cl *REDCAR* TS10 .... 68 C4
Colwyn Rd *HTLPS* TS25 .... 2 A6
   NORTON TS20 .... 75 E1 ◨
Comfrey Mnr *CNHM/HEM* TS8 ... 143 E2
Commerce Wy *ESTON* TS6 .... 80 C5
Commercial St *DARLW* DL3 .... 9 F4
   FYHL DL17 .... 21 F4
   HTLP TS24 .... 19 E1 ◨
   STOCS TS18 .... 7 H3
   TEESM TS2 .... 78 B2
Commondale Av *STOCN* TS19 .... 74 A4
Commondale Dr *HTLPS* TS25......... 32 C1
Commondale Gv *REDCAR* TS10...... 67 F2
Compton Av *BAUK* DL14 .... 26 C3 ◨
   DARLW DL3 .... 115 D5
Compton Rd *HTLPS* TS25 .... 22 C3
Comrie Rd *HTLPS* TS25 .... 31 E1
Concorde Wy *STOCS* TS18 .... 120 A1
Coney Cl *THNBY* TS17 .... 139 E1 ◨
Congreve Ter *NACLF* DL5 .... 55 D5
Conifer Av *SEDG* TS21 .... 29 E3
Conifer Cl *MTN/NUN* TS7 .... 101 D5 ◨
Conifer Crs *BLGHM* TS23 .... 58 B3
Conifer Dr *STOCN* TS19 .... 74 A3 ◨
Conifer Gv *BLGHM* TS23 .... 58 B3
Coningsby Cl *HTLPS* TS25 .... 32 C1
Conisborough Dr *REDCAR* TS10 ... 69 D3 ◨
Coniscliffe Ms *DARLW* DL3 .... 130 B3
Coniscliffe Rd *DARLW* DL3 .... 9 E5
   HTLPW TS26 .... 16 B5
   STOCN TS19 .... 73 D3
Coniston Av *REDCAR* TS10 .... 68 B1
Coniston Gv *ACK/BRKF* TS5 .... 97 E5
Coniston Rd *ESTON* TS6 .... 82 B5

FYHL DL17 .... 20 C2
HTLPS TS25 .... 24 B3
SALT/BTN/SK TS12 .... 109 D1
STOCS TS18 .... 73 F5
Coniston St DARLW DL3 .... 115 E4
Connaught Cl MTN/NUN TS7 .. 127 D4 ⑤
Connaught Rd ACK/BRKF TS5 .. 97 D1
MTN/NUN TS7 .... 126 C4
Consett Cl STOCN TS19 .... 73 D3
Consett Dryden Cl ESTON TS6 101 F3 ⑪
Consort Cl STOCN TS19 .... 93 E1 ①
Constable Gv BLGHM TS23 ...... 41 F3
Constance St NORM/PKE TS3 .. 79 D5 ③
Convalescent St
SALT/BTN/SK TS12 .... 89 E1 ①
Conway Av BLGHM TS23 .... 59 D3
Conway Gv BAUK DL14 .... 27 D3
Conway Rd REDCAR TS10 .... 68 C1
Conwy Gv THNBY TS17 .... 138 B2 ②
Conyers Av DARLW DL3 .... 114 B5
Conyers Cl DARLW DL3 .... 114 C5 ③
Conyers Ct SALT/BTN/SK TS12.. 91 E5
Conyers Gv DARLW DL3 .... 114 C5 ③
Cook Crs NORTON TS20 .... 74 C2
Cookgate MTN/NUN TS7 .... 126 B5
Cook's Ct MTN/NUN TS7 .... 101 D5 ③
Coombe HI MARSKE TS11 .... 86 C3
Coombe Wy STOCS TS18 .... 92 C5
Co-operative St SHIL DL4 .... 35 D2 ⑥
Cooper Ct ESTON TS6 .... 102 A2
Copgrove Cl NORM/PKE TS3 ...... 99 D2
Copley Cl STOCN TS19 .... 73 D3
Copperwood NORM/PKE TS3 .. 100 B3 ⑪
Copperwood Cl RHTLP TS27 .... 11 E5 ③
Coppice Rd MGRV/ESTR TS4 .... 98 C3
The Coppice CNHM/HEM TS8 .. 124 B4
Coppice Wk DARLW DL3 .... 114 B4 ①
Copse La THNBY TS17 .... 139 D1 ①
Copse Side DARLW DL3.......... 130 B2
The Copse BAUK DL14............ 27 D2
HTLP TS24 .... 17 F2 ①
Copsewood Wk GTAY/STK TS9 .. 152 B1 ②
Coquet Cl REDCAR TS10 .... 69 E3
THNBY TS17............................ 139 D3
Coral St MBORO TS1 .... 5 E5 ③
SALT/BTN/SK TS12 .... 89 E1
Coral Wy REDCAR TS10.......... 69 D3
Corbridge Cl CNHM/HEM TS8 .. 124 A5 ③
Corbridge Crs DARLE DL1...... 117 D3
Corby Av ACK/BRKF TS5 .... 96 C5
Corder Rd ACK/BRKF TS5 .... 97 D1
Corfe Crs BLGHM TS23 .... 58 C1
Corfu Wy REDCAR TS10 .... 67 E4
Coris Cl MTN/NUN TS7 .... 125 E3
Cormland Cl NORTON TS20 ...... 75 E2
Cormorant Dr REDCAR TS10 .... 69 D3 ④
Corncroft Ms ESTON TS6 .... 82 A3 ⑥
Cornfield Rd ACK/BRKF TS5 .... 98 A3
STOCN TS19............................ 92 C1
THNBY TS17............................ 95 D4
Cornforth Av NORM/PKE TS3 .... 99 F4
Cornforth Cl STOCN TS19 ...... 73 D3
Cornforth Gv BLGHM TS23 ...... 42 B4 ①
Corngrave Cl MARSKE TS11 ...... 71 D5 ⑪
Cornsay Cl STOCN TS19.......... 123 D1
STOCN TS19............................ 73 D3
Cornwall Av DARLE DL1 .... 117 D4
Cornwall Cl MTN/NUN TS7 .... 126 C5
Cornwall Crs BLGHM TS23 ...... 59 E3
Cornwall Gv NORTON TS20 ...... 75 E3
Cornwallis Cl SALT/BTN/SK TS12 .. 91 E4 ①
Cornwall Rd GUIS TS14.......... 128 C4
Cornwall St HTLPS TS25 .... 23 F2
Coronation Av SHIL DL4 .... 35 F3
Coronation Dr HTLPS TS25 ...... 3 G6
Coronation Gn NORM/PKE TS3 .. 100 B4 ②
Coronation Rd LOFT/ST TS13 .. 113 D3
Coronation St DARLW DL3 .... 115 F4 ③
LOFT/ST TS13........................ 112 B1
NORM/PKE TS3...................... 79 E5 ③
Corporation Rd DARLW DL3 .... 9 E2
HTLP TS24 .... 19 D1
MBORO TS1 .... 5 G3
REDCAR TS10 .... 50 C5
Corporation St STOCS TS18 .... 7 E5
Corscombe Cl FYHL DL17 ...... 21 F2
Cortland Av MTN/NUN TS7 .... 127 E4
Cosgrove Av BAUK DL14 .... 26 C5
Cosin Cl NACLF DL5 .... 55 D2
Costain Gv NORTON TS20 ...... 58 B5
Costa St ESTON TS6................ 80 B3
MBORO TS1 .... 97 F1
Cotgarth Wy STOCN TS19 ...... 72 C3 ①
Cotherstone Dr ACK/BRKF TS5 .. 123 E3
Cotherstone Moor Dr
DARLE DL1 .... 133 E3 ②
Cotherstone Rd STOCS TS18 .... 94 B4
Cotswold Av NORM/PKE TS3.... 99 F1
Cotswold Crs BLGHM TS23...... 58 B3
Cotswold Dr REDCAR TS10...... 67 F2
SALT/BTN/SK TS12 .... 109 E1
Cottage Farm STOCN TS19 ...... 93 E2
Cottage Ms DARLE DL1.......... 117 E4
Cottage Rd SHIL DL4 .... 35 E5 ⑪
Cottersloe Rd NORTON TS20 .... 58 A5

Cottingham Ct DARLW DL3 ...... 114 C4
Cottingham Dr NORM/PKE TS3 .. 99 F1
Cottonwood NORM/PKE TS3 .... 100 B2 ⑩
Coulby Farm Wy CNHM/HEM TS8 .. 143 D1
Coulby Manor Farm
CNHM/HEM TS8 .... 124 C4 ⑪
Coulby Manor Wy
CNHM/HEM TS8 .... 124 B4
Coulson Cl YARM TS15 .... 146 A2
Coulson St SPEN DL16 .... 15 F3
Coulthard Ct ESTON TS6 .... 80 C3 ⑥
Coulton Gv BLGHMW/WYN TS22 .. 57 F1
Countisbury Rd NORTON TS20 .. 57 D4
Courageous St HTLPS TS25 ...... 24 C4
Courtlands Rd DARLW DL3 .... 115 E4
Court Rd MGRV/ESTR TS4 .... 98 C3
Covent Cl ESTON TS6 .... 101 E5 ⑪
Coverdale Ct NACLF DL5.......... 38 A4
Coverdale Rd STOCN TS19 ...... 93 E2
The Covert NACLF DL5 .... 37 E4 ①
Cowdray Cl GUIS TS14 .... 129 E5 ③
Cowley Ct EGG/EAG TS16 ...... 119 F2
HTLPS TS25 .... 25 D3 ①
Cowley Rd ACK/BRKF TS5 ...... 123 F1
Cowpen Bewley Rd BLGHM TS23.. 60 B1
Cowpen Crs STOCN TS19 .... 73 D3
Cowpen La BLGHM TS23 .... 59 D3
Cowper Gv HTLPS TS25 .... 22 C3
Cowper Rd NORTON TS20 ...... 75 E4
Cowscote Crs LOFT/ST TS13 .. 112 C2
Cowton Wy EGG/EAG TS16 .... 119 D4
Coxgreen Cl STOCN TS19 .... 73 D3
Coxhoe Rd BLGHM TS23 .... 59 E1 ⑪
Coxmoor Wy MARSKE TS11 .... 86 B3
Coxwold Cl ACK/BRKF TS5 .... 124 A1
Coxwold Dr DARLE DL1 .... 132 C3
Coxwold Rd STOCS TS18 .... 93 F2
Coxwold Wy BLGHM TS23 ...... 60 A3
Craddock St SPEN DL16 .... 14 C4
Cradley Dr ACK/BRKF TS5........ 123 E4
Cradoc Gv THNBY TS17.......... 138 B2
Cradock St BAUK DL14 .... 27 E3
Cragdale Rd NORM/PKE TS3 .... 99 E2
Craggs St MGRV/ESTR TS4...... 78 C4
STOCN TS19............................ 6 D2
Cragside SALT/BTN/SK TS12.... 91 E5
SEDG TS21 .... 29 D5
Cragside Cl SPEN DL16 .... 15 D4
Cragside Ct THNBY TS17 .... 139 D2
Cragston Cl HTLPW TS26 .... 16 C3
Cragweliside DARLE DL1 .... 117 D3 ⑪
Craigearn Rd ESTON TS6 .... 101 E2
Craig St DARLW DL3 .... 8 C1
Crail Gdns DARLE DL1 .... 116 C1
Craister Rd NORTON TS20 ...... 75 D1
Cramlington Cl CNHM/HEM TS8 .. 124 A5 ⑤
Cramond Cl DARLW DL3 .... 130 B2
Cranage Cl ACK/BRKF TS5 ...... 97 D4
Cranberry CNHM/HEM TS8 .... 143 E1
Cranbourne Ter STOCS TS18 .... 94 B3
Cranbrook MTN/NUN TS7...... 126 A5
Cranfield Av NORM/PKE TS3 .... 80 A5
Cranford Av ESTON TS6 .... 81 D5
Cranford Gdns ACK/BRKF TS5 .. 97 D5
Cranleigh Rd STOCS TS18 .... 6 B5
Cranmore Rd NORM/PKE TS3 .... 99 E1
Cranstock Cl BLGHMW/WYN TS22 57 F1 ③
Cranswick Cl BLGHM TS23 ...... 42 B3
Cranswick Dr ACK/BRKF TS5 .. 124 A1
Cranwell Gv THNBY TS17 ...... 121 F4
Cranwell Rd HTLPS TS25 .... 30 C1
Cranworth Gn THNBY TS17 .... 95 F3 ⑧
Cranworth St THNBY TS17 ...... 95 E3 ⑨
Crathorne Ct ACK/BRKF TS5 .... 97 D2
Crathorne Pk ESTON TS6 .... 101 E3
Crathorne Rd NORTON TS20 .... 75 D1 ②
Craven St MBORO TS1 .... 97 F1
Craven V GUIS TS14................ 129 D4
Crawford Cl BAUK DL14 .... 26 C5 ③
Crawford Rd NACLF DL5.......... 54 C1
Crawford St HTLPS TS25 .... 33 D1
Crawley Rd THNBY TS17.......... 96 A5
Crayke Rd STOCS TS18 .... 93 F3
Creekwood NORM/PKE TS3 .... 100 B2
Creighton Rd NACLF DL5 .... 55 D1
Cremorne Cl MTN/NUN TS7 .... 125 E3
The Crescent ACK/BRKF TS5 .... 97 F5
EGG/EAG TS16........................ 137 D2
HTLPW TS26 .... 17 D4
MTN/NUN TS7 .... 127 D5
SALT/BTN/SK TS12 .... 89 E3
THNBY TS17............................ 95 E5 ①
Cresswell Cl CNHM/HEM TS8 .. 124 A5 ②
Cresswell Ct HTLPW TS26........ 16 C4
Cresswell Dr HTLPW TS26 ...... 17 D4 ③
Cresswell Rd ESTON TS6.......... 82 A3
HTLPW TS26 .... 16 C4
The Crest HTLPW TS26 .... 16 C4 ①
Crestwood NORM/PKE TS3 .... 100 B2 ⑪
REDCAR TS10 .... 68 C5
Crewe Rd NACLF DL5 .... 55 D2
Cribyn Cl THNBY TS17............ 138 B2
Cricket La ESTON TS6 .... 101 E4
Crimdon Cl CNHM/HEM TS8 .. 142 A1 ②
Cringlemoor Crs DARLE DL1 .... 133 E4

Crinklewood NORM/PKE TS3 ...... 100 B3 ②
Crispin Ct SALT/BTN/SK TS12 .... 91 E5
Croft Av ACK/BRKF TS5 .... 97 C5
Crofton Av MGRV/ESTR TS4 ...... 98 B3 ③
Crofton Rd STOCS TS18 .... 75 F5
Croft Rd EGG/EAG TS16.......... 137 D2
Croft Ter HTLP TS24 .... 19 E2
The Croft FYHL DL17 .... 39 D2
MTN/NUN TS7 .... 125 F4
Cromarty Cl DARLE DL1.......... 117 F1
Cromer Ct EGG/EAG TS16 ...... 137 E2
Cromer St MGRV/ESTR TS4 ...... 78 C5
Cromore Cl THNBY TS17........ 121 E5
Crompton Cl FYHL DL17 .... 20 B2 ③
Cromwell Av LOFT/ST TS13 .... 113 F3
STOCS TS18 .... 7 G2
Cromwell Rd ESTON TS6 .... 80 C4
Cromwell St HTLPS TS25.......... 3 E5
NORM/PKE TS3 .... 79 D5 ③
Cromwell Ter THNBY TS17 ...... 95 E4
Crookers Hill Cl MTN/NUN TS7 .. 144 C1
Crooks Barn La NORTON TS20 .. 57 F4
Crook St NORTON TS20 .... 57 F5 ③
Cropton Cl REDCAR TS10 .... 68 A4
Cropton Wy CNHM/HEM TS8 .. 125 D5
Crosby Ct EGG/EAG TS16 ...... 137 E1 ③
Crosby Rd NACLF DL5 .... 54 B2
Crosby St DARLW DL3 .... 116 A2
NORTON TS20 .... 75 D4 ⑥
Crossbeck Wy MTN/NUN TS7 .. 101 D5
Crosscliff CNHM/HEM TS8 ...... 124 A5
Cross Fell REDCAR TS10 .... 68 A2 ②
Crossfield Rd NORM/PKE TS3 .... 99 D3
Crossfield Rd DARLE DL3 .... 115 D3
Crossfields CNHM/HEM TS8 .... 142 C2
Crosskirk Cl NORM/PKE TS3 .. 100 B3 ③
Cross La GTAY/STK TS9 .... 151 D4
LOFT/ST TS13 .... 113 D4
Cross St DARLW DL3 .... 116 A3
GUIS TS14 .... 129 D3 ③
NORTON TS20 .... 75 D1
SEDG TS21 .... 29 E4 ⑪
SHIL DL4.................................. 35 F4
The Crossway DARLE DL1 ...... 133 D1
Crosswell Pk THNBY TS17 ...... 138 B3 ②
Crosthwaite Av MGRV/ESTR TS4 .. 98 B4 ⑥
Crowhurst Cl GUIS TS14 .... 128 C5 ③
GUIS TS14 .... 129 D4 ⑪
Crowland Rd HTLPS TS25 .... 30 C1
Crow La ESTON TS6 .... 102 C1
Crown St BAUK DL14................ 27 F4
DARLE DL1 .... 9 C4
Crowood Av GTAY/STK TS9 .... 152 B1
Croxdale Gv STOCN TS19 .... 93 D2
Croxdale Rd BLGHM TS23 ...... 59 D1 ③
Croxton Av HTLPS TS25 .... 31 E2
Croxton Cl STOCN TS19.......... 92 B1
Croydon Rd MBORO TS1 .... 98 C1
Crummackdale THNBY TS17 .... 139 D4 ②
Crummock Rd REDCAR TS10 .... 68 A3 ②
Culgaith Av NORM/PKE TS3...... 99 E3
Cullen Cl DARLE DL1 .... 117 E2 ③
Cullen Rd HTLPS TS25 .... 23 E5 ①
Culloden Wy BLGHM TS23 ...... 42 C5 ①
Culross Gv STOCN TS19 .... 92 B1
Cumberland Crs BLGHM TS23 .. 58 C4
Cumberland Gv NORTON TS20 .. 57 E5
Cumberland Rd ACK/BRKF TS5 .. 98 A2
Cumberland St DARLW DL3 .... 116 A2 ③
Cumbernauld Rd THNBY TS17 .. 96 A5
Cumbie Wy NACLF DL5 .... 54 B5
Cumby Rd NACLF DL5 .... 54 B2
Cundall Rd HTLPW TS26 .... 17 E4
Cunningham Av THNBY TS17 .. 121 F4
Cunningham Cl
SALT/BTN/SK TS12 .... 91 D4 ③
Cunningham St ACK/BRKF TS5 .. 97 D1
Curlew Cl DARLW DL3 .... 115 D2
Curlew La NORTON TS20 .... 57 F4
Curran Av ACK/BRKF TS5 .... 97 D3 ⑤
Curson St ESTON TS6 .... 102 C3
Curthwaite ACK/BRKF TS5 ...... 122 C3
Cuthbert Cl THNBY TS17.......... 95 E4
Cuthbert St SPEN DL16 .... 15 E1
Cutler Cl MTN/NUN TS7 .... 126 A3
Cyclamen Gv DARLE DL1 .... 133 D2 ⑪
Cypress Cl DARLW DL3 .... 131 D4
Cypress Rd MTN/NUN TS7 ...... 126 A3
REDCAR TS10 .... 69 E1

D

Dacre Cl THNBY TS17 .... 121 E1 ③
Daimler Dr BLGHM TS23.......... 60 A1
Daisy Ct STOCN TS19 .... 73 E4 ⑪
Dalby Cl BLGHMW/WYN TS22 .. 57 F1 ③
REDCAR TS10 .... 68 A4
Dalby Ct CNHM/HEM TS8 ...... 125 E5 ①
Dalby Wy CNHM/HEM TS8...... 143 D1
Dalcross Ct CNHM/HEM TS8 .. 142 A1 ③
Dale Cl STOCN TS19 .... 72 C3
Dale Garth MARSKE TS11 .... 70 C5

Dale Gv *SHIL* DL4 .... 36 A4
   STOCN TS19 .... 93 D2
Dale Rd *DARLW* DL3 .... 8 A4
   SHIL DL4 .... 35 F5
Dales Park Rd *CNHM/HEM* TS8 ...... 141 F1
Daleston Av *ACK/BRKF* TS5 .... 97 F4 🔲
Daleston Cl *HTLPW* TS26 .... 16 B3 🔲
Dale St *MARSKE* TS11 .... 86 C2
Daleville Cl *MGRV/ESTR* TS4 .... 98 C4
Dalewood Wk *GTAY/STK* TS9 ...... 152 B1 🔲
Dalkeith Cl *DARLW* DL3 .... 130 B2
Dalkeith Crs *CNHM/HEM* TS8 .... 124 A4
Dalkeith Rd *HTLPS* TS25 .... 23 D4
Dallas Ct *CNHM/HEM* TS8 .... 142 A1
Dalmuir Cl *EGG/EAG* TS16 .... 137 E1
Dalry Gv *HTLPS* TS25 .... 23 D5 🔲
Daisy La *MTN/NUN* TS7 .... 101 D5
Dalton Back La
   BLGHMW/WYN TS22 .... 30 A2
Dalton Crs *SHIL* DL4 .... 35 F5
Dalton Gv *BLGHM* TS23 .... 42 A4
   NORTON TS20 .... 74 C3
Dalton St *DARLE* DL1 .... 9 H4
   HTLPW TS26 .... 2 A4
Dalton Wy *NACLF* DL5 .... 38 C5
Daltry Cl *YARM* TS15 .... 147 D1 🔲
Dam St *LOFT/ST* TS13 .... 113 E3
Danby Ct *DARLE* DL1 .... 117 D3
Danby Dale Av *REDCAR* TS10 .... 67 F2
Danby Gv *HTLPS* TS25 .... 25 D3 🔲
   THNBY TS17 .... 95 F5
Danby Rd *ESTON* TS6 .... 102 B1
   NORTON TS20 .... 75 D4
Danesbrook Ct *THNBY* TS17 .... 139 D4
Danesfort Av *GUIS* TS14 .... 128 C3 🔲
Danesmoor Crs *DARLW* DL3 .... 131 D1
Dante Rd *MTN/NUN* TS7 .... 125 D3
Daphne Rd *STOCN* TS19 .... 74 C4 🔲
Darenth Rd *NORM/PKE* TS3 .... 99 F3
Darlington Back La *SEDG* TS21 ..... 72 A5
   STOCN TS19 .... 72 B4
Darlington La *NORTON* TS20 .... 74 B2 🔲
   STOCN TS19 .... 73 D4
Darlington Rd *FYHL* DL17 .... 20 C1
   STOCS TS18 .... 93 E4
Darlington St *HTLP* TS24 .... 19 E2 🔲
Darnbrook Wy *MTN/NUN* TS7 ..... 126 B5
Darnell Gn *MGRV/ESTR* TS4 .... 125 D1
Darnton Dr *MGRV/ESTR* TS4 .... 125 D1
Darrowby Dr *DARLW* DL3 .... 115 F3
Dartmouth Gv *REDCAR* TS10 .... 68 C3
Darwen Ct *CNHM/HEM* TS8 .... 142 A1 🔲
Darwin Ct *DARLE* DL1 .... 133 D4
   HTLPS TS25 .... 22 C2
Daryngton Cl *DARLE* DL1 .... 117 L2 🔲
Dauntless Cl *HTLPS* TS25 .... 25 D4
Davenport Rd *YARM* TS15 .... 146 A2
Daventry Av *STOCN* TS19 .... 74 A3
Davey Rd *NORM/PKE* TS3 .... 80 B5
David Rd *NORTON* TS20 .... 75 E3
Davison Dr *HTLP* TS24 .... 12 B5
Davison Rd *DARLE* DL1 .... 116 C2
Davison St *MBORO* TS1 .... 5 F4
Davy St *FYHL* DL17 .... 20 B1 🔲
Dawdon Cl *STOCN* TS19 .... 73 D2 🔲
Dawley Cl *THNBY* TS17 .... 96 A5 🔲
Dawlish Dr *HTLPS* TS25 .... 31 F1
Dawn Cl *NORTON* TS20 .... 57 F4
Daylesford Gv *DARLW* DL3 .... 115 D1
Daylight Rd *STOCN* TS19 .... 73 F4 🔲
Day St *SALT/BTN/SK* TS12 .... 111 D1
Deacon Gdns *HTLPS* TS25 .... 33 D1 🔲
Deacon St *NORM/PKE* TS3 .... 79 E5 🔲
Deal Cl *STOCN* TS19 .... 74 A3
Deal Ct *MGRV/ESTR* TS4 .... 98 C5
Deal Rd *BLGHM* TS23 .... 41 F5 🔲
   REDCAR TS10 .... 69 D3
Dean Cl *SHIL* DL4 .... 35 E2
Dean Gdns *SHIL* DL4 .... 35 E3
Dean Rd *FYHL* DL17 .... 20 C2
Deansgate *ESTON* TS6 .... 102 C2
Dean St *SHIL* DL4 .... 35 E2
   STOCS TS18 .... 7 E5
De Brus Pk *CNHM/HEM* TS8 .... 144 A3
De Brus Wy *GUIS* TS14 .... 129 D2
Deepdale Av *ESTON* TS6 .... 82 B5 🔲
   MGRV/ESTR TS4 .... 98 B4
Deepdale La *LOFT/ST* TS13 .... 112 C1
Deepdale Rd *LOFT/ST* TS13 .... 112 C2
Deerness Rd *BAUK* DL14 .... 26 C3
Dee Rd *ESTON* TS6 .... 101 F1
Deerpool Cl *HTLP* TS24 .... 18 B1 🔲
Defoe Crs *NACLF* DL5 .... 39 D4
De Havilland Dr *MARSKE* TS11 ..... 69 F4 🔲
Deighton Gv *BLGHM* TS23 .... 41 F5 🔲
Deighton Rd *MGRV/ESTR* TS4 ..... 125 D2
De La Mare Dr *BLGHM* TS23 .... 41 F3
Delamere Dr *MARSKE* TS11 .... 87 D1
Delamere Rd *NORM/PKE* TS3 .... 99 F1 🔲
Delarden Rd *NORM/PKE* TS3 .... 99 F1 🔲
Delaval Rd *BLGHM* TS23 .... 59 E1
Dell Cl *MTN/NUN* TS7 .... 125 E4
Dellfield Cl *NORM/PKE* TS3 .... 99 E4
The Dell *BAUK* DL14 .... 27 E1
Del'strother Av *STOCS* TS18 .... 6 A2

Denbigh Rd *BLGHM* TS23 .... 42 A5
Dene Gv *BAUK* DL14 .... 27 E2 🔲
   DARLW DL3 .... 8 A2
   REDCAR TS10 .... 51 F5
Dene Rd *MGRV/ESTR* TS4 .... 98 C3
Deneside *SPEN* DL16 .... 15 D2
Deneside Cl *YARM* TS15 .... 137 F5 🔲
Deneside Rd *DARLW* DL3 .... 8 A1
Denevale *YARM* TS15 .... 137 F5
Dene Wk *MARSKE* TS11 .... 70 A5
Denham Gn *NORM/PKE* TS3 .... 99 F1
Denham Pl *NACLF* DL5 .... 39 D5
Denholme Av *STOCS* TS18 .... 94 A4 🔲
Denmark St *DARLW* DL3 .... 116 A3
   TEESM TS2 .... 4 D2 🔲
Dennison St *STOCS* TS18 .... 94 B4
Denshaw Cl *STOCN* TS19 .... 92 C1
Dentdale Cl *YARM* TS15 .... 146 A2
Denton Av *NACLF* DL5 .... 54 C5
Denton Cl *ACK/BRKF* TS5 .... 123 D3
   DARLW DL3 .... 114 C4 🔲
   STOCN TS19 .... 73 D2 🔲
Dent St *HTLPW* TS26 .... 2 B1
   SHIL DL4 .... 35 F2
Depot Rd *TEESM* TS2 .... 78 A2
Derby Av *ACK/BRKF* TS5 .... 96 C3
Derby Cl *THNBY* TS17 .... 95 F4
Derby Gv *GUIS* TS14 .... 128 C4
Derby St *DARLW* DL3 .... 116 A3 🔲
   HTLPS TS25 .... 24 A2
The Derby *MTN/NUN* TS7 .... 125 D2
Derwent Av *GUIS* TS14 .... 128 B4
Derwent Rd *FYHL* DL17 .... 20 C1
   REDCAR TS10 .... 67 F1
   SALT/BTN/SK TS12 .... 109 D1
   THNBY TS17 .... 121 F1
Derwent St *HTLPW* TS26 .... 2 A2
   MBORO TS1 .... 4 C5
   NORM/PKE TS3 .... 79 E5 🔲
   NORTON TS20 .... 74 C3
Derwent Ter *SPEN* DL16 .... 15 E2
Derwentwater Av *ACK/BRKF* TS5 .. 97 E5 🔲
Derwentwater Rd *ESTON* TS6 .... 82 B5
Desford Gn *NORM/PKE* TS3 .... 99 F2 🔲
Deva Cl *MGRV/ESTR* TS4 .... 99 D3
Devon Cl *REDCAR* TS10 .... 68 A2
Devon Crs *BLGHM* TS23 .... 59 E3
   SALT/BTN/SK TS12 .... 108 C2 🔲
Devonport Rd *ACK/BRKF* TS5 .... 98 B3
   STOCS TS18 .... 75 E5
Devon Rd *ESTON* TS6 .... 82 A5 🔲
   GUIS TS14 .... 128 C4
Devonshire Rd *ACK/BRKF* TS5 ..... 97 F2 🔲
   DARLE DL1 .... 117 D4
Devonshire St *STOCS* TS18 .... 94 B4
Dewberry *CNHM/HEM* TS8 .... 143 E2
Dew La *MTN/NUN* TS7 .... 126 C1
Diamond Ct *STOCS* TS18 .... 120 B1
Diamond Rd *MBORO* TS1 .... 5 E5
   THNBY TS17 .... 95 F5
Diamond St *SALT/BTN/SK* TS12 .... 89 E1
   SHIL DL4 .... 35 E3
Dickens Gv *HTLPS* TS25 .... 23 E2
Dickens St *HTLP* TS24 .... 12 B4
   SPEN DL16 .... 15 D3
Dickinson St *DARLE* DL1 .... 132 C2 🔲
Didcot Cl *DARLW* DL3 .... 114 C1
Digby Cl *DARLW* DL3 .... 8 A2
Diligence Wy *EGG/EAG* TS16 .... 118 C5
Dillside *STOCN* TS19 .... 73 E4
Dinas Ct *THNBY* TS17 .... 138 B2
Dinsdale Av *ACK/BRKF* TS5 .... 123 E1
Dinsdale Ct *BLGHM* TS23 .... 42 B5 🔲
Dinsdale Crs *DARLE* DL1 .... 133 D2
Dinsdale Dr *EGG/EAG* TS16 .... 137 E1
Dinsdale Rd *STOCN* TS19 .... 73 D2
Diomed Ct *MTN/NUN* TS7 .... 125 E2
Dionysia Rd *NORM/PKE* TS3 .... 99 E1
Dipton Rd *STOCN* TS19 .... 72 C2
Dishforth Cl *THNBY* TS17 .... 121 F4
Dixon Gv *NORM/PKE* TS3 .... 99 E1
Dixon Rd *NACLF* DL5 .... 54 C2
Dixons Bank *CNHM/HEM* TS8 ..... 126 B5
   MTN/NUN TS7 .... 126 A4
Dixon St *BAUK* DL14 .... 27 E2 🔲
   SALT/BTN/SK TS12 .... 91 D5
   SALT/BTN/SK TS12 .... 109 E1
   STOCS TS18 .... 7 E4
Dobson Pl *HTLP* TS24 .... 12 A4 🔲
Dockside Rd *ESTON* TS6 .... 80 B2
   NORM/PKE TS3 .... 79 E3
Dock St *TEESM* TS2 .... 5 H1
Dodds St *DARLW* DL3 .... 8 E2
Dodford Rd *CNHM/HEM* TS8 ...... 142 A1
Dodsworth St *DARLE* DL1 .... 116 C4
Doncaster Crs *STOCN* TS19 .... 73 D2 🔲
Donegal Ter *MBORO* TS1 .... 97 E1 🔲
Dorchester Cl *CNHM/HEM* TS8 ... 125 D2 🔲
   STOCN TS19 .... 74 A3 🔲
Dorchester Dr *HTLP* TS24 .... 11 F3
Dorlcote Pl *NORTON* TS20 .... 75 D3 🔲
Dorman Rd *ESTON* TS6 .... 102 A2
Dorman's Crs *REDCAR* TS10 .... 67 E1 🔲
Dornoch Sands *THNBY* TS17 .... 123 D4

Dorothy St *NORM/PKE* TS3 .... 79 E5 🔲
Dorset Cl *ACK/BRKF* TS5 .... 97 F2 🔲
   REDCAR TS10 .... 68 A2
Dorset Crs *BLGHM* TS23 .... 59 E2 🔲
Dorset Dr *DARLE* DL1 .... 117 D4
Dorset Rd *GUIS* TS14 .... 128 C5
   NORTON TS20 .... 75 E2
   SALT/BTN/SK TS12 .... 108 C2
Douglas Cl *STOCS* TS18 .... 120 B1
Douglas St *MGRV/ESTR* TS4 .... 78 C5
Douthwaite Rd *BAUK* DL14 .... 26 C5
Dovecote Cl *MARSKE* TS11 .... 70 B5
Dovecot Hl *BAUK* DL14 .... 27 E5
Dovecot St *STOCS* TS18 .... 7 E5
Dovedale Av *ESTON* TS6 .... 82 B5
Dovedale Cl *NORTON* TS20 .... 75 E1
Dovedale Rd *NORTON* TS20 .... 75 D2
Dover Cl *BLGHM* TS23 .... 58 B1 🔲
   REDCAR TS10 .... 68 C3
Dover Rd *STOCN* TS19 .... 74 B3
Dover St *HTLP* TS24 .... 2 D2
Downe St *LOFT/ST* TS13 .... 112 C3
Downfield Wy *MARSKE* TS11 .... 86 B3 🔲
Downham Av *NORM/PKE* TS3 .... 99 F4
Downham Gv *HTLPS* TS25 .... 31 D1
Downholme Gv *STOCS* TS18 .... 93 E4 🔲
Downing Ct *DARLE* DL1 .... 116 C3
Downside Rd *ACK/BRKF* TS5 .... 96 C4
Dowson Rd *HTLP* TS24 .... 12 B4
Doxford Cl *NACLF* DL5 .... 54 B2
Doyle Wy *STOCN* TS19 .... 72 C5 🔲
Drake Cl *MARSKE* TS11 .... 71 D5
Drake Ct *TEESM* TS2 .... 4 B1
Drake Rd *NORTON* TS20 .... 75 D2
Drake St *SPEN* DL16 .... 15 D3
Draycote Crs *DARLW* DL3 .... 131 E4
Draycote Av *ACK/BRKF* TS5 .... 123 F4
Draycott Cl *NORTON* TS20 .... 57 D5 🔲
   REDCAR TS10 .... 68 A4 🔲
Drayton Rd *HTLPS* TS25 .... 22 C3
Driffield Wy *BLGHM* TS23 .... 42 A3
Driftwell Dr *STOCN* TS19 .... 72 C5 🔲
Drinkfield Crs *DARLW* DL3 .... 116 A1
The Drive *CNHM/HEM* TS8 .... 141 E2 🔲
   HTLPS TS25 .... 31 D4
   MARSKE TS11 .... 70 A5
   THNBY TS17 .... 121 D3
Droitwich Av *STOCN* TS19 .... 74 A3
Drummond Cl *DARLE* DL1 .... 117 F1 🔲
Druridge Gv *REDCAR* TS10 .... 69 E3 🔲
Drury St *DARLW* DL3 .... 8 C2
Drybourne Av *SHIL* DL4 .... 35 E3
Drybourne Pk *SHIL* DL4 .... 35 E3 🔲
Dryburgh Vw *DARLW* DL3 .... 114 C4
Dryburn Rd *STOCN* TS19 .... 72 C2
Dryden Cl *BLGHM* TS23 .... 42 A3 🔲
Dryden Rd *HTLPS* TS25 .... 23 D3
Dublin St *DARLW* DL3 .... 116 B2
Duchy Rd *HTLPW* TS26 .... 16 B4
Dudley Dr *NACLF* DL5 .... 38 C2
Dudley Gv *BAUK* DL14 .... 26 C3 🔲
Dudley Rd *BLGHM* TS23 .... 41 F5 🔲
Dufton Rd *ACK/BRKF* TS5 .... 97 E2
Dugdale St *STOCS* TS18 .... 75 E5
Duhallow Cl *GUIS* TS14 .... 129 D5
Duke St *BAUK* DL14 .... 27 D3
   DARLW DL3 .... 8 D4
   HTLPW TS26 .... 17 E4
Dukesway *THNBY* TS17 .... 139 F1
Dulverton Cl *THNBY* TS17 .... 139 D4 🔲
Dulverton Wy *GUIS* TS14 .... 129 D4
Dumbarton Av *STOCN* TS19 .... 74 B3
Dumfries Rd *HTLPS* TS25 .... 23 E5
Dumfries St *DARLE* DL1 .... 9 H2
Dunbar Av *MGRV/ESTR* TS4 .... 125 D3
Dunbar Dr *EGG/EAG* TS16 .... 137 E2
Dunbar Rd *BLGHM* TS23 .... 58 B1
   HTLPS TS25 .... 23 E4
Duncan Av *REDCAR* TS10 .... 67 E1
Duncan Pl *LOFT/ST* TS13 .... 113 D3
Duncan Rd *HTLPS* TS25 .... 23 D4
Duncombe Bank *FYHL* DL17 .... 21 F2
Duncombe Cl *SPEN* DL16 .... 14 B4 🔲
Dundas Ms *MBORO* TS1 .... 5 G3
Dundas St *HTLP* TS24 .... 3 E4
   LOFT/ST TS13 .... 113 D3
   MBORO TS1 .... 5 G2
   REDCAR TS10 .... 51 E4 🔲
   SPEN DL16 .... 14 C2
   STOCN TS19 .... 73 D3
Dundas St East
   SALT/BTN/SK TS12 .... 89 F2 🔲
Dundas St West *SALT/BTN/SK* TS12 .. 89 E2
Dundee Rd *HTLPS* TS25 .... 23 D5
Dundee St *DARLE* DL1 .... 9 H2
Dunedin Av *STOCS* TS18 .... 93 D3
Dunelm Ct *SEDG* TS21 .... 29 D4 🔲
Dunelm Gv *SHIL* DL4 .... 35 D2 🔲
Dunelm Rd *STOCN* TS19 .... 73 E4
Dunelm Wk *DARLE* DL1 .... 117 E3
Dunford Cl *STOCN* TS19 .... 73 D2 🔲
Dunholm Av *NORM/PKE* TS3 .... 100 C4
Dunkeld Cl *STOCN* TS19 .... 73 D2
Dunkery Cl *THNBY* TS17 .... 138 C4 🔲
Dunlane Cl *ACK/BRKF* TS5 .... 97 D1

Dunlin Cl *NORTON* TS20 .... 57 F4
Dunlin Rd *HTLPW* TS26 .... 17 D1 ⊞
Dunmail Rd *REDCAR* TS10 .... 68 A2 ⊞
   STOCN TS19 .... 6 C3
Dunmoor Gv *THNBY* TS17 .... 138 C3
Dunmow Av *NORM/PKE* TS3 ...... 100 A4 ⊞
Dunnet Cl *REDCAR* TS10 .... 68 B5 ⊞
Dunning Rd *FYHL* DL17 .... 20 C1
   MBORO TS1 .... 5 G4
Dunning St *MBORO* TS1 .... 5 G3
Dunoon Cl *STOCN* TS19 .... 74 B3
Dunottar Av *EGG/EAG* TS16 ...... 119 E4
Dunrobin Cl *DARLE* DL1 .... 117 F1 ⊞
Dunsdale Cl *ESTON* TS6 .... 102 A3 ⊞
   MARSKE TS11 .... 71 D5 ⊞
Dunsley Ct *GUIS* TS14 .... 129 D2 ⊞
Dunsley Dr *BLGHM* TS23 .... 42 A5
Dunsmore Cl *CNHM/HEM* TS8 ... 140 B3
Dunsop Av *MGRV/ESTR* TS4 ..... 125 D1 ⊞
Dunstable Rd *STOCN* TS19 .... 74 A3 ⊞
Dunstable Rd *ACK/BRKF* TS5 ..... 97 D1
   MTN/NUN TS7 .... 101 D5
Dunster Cl *DARLW* DL3 .... 114 B3
Dunster Rd *BLGHM* TS23 .... 42 A5
Dunston Cl *GUIS* TS14 .... 129 D5
Dunston Rd *HTLPW* TS26 .... 16 C3
   STOCN TS19 .... 73 D2 ⊞
Durham Chare *BAUK* DL14 .... 27 E1 ⊞
Durham Coast Pth *RHTLP* TS27 .. 11 E2
Durham La *EGG/EAG* TS16 .... 118 C5
   SEDG TS21 .... 92 C5
Durham Rd *BAUK* DL14 .... 27 F1
   BLGHMW/WYN TS22 .... 41 E3
   ESTON TS6 .... 102 A1
   FYHL DL17 .... 20 C1
   NACLF DL5 .... 55 D5
   REDCAR TS10 .... 69 E2
   SALT/BTN/SK TS12 .... 91 E5
   SEDG TS21 .... 29 D3
   SEDG TS21 .... 56 A5
   SPEN DL16 .... 15 E1
   STOCN TS19 .... 73 E1
Durham St *BAUK* DL14 .... 27 D1
   HTLP TS24 .... 19 D1
   SPEN DL16 .... 14 A5
   STOCS TS18 .... 7 E3
   TEESM TS2 .... 78 B2
Durham Wy *NACLF* DL5 .... 54 C4
Durham Wy North *NACLF* DL5..... 55 D4
Durham Wy South *NACLF* DL5..... 54 C5
Durnford Rd *NORM/PKE* TS3 ..... 100 B3

E

Eade Cl *NACLF* DL5 .... 38 A3
Eagle Pk *CNHM/HEM* TS8 .... 144 B1 ⊞
Eaglescliffe Cl *MARSKE* TS11 ...... 86 B3 ⊞
Eaglesfield Rd *HTLPS* TS25 .... 22 C4
Eamont Gdns *HTLPW* TS26 .... 17 F5
Eamont Rd *FYHL* DL17 .... 20 C1
   NORTON TS20 .... 74 C1
Earl Cl *DARLE* DL1 .... 116 C1 ⊞
Earle Cl *YARM* TS15 .... 138 A5
Earls Court Rd *CNHM/HEM* TS8 142 A1
Earlsdon Av *ACK/BRKF* TS5 .... 123 D2
Earlsferry Rd *HTLPS* TS25 .... 22 C4
Earl's Nook *BLGHM* TS23 .... 59 F3
Earl St *HTLP* TS24 .... 13 F5
Earlsway *THNBY* TS17 .... 122 A5
Earsdon Rd *NORTON* TS20 .... 74 A1 ⊞
Easby Av *ACK/BRKF* TS5 .... 98 A4
Easby Cl *ESTON* TS6 .... 102 C1
   GUIS TS14 .... 129 E3
   REDCAR TS10 .... 68 A3
Easby Gv *ESTON* TS6 .... 101 F2
   THNBY TS17 .... 95 F5
Easby La *GTAY/STK* TS9 .... 150 B4
Easby Pl *DARLW* DL3 .... 114 C4
Easby Rd *BLGHM* TS23 .... 59 D2 ⊞
Easington Rd *HTLP* TS24 .... 17 E1
   HTLPW TS26 .... 12 A5
   RHTLP TS27 .... 11 D2
   STOCN TS19 .... 73 D1
Easson Rd *DARLW* DL3 .... 114 ... ⊞
   REDCAR TS10 .... 68 B1
Easson St *MGRV/ESTR* TS4 .... 98 C2
East Av *BLGHM* TS23 .... 58 C5
Eastbank Rd *MTN/NUN* TS7 ..... 127 D1 ⊞
Eastbourne Av *EGG/EAG* TS16 . 137 E3 ⊞
Eastbourne Gdns *NORM/PKE* TS3 . 100 B4
Eastbourne Rd *ACK/BRKF* TS5 .. 98 A5
   DARLE DL1 .... 133 D2
   STOCN TS19 .... 74 C4 ⊞
Eastbury Cl *THNBY* TS17 .... 139 E2
East Crs *ACK/BRKF* TS5 .... 97 D3
   LOFT/ST TS13 .... 113 F3
Eastcroft Rd *ESTON* TS6 .... 82 A3
East Dr *THNBY* TS17 .... 95 F2
East End *SEDG* TS21 .... 29 E4
Easterside Rd *MGRV/ESTR* TS4 . 125 D1
Eastfield Rd *MARSKE* TS11 .... 70 A5
Eastfields *GTAY/STK* TS9 .... 152 B2
Eastfields Rd *NACLF* DL5 .... 53 E3
Eastgate Rd *ACK/BRKF* TS5 .... 97 E4
Eastham Sands *ACK/BRKF* TS5 .. 123 D4
Eastland Av *HTLPW* TS26 .... 23 E1 ⊞
Eastlea Av *BAUK* DL14 .... 27 E3
Eastleigh *THNBY* TS17 .... 122 A2
East Lodge Gdns *REDCAR* TS10.. 68 A5
Eastlowthian St *TEESM* TS2 .... 78 B1 ⊞
East Mdw *MARSKE* TS11 .... 70 C5
East Mount Rd *DARLE* DL1 .... 9 H1
Easton St *THNBY* TS17 .... 95 F4
East Pde *BAUK* DL14 .... 27 D1
   HTLP TS24 .... 13 F5 ⊞
   SALT/BTN/SK TS12 .... 109 D2
Eastport Rd *STOCS* TS18 .... 75 E5
East Raby St *DARLW* DL3 .... 9 E5
East Rw *ACK/BRKF* TS5 .... 97 D3
   DARLE DL1 .... 9 F5 ⊞
East Scar *REDCAR* TS10 .... 69 D3
East St *DARLE* DL1 .... 9 G4
   MARSKE TS11 .... 70 C5
   STOCS TS18 .... 7 F3
   TEESM TS2 .... 78 B2
East View Ter *HTLPS* TS25 .... 25 D4 ⊞
   MGRV/ESTR TS4 .... 98 C2 ⊞
   SHIL DL4 .... 35 E2
Eastwell Cl *SEDG* TS21 .... 29 E4 ⊞
Eastwood Rd *NORM/PKE* TS3 .. 100 C3 ⊞
Ebba Cl *NACLF* DL5 .... 54 B1
Ebchester Cl *STOCN* TS19 .... 73 D1
Eccleston Wk *MGRV/ESTR* TS4 . 125 D1 ⊞
Eckert Av *ACK/BRKF* TS5 .... 96 C3
Eden Crs *DARLE* DL1 .... 132 A4
Eden Dr *SEDG* TS21 .... 29 E5 ⊞
Eden Gv *NACLF* DL5 .... 37 D3
Edenhall Gv *REDCAR* TS10 .... 68 B3
Eden Rd *MGRV/ESTR* TS4 .... 98 B2
   NACLF DL5 .... 39 D5
   SALT/BTN/SK TS12 .... 109 E1
   SPEN DL16 .... 15 D4
Eden St *HTLP* TS24 .... 2 C4
   SALT/BTN/SK TS12 .... 89 E2
Eden Wy *BLGHMW/WYN* TS22 .. 40 C5
Eder Rd *NORTON* TS20 .... 75 D3 ⊞
Edgar St *HTLPS* TS25 .... 24 A2
   NORTON TS20 .... 75 D3
Edgecombe Dr *DARLW* DL3 ...... 114 B5
Edgecombe Gv *DARLW* DL3 ...... 114 B5
Edge Hl *BAUK* DL14 .... 26 C1
Edgehill Wy *BLGHM* TS23 .... 42 C5 ⊞
Edgley St *STOCS* TS18 .... 93 D5 ⊞
Edinburgh Av *ACK/BRKF* TS5 ..... 97 F4
Edmondbyers Rd *STOCN* TS19 ... 73 D1 ⊞
Edmundsbury Rd *ACK/BRKF* TS5 98 B2 ⊞
Edmund St *DARLE* DL1 .... 116 B4 ⊞
Ednam Gv *HTLPS* TS25 .... 23 D4 ⊞
Edridge Gn *NORM/PKE* TS3 ..... 100 A1 ⊞
Edwards St *ESTON* TS6 .... 102 A3 ⊞
   STOCS TS18 .... 94 C3
Edward St *BAUK* DL14 .... 27 D1
   DARLE DL1 .... 116 C4 ⊞
   ESTON TS6 .... 81 D4 ⊞
   NORM/PKE TS3 .... 79 E5
   SPEN DL16 .... 14 C3
Egerton Cl *NORTON* TS20 .... 57 D5 ⊞
Egerton Gv *NACLF* DL5 .... 38 C3
Egerton Rd *HTLPW* TS26 .... 16 B5
Egerton Ter *HTLPS* TS25 .... 31 D4
Egglescliffe Cl *STOCN* TS19 .... 73 E1 ⊞
Egglestone Cl *BLGHM* TS23 .... 42 B5 ⊞
Egglestone Rd *REDCAR* TS10 ..... 68 B4
Eggleston Vw *DARLW* DL3 .... 114 B4
Eglington Av *GUIS* TS14 .... 129 D4
Eglington Rd *ESTON* TS6 .... 82 A3
Egmont Rd *MGRV/ESTR* TS4 ...... 98 C1
Egton Av *CNHM/HEM* TS8 .... 126 B5
Egton Cl *REDCAR* TS10 .... 68 B4
Egton Dr *HTLPS* TS25 .... 32 C1
Egton Rd *NORTON* TS20 .... 75 D3 ⊞
Egton Wy *DARLE* DL1 .... 117 F2 ⊞
Eider Cl *THNBY* TS17 .... 139 D1 ⊞
Elcho St *HTLPW* TS26 .... 2 A2
Elcoat Rd *NORTON* TS20 .... 58 A5
Elder Ct *MBORO* TS1 .... 5 H4
Elder Gv *STOCN* TS19 .... 74 A3
Elderwood Ct *MGRV/ESTR* TS4 .. 98 B4 ⊞
Eldon Bank *SHIL* DL4 .... 35 F1
Eldon Cl *NACLF* DL5 .... 39 D5 ⊞
Eldon Gv *HTLPW* TS26 .... 17 E5
Eldon Pl *DARLW* DL3 .... 116 A3
Eldon Rd *NACLF* DL5 .... 54 C3
Eldon St *DARLW* DL3 .... 116 A5
   THNBY TS17 .... 95 E4 ⊞
Eleanor Pl *STOCS* TS18 .... 94 C3 ⊞
Elemere St *BLGHM* TS23 .... 42 A5 ⊞
Elgin Av *ESTON* TS6 .... 81 E4
   NORM/PKE TS3 .... 99 F4 ⊞
Elgin Ct *DARLE* DL1 .... 117 F1 ⊞
Elgin Rd *HTLPS* TS25 .... 23 D4
   THNBY TS17 .... 121 F4
Elishaw Gn *THNBY* TS17 .... 138 C3 ⊞
Elizabeth St *THNBY* TS17 .... 95 E4 ⊞
Elizabeth Ter *NORM/PKE* TS3 .... 79 D5 ⊞
Elizabeth Wy *HTLPS* TS25 .... 33 D1
Elland Av *MGRV/ESTR* TS4 ...... 124 C1
Ellen Av *STOCS* TS18 .... 94 B4
Ellerbeck Ct *GTAY/STK* TS9 ...... 152 C4
Ellerbeck Wy *GTAY/STK* TS9 .... 152 C4
   MTN/NUN TS7 .... 101 D5
Ellerburne St *THNBY* TS17 .... 95 F4 ⊞
Ellerby Cl *REDCAR* TS10 .... 68 B3
Ellerby Gn *NORM/PKE* TS3 .... 99 E2
Ellerby Rd *ESTON* TS6 .... 102 B1
Ellers Bank *MARSKE* TS11 .... 107 E5
Ellerton Cl *ACK/BRKF* TS5 .... 124 A1 ⊞
   DARLW DL3 .... 114 B3
Ellerton Rd *STOCS* TS18 .... 93 D4
Ellesmere *SPEN* DL16 .... 14 C1 ⊞
Eliett Ct *HTLP* TS24 .... 12 B5
Elliot St *MBORO* TS1 .... 5 H3 ⊞
   REDCAR TS10 .... 51 D4
Elliott St *HTLPW* TS26 .... 2 A2
Ellis Gdns *CNHM/HEM* TS8 ...... 142 A1
Ellison St *HTLPW* TS26 .... 2 A5
Elm Av *SEDG* TS21 .... 29 E3
Elm Cl *ESTON* TS6 .... 101 E1 ⊞
   SALT/BTN/SK TS12 .... 88 C2
Elmcroft *DARLE* DL1 .... 116 B1
Elm Dr *MTN/NUN* TS7 .... 125 F3
   SHIL DL4 .... 35 D2
Elmfield Pl *NACLF* DL5 .... 54 A1
Elmfield St *DARLW* DL3 .... 9 F2 ⊞
Elmfield Ter *DARLW* DL3 .... 9 F2
   SHIL DL4 .... 35 D2
Elm Gv *HTLPW* TS26 .... 17 F1
   THNBY TS17 .... 95 E5
Elm Rd *FYHL* DL17 .... 21 D2
   GUIS TS14 .... 129 D2
   SHIL DL4 .... 35 D2
Elms Rd *DARLW* DL3 .... 8 D3
Elm St *ESTON* TS6 .... 80 C3 ⊞
   MBORO TS1 .... 5 H3
   TEESM TS2 .... 61 D4
Elm Ter *BAUK* DL14 .... 27 E3
Elm Tree Av *STOCN* TS19 .... 73 D4
Elmtree St *DARLW* DL3 .... 116 A2 ⊞
Elmwood *CNHM/HEM* TS8 .... 125 D5 ⊞
Elmwood Cl *GTAY/STK* TS9 ...... 152 B1
Elmwood Pl *HTLPW* TS26 .... 17 D3
Elmwood Rd *EGG/EAG* TS16 .... 119 F3 ⊞
   HTLPW TS26 .... 17 D3
Elsdon Gdns *THNBY* TS17 .... 138 C3 ⊞
Elsdon St *STOCS* TS18 .... 6 C5
Elstob Cl *NACLF* DL5 .... 38 C4
Elstone Rd *MGRV/ESTR* TS4 ...... 78 C4
Elterwater Cl *REDCAR* TS10 .... 68 A1 ⊞
Eltham Crs *THNBY* TS17 .... 122 A4
Elton Cl *STOCN* TS19 .... 73 E1
Elton Gv *DARLW* DL3 .... 8 B6
   STOCN TS19 .... 92 C2 ⊞
Elton La *EGG/EAG* TS16 .... 137 D2
Elton Pde *DARLW* DL3 .... 8 A6
Elton Rd *BLGHMW/WYN* TS22 .. 41 D5
   DARLW DL3 .... 8 A5
Elton St *REDCAR* TS10 .... 51 E5
Eltringham Rd *HTLPW* TS26 .... 17 F5
Elvan Gv *HTLPS* TS25 .... 23 D4
Elvet Pl *DARLW* DL3 .... 114 C4
Elvington Cl *BLGHM* TS23 .... 42 B2
Elvington Gn *NORM/PKE* TS3 ... 100 A2 ⊞
Elwick Av *ACK/BRKF* TS5 .... 123 E1
   NACLF DL5 .... 37 F3
Elwick Cl *STOCN* TS19 .... 73 D1
Elwick Rd *HTLPS* TS25 .... 2 E5
   HTLPW TS26 .... 16 A4
Ely Crs *REDCAR* TS10 .... 69 E1
   SALT/BTN/SK TS12 .... 91 E5 ⊞
Ely St *MGRV/ESTR* TS4 .... 78 C5 ⊞
Embles La *NACLF* DL5 .... 55 E5 ⊞
Embleton Av *ACK/BRKF* TS5 ...... 97 E5
Embleton Cl *STOCN* TS19 .... 73 D1 ⊞
Embleton Rd
   BLGHMW/WYN TS22 .... 41 D5 ⊞
   THNBY TS17 .... 139 D3 ⊞
Embsay Cl *MGRV/ESTR* TS4 .... 98 C4
Emerald St *MBORO* TS1 .... 5 E5
   SALT/BTN/SK TS12 .... 89 E1
Emerson Av *ACK/BRKF* TS5 .... 98 A4
Emerson Ct *HTLP* TS24 .... 12 B5
Emerson Wy *NACLF* DL5 .... 54 B1
Emily St *MBORO* TS1 .... 5 G4
Emley Moor Rd *DARLE* DL1 ...... 133 D4
Emmanuel Cl *DARLE* DL1 .... 116 C4
Emma Simpson Ct *STOCS* TS18 . 93 E4 ⊞
Emmerson St *ACK/BRKF* TS5 ..... 98 A2 ⊞
Emmetts Gdns *THNBY* TS17 ...... 139 D2
Emsworth Dr *EGG/EAG* TS16 ... 136 C1
Endeavour Cl *HTLPS* TS25 .... 25 D4
Endeavour Dr *MTN/NUN* TS7 ... 127 D1
The Endeavour *MTN/NUN* TS7 .. 126 C4
Enderby Gdns *CNHM/HEM* TS8. 142 A1
Endeston Rd *NORM/PKE* TS3 .... 100 A4
Endrick Rd *HTLPS* TS25 .... 22 C4
Endsleigh Dr *ACK/BRKF* TS5...... 96 C4

Enfield Cha *GUIS* TS14 .... **128** C4
Enfield Gv *ESTON* TS6 .... **101** E5
Enfield St *MBORO* TS1 .... **4** D6
Ennerdale Av *ACK/BRKF* TS5 .... **97** E5
Ennerdale Crs *SALT/BTN/SK* TS12 .. **109** D1
Ennerdale Rd *DARLE* DL1 .... **132** C3
   STOCS TS18 .... **93** F1 ◻
Ennis Rd *REDCAR* TS10 .... **67** D1
Ensign Ct *HTLP* TS24 .... **3** F2
Enterpen Cl *YARM* TS15 .... **138** A5
Epping Av *NORM/PKE* TS3 .... **99** F4
Epping Cl *MARSKE* TS11 .... **70** B5
   THNBY TS17 .... **121** E3
Epsom Av *MGRV/ESTR* TS4 .... **125** D1 ◻
Epsom Ct *FYHL* DL17 .... **39** D2 ◻
Epsom Rd *REDCAR* TS10 .... **68** C2
   STOCS TS18 .... **76** A4
Erica Gv *MTN/NUN* TS7 .... **125** E2
Eric Av *THNBY* TS17 .... **95** F4
Eridge Rd *GUIS* TS14 .... **129** C4
Erith Gv *MGRV/ESTR* TS4 .... **125** D2 ◻
Ernest St *HTLPW* TS26 .... **17** F3
Errington St *SALT/BTN/SK* TS12 ...... **91** D5
Errol St *HTLPW* TS26 .... **2** B2
Erskine Rd *HTLPS* TS25 .... **22** C4
Escomb Cl *NACLF* DL5 .... **39** E4
   STOCN TS19 .... **73** D1 ◻
Escombe Av *MGRV/ESTR* TS4 .... **125** D1
Escombe Rd *BLGHM* TS23 .... **42** A3 ◻
Escomb Rd *BAUK* DL14 .... **26** C2
Esher Av *ESTON* TS6 .... **101** E5
Esher St *MBORO* TS1 .... **78** C5
Eshwood Sq *MBORO* TS1 .... **4** D4
Eskdale Cl *YARM* TS15 .... **146** A3
Eskdale Gdns *SHIL* DL4 .... **36** A3
Eskdale Pl *NACLF* DL5 .... **53** F1
Eskdale Rd *HTLPS* TS25 .... **22** C5
   REDCAR TS10 .... **67** E2
Eskdale St *DARLW* DL3 .... **8** D4
Esk Cn *EGG/EAG* TS16 .... **137** D2 ◻
Esk Gv *HTLPS* TS25 .... **23** D4
Esk Rd *DARLE* DL1 .... **132** B5
   NORTON TS20 .... **74** C2
Esk St *NORM/PKE* TS3 .... **79** E5
Esplanade *REDCAR* TS10 .... **51** F4
Essex Av *ESTON* TS6 .... **81** E4
Essex Cl *REDCAR* TS10 .... **68** A2
Essex Crs *BLGHM* TS23 .... **59** E3
Essex Gv *NORTON* TS20 .... **75** E2
Essexport Rd *STOCS* TS18 .... **75** E5 ◻
Essex St *MBORO* TS1 .... **97** F1
Essex Wy *DARLE* DL1 .... **117** D4
Eston Cl *THNBY* TS17 .... **95** F5
Eston Moor Crs *DARLE* DL1 .... **133** F4 ◻
Eston Rd *ESTON* TS6 .... **81** E3
   ESTON TS6 .... **83** E5
Eston Vw *NORM/PKE* TS3 .... **99** F3
Estoril Rd South *DARLE* DL1 .... **133** F2
Etherley Cl *STOCN* TS19 .... **73** D1
Etherley La *BAUK* DL14 .... **26** C2
Eton Rd *ACK/BRKF* TS5 .... **97** E5
   STOCS TS18 .... **94** B3
Eton St *HTLPS* TS25 .... **23** F2
Ettersgill Dr *DARLW* DL3 .... **130** B1
Ettington Av *NORM/PKE* TS3 .... **99** F5
Etton Rd *BLGHM* TS23 .... **42** A2
Evenwood Cl *STOCN* TS19 .... **73** D1 ◻
Evenwood Gdns *ACK/BRKF* TS5 .. **123** F3 ◻
Everett St *HTLPW* TS26 .... **17** E3
Evergreen Wk *MGRV/ESTR* TS4 .... **98** B4 ◻
Everingham Rd *YARM* TS15 .... **146** A2
Eversham Rd *ESTON* TS6 .... **82** A3
Evesham Rd *NORM/PKE* TS3 .... **99** F4
Evesham Wy *BLGHM* TS23 .... **42** C4
Ewbank Cl *NACLF* DL5 .... **39** D4 ◻
Ewbank Dr *STOCS* TS18 .... **6** D5
Ewbank Gdns *STOCS* TS18 .... **6** D5 ◻
Exchange Sq *TEESM* TS2 .... **5** G2 ◻
Exeter Rd *ACK/BRKF* TS5 .... **98** B2
   ESTON TS6 .... **102** A2
Exeter St *HTLP* TS24 .... **2** D3
   SALT/BTN/SK TS12 .... **89** E2
Exford Cl *THNBY* TS17 .... **139** D4
Exmoor Gv *HTLPW* TS26 .... **16** C2
Ezard St *STOCN* TS19........................... **6** D2

F

Faber Cl *NACLF* DL5 .... **38** C4
Fabian Rd *ESTON* TS6 .... **101** F1
Faceby Pl *NORTON* TS20 .... **75** D4 ◻
Fagg St *STOCS* TS18 .... **7** F4
Fairbridge St *MBORO* TS1 .... **5** F4
Fairburn Cl *STOCN* TS19 .... **92** C1
Fairdene Av *STOCN* TS19 .... **92** C1 ◻
Fairfield Av *ACK/BRKF* TS5 .... **97** D5
   MTN/NUN TS7 .... **126** C1
Fairfield Cl *REDCAR* TS10 .... **68** D2
   STOCN TS19 .... **93** D1
Fairfield Rd *GTAY/STK* TS9 .... **152** A2
   MGRV/ESTR TS4 .... **98** B3
   STOCN TS19 .... **93** D1

Fairfield St *DARLW* DL3 .... **115** F4
Fairmead *REDCAR* TS10 .... **67** F4 ◻
Fairstone Av *STOCN* TS19 .... **72** C5 ◻
Fairthorn Av *STOCN* TS19 .... **92** C1 ◻
Fairview Dr *SPEN* DL16 .... **15** E3
Fairville Rd *STOCN* TS19 .... **72** C5 ◻
The Fairway *CNHM/HEM* TS8 .... **126** A5
   DARLE DL1 .... **133** D2
   EGG/EAG TS16 .... **137** E1 ◻
   SALT/BTN/SK TS12 .... **89** D4
Fairwell Rd *STOCN* TS19 .... **72** C4
Fairwood Pk *CNHM/HEM* TS8 .... **144** A1
Fairydell *MTN/NUN* TS7 .... **125** E5 ◻
Fakenham Av *ACK/BRKF* TS5 .... **97** D4
Falcon La *NORTON* TS20 .... **57** F4
Falcon Rd *DARLE* DL1 .... **133** F1
   HTLPW TS26 .... **16** C2
   NORM/PKE TS3 .... **79** F5
Falkirk St *THNBY* TS17 .... **95** E4
Falklands Cl *MARSKE* TS11 .... **70** A5
Falkland St *MBORO* TS1 .... **4** D6
Fallow Cl *THNBY* TS17 .... **139** D1
Fallow Rd *NACLF* DL5 .... **39** D2 ◻
Fallows Ct *MBORO* TS1 .... **4** D4
Fall Wy *ESTON* TS6 .... **101** E5
Falmer Rd *DARLE* DL1 .... **132** C3
Falmouth St *MBORO* TS1 .... **98** C1
Falston Cl *BLGHM* TS23 .... **41** E5 ◻
Fanacurt Rd *GUIS* TS14 .... **128** A4
Fane Cl *STOCN* TS19 .... **93** D1
Faraday St *MBORO* TS1 .... **4** C6
Fareham Cl *HTLPS* TS25 .... **31** E2 ◻
Farington Dr *MTN/NUN* TS7 .... **126** B4
Farleigh Cl *BLGHM* TS23 .... **42** A5 ◻
Farley Dr *ACK/BRKF* TS5 .... **122** C1
Farmbank Rd *MTN/NUN* TS7 .... **127** D2
Farmcote Ct *CNHM/HEM* TS8 .... **141** F2 ◻
Farm La *THNBY* TS17 .... **139** D1
Farnborough Av *ACK/BRKF* TS5 .... **97** E4 ◻
Farndale *SPEN* DL16 .... **14** C1
Farndale Ct *MGRV/ESTR* TS4 .... **98** C5 ◻
Farndale Crs *DARLW* DL3 .... **115** D5
   MGRV/ESTR TS4 .... **98** C3 ◻
Farndale Gdns *SHIL* DL4 .... **36** A3
Farndale Gn *STOCN* TS19 .... **74** A4 ◻
Farndale Rd *HTLPS* TS25 .... **25** D5
   MGRV/ESTR TS4 .... **98** C3
   MTN/NUN TS7 .... **127** D4 ◻
Farndale Sq *REDCAR* TS10 .... **67** E2
Farne Ct *THNBY* TS17 .... **139** D2
Farnell Gv *HTLPS* TS25 .... **22** C4
Farnham Cl *BAUK* DL14 .... **27** F3 ◻
   EGG/EAG TS16 .... **136** C1
   NACLF DL5 .... **39** D3 ◻
Farrer St *DARLW* DL3 .... **116** A4
   STOCS TS18 .... **7** F2 ◻
Farr Holme *RDARL* DL2 .... **131** D5
Farrier Cl *THNBY* TS17 .... **139** D1 ◻
Farthingale Wy *CNHM/HEM* TS8 .... **141** F2
Fastnet Gv *HTLP* TS24 .... **3** E5
Faulder Wk *HTLPS* TS25 .... **24** A3
Faulkner Rd *NACLF* DL5 .... **38** C5
Faverdale *DARLW* DL3 .... **115** E2
Faverdale Av *ACK/BRKF* TS5 .... **123** E3
Faverdale Cl *STOCN* TS19 .... **73** D1 ◻
Faverdale North *DARLW* DL3 .... **115** E2
Faverdale Rd *DARLW* DL3 .... **115** D2
Faverdale West *DARLW* DL3 .... **115** D2
Faversham Pk *DARLW* DL3 .... **115** D2 ◻
Fawcett Av *CNHM/HEM* TS8 .... **141** E1
Fawcett Rd *THNBY* TS17 .... **121** F2 ◻
Fawcus Ct *REDCAR* TS10 .... **67** E2 ◻
Fawn Cl *NACLF* DL5 .... **39** D2 ◻
Faygate Ct *CNHM/HEM* TS8 .... **141** F1
Fearby Rd *STOCS* TS18 .... **92** A1
Fearnhead *CNHM/HEM* TS8 .... **144** B1
Feetham Av *DARLE* DL1 .... **117** F3
Feethams *DARLE* DL1 .... **9** F6
Feethams Rbt. *DARLE* DL1 .... **9** G6
Feethams South *DARLE* DL1 .... **9** F6 ◻
Felbrigg La *THNBY* TS17 .... **139** D2
Felby Av *NORM/PKE* TS3 .... **99** F5
Felixstowe Cl *HTLPS* TS25 .... **31** D2 ◻
Fell Briggs Dr *MARSKE* TS11 .... **70** B5
Fellston Cl *HTLPW* TS26 .... **17** D3 ◻
Felton Cl *NACLF* DL5 .... **39** D4
Felton La *STOCN* TS19 .... **72** C4
Fenby Av *DARLE* DL1 .... **133** D4
Fencote Gdns *STOCN* TS19 .... **93** D1 ◻
Fenham Ct *MTN/NUN* TS7 .... **100** C5
Fenmoor Cl *CNHM/HEM* TS8 .... **123** E5 ◻
Fenner Cl *MARSKE* TS11 .... **88** B1 ◻
Fens Crs *HTLPS* TS25 .... **31** E1
The Fens *RHTLP* TS27 .... **11** D4
Fenton Cl *ESTON* TS6 .... **80** C3 ◻
   THNBY TS17 .... **139** D2 ◻
Fenton Rd *HTLPS* TS25 .... **30** C2
Fenwick St *STOCS* TS18 .... **74** C4
Ferndale *STOCN* TS19 .... **73** E4
Ferndale Av *NORM/PKE* TS3 .... **80** A5 ◻
Ferndale Cl *MARSKE* TS11 .... **88** C5 ◻
Fern Gv *SPEN* DL16 .... **14** B5
Fernhill Rd *ESTON* TS6 .... **102** B3
Fernie Rd *GUIS* TS14 .... **129** D5
   NORTON TS20 .... **58** A5 ◻

Fernlea Ct *DARLE* DL1 .... **132** C4 ◻
Fern St *MBORO* TS1 .... **5** H6
Fernwood Cl *CNHM/HEM* TS8 .... **143** D3
   REDCAR TS10 .... **68** C4
Fernwood Av *HTLPS* TS25 .... **23** F2
Ferry Rd *HTLP* TS24............................ **19** D2
   TEESM TS2 .... **78** B2
Fewston Cl *NACLF* DL5 .... **37** E5
   NORM/PKE TS3 .... **99** E2 ◻
Field Cl *THNBY* TS17 .... **96** A5
Fieldfare La *NORTON* TS20 .... **58** A4
Fieldfare Rd *HTLPW* TS26 .... **17** D1
Field Head *REDCAR* TS10 .... **68** A2 ◻
Field St *DARLE* DL1 .... **116** A3
Fieldview Cl *TEESM* TS2 .... **61** D5
Fife Gv *HTLPS* TS25 .... **22** C5
Fife Rd *DARLW* DL3 .... **8** C5
   NORTON TS20 .... **57** F5 ◻
Fife St *MBORO* TS1 .... **78** C4 ◻
Filey Cl *REDCAR* TS10 .... **69** E5
Finchale Av *BLGHM* TS23 .... **58** C1
Finchale Crs *DARLE* DL1 .... **114** B4
Finchale Rd *NACLF* DL5 .... **54** C2
Fincham Cl *NORTON* TS20 .... **74** A1
Finchfield Cl *EGG/EAG* TS16 .... **137** D1
Finchley Rd *NORTON* TS20 .... **58** A5 ◻
Findlay Gv *HTLPS* TS25 .... **23** D5 ◻
Finkle St *STOCS* TS18............................ **7** C5
Finsbury St *MBORO* TS1 .... **4** D6
Firbeck Wk *THNBY* TS17 .... **121** E4
Firby Cl *HTLP* TS24............................ **18** B1
   NORTON TS20 .... **57** D5
Fir Gv *REDCAR* TS10 .... **67** F4
   THNBY TS17.................................. **95** E5
The Firlands *MARSKE* TS11 .... **70** C4
Fir Rig Dr *MARSKE* TS11 .... **70** B5
The Firs *DARLE* DL1 .... **117** E2
Firthmoor Crs *DARLE* DL1 .... **133** E3
Firtree *SHIL* DL4 .... **35** F5
Firtree Av *ESTON* TS6 .... **101** E4
Firtree Dr *ESTON* TS6 .... **101** E4
Firtree Rd *STOCN* TS19 .... **74** A4 ◻
Fishponds Rd *REDCAR* TS10 .... **85** D1
Fitzwilliam Cl *MARSKE* TS11 .... **70** C5
Fitzwilliam Dr *DARLE* DL1 .... **116** B3
Fitzwilliam St *REDCAR* TS10 .... **51** F5 ◻
Flamingo Cl *DARLE* DL1 .... **133** F2
Flatts La *ESTON* TS6 .... **101** F4
   MTN/NUN TS7 .... **127** E2
Flaxton Ct *HTLPW* TS26 .... **2** A4
Flaxton St *HTLPW* TS26 .... **2** A4
Fleck Wy *THNBY* TS17........................ **121** F5
Fleet Av *HTLP* TS24.............................. **3** F1
Fleet Bridge Rd *NORTON* TS20 ...... **75** F2
Fleetham Gv *STOCS* TS18 .... **92** C3
Fleetham St *MBORO* TS1 .... **4** D4
Fleet St *BAUK* DL14 .... **27** D5
   THNBY TS17.................................. **96** A5
The Fleet *REDCAR* TS10 .... **67** D2
Fleming Rd *ESTON* TS6 .... **80** C5
Fleming St *REDCAR* TS10 .... **51** D4
Flintoff St *BAUK* DL14 .... **27** E2 ◻
Flixton Gv *BLGHMW/WYN* TS22 .... **57** F1
Flodden Wy *BLGHM* TS23 .... **42** C4
Flora Av *DARLW* DL3 .... **8** B6
Flora St *ESTON* TS6 .... **101** F2
   SPEN DL16.................................... **14** C3
Florence Ct *THNBY* TS17 .... **139** D2
Florence St *TEESM* TS2 .... **5** E1
Florida Gdns *ACK/BRKF* TS5 .... **97** E5
Folkstone Cl *CNHM/HEM* TS8 .... **141** F1
Folland Dr *MARSKE* TS11 .... **70** A4 ◻
Fonteyn Ct *CNHM/HEM* TS8 .... **142** A1
Fontwell Cl *STOCN* TS19 .... **72** C4
Forber Rd *MGRV/ESTR* TS4 .... **98** B5
Forbes Av *ACK/BRKF* TS5 .... **97** D3
Forcett Cl *ACK/BRKF* TS5 .... **123** E2
Forcett St *DARLW* DL3 .... **115** D4 ◻
Fordon Pl *MGRV/ESTR* TS4 .... **98** C5
Ford Pl *STOCS* TS18 .... **7** F2
Ford Wy *BAUK* DL14 .... **26** C5 ◻
Fordwell Rd *STOCN* TS19 .... **72** C4 ◻
Fordyce Rd *CNHM/HEM* TS8 .... **141** F2
   HTLPS TS25 .... **22** C5
Fordy Gv *HTLPS* TS25 .... **121** E1
Foreland Point *THNBY* TS17 .... **138** C5
Forest Dr *MTN/NUN* TS7 .... **127** D2
Forester Cl *HTLPS* TS25 .... **24** C4
Forest La *YARM* TS15 .... **146** A5
Forest Moor Rd *DARLE* DL1 .... **133** E4
Forfar Av *MGRV/ESTR* TS4 .... **125** D2 ◻
Forfar Cl *DARLE* DL1 .... **117** E1
Forge Wy *DARLE* DL1 .... **116** C4
Formby Cl *RHTLP* TS27 .... **11** E3 ◻
Formby Gv *RHTLP* TS27 .... **11** F3
Forresters Pth *NACLF* DL5 .... **53** E3
Forster Cl *NACLF* DL5 .... **38** A2
Forster St *DARLW* DL3 .... **9** E2
Forth Av *HTLPS* TS25 .... **23** D5
Forth Rd *REDCAR* TS10 .... **67** F1
Fortrose Cl *EGG/EAG* TS16 .... **137** E2
Forty Foot Rd *TEESM* TS2 .... **4** C1
Forum Ct *NORM/PKE* TS3 .... **79** D5 ◻
Fossfeld *STOCN* TS19 .... **72** C4
Foster St *SALT/BTN/SK* TS12 .... **110** C1

Foston Cl *NORTON* TS20 .... 57 E5
Fother Ingay Dr *DARLE* DL1 .... 117 F1 ⑦
Foundry St *SHIL* DL4 .... 35 F2
Fountains Av *THNBY* TS17 .... 139 E1
Fountains Cl *GUIS* TS14 .... 129 D3 ⑥
    GUIS TS14 .... 129 E3 ⑥
Fountains Crs *ESTON* TS6 .... 101 F2
Fountains Dr *ACK/BRKF* TS5 .... 97 F5
Fountain St *GUIS* TS14 .... 129 D3
Fountains Vw *DARLW* DL3 .... 114 C4
Four Riggs *DARLW* DL3 .... 9 E3
Four Winds Ct *HTLPW* TS26 .... 16 C4 ⑥
Fowler Cl *YARM* TS15 .... 147 D1 ⑥
Fowler Rd *NACLF* DL5 .... 39 D5
Foxberry Av *ACK/BRKF* TS5 .... 122 C3
Fox Cl *THNBY* TS17 .... 121 E5
Foxglove Cl *STOCN* TS19 .... 73 E4 ⑥
Foxgloves *CNHM/HEM* TS8 .... 143 E2
Foxheads Ct *MBORO* TS1 .... 4 A2
Foxrush Cl *REDCAR* TS10 .... 50 B4
Fox St *NORTON* TS20 .... 75 D2 ⑥
Foxton Cl *NACLF* DL5 .... 38 C4
    YARM TS15 .... 138 A5
Foxton Dr *BLGHM* TS23 .... 42 A3
Foxwood Dr *STOCN* TS19 .... 73 E4
Frampton Gn *NORM/PKE* TS3 .... 99 F5
Frances Ter *DARL* DL14 .... 27 D4
France St *REDCAR* TS10 .... 51 F4
Franklin Cl *STOCS* TS18 .... 93 D3
Franklin Ct *THNBY* TS17 .... 121 F3
Fransham Rd *NORM/PKE* TS3 .... 99 F2
Fraser Gv *HTLPS* TS25 .... 22 C4
Fraser Rd *STOCS* TS18 .... 93 F4 ⑥
Frederick St *NORM/PKE* TS3 ...... 79 E5 ⑩
    STOCS TS18 .... 7 F2
    THNBY TS17 .... 95 E3 ⑥
Frederic St *HTLP* TS24 .... 19 D1
Fredric Ter *BLGHM* TS23 .... 60 C4
Freeman's Pl *DARLE* DL1 .... 9 G4
Freemans Pl. Rbt. *DARLE* DL1 .... 9 G4
Freemantle Gv *HTLPS* TS25 .... 24 A5 ⑥
Fremantle Crs *MGRV/ESTR* TS4 ... 98 B4
Fremington Wk
    MGRV/ESTR TS4 .... 125 D2 ⑥
Frensham Dr *HTLPS* TS25 .... 24 A3
Freshingham Cl
    CNHM/HEM TS8 .... 142 A1 ⑥
Freville Gv *DARLW* DL3 .... 130 B1
Freville St *HTLP* TS24 .... 3 E4
    SHIL DL4 .... 35 D3 ⑦
Friar St *HTLP* TS24 .... 19 E2
Friarswood Cl *YARM* TS15 .... 138 A5
Friar Ter *HTLP* TS24 .... 19 E2
Friendship La *HTLP* TS24 .... 19 E2
Frimley Av *NORM/PKE* TS3 .... 99 F2
Frobisher Cl *MARSKE* TS11 .... 88 B1 ⑥
Frobisher Rd *THNBY* TS17 .... 121 F3
Frome Rd *NORTON* TS20 .... 75 D3
Front St *HTLPS* TS25 .... 31 D4
    LOFT/ST TS13 .... 112 B1 ⑥
    RHTLP TS27 .... 10 C5
    SEDG TS21 .... 29 E4
    SPEN DL16 .... 15 E3
The Front *HTLPS* TS25 .... 25 D5
Frosterley Gv *BLGHM* TS23 .... 42 B4 ⑥
Fryer Crs *DARL* DL1 .... 117 F3
Fry St *MBORO* TS1 .... 5 H3
Fryup Crs *GUIS* TS14 .... 128 C5
Fuchsia Rd *STOCN* TS19 .... 93 E1 ⑥
Fudan Wy *THNBY* TS17 .... 95 E2
Fulbeck Cl *BLGHM* TS23 .... 59 E2 ⑦
Fulbeck Rd *NACLF* DL5 .... 54 C4
    NORM/PKE TS3 .... 100 C4
Fulford Gv *MARSKE* TS11 .... 86 B3
Fulford Pl *DARL* DL1 .... 116 B2
Fulford Wy *CNHM/HEM* TS8 ...... 144 B1
Fuller Crs *NORTON* TS20 .... 74 B1
Fulmar Head *GUIS* TS14 .... 128 A3
Fulmar Rd *REDCAR* TS10 .... 50 B5
Fulmerton Crs *REDCAR* TS10 ...... 68 B5
Fulthorp Av *HTLPS* TS24 .... 11 F4
Fulthorpe Av *DARLW* DL3 .... 130 B1
Fulthorpe Cl *DARLW* DL3 .... 130 C1 ⑥
Fulthorpe Gv *DARLW* DL3 .... 114 B5
Fulthorpe Rd *BLGHMW/WYN* TS22 ... 40 A2
    NORTON TS20 .... 74 B1
Fulwood Av *MGRV/ESTR* TS4 .... 98 C4
The Furlongs *REDCAR* TS10 .... 68 C4
Furness Cl *DARLE* DL1 .... 117 D2 ⑥
    HTLP TS24 .... 18 A3
Fylands Br *BAUK* DL14 .... 34 A2
The Gables *MTN/NUN* TS7 .... 125 E4
    SEDG TS21 .... 29 D2

G

Gainford Av *ACK/BRKF* TS5 .... 98 A4 ⑥
Gainford Rd *BLGHM* TS23 .... 59 E1
    STOCN TS19 .... 93 E2
Gainford St *HTLPW* TS26 .... 2 B4
Gainsborough Crs *BLGHM* TS23 ... 41 F4

Gainsborough Rd *MTN/NUN* TS7 ... 125 E3
Gaisgill Cl *MTN/NUN* TS7 .... 100 C5
Galgate Cl *MTN/NUN* TS7 .... 126 A4
Galloway *DARL* DL1 .... 117 F1
Galloway Sands *ACK/BRKF* TS5 ... 123 D4 ⑥
Galsworthy Rd *HTLPS* TS25 .... 22 C3
Ganstead Wy *BLGHM* TS23 .... 42 B3 ⑥
Ganton Cl *BLGHMW/WYN* TS22 ... 57 F1
    MARSKE TS11 .... 86 C2 ⑥
Garbutt Cl *SHIL* DL4 .... 35 D2
Garbutt Sq *DARL* DL1 .... 132 C2
Garbutt St *SHIL* DL4 .... 35 D3
    STOCS TS18 .... 7 G2
Garden Cl *THNBY* TS17 .... 95 D4
Garden Pl *DARLW* DL3 .... 116 B1 ⑦
    ESTON TS6 .... 101 F3
Garden St *DARL* DL1 .... 9 G3
Garforth Cl *NORTON* TS20 .... 57 E5 ⑥
Garmon Cl *THNBY* TS17 .... 138 B2
Garnet Rd *THNBY* TS17 .... 95 E3
Garnet St *MBORO* TS1 .... 5 E5
    THNBY TS17 .... 89 E1
Garrett Wk *MBORO* TS1 .... 4 C5
Garrick Gv *HTLPS* TS25 .... 23 D3
Garrowby Rd *NORM/PKE* TS3 ...... 99 E3
Garsbeck Wy *MTN/NUN* TS7 ...... 101 D5
Garsdale Cl *YARM* TS15 .... 146 A2
Garside Dr *HTLP* TS24 .... 12 C5
Garstang Cl *MTN/NUN* TS7 .... 126 B4
Garston Gv *HTLPS* TS25 .... 24 A5 ⑦
Garthlands Rd *DARLW* DL3 .... 115 D4
Garthorne Av *DARLW* DL3 .... 130 B1
The Garth *CNHM/HEM* TS8 .... 143 D2 ⑥
    FYHL DL17 .... 20 C1
    GTAY/STK TS9 .... 152 A2
    MARSKE TS11 .... 70 B4
    NACLF DL5 .... 53 E5
    NORTON TS20 .... 74 C1 ⑦
    SALT/BTN/SK TS12 .... 91 E5
    SEDG TS21 .... 29 E3 ⑦
    SPEN DL16 .... 15 F2 ⑥
Garvin Cl *NORM/PKE* TS3 .... 99 E3
Gascoyne Cl *MTN/NUN* TS7 ...... 126 A3
Gaskell La *LOFT/ST* TS13 .... 113 D3
Gatehouse Cl *DARLE* DL1 .... 117 F2 ⑦
Gatenby Dr *ACK/BRKF* TS5 .... 123 E3
Gatesgarth Cl *HTLP* TS24 .... 18 A1 ⑥
The Gateway *DARL* DL1 .... 116 C2
Gaunless Ter *BAUK* DL14 .... 27 E1 ⑥
Gayton Sands *ACK/BRKF* TS5 ...... 123 D4
Gedney Av *NORM/PKE* TS3 .... 99 F5
Geltsdale *ACK/BRKF* TS5 .... 123 E3
Geneva Crs *DARL* DL1 .... 132 C4
Geneva Dr *DARLE* DL1 .... 132 C4
    REDCAR TS10 .... 68 B1
Geneva Gdns *DARL* DL1 .... 132 C4
Geneva La *DARLE* DL1 .... 132 C4
Geneva Rd *DARLE* DL1 .... 133 D4
Geneva Ter *DARL* DL1 .... 132 B3 ⑥
Gentian Wy *STOCN* TS19 .... 73 E3
Gent Rd *BAUK* DL14 .... 27 E5
George Short Cl *DARL* DL1 .... 116 B4 ⑥
George St *BAUK* DL14 .... 27 D1 ⑥
    DARLE DL1 .... 9 G6
    FYHL DL17 .... 21 F4
    HTLP TS24 .... 3 E2
    REDCAR TS10 .... 51 F5
    SHIL DL4 .... 35 D3 ⑥
    THNBY TS17 .... 95 E3
George Ter *SALT/BTN/SK* TS12 .... 111 D1
Georgiana Cl *THNBY* TS17 .... 95 E2
    THNBY TS17 .... 95 E4 ⑦
Gerard St *SPEN* DL16 .... 15 E2
Gibbon St *BAUK* DL14 .... 27 D1
Gib Chare *BAUK* DL14 .... 27 E1
Gibson Gv *HTLP* TS24 .... 11 F3 ⑥
Gifford St *ACK/BRKF* TS5 .... 97 F2
Gilberti Pl *HTLP* TS24 .... 12 B4
Gilkes St *MBORO* TS1 .... 5 E3
Gillercomb *REDCAR* TS10 .... 68 B5 ⑥
Gilling Crs *DARLE* DL1 .... 133 D3
    SPEN DL16 .... 15 E3
Gilling Rd *STOCN* TS19 .... 93 E4
Gillpark Gv *HTLPS* TS25 .... 24 C5
Gill St *GUIS* TS14 .... 129 D2
    HTLP TS24 .... 2 B4
    SALT/BTN/SK TS12 .... 89 E3
Gilmonby Rd *NORM/PKE* TS3 ..... 99 F5
Gilmour St *THNBY* TS17 .... 95 E4
Gilpin Rd *NACLF* DL5 .... 55 D1
    THNBY TS17 .... 95 E3
Gilpin Sq *STOCN* TS19 .... 74 B4 ⑥
Gilside Rd *BLGHM* TS23 .... 59 E1
Gilsland Cl *ACK/BRKF* TS5 .... 123 D3 ⑥
Gilsland Crs *DARLE* DL1 .... 117 D2
Gilsland Gv *ESTON* TS6 .... 101 F3
Gilwern Ct *THNBY* TS17 .... 138 B3 ⑥
Girrick Cl *CNHM/HEM* TS8 .... 141 E1 ⑦
Girton Av *NORM/PKE* TS3 .... 99 F5
Girton Wk *DARLE* DL1 .... 116 C3
Gisborne Gv *STOCS* TS18 .... 93 E3
Gisburn Av *NORM/PKE* TS3 .... 99 F4
Gisburn Rd *BLGHM* TS23 .... 59 E1
Gladesfield Rd *NORTON* TS20 ..... 75 D3 ⑥
Gladstone St *DARLW* DL3 .... 9 E3

ESTON TS6 .... 102 B2
HTLP TS24 .... 19 E2 ⑥
LOFT/ST TS13 .... 112 B1
LOFT/ST TS13 .... 113 E3
SALT/BTN/SK TS12 .... 110 C1
STOCS TS18 .... 94 C3
Glaisdale *SPEN* DL16 .... 14 C2
Glaisdale Av *ACK/BRKF* TS5 .... 98 A5
    REDCAR TS10 .... 67 E2
    STOCN TS19 .... 74 A4
Glaisdale Cl *ESTON* TS6 .... 102 C3 ⑥
Glaisdale Gdns *SHIL* DL4 .... 36 A3
Glaisdale Rd *ESTON* TS6 .... 102 C3 ⑥
    YARM TS15 .... 138 A4
Glamis Gv *MGRV/ESTR* TS4 .... 98 C4
Glamis Rd *BLGHM* TS23 .... 58 B1 ⑦
    DARLE DL1 .... 117 E2 ⑦
Glamorgan Gv *HTLPW* TS26 .... 16 C2
Glasgow St *THNBY* TS17 .... 95 E3 ⑥
Glastonbury Av *ESTON* TS6 .... 102 A2
Glastonbury Rd
    SALT/BTN/SK TS12 .... 109 F2 ⑦
Glastonbury Wk *HTLPW* TS26 .... 17 D2 ⑥
Gleaston Crs *MGRV/ESTR* TS4 ..... 98 C5
Glebe Rd *DARLE* DL1 .... 116 C1
    GTAY/STK TS9 .... 152 B3
    MBORO TS1 .... 4 D6
The Glebe *NORTON* TS20 .... 57 D5
Glendale Av *HTLPW* TS26 .... 17 E5
Glendale Dr *DARLW* DL3 .... 131 E4 ⑦
Glendale Rd *ACK/BRKF* TS5 .... 98 A5
Glendue Cl *MTN/NUN* TS7 .... 126 B4
Gleneagles Cl
    BLGHMW/WYN TS22 .... 57 F1 ⑦
    MARSKE TS11 .... 86 C3
    MGRV/ESTR TS4 .... 98 B5
    RHTLP TS27 .... 11 E3
Gleneagles Rd *DARLE* DL1 .... 117 E1
Glenfield Cl *BLGHMW/WYN* TS22 ... 57 F1 ⑦
Glenfield Cl *STOCN* TS19 .... 92 C1 ⑥
Glenfield Dr *ACK/BRKF* TS5 .... 98 A5
Glenfield Rd *DARLW* DL3 .... 131 E4
    STOCN TS19 .... 92 C1
Glenluce Cl *EGG/EAG* TS16 .... 137 E1
Glenmere *SPEN* DL16 .... 14 C1
Glenmor Gv *ESTON* TS6 .... 101 E2
Glenn Crs *MTN/NUN* TS7 .... 125 F4
Glenside *SALT/BTN/SK* TS12 .... 89 F2
Glenston Cl *HTLPW* TS26 .... 16 B3
The Glen *EGG/EAG* TS16 .... 137 E1
Glentower Gv *HTLPS* TS25 .... 24 C5
Glentworth Av *NORM/PKE* TS3 ... 100 C3
Gloucester Rd *GUIS* TS14 .... 128 C5
Gloucester St *HTLPS* TS25 .... 23 F1
Gloucester Ter *BLGHM* TS23 .... 59 E3
Glyder Ct *THNBY* TS17 .... 138 B2 ⑥
Goathland Dr *HTLPS* TS25 .... 32 C1
Goathland Gv *GUIS* TS14 .... 128 C5
Goathland Rd *ESTON* TS6 .... 102 B1
Gofton Pl *ESTON* TS6 .... 81 F5
Gold Crest *GUIS* TS14 .... 128 A3 ⑥
Goldcrest Cl *THNBY* TS17 .... 139 D1
Goldfinch Rd *HTLPW* TS26 .... 16 B2
Goldsmith Av *HTLP* TS24 .... 12 A4
Goldsmith Cl *DARL* DL1 .... 116 B2
Gonville Ct *DARL* DL1 .... 9 F6 ⑥
Goodison Wy *DARLW* DL1 .... 117 F5 ⑥
Goodwin Cl *REDCAR* TS10 .... 68 A5
Goodwood Cl *REDCAR* TS10 .... 68 C3
Goosepastures *YARM* TS15 .... 137 E5
Gooseport Rd *STOCS* TS18 .... 75 D3 ⑦
Gordon Closel *DARLE* DL1 .... 117 F1 ⑩
Gordon Crs *ESTON* TS6 .... 82 A4 ⑥
Gordon Rd *REDCAR* TS10 .... 50 C5
Gordon St *HTLPW* TS26 .... 17 E4
Gordon Ter *FYHL* DL17 .... 21 D2
Gore Sands *ACK/BRKF* TS5 .... 122 C3
Gorman Rd *ACK/BRKF* TS5 .... 97 F2
Gorton Cl *BLGHM* TS23 .... 41 E5 ⑥
Gort Rd *NACLF* DL5 .... 54 C1
Gosforth Rd *NORTON* TS20 .... 74 C3
Gosforth St *TEESM* TS2 .... 5 F1
Gosforth Av *REDCAR* TS10 .... 51 F5 ⑦
Gough Cl *MBORO* TS1 .... 4 C5 ⑥
Gouldsmith Gdns *DARLE* DL1 .... 117 F3
Goulton Cl *YARM* TS15 .... 138 A5
Grace Cl *HTLPS* TS25 .... 33 D1
Graffenberg St *REDCAR* TS10 ..... 51 F4 ⑥
Grafton Cl *GUIS* TS14 .... 129 D4
Graham St *HTLP* TS24 .... 19 D1 ⑥
    LOFT/ST TS13 .... 112 C3
Grainger St *DARLE* DL1 .... 132 B3
    HTLP TS24 .... 18 A3
    SPEN DL16 .... 15 F2
Grammar School La *YARM* TS15 ... 137 D5 ⑥
Grampian Rd *BLGHM* TS23 .... 58 C3
    SALT/BTN/SK TS12 .... 109 E1
Grange Av *BLGHM* TS23 .... 59 D5
    HTLPW TS26 .... 17 E4
    STOCS TS18 .... 6 A3
Grange Cl *ESTON* TS6 .... 82 A4 ⑥
    HTLPW TS26 .... 17 D4 ⑦
Grange Crs *MTN/NUN* TS7 .... 125 F4
Grange Dr *GTAY/STK* TS9 .... 152 A2

Grange Farm Rd *ESTON* TS6 .... 82 A4
Grangefield Rd *STOCS* TS18 .... 6 A4
Grange Rd *DARLE* DL1 .... 9 E6
  DARLE DL1 .... 131 F4
  HTLPW TS26 .... 17 E4
  MBORO TS1 .... 5 E4
  NORTON TS20 .... 75 D2
  THNBY TS17 .... 95 E2
Grange Road Rbt. *DARLE* DL1 .... 9 E6
Grangeside *DARLW* DL3 .... 131 E4
  NACLF DL5 .... 52 B3
The Grange *FYHL* DL17 .... 38 C2
Grangetown Station Rd
  ESTON TS6 .... 81 F1
Grangeville Av *STOCN* TS19 .... 92 C1 ▢
Grange Wd *CNHM/HEM* TS8 .... 124 B4
Grantham Gn *MGRV/ESTR* TS4 ..... 125 D1
Grantham Rd *HTLPW* TS26 .... 17 F5
  NORTON TS20 .... 57 E4
Grantley Av *NORM/PKE* TS3 .... 100 C1
Granton Cl *DARLW* DL3 .... 130 B2
Grant St *REDCAR* TS10 .... 51 E4 ▢
Granville Av *HTLPW* TS26 .... 17 E4
  SHIL DL4 .... 35 E3
Granville Cl *SHIL* DL4 .... 35 E3 ▢
Granville Gv *NORTON* TS20 .... 75 D3
Granville Rd *BAUK* DL14 .... 26 C3
  ESTON TS6 .... 81 F4
  MBORO TS1 .... 98 A1
Granville Ter *REDCAR* TS10 .... 51 F4
Granwood Rd *ESTON* TS6 .... 102 B3
Grasby Cl *NORM/PKE* TS3 .... 100 C3
Grasmere *SPEN* DL16 .... 14 C1
Grasmere Av *ACK/BRKF* TS5 ..... 123 E1 ▢
Grasmere Crs *SALT/BTN/SK* TS12 .. 109 D2
Grasmere Dr *ESTON* TS6 .... 101 E2
Grasmere Rd *DARLE* DL1 .... 132 C3
  FYHL DL17 .... 20 C2
  REDCAR TS10 .... 68 B1
  STOCS TS18 .... 6 A3
Grasmere St *HTLPW* TS26................. 2 A5
Grassholm Rd *NORTON* TS20 .... 75 D2
Grassington Gn *THNBY* TS17 .... 139 D4
Grassington Rd *MGRV/ESTR* TS4 .... 98 C4
Grass St *DARLE* DL1 .... 116 B4
Graygarth Rd *NORM/PKE* TS3 .... 99 E3
Grayson Rd *SPEN* DL16................... 14 B5
Gray's Rd *STOCS* TS18 .... 6 B3
Gray St *HTLP* TS24 .... 18 A3
  TEESM TS2 .... 5 H1
Great Auk *GUIS* TS14 .... 128 A3
Greatham Cl *ACK/BRKF* TS5 .... 123 E3
Greatham St *HTLPS* TS25 .... 24 B2
Greathead Crs *NACLF* DL5 .... 55 D1 ▢
Greenacre *GTAY/STK* TS9 .... 150 B4
Greenacres *CNHM/HEM* TS8 .... 141 D1
Greenacres Cl *MARSKE* TS11 .... 70 B5 ▢
Greenbank Av *ACK/BRKF* TS5 .... 97 D2 ▢
Greenbank Ct *HTLPW* TS26 .... 17 D4
Greenbank Rd *DARLW* DL5 .... 8 D2
Green Cl *MTN/NUN* TS7 .... 126 C5
Greencroft *REDCAR* TS10 .... 67 F4 ▢
Greencroft Cl *DARLW* DL3 .... 8 B6
Greenfield Dr *ECG/EAG* TS16 ...... 137 D1
Greenfields Wy *STOCS* TS18............ 92 C1
Greenfield Wy *NACLF* DL5 .... 37 E5
Greenham Cl *NORM/PKE* TS3 ..... 100 C3 ▢
Greenhead Rd *CNHM/HEM* TS8 .... 124 A4 ▢
Greenhow Rd *NORM/PKE* TS3......... 99 E2
Greenland Av *ACK/BRKF* TS5 .... 96 C5 ▢
Greenland Rd *HTLP* TS24 .... 18 B1
Greenlands Rd *REDCAR* TS10 .... 69 D1
Green La *ACK/BRKF* TS5 .... 97 E4
  BAUK DL14 .... 27 D1
  BAUK DL14 .... 34 A1
  CNHM/HEM TS8 .... 148 A1
  DARLE DL1 .... 117 D1
  NACLF DL5 .... 55 F5
  REDCAR TS10 .... 69 F2
  SHIL DL4 .... 35 F1
  STOCN TS19 .... 6 C1
  STOCN TS19 .... 73 F3
  THNBY TS17 .... 121 D1
  YARM TS15 .... 146 A2
  YARM TS15 .... 147 D1
Greenlee Cl *THNBY* TS17 .... 138 C3 ▢
Greenlee Garth *NACLF* DL5 .... 37 F4
Greenmount Rd *DARLW* DL3 .... 131 F3
Greenock Cl *MARSKE* TS11 .... 86 B3 ▢
Greenock Rd *HTLPS* TS25 .... 23 D5
Greenrigg Cl *DARLW* DL3 .... 115 D1 ▢
Green Rd *SALT/BTN/SK* TS12 .... 109 D2
Green's Beck Rd *STOCS* TS18 .... 93 E3
Green Scar *REDCAR* TS10 .... 69 D4
Greenside *ESTON* TS6 .... 101 E5
  STOCS TS18 .... 93 E3
  THNBY TS17 .... 121 D5 ▢
Green's La *STOCS* TS18 .... 93 E3
Greenstones Rd *REDCAR* TS10 .... 69 D3
Green St *DARLE* DL1 .... 132 C2
  HTLPS TS25 .... 2 C5
Greens Valley Dr *STOCS* TS18 .... 93 E3
Green Ter *HTLPS* TS25 .... 25 D5

The Green *REDCAR* TS10 .... 67 D2
  SALT/BTN/SK TS12 .... 89 D4
  YARM TS15 .... 146 C5
Green Vale Gv *STOCN* TS19 .... 92 C2
Green Wy *MTN/NUN* TS7 .... 126 C5
Greenway *ESTON* TS6 .... 102 A2 ▢
Greenway *THNBY* TS17 .... 139 D1
The Greenway *NORM/PKE* TS3 ... 100 C2 ▢
Greenwell Rd *NACLF* DL5 .... 38 C5
Greenwell St *DARLE* DL1 .... 132 B3
Greenwood Av *ACK/BRKF* TS5 .... 97 F4 ▢
Greenwood Rd *BLGHM* TS23 .... 59 E2
  HTLP TS24 .... 18 A3
  STOCS TS18 .... 93 E5
Grendale Ct *LOFT/ST* TS13 .... 113 E5
Grenville Cl *MARSKE* TS11 .... 88 A1
Grenville Rd *THNBY* TS17 .... 121 F5
Gresham Cl *DARLE* DL1 .... 116 C3
Gresham Rd *MBORO* TS1 .... 4 D6
Greta Av *HTLPS* TS25...................... 23 F3
Greta Rd *NORTON* TS20 .... 74 C1
  REDCAR TS10 .... 67 F1
  SALT/BTN/SK TS12 .... 109 F1
Greta St *MBORO* TS1 .... 4 B5
  SALT/BTN/SK TS12 .... 89 E3
Gretton Av *MGRV/ESTR* TS4 .... 125 D1
Greville Wy *NACLF* DL5 .... 54 C1
Grewgrass La *MARSKE* TS11 .... 69 D5
Greyfriars Cl *DARLW* DL3 .... 130 A2
Greylands Av *NORTON* TS20 .... 75 D2
Greymouth Cl *STOCS* TS18 .... 93 E3 ▢
Greys Ct *THNBY* TS17 .... 139 D2 ▢
Greystoke Gv *REDCAR* TS10 .... 68 B4
Greystoke Rd *REDCAR* TS10............ 68 B4
Greystone Rd *ESTON* TS6 .... 82 B4
Grey St *BAUK* DL14 .... 27 D1
  DARLE DL1 .... 116 C5
  NORTON TS20 .... 75 D3 ▢
Grey Towers Dr *MTN/NUN* TS7 ..... 144 C1
Greywood Cl *RHTLP* TS27 .... 11 E2 ▢
Gribdale Rd *NORM/PKE* TS3 .... 99 F2
Griffin Rd *MGRV/ESTR* TS4 .... 98 C2
Griffiths Cl *YARM* TS15 .... 146 A2
Griffiths Rd *ESTON* TS6 .... 82 A5
Grindon Ct *NACLF* DL5.................... 39 D3
Grinkle Av *NORM/PKE* TS3 .... 99 F4 ▢
Grinkle Ct *GUIS* TS14 .... 129 D2 ▢
Grinkle Rd *REDCAR* TS10 .... 67 E1
Grinton Park Wy *DARLE* DL1 .... 133 D4 ▢
Grinton Rd *STOCS* TS18................... 93 D4
Grisedale Ct *ACK/BRKF* TS5 .... 123 E3 ▢
Grisedale Crs *ECG/EAG* TS16 .... 137 E2
  ESTON TS6 .... 82 B5
Gritten Sq *HTLP* TS24 .... 13 E5
Groat Av *NACLF* DL5....................... 55 D3
Groat Ct *NACLF* DL5 .... 55 D3
Groat Rd *NACLF* DL5 .... 55 D3
Groat Wy *NACLF* DL5 .... 55 D3
Grosmont Cl *REDCAR* TS10 .... 68 B4
Grosmont Dr *BLGHM* TS23 .... 58 B1
Grosmont Rd *ESTON* TS6 .... 102 B1
  HTLPS TS25 .... 33 D1
Gross St *BLGHM* TS23 .... 60 C4 ▢
Grosvenor Gdns *ESTON* TS6 .... 101 F5 ▢
Grosvenor Pl *GUIS* TS14 .... 128 C3
Grosvenor Rd *ACK/BRKF* TS5........ 97 E2
  BLGHMW/WYN TS22 .... 58 A1
  STOCN TS19 .... 93 E2
Grosvenor St *DARLE* DL1 .... 132 B3 ▢
  HTLPW TS26 .... 2 A1 ▢
Grove Bank *YARM* TS15 .... 146 B5
Grove Cl *HTLPW* TS26 .... 17 E5
Grove Rd *NORM/PKE* TS3 .... 79 D5
  REDCAR TS10 .... 50 C5
Groves St *HTLP* TS24 .... 19 E2 ▢
Grove St *STOCS* TS18 .... 94 B3
Grove Ter *NORTON* TS20................. 75 D3
The Grove *ACK/BRKF* TS5 .... 123 F4
  GUIS TS14 .... 128 A5
  HTLPS TS25 .... 31 D4 ▢
  HTLPW TS26 .... 17 E4
  MTN/NUN TS7 .... 125 E2
  YARM TS15 .... 146 B1
Grundales Dr *MARSKE* TS11 .... 70 B5
Gudmunsen Av *DARL* DL14 .... 26 C5
Guildford Cl *DARLE* DL1 .... 117 F3 ▢
Guildford Rd *BLGHM* TS23 .... 58 B1 ▢
  ESTON TS6 .... 101 E5
Guillemot Rd *HTLPW* TS26 .... 16 C1
Guisborough Ct *ESTON* TS6 .... 102 B2 ▢
Guisborough Rd *GTAY/STK* TS9 .... 150 B2
  MTN/NUN TS7 .... 127 D4
  SALT/BTN/SK TS12 .... 89 D4
  THNBY TS17 .... 95 F5
Guisborough St *ESTON* TS6 .... 102 B3
Guiseley Wy *ECG/EAG* TS16 .... 119 D4
Gulliver Rd *HTLPS* TS25.................. 22 C5
Gunnergate Cl
  SALT/BTN/SK TS12 .... 88 C2 ▢
Gunnergate La *CNHM/HEM* TS8 ... 125 E5
  MTN/NUN TS7 .... 125 E5
Gunnerside Rd *STOCN* TS19 .... 92 C1
Gunn La *NACLF* DL5 .... 55 D1
Gurney St *DARLE* DL1 .... 116 B4
  MARSKE TS11 .... 86 C2

  MBORO TS1 .... 5 G3
Gurney Wy *NACLF* DL5 .... 54 B3
Guthrie Av *ACK/BRKF* TS5 .... 96 C4
Gwynn Cl *STOCN* TS19...................... 72 C5
Gypsy La *MTN/NUN* TS7 .... 126 A4

H

Hackforth Rd *STOCS* TS18 .... 93 D4
Hackworth Cl *FYHL* DL17 .... 20 B2
  NACLF DL5 .... 55 D2 ▢
  SHIL DL4 .... 35 F4
Hackworth St *FYHL* DL17 .... 20 B2
  SHIL DL4 .... 35 F3
Hadasia Gdns *STOCN* TS19 .... 93 E1 ▢
Haddon Cl *BLGHM* TS23 .... 58 B1 ▢
Haddon St *MBORO* TS1 .... 5 H6
Hadleigh Cl *SEDG* TS21 .... 29 E5
Hadleigh Crs *MGRV/ESTR* TS4 .... 98 C3 ▢
Hadnall Cl *ACK/BRKF* TS5 .... 122 C1 ▢
Hadrian Ct *DARLW* DL3 .... 131 F3 ▢
Haffron Av *STOCS* TS18 .... 7 G2
Haig St *DARLE* DL1 .... 116 A3
  FYHL DL17 .... 20 B2
Hailsham Av *THNBY* TS17 .... 139 F1
Haldane Gv *HTLPS* TS25 .... 23 D5 ▢
Hale Rd *BLGHM* TS23 .... 42 A5 ▢
Half Moon La *SPEN* DL16 .... 15 F3
Halidon Wy *BLGHM* TS23 .... 42 B5
Halifax Cl *MARSKE* TS11 .... 70 A5
Halifax Rd *THNBY* TS17 .... 121 F5 ▢
  NACLF DL5 .... 70 B5
The Hall Cl *MTN/NUN* TS7 .... 100 C5 ▢
Hallcroft Cl *BLGHM* TS23 .... 58 C5
Hall Dr *ACK/BRKF* TS5 .... 123 E1
Hallgarth Cl *ACK/BRKF* TS5 .... 123 E3
Hallgate Cl *STOCS* TS18 .... 92 C4 ▢
Hall Grounds *LOFT/ST* TS13 .... 113 E4
Hallifield St *NORTON* TS20 .... 75 D3
Hall Lea *SEDG* TS21 .... 29 D3 ▢
Hall Moor Cl *YARM* TS15 .... 146 C5
Hall View Gv *DARLW* DL3 .... 114 B5
Halnaby Av *DARLW* DL3 .... 130 A1
Halton Ct *BLGHM* TS23 .... 42 A3 ▢
Hambledon Crs
  SALT/BTN/SK TS12 .... 109 E1 ▢
Hambledon Rd *ACK/BRKF* TS5 ...... 97 D3
Hambleton Av *REDCAR* TS10........... 67 F3
Hambleton Ct *NACLF* DL5................. 37 F4
Hambleton Crs *MARSKE* TS11 .... 88 A1
Hambleton Ga *GTAY/STK* TS9 ...... 152 B4
Hambletonian Yd *STOCS* TS18 .... 7 F5 ▢
Hambleton Rd *MTN/NUN* TS7 .... 127 D4
Hambleton Sq *BLGHM* TS23 .... 58 B2
Hamilton Dr *DARLE* DL1 .... 117 D1
Hamilton Gv *ESTON* TS6 .... 101 D1 ▢
  REDCAR TS10 .... 50 C5 ▢
Hamilton Rd *HTLPS* TS25 .... 23 D5 ▢
  STOCN TS19 .... 74 B4
Hammond Cl *MTN/NUN* TS7 .... 125 E4
Hammond Dr *DARLE* DL1 .... 132 A5
Hampden St *ESTON* TS6 .... 80 C4
Hampden Wy *THNBY* TS17 .... 121 F5
Hampstead Gv *ESTON* TS6 .... 101 E5 ▢
Hampstead Rd *ESTON* TS6............. 101 E4
The Hampstead *REDCAR* TS10 ...... 69 D3 ▢
Hampton Cl *MTN/NUN* TS7 .... 126 C4
Hampton Gv *REDCAR* TS10 .... 69 E1
Hampton Rd *STOCS* TS18 .... 94 B3
Hamsterley Rd *NACLF* DL5 .... 38 A4
  STOCN TS19 .... 73 D3
Hamsterley St *DARLW* DL3........... 115 F4
Hamsterley Wy
  SALT/BTN/SK TS12 .... 109 E1 ▢
Hanbury Cl *THNBY* TS17 .... 139 D1 ▢
Handale Cl *GUIS* TS14 .... 129 F3
Handley Cl *STOCS* TS18.................. 120 B2
Hankin Rd *NORM/PKE* TS3 .... 79 D5 ▢
Hanover Cl *DARLW* DL3 .... 130 B2 ▢
Hanover Court Gdns *DARL* DL14 ..... 27 E5
Hanover Gdns *ACK/BRKF* TS5 ..... 97 E3 ▢
Hanover Pde *NORTON* TS20 .... 74 B1 ▢
Hansard Ct *NACLF* DL5 .... 53 E5 ▢
Hanson Gv *NORM/PKE* TS3 .... 100 B1 ▢
Hanson St *REDCAR* TS10............... 50 B5 ▢
Hanson St *ESTON* TS6 .... 51 E5
Harbone Gdns *ACK/BRKF* TS5 ..... 123 F5
Harbottle Cl *THNBY* TS17 .... 138 C3 ▢
Harbour Wk *HTLP* TS24 .... 18 B3
Harcourt Rd *ESTON* TS6 .... 80 C4
Harcourt St *DARLW* DL3 .... 116 A4
  HTLPW TS26 .... 17 E4
Hardale Gv *REDCAR* TS10 .... 67 F2
Hardinge Rd *NACLF* DL5 .... 38 C5
Harding Ter *DARLW* DL3 .... 115 F4
Hardisty Crs *BAUK* DL14 .... 26 C4
Hardknott Gv *REDCAR* TS10 .... 68 A1 ▢
Hardwick Av *ACK/BRKF* TS5........... 97 E5
Hardwick Cl *DARLE* DL1 .... 117 E2
Hardwick Ct *HTLPW* TS26............... 22 B1
  NACLF DL5 .... 38 C4
Hardwick Rd *BLGHM* TS23 .... 59 E1
  ESTON TS6 .... 80 C3

SEDG TS21 ..... 29 D3
STOCN TS19 ..... 73 E2
Harebell Cl SALT/BTN/SK TS12 ..... 110 A2
  THNBY TS17 ..... 121 D5
Harebell Mdw NACLF DL5 ..... 38 C2
Harehills Rd ACK/BRKF TS5 ..... 97 D3
Haresfield Wy THNBY TS17 ..... 139 D2
Hareshaw Cl THNBY TS17 ..... 138 C3
Hareson Rd NACLF DL5 ..... 37 F4
Harewood Crs STOCN TS19 ..... 73 D4
Harewood Gv DARLW DL3 ..... 131 F3
Harewood Rd THNBY TS17 ..... 95 E3
Harewood St MBORO TS1 ..... 98 A1
Harewood Ter DARLW DL3 ..... 131 F3
Harford St MBORO TS1 ..... 97 F1
Hargreave Ter DARLE DL1 ..... 9 H6
Harker Cl YARM TS15 ..... 146 A1
Harker St SHIL DL4 ..... 35 D3
Harlech Cl ESTON TS6 ..... 102 A1
Harlech Ct THNBY TS17 ..... 138 B2
Harlech Gv MARSKE TS11 ..... 86 C3
Harley Gv DARLE DL1 ..... 117 F2
Harlow Crs THNBY TS17 ..... 122 A1
Harlsey Crs STOCS TS18 ..... 93 E4
Harlsey Gv STOCS TS18 ..... 93 E4
Harlsey Rd STOCS TS18 ..... 93 E4
Harper Ter STOCS TS18 ..... 93 F4
Harringay Crs DARLE DL1 ..... 117 F5
Harris Gv HTLPS TS25 ..... 23 D5
Harrison Cl SHIL DL4 ..... 35 F5
Harrison Pl HTLP TS24 ..... 12 B5
Harrison St NORM/PKE TS3 ..... 79 E5
Harrison Ter DARLW DL3 ..... 115 F4
Harris St DARLE DL1 ..... 133 D3
  MBORO TS1 ..... 5 E4
Harrogate Crs ACK/BRKF TS5 ..... 98 A3
Harrowgate La STOCN TS19 ..... 72 C3
Harrow Rd ACK/BRKF TS5 ..... 97 E4
  STOCS TS18 ..... 6 B5
Harrow St HTLPS TS25 ..... 23 F2
Harry St DARLW DL3 ..... 116 A3
Harsley Wk NORM/PKE TS3 ..... 99 F2
Hart Av HTLPW TS26 ..... 17 D3
Hartburn Av STOCS TS18 ..... 94 A3
Hartburn La STOCS TS18 ..... 94 A3
Hartburn Village STOCS TS18 ..... 93 F4
Hart Cl STOCN TS19 ..... 73 F3
Harter Cl MTN/NUN TS7 ..... 126 C5
Hartford Rd DARLW DL3 ..... 131 E3
Hartforth Av ACK/BRKF TS5 ..... 123 E3
Hartington Cl THNBY TS17 ..... 95 E4
Hartington Rd MBORO TS1 ..... 4 D3
  STOCS TS18 ..... 7 E5
Hartington St LOFT/ST TS13 ..... 112 C2
  THNBY TS17 ..... 95 E4
Hartington Wy DARLW DL3 ..... 115 F3
Hartland Gv NORM/PKE TS3 ..... 100 A4
Hart La HTLPW TS26 ..... 16 C2
Hartlepool Cl STOCN TS19 ..... 73 F3
Hartley Cl HTLPW TS26 ..... 2 A2
Hartley Rd NACLF DL5 ..... 38 C5
Hartley Ter SPEN DL16 ..... 15 E2
Harton Av BLGHMW/WYN TS22 ..... 57 F1
Hart Pastures RHTLP TS27 ..... 10 C5
Hart Rd RHTLP TS27 ..... 11 F4
Hartsbourne Crs MARSKE TS11 ..... 86 B3
Hartside Gv STOCN TS19 ..... 74 A3
Hartville Rd HTLP TS24 ..... 11 E2
Hartwith Dr STOCN TS19 ..... 72 C1
Harvard Av THNBY TS17 ..... 95 E2
Harvester Ct MTN/NUN TS7 ..... 125 D2
Harvey Ct REDCAR TS10 ..... 67 D2
Harwal Rd REDCAR TS10 ..... 50 C5
Harwell Cl MGRV/ESTR TS4 ..... 98 C4
Harwell Dr STOCN TS19 ..... 73 D4
Harwich Cl REDCAR TS10 ..... 69 E3
Harwich Gv HTLPS TS25 ..... 24 A5
Harwood Ct TEESM TS2 ..... 77 F2
Harwood St HTLP TS24 ..... 17 F2
Haselrigg Cl NACLF DL5 ..... 53 E3
Hasledon Gv SEDG TS21 ..... 29 D5
Haslewood Rd FYHL DL17 ..... 38 B2
Hastings Cl MTN/NUN TS7 ..... 126 C4
  THNBY TS17 ..... 121 F4
Hastings Pl HTLP TS24 ..... 12 B5
Hastings Wy BLGHM TS23 ..... 42 C5
Haswell Av HTLPS TS25 ..... 24 A3
Hatfield Av ACK/BRKF TS5 ..... 97 E5
Hatfield Cl EGG/EAG TS16 ..... 136 C1
Hatfield Rd BLGHM TS23 ..... 59 D1
  NACLF DL5 ..... 55 D1
Hatfield Wy BAUK DL14 ..... 27 F5
Hatherley Ct NORM/PKE TS3 ..... 100 A1
Haughton Rd DARLE DL1 ..... 116 C5
Hauxley Cl REDCAR TS10 ..... 69 E3
Havelock Cl NACLF DL5 ..... 55 D1
Havelock St DARLE DL1 ..... 116 B4
  HTLP TS24 ..... 3 F4
  THNBY TS17 ..... 95 E4
Haverthwaite ACK/BRKF TS5 ..... 123 E5
Haverton Hill Rd BLGHM TS23 ..... 60 B4
  STOCS TS18 ..... 76 B4
Havilland Rd THNBY TS17 ..... 121 F3
Haweswater Rd REDCAR TS10 ..... 68 A1
Hawford Cl THNBY TS17 ..... 139 E1

Hawkesbury Cl STOCS TS18 ..... 93 E3
Hawkins Cl MARSKE TS11 ..... 88 A1
Hawkridge Cl HTLPW TS26 ..... 17 F3
  THNBY TS17 ..... 139 D4
Hawk Rd NORM/PKE TS3 ..... 79 F5
Hawkshead Rd REDCAR TS10 ..... 68 B2
Hawkstone CNHM/HEM TS8 ..... 144 A1
Hawkstone Cl
  BLGHMW/WYN TS22 ..... 57 F1
  GUIS TS14 ..... 129 D4
Hawnby Cl STOCN TS19 ..... 92 C1
Hawnby Rd ACK/BRKF TS5 ..... 98 A4
Hawthorn Av BLGHM TS23 ..... 58 C4
  THNBY TS17 ..... 121 E1
Hawthorn Crs MTN/NUN TS7 ..... 126 A3
Hawthorne Av MGRV/ESTR TS4 ..... 98 B3
Hawthorne Dr GUIS TS14 ..... 128 A4
Hawthorne Rd FYHL DL17 ..... 21 D2
  STOCN TS19 ..... 74 B4
Hawthorn Gv YARM TS15 ..... 137 F5
Hawthorn Rd BAUK DL14 ..... 27 E2
  REDCAR TS10 ..... 69 D1
  SEDG TS21 ..... 29 D2
  SPEN DL16 ..... 14 B4
The Hawthorns GTAY/STK TS9 ..... 150 C2
Hawthorn St DARLE DL1 ..... 132 B3
Haxby Cl ACK/BRKF TS5 ..... 124 A1
Hayburn Cl REDCAR TS10 ..... 69 D5
  THNBY TS17 ..... 139 E2
Hayburn Ct CNHM/HEM TS8 ..... 141 F1
Haydon Gn BLGHM TS23 ..... 41 F3
Hayling Gv REDCAR TS10 ..... 69 D4
Hayling Wy STOCS TS18 ..... 92 B2
Haymore St ACK/BRKF TS5 ..... 98 A2
Hayston Rd HTLPW TS26 ..... 16 B3
Hazel Av DARLW DL3 ..... 115 F4
Hazel Ct MBORO TS1 ..... 5 H4
Hazeldale Av SHIL DL4 ..... 36 A3
Hazeldene Av STOCS TS18 ..... 94 A4
  STOCS TS18 ..... 94 B4
Hazel Gdns SALT/BTN/SK TS12 ..... 90 C5
Hazel Gv HTLP TS24 ..... 17 F2
  MTN/NUN TS7 ..... 126 B4
Hazelmere SPEN DL16 ..... 14 C1
Hazelmere Cl
  BLGHMW/WYN TS22 ..... 40 C5
Hazel Rd MTN/NUN TS7 ..... 126 B3
  STOCN TS19 ..... 74 B4
Hazel Slade EGG/EAG TS16 ..... 137 E1
Hazelwood Cl ACK/BRKF TS5 ..... 124 A3
Headingham Cl MGRV/ESTR TS4 ..... 98 C3
Headingley Ct HTLPS TS25 ..... 33 D1
Headingley Crs DARLE DL1 ..... 117 F5
Headlam Rd BLGHM TS23 ..... 42 B5
  DARLE DL1 ..... 133 D3
  NORTON TS20 ..... 75 D4
The Headlands DARLW DL3 ..... 131 D2
  MARSKE TS11 ..... 70 C4
Head St MBORO TS1 ..... 5 E4
Healaugh Pk YARM TS15 ..... 146 C1
Heatfield Dr HTLPS TS25 ..... 23 F2
Heatherburn Ct NACLF DL5 ..... 38 C4
Heather Cl STOCN TS19 ..... 74 A2
Heather Dr ACK/BRKF TS5 ..... 123 E1
Heatherfields Rd ESTON TS6 ..... 102 A4
Heather Gv HTLPW TS26 ..... 17 E1
  SALT/BTN/SK TS12 ..... 110 A3
  SPEN DL16 ..... 14 B5
Heathfield Cl EGG/EAG TS16 ..... 137 D1
Heath Rd SPEN DL16 ..... 14 B5
Heathrow THNBY TS17 ..... 122 A1
The Heath NORTON TS20 ..... 74 C3
Heaton Rd BLGHM TS23 ..... 41 F3
Hebburn Rd STOCN TS19 ..... 73 E3
Hebron Rd ACK/BRKF TS5 ..... 98 B3
Heddon Gv THNBY TS17 ..... 138 C4
Hedley Cl YARM TS15 ..... 146 A2
Hedley St GUIS TS14 ..... 129 D2
Heighington Cl STOCN TS19 ..... 73 E3
Heighington La NACLF DL5 ..... 53 E5
Heild Cl NACLF DL5 ..... 39 D5
Helena Ter BAUK DL14 ..... 27 D4
Helmsley Cl ACK/BRKF TS5 ..... 98 A5
  FYHL DL17 ..... 21 E2
Helmsley Ct NACLF DL5 ..... 39 D3
Helmsley Dr GUIS TS14 ..... 129 D2
Helmsley Gv STOCN TS19 ..... 73 D5
Helmsley Moor Wy DARLE DL1 ..... 133 E4
Helmsley Rd GTAY/STK TS9 ..... 152 B2
Helmsley St HTLP TS24 ..... 17 F2
Helston Ct THNBY TS17 ..... 122 A1
Hemel Cl THNBY TS17 ..... 96 A5
Hemingford Gdns YARM TS15 ..... 146 C1
Hemlington Hall Rd
  CNHM/HEM TS8 ..... 123 F5
Hemlington La CNHM/HEM TS8 ..... 124 A3
Hemlington Rd CNHM/HEM TS8 ..... 141 E1
Hemlington Village Rd
  CNHM/HEM TS8 ..... 142 C1
Hempstead Cl THNBY TS17 ..... 96 A5
Henderson Gv HTLP TS24 ..... 18 A3
Henderson Rd NACLF DL5 ..... 55 D1
Henderson St DARLE DL1 ..... 132 A3
Hendren Cl DARLW DL3 ..... 116 B1

Henley Gv THNBY TS17 ..... 95 E4
Henley Rd ACK/BRKF TS5 ..... 97 E3
Henrhyd Cl THNBY TS17 ..... 138 B3
Henrietta Cl THNBY TS17 ..... 95 E4
Henrietta St HTLP TS24 ..... 19 D1
Henry St DARLE DL1 ..... 116 E3
  ESTON TS6 ..... 81 D3
  NORM/PKE TS3 ..... 99 E1
  REDCAR TS10 ..... 51 D4
  SHIL DL4 ..... 35 E3
Hensfield Rd DARLW DL3 ..... 115 F3
Henshaw Dr THNBY TS17 ..... 138 C3
Hensley Ct NORTON TS20 ..... 57 D5
Henson Cl BAUK DL14 ..... 27 E5
Henson Gv NACLF DL5 ..... 38 C4
Heortnesse Rd HTLP TS24 ..... 13 E5
Hepple Cl BLGHM TS23 ..... 41 F3
Herbert St DARLE DL1 ..... 9 G6
  NORM/PKE TS3 ..... 79 E5
Hercules St DARLE DL1 ..... 117 D2
Hereford Cl ACK/BRKF TS5 ..... 98 A2
Hereford Rd GUIS TS14 ..... 128 C4
Hereford St HTLPS TS25 ..... 24 A2
Hereford Ter BLGHM TS23 ..... 59 E3
Heriot Gv HTLPS TS25 ..... 23 D5
Heron Dr DARLE DL1 ..... 133 E2
Heron Ga GUIS TS14 ..... 128 A3
Heronspool Cl HTLP TS24 ..... 18 B1
Herrington Ct NACLF DL5 ..... 38 C4
Herrington Rd BLGHM TS23 ..... 42 A3
Herriot Ct DARLE DL1 ..... 117 F1
Herschell St REDCAR TS10 ..... 51 E5
Hershall Dr NORM/PKE TS3 ..... 100 A2
Hertford Rd NORTON TS20 ..... 74 C2
Hesketh Av MGRV/ESTR TS4 ..... 125 D1
Hesleden Av ACK/BRKF TS5 ..... 123 D3
Hesledon Cl STOCN TS19 ..... 73 F3
Heslop Dr DARLE DL1 ..... 132 A4
Heswall Rd BLGHM TS23 ..... 59 E1
Hetton Cl BLGHM TS23 ..... 41 F5
Heugh Chare HTLP TS24 ..... 19 F2
Hewitson Rd DARLE DL1 ..... 133 E2
Hewley St ESTON TS6 ..... 101 F5
Heworth Dr NORTON TS20 ..... 57 D5
Heworth La NACLF DL5 ..... 55 F5
Hexham St BAUK DL14 ..... 27 D1
Hexham Wy DARLW DL3 ..... 114 B3
Heysham Gv REDCAR TS10 ..... 69 E4
Heythrop Dr ACK/BRKF TS5 ..... 96 C5
  GUIS TS14 ..... 129 D4
Hibernian Gv HTLPS TS25 ..... 23 D5
Hickling Gv STOCN TS19 ..... 73 D4
Hickstead Rd NACLF DL5 ..... 39 D2
Hidcote Gdns THNBY TS17 ..... 139 D2
Highbank Rd MTN/NUN TS7 ..... 127 D2
High Barn Rd NACLF DL5 ..... 53 E3
Highbury Av ACK/BRKF TS5 ..... 97 F5
Highbury Rd DARLW DL3 ..... 115 D5
High Church Wynd YARM TS15 ..... 137 D4
Highcliffe Gv MARSKE TS11 ..... 86 C3
Highcroft SPEN DL16 ..... 14 B5
High Fell REDCAR TS10 ..... 68 A2
Highfield Cl EGG/EAG TS16 ..... 137 D1
Highfield Crs STOCS TS18 ..... 93 E3
Highfield Dr EGG/EAG TS16 ..... 137 D1
Highfield Gdns EGG/EAG TS16 ..... 137 E1
Highfield Rd DARLW DL3 ..... 114 C3
  ESTON TS6 ..... 102 A2
  MARSKE TS11 ..... 69 F5
  MGRV/ESTR TS4 ..... 98 C2
  STOCS TS18 ..... 93 E4
Highgate ESTON TS6 ..... 102 C2
High Gill Rd MTN/NUN TS7 ..... 126 C3
High Grange Av BLGHM TS23 ..... 41 F5
High Grange Rd SPEN DL16 ..... 15 D2
High Gn FYHL DL17 ..... 38 C2
Highland Gdns SHIL DL4 ..... 35 D2
Highland Rd HTLPS TS25 ..... 23 D5
High La YARM TS15 ..... 140 A3
The Highlight HTLP TS24 ..... 18 B3
Highmead Wk NORM/PKE TS3 ..... 99 F5
High Melbourne St BAUK DL14 ..... 27 D3
Highmoor Rd DARLE DL1 ..... 133 F4
High Newham Rd STOCN TS19 ..... 73 D2
High Northgate DARLW DL3 ..... 9 G1
High Peak GUIS TS14 ..... 129 E5
High Rifts CNHM/HEM TS8 ..... 141 D1
High Rd NACLF DL5 ..... 53 A4
High Rw DARLE DL1 ..... 9 F5
  LOFT/ST TS13 ..... 112 C2
Highside Rd RDARL DL2 ..... 52 A5
High Stone Cl REDCAR TS10 ..... 69 D3
High St BLGHMW/WYN TS22 ..... 41 E4
  ESTON TS6 ..... 83 E5
  ESTON TS6 ..... 101 F3
  ESTON TS6 ..... 102 C1
  FYHL DL17 ..... 21 F3
  GTAY/STK TS9 ..... 150 B3
  GTAY/STK TS9 ..... 152 A2
  HTLP TS24 ..... 19 E2
  HTLPS TS25 ..... 31 D3
  LOFT/ST TS13 ..... 113 E5
  MARSKE TS11 ..... 70 B5
  NORM/PKE TS3 ..... 100 B3

NORTON TS20 .... 58 A5
REDCAR TS10 .... 51 F4
SALT/BTN/SK TS12 .... 91 D5
SALT/BTN/SK TS12 .... 109 D2
SALT/BTN/SK TS12 .... 109 D5
SEDG TS21 .... 29 E4
SPEN DL16 .... 15 D3
STOCS TS18 .... 7 C4
TEESM TS2 .... 78 B1 🔢
YARM TS15 .... 137 D4
High St East *REDCAR* TS10 .... 51 E4
High St West *REDCAR* TS10 .... 50 C4
Hilda Pl *SALT/BTN/SK* TS12 .... 89 C2
Hilda St *DARLE* DL1 .... 9 H4
Hilderthorpe *MTN/NUN* TS7 .... 126 B4
Hildyard Cl *GTAY/STK* TS9 .... 152 A1
Hillbeck St *BAUK* DL14 .... 27 F4
Hill Cl *SALT/BTN/SK* TS12 .... 109 D2
Hillclose Av *MARSKE* TS11 .... 88 B4
Hillside Cl *SPEN* DL16 .... 15 F2
Hillside Rd *DARLW* DL3 .... 131 E3
NORTON TS20 .... 58 A5
Hillston Cl *HTLPW* TS26 .... 16 B4
Hill St *MBORO* TS1 .... 5 F3
REDCAR TS10 .... 51 D4
Hill St East *STOCS* TS18 .... 95 E1
Hills View Rd *ESTON* TS6 .... 102 B2
Hill Vw *HTLPS* TS25 .... 31 E5
Hilsdon Dr *SHIL* DL4 .... 36 A4
Hilton Rd *BAUK* DL14 .... 27 E3
NACLF DL5 .... 54 C3
Hind Ct *NACLF* DL5 .... 39 D2
Hinderwell Av *REDCAR* TS10 .... 67 F1
Hindhead *EGG/EAG* TS16 .... 137 E1 🔢
Hindpool Cl *HTLP* TS24 .... 18 A1
Hind St *STOCS* TS18 .... 94 B3
Hinton Av *ACK/BRKF* TS5 .... 97 D2 🔢
Hirdman Gv *HTLP* TS24 .... 12 A3
Hird St *DARLE* DL1 .... 9 H5
Hirst Ct *SPEN* DL16 .... 14 A5
Hirst Gv *DARLE* DL1 .... 133 E2
Hive Cl *STOCS* TS19 .... 74 B3
Hob Hill Cl *SALT/BTN/SK* TS12 .... 89 D3
Hob Hill Crs *SALT/BTN/SK* TS12 .... 89 D3
Hob Hill La *SALT/BTN/SK* TS12 .... 88 B4
Hobson Av *REDCAR* TS10 .... 67 D3
Hodgson Ct *ESTON* TS6 .... 102 B3 🔢
The Hoe *HTLP* TS24 .... 3 F1 🔢
Hogarth Cl *BLGHM* TS23 .... 41 F4
Holbeck Av *ACK/BRKF* TS5 .... 123 F3
Holbeck Wk *THNBY* TS17 .... 122 A4
Holborn *SPEN* DL16 .... 15 D2
Holburn Pk *STOCS* TS19 .... 73 E5
Holdenby Dr *NORM/PKE* TS3 .... 99 F5
Holden Cl *ESTON* TS6 .... 81 D3
Holderness *NACLF* DL5 .... 37 E4 🔢
Holder St *REDCAR* TS10 .... 51 E5 🔢
Holdforth Cl *HTLP* TS24 .... 17 E1
Holdforth Rd *HTLP* TS24 .... 17 E1
Holgate Moor Gn *DARLE* DL1 .... 133 E4
The Holgate *ACK/BRKF* TS5 .... 97 F1 🔢
Holindale *SPEN* DL16 .... 15 D4 🔢
Holland Rd *HTLPS* TS25 .... 31 D2
The Hollies *REDCAR* TS10 .... 69 E1
Hollinside Cl *STOCS* TS19 .... 73 E4
Hollinside Rd *BLGHM* TS23 .... 42 B5
Hollins La *ACK/BRKF* TS5 .... 97 C3
Hollin Wy *NACLF* DL5 .... 54 B5
Hollowfield *CNHM/HEM* TS8 .... 124 C5 🔢
Hollybush Av *THNBY* TS17 .... 121 E5
Holly Garth Cl *GTAY/STK* TS9 .... 150 B3
Holly Hl *SHIL* DL4 .... 36 A3
Hollyhurst Av *MGRV/ESTR* TS4 ..... 98 B4 🔢
Hollyhurst Rd *DARLW* DL3 .... 8 C2
Holly La *CNHM/HEM* TS8 .... 141 E1 🔢
Hollymead Dr *GUIS* TS14 .... 129 D2
Hollystone Ct *BLGHM* TS23 .... 42 A4
Holly St *DARLW* DL3 .... 9 F5
MBORO TS1 .... 5 H5
NORTON TS20 .... 75 D2 🔢
Holly Ter *TEESM* TS2 .... 61 D5 🔢
Hollywalk Av *ESTON* TS6 .... 101 F4
Hollywalk Cl *ESTON* TS6 .... 101 E4
Hollywalk Dr *ESTON* TS6 .... 101 F3
Holmebeck Rd *SALT/BTN/SK* TS12 .. 110 A2
Holmefields Rd *ESTON* TS6 .... 102 A4
Holme House Rd *STOCS* TS18 .... 76 A4
Holmes Cl *THNBY* TS17 .... 121 D1
Holmeside Gv *BLGHM* TS23 .... 42 B4 🔢
Holmlands Rd *DARLW* DL3 .... 115 E4
Holmwood Av *MGRV/ESTR* TS4 ...... 98 B4
Holnest Av *NORM/PKE* TS3 .... 99 F3
Holnicote Cl *THNBY* TS17 .... 139 D4 🔢

Holt St *HTLP* TS24 .... 2 B4
The Holt *CNHM/HEM* TS8 .... 124 B4
Holwick Rd *DARLE* DL1 .... 116 B2
TEESM TS2 .... 4 A2
Holyhead Dr *REDCAR* TS10 .... 69 E3
Holyrood Av *DARLW* DL3 .... 130 B2
Holyrood Cl *THNBY* TS17 .... 95 F4
Holyrood Crs *RHTLP* TS27 .... 10 B5 🔢
Holystone Dr *THNBY* TS17 .... 138 C3
Holywell Gn *EGG/EAG* TS16 .... 137 E1
Homerell Cl *DARLE* DL1 .... 69 D3 🔢
Homer Gv *HTLPS* TS25 .... 23 D3
Homerton Ct *DARLE* DL1 .... 116 C3 🔢
Homerton Rd *NORM/PKE* TS3 .... 99 F2
Hondbu Ct *THNBY* TS17 .... 138 B3 🔢
Honey Bee Ct *STOCN* TS19 .... 74 B3 🔢
Honeycomb Av *STOCN* TS19 .... 74 B3
Honeypot Gv *STOCN* TS19 .... 74 B3
Honeypot La *DARLE* DL1 .... 115 F3
Honeysuckle Ct *NORTON* TS20 ...... 74 C2 🔢
Honeywood Gdns *DARLW* DL3 ...... 115 F4 🔢
Honister Cl *STOCN* TS19 .... 6 C1
Honister Gv *ACK/BRKF* TS5 .... 123 D1
Honister Rd *REDCAR* TS10 .... 68 A1 🔢
Honiton Wy *HTLPS* TS25 .... 31 E1
Hood Cl *HTLP* TS24 .... 12 A3
Hood Dr *ESTON* TS6 .... 81 D4
Hoode Cl *NACLF* DL5 .... 37 F4
Hoope Cl *YARM* TS15 .... 146 A2 🔢
Hopemoor Pl *DARLE* DL1 .... 117 D3
Hope St *BLGHM* TS23 .... 60 C4
HTLP TS24 .... 2 D3
STOCS TS18 .... 94 B3 🔢
Hopetown La *DARLW* DL3 .... 116 A4
Hopper Rd *NACLF* DL5 .... 54 C2
Hopps St *HTLPW* TS26 .... 17 F3 🔢
Horcum Ct *CNHM/HEM* TS8 .... 141 F1
Horden Rd *BLGHM* TS23 .... 59 E1
Hornbeam Cl *MTN/NUN* TS7 .... 101 D5 🔢
Hornby Av *SEDG* TS21 .... 29 D5
Hornby Cl *HTLPS* TS25 .... 25 D3
Horndale Av *NACLF* DL5 .... 54 A2
Hornleigh Gv *REDCAR* TS10 .... 50 C5
Hornsea Cl *BLGHM* TS23 .... 42 B3
Hornsea Gv *REDCAR* TS10 .... 50 C5 🔢
Hornsea Rd *CNHM/HEM* TS8 .... 141 E1
Horseclose La *SEDG* TS21 .... 72 A1
Horsefield St *MGRV/ESTR* TS4 .... 78 C4
Horse Market *DARLE* DL1 .... 9 F5
Horsley Pl *HTLP* TS24 .... 12 B5 🔢
Horsley Wy *BLGHM* TS23 .... 42 A4
Hoskins Wy *NORM/PKE* TS3 .... 100 A3
Hough Crs *THNBY* TS17 .... 121 E1 🔢
Houghton St *HTLPS* TS25 .... 2 B5
Houndgate *DARLE* DL1 .... 9 F5
Hoveton Cl *STOCS* TS19 .... 73 E4 🔢
Hovingham St *NORM/PKE* TS3 .... 79 E5 🔢🔢
Howard Cl *BAUK* DL14 .... 26 C5
Howard Ct *MGRV/ESTR* TS4 .... 98 C3 🔢
Howard Dr *MARSKE* TS11 .... 88 A1
Howard Pl *NORTON* TS20 .... 75 D4 🔢
Howard St *HTLP* TS24 .... 13 F5
MBORO TS1 .... 4 C6
Howbeck La *HTLP* TS24 .... 17 F1
Howcroft Av *REDCAR* TS10 .... 67 D3 🔢
Howden Dike *YARM* TS15 .... 146 C1
Howden Rd *HTLP* TS24 .... 12 A3
NACLF DL5 .... 55 D3
Howe St *MBORO* TS1 .... 98 A1
Howlbeck Rd *GUIS* TS14 .... 128 C2
Howson Crs *NACLF* DL5 .... 38 C3
Hoylake Cl *MARSKE* TS11 .... 86 C3 🔢
Hoylake Rd *MGRV/ESTR* TS4 .... 98 B5
Hoylake Wy *EGG/EAG* TS16 .... 137 E2
Huckelhoven Wy *HTLP* TS24 .... 2 D3
Hudson St *FYHL* DL17 .... 20 C1
TEESM TS2 .... 78 B2 🔢
Hudswell Gv *STOCS* TS18 .... 93 E4 🔢
Hugill Gv *YARM* TS15 .... 146 C1
Hulam Cl *STOCN* TS19 .... 73 F3 🔢
Hullock Rd *NACLF* DL5 .... 38 C5 🔢
Hulton Cl *MTN/NUN* TS7 .... 126 B4 🔢
Humber Cl *LOFT/ST* TS13 .... 113 F4
Humber Gv *BLGHMW/WYN* TS22 .. 40 C5 🔢
Humber Pl *DARLE* DL1 .... 132 A4
Humber Rd *HTLPS* TS25 .... 121 F1 🔢
Humbledon Rd *STOCN* TS19 .... 73 F3 🔢
Hume St *STOCS* TS18 .... 7 F2
Humewood Gv *NORTON* TS20 .... 58 A5
Hummersea Cl
SALT/BTN/SK TS12 .... 91 D4 🔢
Hummersea La *LOFT/ST* TS13 .... 113 E1
Hummershill La *MARSKE* TS11 .... 70 C5
Hummersknott Av *DARLW* DL3 ...... 130 C2
Humphrey Cl *NACLF* DL5 .... 38 B5
Hundale Crs *REDCAR* TS10 .... 69 D4
Hunden's La *DARLE* DL1 .... 116 C5
DARLE DL1 .... 133 D1
Hunley Av *SALT/BTN/SK* TS12 .... 91 D4
Hunley Cl *SALT/BTN/SK* TS12 .... 91 D4
Hunstanton Gv *MARSKE* TS11 ...... 86 B3 🔢
Hunstanworth Rd *DARLW* DL3 .... 114 C4
Huntcliffe Av *REDCAR* TS10 .... 67 F2
Huntcliffe Dr *SALT/BTN/SK* TS12 ...... 90 C4
Hunter Rd *NACLF* DL5 .... 54 C1

Huntersgate *ESTON* TS6 .... 102 C2
Hunters Gn *NACLF* DL5 .... 37 E4
Huntershaw Wy *DARLW* DL3 .... 116 A1 🔢
Hunter St *HTLPW* TS26 .... 2 A2
Huntley Cl *NORM/PKE* TS3 .... 100 A5
Huntley St *DARLE* DL1 .... 9 H6
Huntly Rd *HTLPS* TS25 .... 23 D5
Hunwick Cl *ACK/BRKF* TS5 .... 123 D2 🔢
Hurn Wk *THNBY* TS17 .... 122 A2
Hurst Pk *REDCAR* TS10 .... 68 C2
Hurworth Cl *STOCN* TS19 .... 92 C1 🔢
Hurworth Hunt *NACLF* DL5 .... 37 F5
Hurworth Rd *BLGHM* TS23 .... 42 B3
MGRV/ESTR TS4 .... 98 C4 🔢
NACLF DL5 .... 54 B3
Hurworth St *HTLP* TS24 .... 18 A3 🔢
Hury Rd *NORTON* TS20 .... 123 C4
Hustler Rd *ACK/BRKF* TS5 .... 123 E4 🔢
Hutchinson St *BAUK* DL14 .... 27 D2 🔢
SALT/BTN/SK TS12 .... 91 D5
STOCS TS18 .... 7 E3
Hutone Pl *HTLP* TS24 .... 12 A3
Hutton Av *DARLE* DL1 .... 117 D3
HTLPW TS26 .... 17 E4
Hutton Cl *BAUK* DL14 .... 27 E5
THNBY TS17 .... 95 E5
Hutton Gv *REDCAR* TS10 .... 67 D3
STOCS TS18 .... 93 F1 🔢
Hutton La *GUIS* TS14 .... 128 A5
Hutton Rd *ESTON* TS6 .... 102 C1
MGRV/ESTR TS4 .... 99 D1
Hutton St *HTLP* TS24 .... 13 E5
Huxley Gv *DARLE* DL1 .... 133 D2
Huxley Wk *HTLPS* TS25 .... 23 D3
Hylton Cl *NACLF* DL5 .... 39 E4
Hylton Gv *NORTON* TS20 .... 74 C3 🔢
Hylton Rd *BLGHM* TS23 .... 59 E1
HTLPW TS26 .... 16 C5
Hythe Cl *REDCAR* TS10 .... 69 E4

I

Ian Gv *HTLPS* TS25 .... 31 D1
Ianson Sq *DARLE* DL1 .... 9 G3
Ianson St *DARLW* DL3 .... 116 A2
Ian St *THNBY* TS17 .... 95 F4
Ibbetson St *HTLP* TS24 .... 19 E1 🔢
Iber Gv *HTLPS* TS25 .... 31 D1
Ibrox Gv *HTLPS* TS25 .... 31 D1
Ickworth Ct *THNBY* TS17 .... 139 D2
Idaho Gdns *DARLE* DL1 .... 116 C2 🔢
Ida Rd *NORM/PKE* TS3 .... 99 D1
Ida St *NORTON* TS20 .... 74 C3
Ilam Ct *THNBY* TS17 .... 139 D2 🔢
Ilford Rd *STOCN* TS19 .... 73 E1
Ilford Wy *NORM/PKE* TS3 .... 99 F4 🔢
Ilkley Gv *GUIS* TS14 .... 128 C5
HTLPS TS25 .... 24 A5 🔢
Imeson St *ESTON* TS6 .... 102 B3 🔢
Imperial Av *NORTON* TS20 .... 75 D3
THNBY TS17 .... 95 F4
Imperial Crs *NORTON* TS20 .... 75 D3
Imperial Rd *BLGHM* TS23 .... 75 F1
Inchcape Rd *HTLPS* TS25 .... 31 D1
Inch Gv *HTLPS* TS25 .... 31 D1
Ingham Gv *HTLPS* TS25 .... 30 C2
Ingleborough La *THNBY* TS17 .... 139 D3
Ingleby Cl *ESTON* TS6 .... 102 C1
Ingleby Gv *STOCS* TS18 .... 93 F3
Ingleby Moor Crs *DARLE* DL1 .... 133 E4
Ingleby Rd *HTLPS* TS25 .... 33 D1 🔢
MGRV/ESTR TS4 .... 99 D1
Ingleby Wy *THNBY* TS17 .... 138 C1
Inglesgarth Ct *SPEN* DL16 .... 14 C4
Ingleside Ms *SALT/BTN/SK* TS12 .. 89 E2 🔢
Ingleton Rd *STOCN* TS19 .... 73 E1
Inglewood Av *MARSKE* TS11 .... 70 B5 🔢
Inglewood Cl *DARLE* DL1 .... 116 C3
NORM/PKE TS3 .... 100 C2
Ingoldsby Rd *NORM/PKE* TS3 .... 100 C2
Ingram Gv *THNBY* TS17 .... 138 C3 🔢
Ingram Rd *NORM/PKE* TS3 .... 99 E2
Ingrove Cl *STOCN* TS19 .... 73 E1 🔢
Ings La *SALT/BTN/SK* TS12 .... 91 E4
Ings Rd *REDCAR* TS10 .... 51 F5
Inkerman St *STOCS* TS18 .... 7 F5 🔢
Innes Rd *HTLPS* TS25 .... 31 D1
Innes St *TEESM* TS2 .... 78 A2
Institute Ter *ESTON* TS6 .... 81 F3
Instow Cl *STOCN* TS19 .... 73 E2 🔢
Inveraray Cl *DARLE* DL1 .... 117 F1 🔢
Inverness Rd *HTLPS* TS25 .... 31 D1
Ipswich Av *NORM/PKE* TS3 .... 99 F4
Irene St *LOFT/ST* TS13 .... 112 B1 🔢
Irthing Cl *THNBY* TS17 .... 138 C3 🔢
Irvin Av *BAUK* DL14 .... 26 C4
SALT/BTN/SK TS12 .... 91 D4
Irvine Rd *HTLPS* TS25 .... 31 D1
NORM/PKE TS3 .... 99 E1 🔢
Isherwood Cl *NACLF* DL5 .... 54 C1
Islay Gv *HTLPS* TS25 .... 31 D1 🔢
Italy St *TEESM* TS2 .... 5 E1

Ivanhoe Crs *HTLPS* TS25 .... 31 D1
Iveston Gv *BLGHMW/WYN* TS22 .... 57 F1
Ivy Cl *NORTON* TS20 .... 74 C3
   SPEN DL16 .... 15 D4
Ivy Gv *HTLP* TS24 .... 17 E1
Ivywood Ct *DARLW* DL3 .... 115 F3 🗗

J

Jackson Dr *GTAY/STK* TS9 .... 152 A1
Jackson Pl *NACLF* DL5 .... 39 E5 🗗
Jackson St *HTLPS* TS25 .... 23 F2
   SALT/BTN/SK TS12 .... 111 D1
   SPEN DL16 .... 14 C3
Jameson Rd *HTLPS* TS25 .... 22 C5
   NORTON TS20 .... 57 F5
James St *DARLE* DL1 .... 116 B4
   HTLP TS24 .... 3 E4
   NORM/PKE TS3 .... 79 D5
   SPEN DL16 .... 15 D3
Japonica Wy *NORTON* TS20 .... 74 C3
Jasmine Av *SHIL* DL4 .... 35 F3
Jasmine Gv *MTN/NUN* TS7 .... 125 E3 🗗
Jasmine Rd *STOCN* TS19 .... 74 B4
Jay Av *THNBY* TS17 .... 139 F2
Jaywood Cl *RHTLP* TS27 .... 11 D3
Jedburgh Dr *DARLW* DL3 .... 114 A3
Jedburgh Rd *HTLPS* TS25 .... 22 C5 🗗
Jedburgh St *MBORO* TS1 .... 5 H5
Jefferson St *NORM/PKE* TS3 ...... 79 E5 🔟
Jenison Cl *NACLF* DL5 .... 53 E3
Jenkins Dr *BAUK* DL14 .... 27 D5
The Jennings *ESTON* TS6 .... 101 F3 🗗
Jersey St *HTLP* TS24 .... 2 D2
Jervaulx Rd *SALT/BTN/SK* TS12 .. 109 F2
Jesmond Av *ACK/BRKF* TS5 .... 97 E4
Jesmond Ct *NACLF* DL5 .... 37 F4
Jesmond Gdns *HTLPW* TS26 .... 17 E2
Jesmond Gv *STOCS* TS18 .... 93 E4
Jesmond Ms *HTLP* TS24 .... 17 F3
Jesmond Rd *DARLE* DL1 .... 117 F2
   HTLP TS24 .... 17 E3
Jobson St *HTLPW* TS26 .... 17 F3 🗗
John Dixon La *DARLE* DL1 .... 132 C1
John Dobbin Rd *DARLE* DL1 .... 9 G3
Johnson Gv *NORTON* TS20 .... 74 B3
Johnson St *HTLPW* TS26 .... 2 B3
   MBORO TS1 .... 5 E3
Johnston Av *SALT/BTN/SK* TS12 ... 89 D2
John St *DARLE* DL1 .... 9 G1
   GTAY/STK TS9 .... 150 C2
   HTLP TS24 .... 3 E2 🗗
   LOFT/ST TS13 .... 113 E5
   SALT/BTN/SK TS12 .... 109 F2
   SHIL DL4 .... 35 E2
Joicey Cl *HTLPW* TS26 .... 2 A1 🗗
Jones Rd *ESTON* TS6 .... 81 D3
   HTLP TS24 .... 12 B5
Joppa Gv *HTLPS* TS25 .... 23 D5
Jowitt Rd *HTLP* TS24 .... 12 B5
Joyce Rd *HTLP* TS24 .... 12 A4
Jubilee Bank *MTN/NUN* TS7 .... 100 C5
Jubilee Crs *SHIL* DL4 .... 36 A3
Jubilee Gv *BLGHMW/WYN* TS22 .... 58 B1
Jubilee Rd *ESTON* TS6 .... 102 B3
   SHIL DL4 .... 35 F3 🗗
Jubilee St *NORM/PKE* TS3 .... 79 E5
Junction Rd *STOCN* TS19 .... 56 C5
Juniper Gv *MTN/NUN* TS7 .... 126 B3
   SEDG TS21 .... 92 A5
Jura Dr *DARLE* DL1 .... 117 E1
Jura Gv *HTLPS* TS25 .... 23 D5
Jute Gv *HTLPS* TS25 .... 22 C5 🗗
Jutland Rd *HTLPS* TS25 .... 24 A5

K

Kader Av *ACK/BRKF* TS5 .... 123 D2
Kader Farm Rd *ACK/BRKF* TS5 .... 123 E2
Karles Cl *NACLF* DL5 .... 38 B2
Katherine St *DARLE* DL1 .... 116 B4
Kathleen St *HTLPS* TS25 .... 24 A2
Kay Gv *DARLE* DL1 .... 133 D2 🗗
Kearsley Cl *EGG/EAG* TS16 .... 119 F2 🗗
Keasdon Cl *NORM/PKE* TS3 .... 99 D2 🗗
Keats Ct *DARLE* DL1 .... 133 D3
Keats Rd *ESTON* TS6 .... 101 F3
Keay St *ACK/BRKF* TS5 .... 97 E1 🗗
Kedleston Cl *STOCN* TS19 .... 73 F4 🗗
Kedleston Pk *CNHM/HEM* TS8 .... 144 A1
Kedward Av *NORM/PKE* TS3 .... 100 A1
Keepers La *THNBY* TS17 .... 139 D1
Keighley Av *CNHM/HEM* TS8 .... 125 D2
Keilder Cl *REDCAR* TS10 .... 68 A4
Keilder Ri *CNHM/HEM* TS8 .... 124 A5
Keir Hardie Crs *ESTON* TS6 .... 81 D3
Keithlands Av *NORTON* TS20 .... 75 D2
Keith Rd *MGRV/ESTR* TS4 .... 98 B4 🗗
Keithwood Cl *MGRV/ESTR* TS4 ... 98 B4 🗗
Keld Cl *THNBY* TS17 .... 139 D4 🗗

Keld Gv *STOCN* TS19 .... 92 C2
Keldmere *SPEN* DL16 .... 14 B1 🗗
Keld Rd *NACLF* DL5 .... 38 A5
Kelfield Av *NORM/PKE* TS3 .... 100 A2
Kelling Cl *BLGHM* TS23 .... 42 A4
Kelloe Cl *STOCN* TS19 .... 73 E2 🗗
Kells Gv *HTLPS* TS25 .... 22 C5
Kelsall Cl *NORM/PKE* TS3 .... 100 A4
Kelso Ct *NORM/PKE* TS3 .... 99 E3
Kelso Gv *HTLPS* TS25 .... 22 C5
Kelsterne Cl *YARM* TS15 .... 146 C1
Kelvin Gv *HTLPS* TS25 .... 22 C5
   NORM/PKE TS3 .... 99 F4
Kelvin St *FYHL* DL17 .... 20 B1
Kempston Wy *NORTON* TS20 .... 74 A1
Kempton Cl *FYHL* DL17 .... 39 D2
Kendal Cl *DARLE* DL1 .... 131 F3
Kendal Ct *MGRV/ESTR* TS4 .... 98 C3
Kendal Gv *REDCAR* TS10 .... 68 B2
Kendal Rd *HTLPS* TS25 .... 24 A2
   STOCS TS18 .... 93 E4
Kendrew Cl *NACLF* DL5 .... 38 C4
Kendrew St *DARLW* DL3 .... 9 F5 🗗
Kenilworth Av *NORM/PKE* TS3 ... 100 A4
Kenilworth Ct *NACLF* DL5 .... 39 D3 🗗
Kenilworth Dr *DARLW* DL3 .... 114 C3
Kenilworth Rd *BLGHM* TS23 .... 59 D1
Kenilworth Wy *REDCAR* TS10 .... 69 E3
Kenley Gdns *NORTON* TS20 .... 57 D5
Kenmir St *SPEN* DL16 .... 15 E3 🗗
Kenmore Rd *NORM/PKE* TS3 ...... 100 B3
Kennedy Gv *NORTON* TS20 .... 74 B2 🗗
Kennel La *DARLE* DL1 .... 117 F4
Kennthorpe *MTN/NUN* TS7 .... 126 B4 🗗
Kensington Av *ESTON* TS6 .... 101 F4
Kensington Gdns *DARLE* DL1 ...... 133 D2
Kensington Rd *ACK/BRKF* TS5 .... 97 F1
   STOCS TS18 .... 94 B3
Kent Av *HTLPS* TS25 .... 24 A2
Kent Cl *MTN/NUN* TS7 .... 127 D4
   REDCAR TS10 .... 68 A2
Kent Gv *NORTON* TS20 .... 75 E2 🗗
Kentmere *SPEN* DL16 .... 14 C1
Kentmere Rd *NORM/PKE* TS3 ...... 99 E3
Kenton Cl *STOCS* TS18 .... 93 E4
Kent Rd *GUIS* TS14 .... 128 C4 🗗
Kenville Gv *STOCN* TS19 .... 72 C5
Kepier Cl *STOCN* TS19 .... 73 E2
Kepple Av *NORM/PKE* TS3 .... 99 E3
Kepwick Cl *ACK/BRKF* TS5 .... 124 A1 🗗
Kerridge Cl *MARSKE* TS11 .... 70 B5 🗗
Kesteven Rd *HTLPS* TS25 .... 30 C1
   MGRV/ESTR TS4 .... 125 D2
Kestrel Av *NORM/PKE* TS3 .... 79 F5
Kestrel Cl *HTLPW* TS26 .... 16 B2
   NORTON TS20 .... 57 F4
Kestrel Hide *GUIS* TS14 .... 128 A3 🗗
Keswick Dr *SPEN* DL16 .... 15 F2 🗗
Keswick Gv *ACK/BRKF* TS5 .... 123 E1
Keswick Rd *BLGHM* TS23 .... 58 C5
   ESTON TS6 .... 101 E2
   REDCAR TS10 .... 68 B2
Keswick St *HTLPW* TS26 .... 2 A5
Kettleness Av *REDCAR* TS10 .... 67 F1
Kettlewell Cl *BLGHM* TS23 .... 41 F5
Ketton Rd *STOCN* TS19 .... 73 E2
Ketton Wy *NACLF* DL5 .... 54 C5
Keverstone Cl *STOCN* TS19 .... 73 F2 🗗
Keverstone Gv *BLGHM* TS23 ...... 42 B3 🗗
Kew Gdns *NORTON* TS20 .... 57 D5
Kew Ri *DARLW* DL3 .... 114 C5
   ESTON TS6 .... 101 E5
Kielder Cl *BLGHMW/WYN* TS22 ... 57 F1
Kielder Dr *DARLE* DL1 .... 117 E3
Kilbride Cl *THNBY* TS17 .... 96 A5 🗗
Kilburn Rd *MGRV/ESTR* TS4 .... 98 C4
   STOCS TS18 .... 93 F3
Kilburn St *SHIL* DL4 .... 35 F5 🗗
Kildale Gv *HTLPS* TS25 .... 32 C1
   REDCAR TS10 .... 67 F2
   STOCN TS19 .... 92 C2
Kildale Moor Pl *DARLE* DL1 .... 133 E3 🗗
Kildale Rd *BLGHM* TS23 .... 58 C3
   MGRV/ESTR TS4 .... 99 D2
Kildare St *MBORO* TS1 .... 97 F1
Kildwick Gv *NORM/PKE* TS3 .... 100 A4
Kilkenny Rd *GUIS* TS14 .... 129 D4
Killinghall Gv *STOCS* TS18 .... 92 C2
Killinghall St *DARLE* DL1 .... 116 C5
Killin Rd *DARLE* DL1 .... 117 E2
Kilmarnock Rd *DARLE* DL1 .... 117 E1
   HTLPS TS25 .... 30 C1
Kilmarsh Cl *BLGHM* TS23 .... 42 B3
Kilnwick Cl *BLGHM* TS23 .... 58 B3
   MGRV/ESTR TS4 .... 99 D2
Kilton Cl *REDCAR* TS10 .... 69 D2
   STOCN TS19 .... 73 F2 🗗
Kilton Ct *MGRV/ESTR* TS4 .... 98 B3
Kilton Dro *SALT/BTN/SK* TS12 .... 91 E5 🗗
Kilton La *LOFT/ST* TS13 .... 111 F4
   SALT/BTN/SK TS12 .... 91 E5
Kilton Thorpe La
   SALT/BTN/SK TS12 .... 111 E3

Kilwick St *HTLP* TS24........................ 2 B4
Kimberley Dr *NORM/PKE* TS3 ...... 99 F2
Kimberley St *HTLPW* TS26 .... 23 F1
Kimble Dr *THNBY* TS17 .... 121 E3
Kimmerton Av *ACK/BRKF* TS5 ..... 123 E2
Kinbrace Rd *HTLPS* TS25 .... 30 C1
Kindersley St *NORM/PKE* TS3 .... 79 E5 🔟
Kinderton Gv *NORTON* TS20 .... 74 A1
Kingcraft Rd *CNHM/HEM* TS8 .... 125 D2
King Edward's Rd *MBORO* TS1 ...... 5 F5 🗗
King Edward St *SHIL* DL4 .... 35 F2 🗗
King James St *SPEN* DL16 .... 15 D2 🗗
King Oswy Dr *HTLP* TS24 .... 11 F3
Kings Ct *NORTON* TS20 .... 75 D1
Kingsdale Cl *YARM* TS15 .... 146 A2
Kingsdown Wy *MARSKE* TS11 ..... 86 C3
Kings Dr *NACLF* DL5 .... 38 B4
Kingsley Av *HTLPS* TS25 .... 23 E2
Kingsley Cl *ESTON* TS6 .... 82 A5
Kingsley Rd *ESTON* TS6 .... 82 A5
   STOCS TS18 .... 93 F2
Kings Ms East *NORM/PKE* TS3 ... 79 D5 🔟
Kings Ms West *NORM/PKE* TS3 ... 79 D5 🔟
Kingsport Cl *STOCS* TS18 .... 75 F5 🗗
Kings Rd *ACK/BRKF* TS5 .... 97 E2
   BLGHMW/WYN TS22 .... 58 B1 🗗
   NORM/PKE TS3 .... 79 D5
Kingston Av *ACK/BRKF* TS5 .... 97 F4
Kingston Rd *NORTON* TS20 .... 75 D4
Kingston St *DARLW* DL3 .... 9 E2
   MBORO TS1 .... 5 E5
King St *DARLW* DL3 .... 9 F3
   ESTON TS6 .... 81 D4
   HTLPS TS25 .... 24 B2
   REDCAR TS10 .... 51 F4 🗗
   SPEN DL16 .... 15 D2
   STOCS TS18 .... 7 G3
   THNBY TS17 .... 95 E4 🗗
Kingsway *BAUK* DL14 .... 27 E1
Kingsway *BLGHM* TS23 .... 58 C2
   DARLE DL1 .... 116 C2 🗗
Kingsway Av *ESTON* TS6 .... 82 A5 🗗
King William St *DARLE* DL1 .... 132 C2 🗗
   SPEN DL16 .... 15 D2 🗗
Kininvie Cl *REDCAR* TS10 .... 68 B5 🗗
Kinloch Rd *ESTON* TS6 .... 101 E2
Kinloss Cl *THNBY* TS17 .... 122 A2
Kinmel Cl *REDCAR* TS10 .... 69 D4 🗗
Kinross Av *NORM/PKE* TS3 .... 100 A4 🗗
Kinross Gv *HTLPS* TS25 .... 22 C5
Kintra Rd *HTLPS* TS25 .... 22 C5
Kintyre Cl *DARLE* DL1 .... 117 F1 🗗
Kintyre Dr *THNBY* TS17 .... 121 E5
Kinver Cl *NORM/PKE* TS3 .... 99 E3
Kipling Gv *STOCN* TS19 .... 93 D2
Kipling Rd *HTLPS* TS25 .... 23 D2
Kirby Av *ACK/BRKF* TS5 .... 97 D3
Kirby Br *GTAY/STK* TS9 .... 152 C4
Kirby Cl *BLGHM* TS23 .... 59 E1 🗗
   ESTON TS6 .... 102 C1
Kirkby La *GTAY/STK* TS9 .... 152 C5
Kirkdale *SPEN* DL16 .... 14 C1
Kirkdale Cl *STOCN* TS19 .... 6 B2
Kirkdale Wy *ACK/BRKF* TS5 .... 124 A1
Kirkfell Cl *EGG/EAG* TS16 .... 119 D5 🗗
Kirkfield Rd *DARLW* DL3 .... 116 B1
Kirkgate Rd *ACK/BRKF* TS5 .... 97 E4
Kirkham Cl *NACLF* DL5 .... 38 C3
Kirkham Rd *MTN/NUN* TS7 .... 127 D4
Kirkham Rw *MGRV/ESTR* TS4 ...... 99 D5
Kirkham Wy *BAUK* DL14 .... 27 F3
The Kirklands *MARSKE* TS11 .... 70 C4
Kirkland Wk *NORM/PKE* TS3 ..... 99 F4 🗗
Kirkleatham Av *MARSKE* TS11 ...... 70 C4
Kirkleatham La *REDCAR* TS10 ...... 50 C5
   REDCAR TS10 .... 67 F5
Kirkleatham St *REDCAR* TS10 ...... 50 C5
Kirknewton Cl *STOCN* TS19 .... 73 E2 🗗
Kirknewton Gv *THNBY* TS17 ...... 138 C3 🗗
Kirknewton Rd *ESTON* TS6 .... 101 E3
Kirk Rd *YARM* TS15 .... 147 D1
Kirkstall Crs *DARLW* DL3 .... 114 C4
Kirkstone Cl *HTLP* TS24 .... 17 F1 🗗
Kirkstone Gv *HTLP* TS24 .... 17 E1
   REDCAR TS10 .... 68 B2 🗗
Kirkstone Pl *NACLF* DL5 .... 54 A1
Kirkstone Rd *NORM/PKE* TS3 .... 99 E3
Kirkwall Cl *STOCN* TS19 .... 72 B5
Kirriemuir Rd *HTLPS* TS25 .... 22 C5 🗗
Kitchen Av *BAUK* DL14 .... 26 C4
Kitchener St *DARLW* DL3 .... 9 E1
Kitchener Ter *FYHL* DL17 .... 21 D2
Kitching Gv *DARLW* DL3 .... 116 A3 🗗
Kittiwake Cl *HTLPW* TS26 .... 16 C2
Knapton Av *BLGHMW/WYN* TS22 .. 57 F1
Knaresborough Av *MTN/NUN* TS7 .. 125 F5
Knaresborough Cl *RHTLP* TS27 ... 11 F4 🗗
Knayton Gv *STOCN* TS19 .... 92 C2
Knighton Ct *THNBY* TS17 .... 122 A1
Knightport Rd *STOCS* TS18 .... 75 E5 🗗
Knightsbridge Av *DARLE* DL1 .... 117 F2 🗗
Knightsbridge Gdns
   HTLPW TS26 .... 17 D4 🗗
Knitsley Wk *STOCN* TS19 .... 73 E2
Knole Rd *BLGHM* TS23 .... 59 D1 🗗

Knoll Av *DARLW* DL3 .... 131 E3
Knowles Cl *YARM* TS15 .... 146 B5
Knowles St *STOCS* TS18 .... 7 C4
Kyle Av *HTLPS* TS25 .... 23 F2

L

Laburnum Av *THNBY* TS17 .... 121 E1
Laburnum Gv *TEESM* TS2 .... 78 B1 🔲
Laburnum Rd *BAUK* DL14 .... 27 E2 🔲
  EGG/EAG TS16 .... 119 E5 🔲
  ESTON TS6 .... 101 E1 🔲
  FYHL DL17 .... 21 F5
  MTN/NUN TS7 .... 101 D5
  SALT/BTN/SK TS12 .... 90 C5
Laburnum St *HTLPW* TS26 .... 2 A1 🔲
Lacey Gv *HTLPW* TS26 .... 17 E3 🔲
Lackenby La *ESTON* TS6 .... 102 C1
Ladgate Gra *NORM/PKE* TS3 .... 99 F3
Ladgate La *ACK/BRKF* TS5 .... 124 A4
  MGRV/ESTR TS4 .... 125 D2
Ladyfern Wy *NORTON* TS20 .... 74 B2
Lady Kathryn Gv *DARLW* DL3 .... 115 F4
Ladysmith St *BAUK* DL14 .... 26 C2
  HTLPS TS25 .... 24 B2
Lagonda Ct *BLGHM* TS23 .... 60 B1 🔲
Lagonda Rd *BLGHM* TS23 .... 60 B1
Laindon Av *MGRV/ESTR* TS4 .... 125 E2 🔲
Laing Cl *ESTON* TS6 .... 81 F3
Laing St *DARLW* DL3 .... 115 D4
  STOCS TS19 .... 7 F3
Laird Rd *HTLPS* TS25 .... 22 C5
Lakes Av *REDCAR* TS10 .... 68 B1
Lakeside *DARLE* DL1 .... 131 F4
Lakeside Ct *SPEN* DL16 .... 15 F2
Lakeston Cl *HTLPW* TS26 .... 16 C5 🔲
Lamb Cl *NACLF* DL5 .... 39 D4 🔲
Lambert Rd *HTLP* TS24 .... 12 B4
Lambeth Rd *ACK/BRKF* TS5 .... 97 F3
Lamb La *THNBY* TS17 .... 138 C2
Lambourne Dr *MTN/NUN* TS7 .... 126 A3
Lambton Cl *NACLF* DL5 .... 54 C2 🔲
Lambton Crs *SEDG* TS21 .... 29 D4 🔲
Lambton Dr *BAUK* DL14 .... 26 C3
Lambton Rd *BLGHM* TS23 .... 59 E1 🔲
  FYHL DL17 .... 21 E2
  MGRV/ESTR TS4 .... 98 C2
  STOCS TS19 .... 6 D1
Lambton St *ESTON* TS6 .... 101 F3 🔲
  SHIL DL4 .... 35 D3
Lammermuir Rd *BLGHM* TS23 .... 58 B2
Lamonby Cl *MTN/NUN* TS7 .... 126 B5
Lamont Gv *HTLPS* TS25 .... 22 B5
Lamport Cl *STOCS* TS18 .... 75 F5 🔲
Lamport St *MBORO* TS1 .... 4 B5
Lanark Cl *STOCS* TS19 .... 73 C5 🔲
Lanark Rd *HTLPS* TS25 .... 22 C5
Lancaster Dr *MARSKE* TS11 .... 70 A4 🔲
Lancaster Rd *ACK/BRKF* TS5 .... 98 A3
  HTLP TS24 .... 18 A1 🔲
Lancaster Wy *THNBY* TS17 .... 121 F4
Lancefield Rd *NORTON* TS20 ...... 58 A5 🔲
Lancelot Cl *NACLF* DL5 .... 38 A3
Lancelot St *HTLPW* TS26 .... 17 E4
Lanchester Av *BLGHM* TS23 .... 41 E5
Lanchester Rd *ESTON* TS6 .... 82 A3
The Lanchesters *MARSKE* TS11 ... 70 A5 🔲
Landseer Dr *BLGHM* TS23 .... 41 E5
Lanehouse Rd *THNBY* TS17 .... 95 E5
Laneside Rd *STOCS* TS18 .... 93 E5
The Lane *SEDG* TS21 .... 29 E3
Lanethorpe Crs *DARLE* DL1 .... 133 E3
Lanethorpe Rd *DARLE* DL1 .... 133 E3
Langbaurgh Cl *GTAY/STK* TS9 ..... 150 C2
Langdale Cl *EGG/EAG* TS16 ...... 137 D2 🔲
Langdale Cls *ESTON* TS6 .... 102 A1
Langdale Gv *ACK/BRKF* TS5 ...... 97 F5 🔲
Langdale Pl *NACLF* DL5 .... 53 F1
Langdale Rd *BLGHM* TS23 .... 59 D5 🔲
  DARLE DL1 .... 132 C3
Langdowne Rd
  SALT/BTN/SK TS12 .... 111 E1 🔲
Langholm Crs *DARLW* DL3 .... 8 C6
Langleeford Wy *THNBY* TS17 ...... 138 C3
Langley Av *THNBY* TS17 .... 95 F4
Langley Cl *REDCAR* TS10 .... 68 B4
Langley Gv *BAUK* DL14 .... 26 C3
Langley Rd *NACLF* DL5 .... 39 D5
Langmere *SPEN* DL16 .... 14 C1 🔲
Langridge Crs *NORM/PKE* TS3 ...... 99 E3
Langsett Av *NORM/PKE* TS3 .... 99 E3
Langthorne Gv *STOCS* TS18 .... 92 C3
Langthorpe *MTN/NUN* TS7 .... 126 B4 🔲
Langton Av *BLGHMW/WYN* TS22 .... 57 F1
Langton Cl *MGRV/ESTR* TS4 .... 98 B2
Lansbury Cl *ESTON* TS6 .... 80 C4 🔲
Lansbury Gv *HTLP* TS24 .... 18 A3
Lansdowne Rd *HTLPW* TS26 .... 2 A4
  MGRV/ESTR TS4 .... 98 C1
  THNBY TS17 .... 96 A5
  YARM TS15 .... 137 F5
Lansdowne St *DARLW* DL3 .... 116 A3

Lansdown Wy *BLGHM* TS23 .... 42 B4
Lantsbery Dr *LOFT/ST* TS13 .... 112 C4
The Lanyard *HTLP* TS24 .... 2 D1
Lapwing La *NORTON* TS20 .... 57 F4
Lapwing Rd *HTLPW* TS26 .... 16 C2
Larch Av *SHIL* DL4 .... 36 A3
Larch Cl *MTN/NUN* TS7 .... 126 B3
The Larches *ESTON* TS6 .... 101 D1
  MTN/NUN TS7 .... 127 D1
  REDCAR TS10 .... 69 D3 🔲
Larchfield St *DARLW* DL3 .... 9 E4
Larch Gv *HTLP* TS24 .... 17 F1 🔲
Larch Rd *GUIS* TS14 .... 128 C2 🔲
  STOCS TS19 .... 74 C4 🔲
Larch Ter *TEESM* TS2 .... 78 B1 🔲
Largo Gdns *DARLE* DL1 .... 117 D1
Larkhall Sq *NORTON* TS20 .... 75 D3 🔲
Larkspur Dr *DARLE* DL1 .... 133 D1
Larkspur Rd *CNHM/HEM* TS8 ..... 125 D3
Larkswood Rd *REDCAR* TS10 .... 68 B5
The Larun Beat *YARM* TS15 .... 146 B1
Lascelles Av *NACLF* DL5 .... 37 F4
Lastingham Av *ESTON* TS6 .... 101 F2 🔲
Latham Rd *ACK/BRKF* TS5 .... 97 F2
Latimer La *GUIS* TS14 .... 128 B4
Latimer Rd *DARLE* DL1 .... 117 D4
Lauder Cl *STOCS* TS19 .... 73 D5
Lauderdale Dr *GUIS* TS14 .... 129 E4
Lauder St *HTLPW* TS26 .... 2 B2 🔲
Laura St *MBORO* TS1 .... 98 B1
Laurel Av *MGRV/ESTR* TS4 .... 98 C4
  THNBY TS17 .... 121 E1
Laurel Cl *SALT/BTN/SK* TS12 .... 89 E3
Laurel Crs *SALT/BTN/SK* TS12 .... 90 C5
Laurel Pk *LOFT/ST* TS13 .... 113 D3
Laurel Rd *EGG/EAG* TS16 .... 119 E3 🔲
  FYHL DL17 .... 21 F5
  MTN/NUN TS7 .... 125 F4
  REDCAR TS10 .... 69 E2
  SALT/BTN/SK TS12 .... 89 E3
  STOCS TS19 .... 74 B4
Laurel St *DARLW* DL3 .... 8 C1 🔲
  MBORO TS1 .... 5 H5
Lauriston Cl *DARLW* DL3 .... 130 B2
Lavan Cl *REDCAR* TS10 .... 69 D4
Lavan Sands *ACK/BRKF* TS5 .... 123 D4 🔲
Lavender Ct *MARSKE* TS11 .... 87 F1
Lavender Rd *NORM/PKE* TS3 ...... 99 E1 🔲
Lavender Wy *NORTON* TS20 .... 74 C2 🔲
Lavernock Cl *REDCAR* TS10 .... 69 D5
Lawns Gill *SALT/BTN/SK* TS12 ..... 108 C2
The Lawns *HTLP* TS24 .... 19 E2 🔲
Lawnswood Rd *NORM/PKE* TS3 .... 100 C2
Lawrence Av *THNBY* TS17 .... 121 D1
Lawrence St *DARLE* DL1 .... 132 C2
  REDCAR TS10 .... 51 F5 🔲
  STOCS TS18 .... 94 C3
Lawrenny Gv *THNBY* TS17 .... 138 B3
Lawson Cl *ESTON* TS6 .... 81 D4
  NORM/PKE TS3 .... 79 D5
Lawson Rd *BLGHM* TS23 .... 25 D4
Lawson St *STOCS* TS18 .... 7 E6 🔲
Lawson Wy *NORM/PKE* TS3 .... 79 E4
Lax Ter *BLGHMW/WYN* TS22 .... 41 E3
Laxton Cl *BLGHM* TS23 .... 41 F5 🔲
Laycock St *MBORO* TS1 .... 4 B6
Layland Rd *SALT/BTN/SK* TS12 .... 110 A2
Layton Ct *NACLF* DL5 .... 38 C3
Lazenby Cl *DARLW* DL3 .... 114 C5
Lazenby Crs *DARLW* DL3 .... 114 C5
Lazenby Gv *DARLW* DL3 .... 114 C5 🔲
Lazenby Rd *HTLP* TS24 .... 12 A3
Leach Gv *DARLW* DL3 .... 115 D3
Leadenhall St *DARLE* DL1 .... 9 G2 🔲
Leafield Rd *DARLE* DL1 .... 132 B3
Leahope Ct *THNBY* TS17 .... 122 A3 🔲
Lealholm Crs *NORM/PKE* TS3 ...... 100 A4
Lealholm Gv *STOCS* TS19 .... 93 D2
Lealholm Rd *HTLPS* TS25 .... 23 F5
Lealholm Wy *GUIS* TS14 .... 128 C5
Leamington Dr *HTLPS* TS25 .... 24 A2 🔲
Leamington Gv *NORM/PKE* TS3 .... 100 B4
Leamington Pde *HTLPS* TS25 .... 24 A2
Leam La *STOCS* TS19 .... 72 C3
Leas Gv *HTLP* TS24 .... 13 F5
Leaside *NACLF* DL5 .... 54 C3
Leaside North *NACLF* DL5 .... 54 C3
The Leas *DARLE* DL1 .... 116 B1
  REDCAR TS10 .... 69 D5
  SEDG TS21 .... 29 E5
Leckfell Cl *MTN/NUN* TS7 .... 126 B5 🔲
Ledbury Dr *ACK/BRKF* TS5 .... 123 F4
  THNBY TS17 .... 121 E1 🔲
Ledbury Wy *GUIS* TS14 .... 128 C5
Lee Gn *NACLF* DL5 .... 54 C2
Leeholme Rd *BLGHM* TS23 .... 59 E2
Leeming Rd *ACK/BRKF* TS5 .... 97 E3
Lee Rd *ESTON* TS6 .... 82 A3 🔲
Lees Rd *MBORO* TS1 .... 4 C5
Leicester Gv *DARLE* DL1 .... 117 F3 🔲
Leicester Rd *NORTON* TS20 .... 75 E2
Leicester Wy *EGG/EAG* TS16 ...... 137 D3 🔲
Leighton Rd *ESTON* TS6 .... 82 A4
  STOCS TS19 .... 92 C4
Leinster Rd *MBORO* TS1 .... 97 E1

Leith Rd *DARLW* DL3 .... 130 B2
Lenham Cl *BLGHMW/WYN* TS22 ..... 40 C5
Lennox Crs *BLCHM* TS23 .... 58 C5 🔲
Leonard Ropner Dr *STOCN* TS19 ... 72 B5
Leonard St *DARLE* DL1 .... 132 C3
Lerwick Cl *STOCN* TS19 .... 92 B1
Letch La *SEDG* TS21 .... 72 B1
Letch Rd *NORTON* TS20 .... 58 A5
Leven Bank Rd *YARM* TS15 .... 147 E1
Leven Cl *EGG/EAG* TS16 .... 137 D3
Leven Ct *GTAY/STK* TS9 .... 151 D4 🔲
Levendale Cl *YARM* TS15 .... 138 A3
Leven Gdns *DARLE* DL1 .... 117 D3 🔲
Leven Gv *HTLPS* TS25 .... 22 C5
  THNBY TS17 .... 121 F1 🔲
Leven Rd *GUIS* TS14 .... 128 C4
  NORM/PKE TS3 .... 79 E5
  NORTON TS20 .... 74 C1
  YARM TS15 .... 137 F5
Levenside *GTAY/STK* TS9 .... 150 B3
  GTAY/STK TS9 .... 152 A3
Leven St *BLGHM* TS23 .... 58 C5
  ESTON TS6 .... 80 C3
  MBORO TS1 .... 4 B6
  SALT/BTN/SK TS12 .... 89 E2
Levens Wk *REDCAR* TS10 .... 68 B2 🔲
Leven Wynd *GTAY/STK* TS9 .... 152 A3 🔲
Leveret Cl *THNBY* TS17 .... 121 E5 🔲
Levick Crs *ACK/BRKF* TS5 .... 96 C5
Levington Wynd *MTN/NUN* TS7 ... 126 B5
Levisham Cl *ACK/BRKF* TS5 .... 124 A1 🔲
  STOCS TS18 .... 93 F3 🔲
Lewes Rd *DARLE* DL1 .... 132 C3
Lewes Wy *BLGHM* TS23 .... 42 C3
Lewis Gv *HTLPS* TS25 .... 22 C3
Lewis Rd *ACK/BRKF* TS5 .... 97 F2
Lexden Av *ACK/BRKF* TS5 .... 96 C5
Leybourne Ter *STOCS* TS18 .... 6 D6 🔲
Leyburn Gv *STOCS* TS18 .... 93 D4
Leyburn Rd *DARLE* DL1 .... 116 B3
Leyburn St *HTLPW* TS26 .... 2 A5
Libanus Ct *THNBY* TS17 .... 138 B2 🔲
Lichfield Av *EGG/EAG* TS16 .... 136 C1 🔲
  ESTON TS6 .... 102 A1
Lichfield Rd *ACK/BRKF* TS5 .... 98 B3
Liddell Cl *NACLF* DL5 .... 39 E5
Lightfoot Crs *HTLP* TS24 .... 12 B5
Lightfoot Gv *STOCS* TS18 .... 7 E6
Lightfoot Rd *NACLF* DL5 .... 38 B5
Light Pipe Hall Rd *STOCS* TS18 ..... 6 C5
Lilac Av *THNBY* TS17 .... 121 E1
Lilac Cl *ESTON* TS6 .... 83 E5
  SALT/BTN/SK TS12 .... 88 C3
  SPEN DL16 .... 14 B5
Lilac Crs *SALT/BTN/SK* TS12 .... 90 C5
Lilac Gv *NORM/PKE* TS3 .... 100 A1 🔲
  REDCAR TS10 .... 69 D1
Lilac Rd *EGG/EAG* TS16 .... 119 E3
  ESTON TS6 .... 101 E1
  FYHL DL17 .... 21 F5
  MTN/NUN TS7 .... 126 C1
  STOCN TS19 .... 74 A4
Lilburne Crs *NACLF* DL5 .... 38 C5
Limbrick Av *STOCN* TS19 .... 92 C1
Lime Cl *MTN/NUN* TS7 .... 125 F3 🔲
Lime Crs *ESTON* TS6 .... 101 E2 🔲
  HTLP TS24 .... 17 F2
Lime Gv *BAUK* DL14 .... 27 D5
  SHIL DL4 .... 36 A3
  STOCN TS19 .... 93 D1
Limehurst Rd *DARLW* DL3 .... 8 C1
Limeoak Wy *STOCS* TS18 .... 75 E5
Limerick Rd *REDCAR* TS10 .... 66 C5
Lime Rd *EGG/EAG* TS16 .... 119 F3
  ESTON TS6 .... 101 D1
  FYHL DL17 .... 20 C1
  GUIS TS14 .... 128 C2
Limes Crs *MARSKE* TS11 .... 87 F1
Limes Rd *ACK/BRKF* TS5 .... 98 A3
Lime Tree Cl *TEESM* TS2 .... 61 D5
Limetree Ct *MGRV/ESTR* TS4 ..... 98 B4 🔲
Limpton Ga *YARM* TS15 .... 146 B1
Linacre Wy *DARLE* DL1 .... 116 C2
Linby Av *NORM/PKE* TS3 .... 99 E4
Lincoln Cl *NACLF* DL5 .... 38 B5 🔲
Lincoln Ct *DARLE* DL1 .... 117 F4 🔲
Lincoln Crs *BLGHM* TS23 .... 59 E3 🔲
Lincoln Gv *NORTON* TS20 .... 75 E2
Lincoln Pl *THNBY* TS17 .... 95 E5 🔲
Lincoln Rd *GUIS* TS14 .... 128 C4
  HTLPS TS25 .... 30 C1
Lincombe Dr *ACK/BRKF* TS5 .... 123 F4 🔲
Linden Av *DARLW* DL3 .... 8 A6
  GTAY/STK TS9 .... 150 B3
  STOCS TS18 .... 93 D1
Linden Cl *GTAY/STK* TS9 .... 150 B2 🔲
  SHIL DL4 .... 36 A4
Linden Ct *SPEN* DL16 .... 15 E3
Linden Crs *GTAY/STK* TS9 .... 150 B3
  MTN/NUN TS7 .... 125 E4
Linden Dr *DARLW* DL3 .... 131 E3
Linden Gv *ACK/BRKF* TS5 .... 97 F5
  GTAY/STK TS9 .... 150 B2
  HTLPW TS26 .... 17 E4
  THNBY TS17 .... 95 E5

Linden Pl *NACLF* DL5 .... 53 F1
Linden Rd *BAUK* DL14 .... 27 D3 🔟
FYHL DL17 .... 21 E2
GTAY/STK TS9 .... 150 B3
SALT/BTN/SK TS12 .... 90 C5
Lindisfarne Cl *RHTLP* TS27 .... 11 F4 �
Lindisfarne Rd *NORM/PKE* TS3 .... 100 B4 🞮
Lindrick *CNHM/HEM* TS8 .... 144 C5
Lindrick Cl *ESTON* TS6 .... 102 A3 🞮
Lindrick Dr *RHTLP* TS27 .... 11 E3
Lindrick Rd *MARSKE* TS11 .... 86 B3
Lindsay Rd *HTLPS* TS25 .... 22 B5
Lindsay St *BAUK* DL14 .... 26 C2
STOCS TS18 .... 94 C3 🞮
Lindsey Ct *SALT/BTN/SK* TS12 .... 91 E5
Ling Cl *MTN/NUN* TS7 .... 125 E2 🞮
Lingdale Cl *STOCN* TS19 .... 6 A1
STOCN TS19 .... 74 A4 🞮
Lingdale Dr *HTLPS* TS25 .... 32 C1
Lingdale Gv *REDCAR* TS10 .... 67 E2
Lingdale Rd *THNBY* TS17 .... 121 F2
Lingfield Ash *CNHM/HEM* TS8 .... 143 D1
Lingfield Dr *EGG/EAG* TS16 .... 136 C2
Lingfield Gn *DARLE* DL1 .... 133 F2 🞮
Lingfield Rd *STOCN* TS19 .... 92 C1
YARM TS15 .... 138 A5
Lingfield Wy *CNHM/HEM* TS8 .... 143 E1
Lingholme *REDCAR* TS10 .... 68 A2 🞮
Lingmell Rd *REDCAR* TS10 .... 68 B3
The Links *HTLPS* TS25 .... 33 D1
SALT/BTN/SK TS12 .... 91 E5
The Link *NORM/PKE* TS3 .... 100 B4 🞮
The Linkway *BLGHM* TS23 .... 59 D2
Linley Ct *NORTON* TS20 .... 57 F4 🞮
Linlithgow Cl *GUIS* TS14 .... 128 C5 🞮
Linmoor Av *NORM/PKE* TS3 .... 100 A2 🞮
Linnet Ct *NORTON* TS20 .... 58 A4
Linnet Rd *HTLPW* TS26 .... 17 D1
Linshiels Gv *THNBY* TS17 .... 138 C3
Linthorpe Rd *ACK/BRKF* TS5 .... 98 A2 🞮
MBORO TS1 .... 5 F3
Linton Av *MTN/NUN* TS7 .... 125 E4
Linton Cl *STOCN* TS19 .... 73 D3
Linton Rd *ESTON* TS6 .... 101 D3
Linwood Av *GTAY/STK* TS9 .... 152 B1
Linwood Gv *DARLW* DL3 .... 131 E4 🞮
Lisle Rd *NACLF* DL5 .... 37 F4
Lismore Dr *DARLE* DL1 .... 117 E1
Lister St *HTLPW* TS26 .... 2 A1
Lithgo Cl *HTLPS* TS25 .... 25 D3
Little Ayton La *GTAY/STK* TS9 .... 151 D3
Littlebeck Dr *DARLE* DL1 .... 117 D3
Littleboy Dr *THNBY* TS17 .... 96 A5
Little Crake *GUIS* TS14 .... 128 A3
Little La *NACLF* DL5 .... 55 D5
Littondale Ct *THNBY* TS17 .... 138 C4 🞮
Liverton Av *ACK/BRKF* TS5 .... 97 E5 🞮
Liverton Crs *BLGHMW/WYN* TS22 .... 41 D5
THNBY TS17 .... 121 D4
Liverton Rd *LOFT/ST* TS13 .... 113 D3 🞮
Liverton Ter *LOFT/ST* TS13 .... 112 C4
Liverton Whin *SALT/BTN/SK* TS12 .... 88 C2
Livingstone Rd *NORM/PKE* TS3 .... 79 E5
Lizard Gv *HTLP* TS24 .... 2 D4
Lloyd St *TEESM* TS2 .... 4 D1
Lobelia Ct *MTN/NUN* TS7 .... 101 D5 🞮
Lobster Rd *REDCAR* TS10 .... 51 D4
Loch Gv *HTLPS* TS25 .... 22 C5 🞮
Locke Rd *REDCAR* TS10 .... 51 D5
Lockheed Cl *STOCS* TS18 .... 120 B2
Lockton Cl *CNHM/HEM* TS8 .... 141 E1 🞮
Lockton Crs *THNBY* TS17 .... 121 D4
Lockwood Ct *ESTON* TS6 .... 102 A3
Lockyer Cl *NACLF* DL5 .... 38 A5
Locomotive St *DARLE* DL1 .... 117 D2
Lodge Rd *ESTON* TS6 .... 102 A2
Lodge St *DARLE* DL1 .... 9 H3
STOCS TS18 .... 7 F5
Lodore Gv *ACK/BRKF* TS5 .... 123 D1
Loftus Bank *LOFT/ST* TS13 .... 112 C2
Loftus Rd *THNBY* TS17 .... 95 F5
Logan Dr *STOCN* TS19 .... 93 E1
Logan Gv *HTLPS* TS25 .... 22 C5
Lomond Av *BLGHM* TS23 .... 59 D3
Londonderry Rd *STOCN* TS19 .... 6 C1
Londonderry St *HTLP* TS24 .... 19 E2 🞮
Longacre Cl *SALT/BTN/SK* TS12 ...... 89 E5 🞮
Longbank Rd *MTN/NUN* TS7 .... 127 D1
Longbeck La *MARSKE* TS11 .... 86 A3
Longbeck Rd *MARSKE* TS11 .... 87 D1
Longbeck Wy *THNBY* TS17 .... 122 A4
Longfellow Rd *BLGHM* TS23 .... 41 F3
Longfield Rd *BAUK* DL14 .... 27 E4
DARLW DL3 .... 116 A1
Longfield Vw *ESTON* TS6 .... 101 E5
Longford Cl *BLGHM* TS23 .... 42 A5 🞮
Longford St *MBORO* TS1 .... 97 E1
Longhurst *CNHM/HEM* TS8 .... 143 E1
Longlands Rd *MGRV/ESTR* TS4 .... 98 C1
NORM/PKE TS3 .... 79 F5
Longshaw Cl *THNBY* TS17 .... 139 E1 🞮
Longworth Wy *GUIS* TS14 .... 129 E1 🞮
Lonsdale Gv *REDCAR* TS10 .... 67 D3
Lonsdale St *MBORO* TS1 .... 97 F1
Loraine Cl *MARSKE* TS11 .... 88 A1

Loraine Crs *DARLE* DL1 .... 132 A4
Lord Av *THNBY* TS17 .... 121 F5
Lord Neville Dr *NACLF* DL5 .... 53 E5
Lord St *REDCAR* TS10 .... 51 F4
Lorimer Cl *THNBY* TS17 .... 139 D1 🞮
Lorne St *MBORO* TS1 .... 4 C6
Lorrain Gv *NORTON* TS20 .... 58 B5
Lorton Rd *REDCAR* TS10 .... 68 B3
Lothian Cl *SPEN* DL16 .... 14 C4
Lothian Gv *NACLF* DL5 .... 67 F1 🞮
Lothian Rd *MGRV/ESTR* TS4 .... 98 C1
Lough House Bank *FYHL* DL17 .... 21 F3
Louisa St *DARLE* DL1 .... 132 C2
Lovaine St *MBORO* TS1 .... 4 D6
Lovat Av *REDCAR* TS10 .... 67 E1
Lovat Gv *HTLPS* TS25 .... 22 C5 🞮
Low Church Wynd *YARM* TS15 ...... 137 D3 🞮
Low Cleveland St *LOFT/ST* TS13 .... 112 C3
Lowcross Av *GUIS* TS14 .... 128 B5
Lowdale La *HTLP* TS24 .... 11 E3
Lowell Cl *BLGHM* TS23 .... 42 A5 🔟
Lower East St *TEESM* TS2 .... 5 C1
Lower Feversham St *TEESM* TS2 .... 5 C1
Lower Gosford St *TEESM* TS2 .... 5 C1
Lowery Rd *NACLF* DL5 .... 54 B1
Lowe St *DARLW* DL3 .... 9 E3
Loweswater Crs *STOCS* TS18 .... 93 F1 🞮
Loweswater Gv *REDCAR* TS10 .... 68 B3 🞮
Low Farm Dr *REDCAR* TS10 .... 68 A3
Lowfield Av *NORM/PKE* TS3 .... 100 A1 🞮
Lowfields *NACLF* DL5 .... 53 E3 🞮
Lowfields Av *THNBY* TS17 .... 121 D5
Low Fold *REDCAR* TS10 .... 68 A2 🞮
Low Grange Av *BLGHM* TS23 .... 42 A3
Low Grange Rd *SPEN* DL16 .... 15 E2
Low Gn *FYHL* DL17 .... 38 C2
GTAY/STK TS9 .... 150 A3
Lowick Cl *STOCN* TS19 .... 75 D4
Low La *CNHM/HEM* TS8 .... 124 A4
CNHM/HEM TS8 .... 140 C1
YARM TS15 .... 139 F4
Lowood Av *MTN/NUN* TS7 .... 125 E4 🔟
Lowson St *DARLW* DL3 .... 116 B2 🔟
Low Stanghow Rd
SALT/BTN/SK TS12 .... 109 F2
Lowther Cl *BLGHMW/WYN* TS22 .... 40 C5 🞮
Lowther Dr *NACLF* DL5 .... 39 D3
Lowther Rd *BAUK* DL14 .... 26 C5
Lowthian Rd *HTLPW* TS26 .... 2 A1
Loxley Rd *NORM/PKE* TS3 .... 100 C2
Loyalty Cl *HTLPS* TS25 .... 24 A3
Loyalty Rd *HTLPS* TS25 .... 24 A4
Lucan St *HTLPW* TS26 .... 2 B2
Luccombe Cl *THNBY* TS17 .... 139 D4 🞮
Lucerne Ct *MTN/NUN* TS7 .... 125 E3 🞮
Lucerne Dr *REDCAR* TS10 .... 68 A4
Lucerne Rd *REDCAR* TS10 .... 68 A4
Luce Sands *ACK/BRKF* TS5 .... 123 D4
Lucia La *GUIS* TS14 .... 128 B4
Lucknow St *DARLE* DL1 .... 116 C5 🔟
Ludford Av *NORM/PKE* TS3 .... 99 F4
Ludham Gv *STOCN* TS19 .... 73 E4
Ludlow Crs *REDCAR* TS10 .... 69 D2
Ludlow Rd *BLGHM* TS23 .... 58 C1 🞮
Luff Wy *REDCAR* TS10 .... 69 D3 🞮
Lulsgate *THNBY* TS17 .... 122 A2
Lulworth Gv *HTLP* TS24 .... 11 F3 🞮
Lumley Cl *NACLF* DL5 .... 54 C1
SPEN DL16 .... 15 E1
Lumley Crs *FYHL* DL17 .... 21 E2
Lumley Gv *BAUK* DL14 .... 26 C3 🞮
Lumley Rd *BLGHM* TS23 .... 59 D1 🞮
REDCAR TS10 .... 51 F5
Lumley St *LOFT/ST* TS13 .... 112 C2
Lumpsey Cl *SALT/BTN/SK* TS12 .... 91 D5
Lundy Ct *THNBY* TS17 .... 139 D2 🞮
Lunebeck Wk *THNBY* TS17 .... 122 A4
Lunedale Av *ACK/BRKF* TS5 .... 97 E5
Lunedale Rd *BLGHM* TS23 .... 58 C5
DARLW DL3 .... 130 C1 🞮
Lune Rd *EGG/EAG* TS16 .... 137 D3
NORTON TS20 .... 74 C2
Lune St *SALT/BTN/SK* TS12 .... 89 E2
Lusby Crs *BAUK* DL14 .... 26 C5
Lustrum Av *STOCS* TS18 .... 76 B4
Lutton Crs *BLGHMW/WYN* TS22 .... 57 F1
Luttryngton Ct *NACLF* DL5 .... 37 F4
Lycium Cl *MTN/NUN* TS7 .... 125 E2
Lydbrook Rd *ACK/BRKF* TS5 .... 97 D2
Lyn Cl *THNBY* TS17 .... 139 D4
Lyndon Wy *STOCN* TS19 .... 92 C1
Lyne Rd *SPEN* DL16 .... 14 B5
Lynmouth Cl *CNHM/HEM* TS8 .... 123 E5
Lynmouth Rd *NORTON* TS20 .... 57 F5
Lynne Cl *DARLW* DL3 .... 116 B1 🞮
Lynnfield Rd *HTLPW* TS26 .... 2 B1 🞮
Lynn St *HTLP* TS24 .... 3 E2
Lynn St South *HTLP* TS24 .... 3 E4
Lynton Gdns *DARLE* DL1 .... 133 E2 🞮
Lynwood Av *ACK/BRKF* TS5 .... 98 A5 🞮
Lyonette Rd *DARLE* DL1 .... 117 D2
Lyon St *NACLF* DL5 .... 54 C1
Lysander Ct *MARSKE* TS11 .... 70 A5 🞮
Lytham Rd *DARLE* DL1 .... 116 C1
Lythe Pl *MGRV/ESTR* TS4 .... 98 C5

Lyttleton Dr *STOCS* TS18 .... 93 E3
Lytton St *MGRV/ESTR* TS4 .... 78 C5

M

Macaulay Rd *HTLPS* TS25 .... 22 C3
Mac Bean St *NORM/PKE* TS3 .... 79 E5
Mackie Dr *GUIS* TS14 .... 129 E2
Macklin Av *BLGHM* TS23 .... 60 A1
Macmillan Rd *NACLF* DL5 .... 38 B5
Macnay St *SALT/BTN/SK* TS12 .... 89 E2 🞮
Macrae Rd *BLGHMW/WYN* TS22 .... 30 B1
Maddison St *SHIL* DL4 .... 35 E4 🔟
Mafeking Pl *SHIL* DL4 .... 35 F4
Magdalene Dr *RHTLP* TS27 .... 10 B4
Magdalen St *NORM/PKE* TS3 ...... 79 D5 🔟Ⅎ
Magister Rd *THNBY* TS17 .... 121 D2
Magnet St *SHIL* DL4 .... 35 F4 🞮
Magnolia Wy *SHIL* DL4 .... 36 A3
Maidstone Dr *MTN/NUN* TS7 .... 126 A3
Main Rd *NACLF* DL5 .... 52 B4
Mainsforth Dr *ACK/BRKF* TS5 .... 123 F2
BLGHM TS23 .... 42 B3
Mainsforth Rd *HTLP* DL17 .... 21 F4
Mainsforth Ter *HTLP* TS24 .... 3 E2
HTLPS TS25 .... 3 F6
Main St *BAUK* DL14 .... 27 F4 🔟
FYHL DL17 .... 20 C1
SHIL DL4 .... 35 E3
Major St *DARLW* DL3 .... 115 F4
STOCS TS18 .... 7 G2
Malcolm Gv *REDCAR* TS10 .... 69 D3 🞮
THNBY TS17 .... 121 F1
Malcom Rd *HTLPS* TS25 .... 30 C1
Malden Rd *NORTON* TS20 .... 75 D1 🞮
Maldon Rd *ACK/BRKF* TS5 .... 97 D2
Malham Crs *NACLF* DL5 .... 38 A5 🞮
Malham Gill *REDCAR* TS10 .... 68 A2 🞮
Malham Gv *THNBY* TS17 .... 139 E1
Malim Rd *DARLE* DL1 .... 133 F2
Maling Gn *NACLF* DL5 .... 39 D5 🞮
Malin Gv *REDCAR* TS10 .... 68 B5
Mallard La *NORTON* TS20 .... 57 F5 🞮
Mallard Rd *DARLE* DL1 .... 133 F2
Maling Rd *NORTON* TS20 .... 75 D3
Mallory Cl *MBORO* TS1 .... 4 D4 🞮
Mallory Ct *DARLE* DL1 .... 117 F4
Mallory Rd *NORTON* TS20 .... 74 C1 🞮
Mallowdale *MTN/NUN* TS7 .... 126 B5
Maltraeth Sands *ACK/BRKF* TS5 ...... 122 C3
Maltby Cl *GUIS* TS14 .... 128 C2
Maltby Pl *THNBY* TS17 .... 95 E5 🞮
Maltby Rd *CNHM/HEM* TS8 .... 140 C2
Maltby St *NORM/PKE* TS3 .... 79 E5 🞮
The Maltings *HTLPS* TS25 .... 2 A6
Malton Cl *THNBY* TS17 .... 95 F5
Malton Dr *STOCN* TS19 .... 72 C4
Malvern Av *REDCAR* TS10 .... 67 E2
SALT/BTN/SK TS12 .... 109 E1 🞮
Malvern Cl *GTAY/STK* TS9 .... 152 A3
Malvern Crs *DARLW* DL3 .... 114 A3
Malvern Dr *ACK/BRKF* TS5 .... 123 E3
GTAY/STK TS9 .... 152 A3
Malvern Rd *BLGHM* TS23 .... 58 C2
STOCS TS18 .... 6 B6
Malvern Wy *NACLF* DL5 .... 37 E5
Mandale Rd *ACK/BRKF* TS5 .... 96 C5
THNBY TS17 .... 95 E5
Manfield Av *ACK/BRKF* TS5 .... 96 C5
Manfield St *STOCS* TS18 .... 6 D6
Manitoba Crs *MGRV/ESTR* TS4 .... 98 C1 🞮
Manless Ter *SALT/BTN/SK* TS12 ...... 109 D3
Manners St *HTLP* TS24 .... 19 E2 🔟Ⅎ
Manning Cl *THNBY* TS17 .... 121 F2 🞮
Mannion Ct *ESTON* TS6 .... 81 D3
Manor Cl *BLGHMW/WYN* TS22 .... 41 E4
GTAY/STK TS9 .... 152 B2
Manor Ct *BLGHMW/WYN* TS22 .... 41 E4
Manor Farm Wy *CNHM/HEM* TS8 .... 124 C5
Manor Garth *YARM* TS15 .... 146 C5
Manor Gn *ESTON* TS6 .... 101 E2
Manor Pl *STOCN* TS19 .... 73 D5
Manor Rd *DARLW* DL3 .... 131 F3
HTLPW TS26 .... 16 C4
Manor St *MBORO* TS1 .... 4 D5
Manor Wd *CNHM/HEM* TS8 .... 124 B4
Mansepool Cl *HTLP* TS24 .... 13 D5 🔟
Mansfield Av *THNBY* TS17 .... 95 F3
Mansfield Rd *ESTON* TS6 .... 102 A3
Mansley Ct *DARLW* DL3 .... 115 F4 🞮
Manton Av *ACK/BRKF* TS5 .... 96 C4
Maple Av *MGRV/ESTR* TS4 .... 98 B4
SHIL DL4 .... 36 A3
THNBY TS17 .... 121 E1
Maple Gv *SALT/BTN/SK* TS12 .... 90 C5
Maple Rd *STOCN* TS19 .... 74 B3
Maple Sq *REDCAR* TS10 .... 51 F5
Maple St *MBORO* TS1 .... 5 H5
NORM/PKE TS3 .... 79 E4 🞮
Mapleton Cl *REDCAR* TS10 .... 68 B5 🞮
Mapleton Crs *REDCAR* TS10 .... 68 B4 🔟
Mapleton Dr *CNHM/HEM* TS8 .... 123 F5

NORTON TS20 .... 57 E5
Mapleton Rd *HTLP* TS24 .... 18 A2 🔢
Marchlyn Crs *THNBY* TS17 .... 138 A2
Mardale *CNHM/HEM* TS8 .... 141 F1 🔢
Mardale Av *HTLPS* TS25 .... 31 E1
Margaret St *NORM/PKE* TS3 .... 79 D5 🔢
Margill Cl *MTN/NUN* TS7 .... 126 A3
Margrove Wk *NORM/PKE* TS3 ..... 99 F4 🔢
Margrove Wy *SALT/BTN/SK* TS12 ...... 90 C4
Marham Cl *NORM/PKE* TS3 .... 100 B4
Maria Dr *STOCN* TS19 .... 72 C5
Maria St *NORM/PKE* TS3 .... 79 E5 🔢
Marigold Ct *DARLE* DL1 .... 133 D1 🔢
Marigold Gv *STOCN* TS19 .... 73 E4
Marina Av *REDCAR* TS10 .... 50 B4
Marina Wy *HTLP* TS24 .... 18 A2
Marine Crs *HTLP* TS24 .... 19 E2 🔢
Marine Dr *HTLP* TS24 .... 13 F5
Marine Pde *SALT/BTN/SK* TS12 ...... 89 E1
Mariners Cl *MARSKE* TS11 .... 70 B4 🔢
Marion Av *ACK/BRKF* TS5 .... 97 D4
EGG/EAG TS16 .... 137 D2
Maritime Av *HTLP* TS24 .... 2 D1
Maritime Cl *STOCS* TS18 .... 7 H2 🔢
Maritime Rd *STOCS* TS18 .... 7 G2
Mark Av *NORTON* TS20 .... 57 F5 🔢
Market Pl *SHIL* DL4 .... 35 F2
Market St *ESTON* TS6 .... 80 C3 🔢
FYHL DL17 .... 20 C1
Marlborough Av *MARSKE* TS11 ..... 70 A4
Marlborough Cl *BLGHM* TS23 ... 58 C5 🔢
Marlborough Ct *DARLE* DL1 ..... 131 F3 🔢
Marlborough Dr *DARLE* DL1 ...... 131 F3
Marlborough Gdns *TEESM* TS2 ... 78 A2 🔢
Marlborough Rd *MTN/NUN* TS7 ... 125 E4
SALT/BTN/SK TS12 .... 109 E1
STOCS TS18 .... 94 B3
Marlborough St *HTLPS* TS25 .... 23 F2
Marley Cl *STOCN* TS19 .... 73 E5
Marley Rd *NACLF* DL5 .... 54 C1
Marley Wy *RHTLP* TS27 .... 11 F4
Marlowe Rd *HTLPS* TS25 .... 22 C3
Marlsford Gv *ACK/BRKF* TS5 ... 97 D5 🔢
Marmaduke Pl *NORTON* TS20 .... 57 F5 🔢
Marmaduke St *SPEN* DL16 .... 15 F2
Marmion Cl *HTLPS* TS25 .... 24 A3
Marquand Rd *ESTON* TS6 .... 81 D4
Marquis Gv *NORTON* TS20 .... 57 E5 🔢
Marquis St *HTLP* TS24 .... 19 E2 🔢
Marrick Av *DARLW* DL3 .... 114 A3
Marrick Rd *NORM/PKE* TS3 .... 99 F4
STOCS TS18 .... 93 D4
Marsden Cl *MGRV/ESTR* TS4 ..... 98 C4 🔢
THNBY TS17 .... 139 E2 🔢
Marshall Av *NORM/PKE* TS3 .... 100 A1
Marshall Cl *HTLP* TS24 .... 12 A4
SALT/BTN/SK TS12 .... 89 D2 🔢
Marshall Dr *SALT/BTN/SK* TS12 ..... 90 C4
Marshall Gv *STOCN* TS19 .... 6 A1
Marshall Rd *NACLF* DL5 .... 38 B5
Marshall St *DARLW* DL3 .... 9 E1
Marsh House Av *BLGHM* TS23 ...... 42 A2
BLGHM TS23 .... 59 D2
Marsh House La *HTLPS* TS25 .... 31 E5
Marsh La *BLGHM* TS23 .... 43 E5
Marsh Rd *MBORO* TS1 .... 4 C3
NORM/PKE TS3 .... 79 E4
Marsh St *MBORO* TS1 .... 4 C3
Marske Gv *DARLW* DL3 .... 116 A3
Marske La *SALT/BTN/SK* TS12 ...... 88 C5
STOCS TS19 .... 72 C3
Marske Mill La *SALT/BTN/SK* TS12 .. 89 D2
Marske Rd *MARSKE* TS11 .... 88 A2
SALT/BTN/SK TS12 .... 89 D2
THNBY TS17 .... 95 F5 🔢
Marske St *HTLPS* TS25 .... 2 B6
Marston Gdns *HTLP* TS24 .... 17 F2
Marston Moor Rd *DARLE* DL1 ...... 133 E5
Marston Rd *SALT/BTN/SK* TS12 ..... 91 E5
STOCS TS18 .... 76 A5
Martham Cl *STOCN* TS19 .... 73 E4
Martindale *ACK/BRKF* TS5 ...... 123 D3 🔢
Martindale Gv *EGG/EAG* TS16 .... 137 D5
Martindale Rd *DARLE* DL1 .... 117 D3
ESTON TS6 .... 102 A1
Martindale Wy *REDCAR* TS10 .... 68 B5
Martinet Cl *THNBY* TS17 .... 121 E2
Martinet Rd *THNBY* TS17 .... 121 E2
Martin Gv *HTLPS* TS25 .... 23 E2
Martinhoe Cl *THNBY* TS17 .... 139 D5 🔢
Marton Av *MGRV/ESTR* TS4 .... 99 F5
NORM/PKE TS3 .... 100 B4
Marton Burn Rd *MGRV/ESTR* TS4 ... 98 B3
Marton Crs *ESTON* TS6 .... 102 A3
Marton Dr *BLGHMW/WYN* TS22 ... 58 A1
Marton Gill *SALT/BTN/SK* TS12 ...... 88 C2
Marton Gv *SALT/BTN/SK* TS12 ...... 90 C4
Marton Grove Rd *MGRV/ESTR* TS4 ... 98 B2
Marton Moor Rd *MTN/NUN* TS7 ... 127 D5
Marton Rd *MBORO* TS1 .... 78 C4
MGRV/ESTR TS4 .... 98 C2
Marton St *HTLP* TS24 .... 17 F3
Marway Rd *SALT/BTN/SK* TS12 ...... 90 C4
Marwood Crs *DARLW* DL3 .... 115 E3
Marwood Dr *GTAY/STK* TS9 .... 150 B3

Mary Ct *DARLW* DL3 .... 114 C4
Marykirk Rd *THNBY* TS17 .... 121 F4
Maryport Cl *STOCS* TS18 .... 75 E5
Mary St *HTLPW* TS26 .... 2 A2 🔢
STOCS TS18 .... 6 D6
Masefield Rd *HTLPS* TS25 .... 22 C2
Masham Gv *STOCS* TS18 .... 92 C2
Masham Moor Wy *DARLE* DL1 ... 133 E4 🔢
Mason St *ESTON* TS6 .... 101 F3 🔢
Massey Rd *THNBY* TS17 .... 95 E2
Master Rd *THNBY* TS17 .... 121 E2
Masterton Dr *STOCS* TS18 .... 93 D3
Mastiles Cl *THNBY* TS17 .... 138 C4
Matfen Av *MTN/NUN* TS7 .... 126 C4
Matfen Ct *SEDG* TS21 .... 29 D3
Matlock Av *MTN/NUN* TS7 .... 125 F5
Matlock Gdns *BLGHMW/WYN* TS22 .. 41 E5
Matthew Cl *NACLF* DL5 .... 39 E4 🔢
Mattison Av *ACK/BRKF* TS5 .... 97 D2
Maude St *DARLW* DL3 .... 9 E3
Maughan St *SHIL* DL4 .... 35 E3 🔢
Maxton Rd *ESTON* TS6 .... 80 C4
Maxwell Cl *DARLE* DL1 .... 133 E3
Maxwell Pl *REDCAR* TS10 .... 67 D2
Maxwell Rd *HTLPS* TS25 .... 30 C1
Mayberry Gv *ACK/BRKF* TS5 .... 98 A4 🔢
Mayfair Av *ESTON* TS6 .... 101 E5
MGRV/ESTR TS4 .... 98 C2
Mayfair Rd *DARLE* DL1 .... 116 B1
Mayfair St *HTLPW* TS26 .... 17 F4
Mayfield *DARLW* DL3 .... 8 D5
Mayfield Cl *EGG/EAG* TS16 .... 136 C1 🔢
Mayfield Crs *EGG/EAG* TS16 .... 136 C2
Mayfield Rd *MTN/NUN* TS7 .... 126 C3
Mayflower Cl *HTLP* TS24 .... 3 F1 🔢
Maygate *ESTON* TS6 .... 102 C2
Maynard St *LOFT/ST* TS13 .... 112 B1 🔢
May St *BAUK* DL14 .... 27 D1
HTLP TS24 .... 18 A2
Maze La *THNBY* TS17 .... 96 A2
Mc Clean Av *REDCAR* TS10 .... 67 E1
Mcclean Rd *SALT/BTN/SK* TS12 ... 91 E5 🔢
Mcintyre Ter *BAUK* DL14 .... 27 E3
Mcmullen Rd *DARLE* DL1 .... 133 F1
Mcnay St *DARLW* DL3 .... 116 A4
Mead Crs *THNBY* TS17 .... 96 A5
Meadford Dr *ACK/BRKF* TS5 .... 123 E3
Meadowbank Rd
  MTN/NUN TS7 .... 127 D1 🔢
Meadow Cl *GUIS* TS14 .... 129 D3 🔢
  MTN/NUN TS7 .... 126 C1 🔢
Meadowcroft Rd *STOCN* TS6 .... 101 D3
Meadowdale Cl *TEESM* TS2 .... 61 D5
Meadow Dr *HTLPW* TS26 .... 16 C5
  MTN/NUN TS7 .... 127 D1 🔢
Meadow End *EGG/EAG* TS16 .... 119 D5 🔢
Meadowfield *GTAY/STK* TS9 .... 152 C1 🔢
Meadowfield Av *MGRV/ESTR* TS4 ... 98 B3
Meadowfield Dr *EGG/EAG* TS16 ... 119 D5
Meadowfield Rd *DARLW* DL3 ...... 114 C3
Meadowfield Wy *NACLF* DL5 .... 37 F4
Meadowgate *ESTON* TS6 .... 102 B2
The Meadowings *YARM* TS15 ...... 137 D5
Meadow Ri *DARLW* DL3 .... 130 C1
Meadow Rd *MARSKE* TS11 .... 87 F1
  STOCN TS19 .... 93 D1
The Meadows *CNHM/HEM* TS8 ... 143 E1
  NACLF DL5 .... 37 D3
  SEDG TS21 .... 29 E5
The Meadow *HTLPS* TS25 .... 23 F3
Meadow View Rd *ACK/BRKF* TS5 ... 97 D2
Meadway *REDCAR* TS10 .... 68 A4
Meath St *MBORO* TS1 .... 97 E1
Meath Wy *GUIS* TS14 .... 128 C4 🔢
Meatlesburn Cl *NACLF* DL5 .... 53 E3 🔢
Medbourne Cl *ESTON* TS6 .... 102 B3 🔢
Medbourne Gdns *ACK/BRKF* TS5 .. 123 F3
Medina Cl *STOCN* TS19 .... 73 D5 🔢
Medway Cl *SALT/BTN/SK* TS12 ...... 89 E5
Medwin Cl *SALT/BTN/SK* TS12 ...... 90 C4
The Meet *NACLF* DL5 .... 37 E4 🔢
Megarth Rd *ACK/BRKF* TS5 .... 97 F2 🔢
Meggitts Av *REDCAR* TS10 .... 67 D3
Melbourne Cl *MTN/NUN* TS7 ...... 126 A4
Melbourne St *STOCS* TS18 .... 7 E4
Melbreak Av *ACK/BRKF* TS5 ..... 123 D1 🔢
Meldon Cl *DARLE* DL1 .... 117 E3
Meldyke La *CNHM/HEM* TS8 .... 141 E1
Meldyke Pl *CNHM/HEM* TS8 ..... 141 E1 🔢
Melford Gv *THNBY* TS17 .... 139 D2
Melgrove Wy *SEDG* TS21 .... 29 D5
Mellanby Crs *NACLF* DL5 .... 55 E1
Mellanby La *HTLPS* TS25 .... 31 D4 🔢
Melland St *DARLE* DL1 .... 9 H5
Mellor Ct *DARLW* DL3 .... 116 B3 🔢
Mellor St *STOCN* TS19 .... 6 D2
Melrose Av *ACK/BRKF* TS5 .... 97 E4
  BLGHM TS23 .... 59 D1
  DARLW DL3 .... 116 B1 🔢
Melrose Crs *GUIS* TS14 .... 129 F3
Melrose St *HTLPS* TS25 .... 23 F2
  MBORO TS1 .... 5 H5
Melsonby Av *NORM/PKE* TS3 ..... 100 A4 🔢
Melsonby Crs *DARLE* DL1 .... 133 D3

Melsonby Gv *STOCS* TS18 .... 92 C3
Melton Rd *STOCN* TS19 .... 73 D5
Melville St *DARLW* DL3 .... 9 F1
Mendip Av *SALT/BTN/SK* TS12 ... 109 E1 🔢
Mendip Dr *REDCAR* TS10 .... 67 F3
Mendip Gv *DARLE* DL1 .... 117 D3
Mendip Rd *BLGHM* TS23 .... 58 C3
Menom Rd *NACLF* DL5 .... 54 C5
Menville Cl *NACLF* DL5 .... 53 E3 🔢
Meredith Av *ESTON* TS6 .... 101 E4
Meresled Cl *BLGHM* TS23 .... 42 B3 🔢
Mereston Cl *HTLPW* TS26 .... 16 B3 🔢
Merion Dr *MARSKE* TS11 .... 86 A3
Merlin Cl *GUIS* TS14 .... 128 A3 🔢
Merlin Rd *NORM/PKE* TS3 .... 79 F5
  STOCN TS19 .... 73 D5
Merring Cl *STOCS* TS18 .... 92 C2
Merrington Av *ACK/BRKF* TS5 .... 123 D3
Merrington Rd *FYHL* DL17 .... 20 A2
Merrington Vw *SPEN* DL16 .... 15 D3
Mersehead Sands
  ACK/BRKF TS5 .... 123 D3 🔢
Mersey Rd *REDCAR* TS10 .... 68 A2
Merton Cl *DARLE* DL1 .... 116 C2 🔢
Merville Av *STOCN* TS19 .... 93 E2
Merz Rd *NACLF* DL5 .... 54 C1
Metcalfe Cl *YARM* TS15 .... 146 A2
Metcalfe Rd *ESTON* TS6 .... 80 B4
Mewburn Ct *DARLW* DL3 .... 116 A2 🔢
Mewburn Rd *DARLW* DL3 .... 115 F1
Mexborough Cl *STOCN* TS19 ..... 73 F4 🔢
Meynell Av *GUIS* TS14 .... 128 A5
Meynell Rd *DARLW* DL3 .... 116 A3
Meynell's Wk *YARM* TS15 .... 146 A1
Mickleby Cl *MTN/NUN* TS7 .... 126 B5
Mickledales Dr *MARSKE* TS11 .... 70 B5
Micklemire La *HTLPS* TS25 .... 31 E5
Mickleton Rd *TEESM* TS2 .... 77 E1
Micklow Cl *REDCAR* TS10 .... 68 B4
Micklow La *LOFT/ST* TS13 .... 113 E3
Midbourne Rd *STOCN* TS19 ...... 74 C4 🔢
Middle Av *BLGHM* TS23 .... 58 C5
Middle Bank Rd *MTN/NUN* TS7 ... 127 D1
Middlefield Rd *MARSKE* TS11 .... 70 A5
  STOCN TS19 .... 73 E3
Middlegate *HTLP* TS24 .... 19 E2 🔢
Middleham Rd *DARLE* DL1 .... 116 C2 🔢
  STOCN TS19 .... 93 E2
Middleham Wk *SPEN* DL16 .... 15 E1 🔢
Middleham Rd *NACLF* DL5 .... 39 D3
Middle Rd *THNBY* TS17 .... 139 D1
Middlesbrough Rd *ESTON* TS6 ...... 80 B3
  GUIS TS14 .... 128 A3 🔢
  MTN/NUN TS7 .... 127 F3
  THNBY TS17 .... 121 E4
Middlesbrough Rd East *ESTON* TS6 .. 81 D3
Middle St *STOCS* TS18 .... 7 F3
Middleton Av *ACK/BRKF* TS5 .... 97 D4 🔢
  BLGHMW/WYN TS22 .... 58 A1
  THNBY TS17 .... 121 E4
Middleton Dr *GUIS* TS14 .... 129 E4
Middleton Grange La *HTLPW* TS26 ... 2 B2 🔢
  HTLPW TS26 .... 2 C2 🔢
Middleton Rd *HTLP* TS24 .... 18 A3
  SHIL DL4 .... 35 E4
Middleton St *DARLE* DL1 .... 9 H4
Middleton Wk *STOCS* TS18 .... 7 E5
Middleway *THNBY* TS17 .... 95 E3 🔢
Middlewood Cl *RHTLP* TS27 ...... 11 E3 🔢
Middridge Gv *BLGHM* TS23 .... 42 B4
Middridge La *SHIL* DL4 .... 36 B3
Middridge Rd *NACLF* DL5 .... 37 E3 🔢
Midfields *NACLF* DL5 .... 53 E3
The Midfield *ACK/BRKF* TS5 ...... 97 F1 🔢
Midhurst Rd *NORM/PKE* TS3 .... 100 C2
Midlothian Rd *HTLPS* TS25 .... 22 B5
Miers Av *HTLP* TS24 .... 12 C5
Milbank Ct *DARLW* DL3 .... 131 D1 🔢
  STOCS TS18 .... 7 F4
Milbank Crs *DARLW* DL3 .... 8 B3
Milbank Rd *DARLW* DL3 .... 8 A3
  HTLP TS24 .... 18 A2
Milbank St *ESTON* TS6 .... 80 C3 🔢
  STOCS TS18 .... 7 F4 🔢
Milbank Ter *REDCAR* TS10 .... 51 E4 🔢
Milbourne Ct *SEDG* TS21 .... 29 D2 🔢
Milburn Crs *NORTON* TS20 .... 57 D3
Mildenhall Cl *HTLPS* TS25 .... 31 D3
Mildred St *DARLW* DL3 .... 9 E1
  HTLPW TS26 .... 17 F3
Milfoil Cl *MTN/NUN* TS7 .... 125 D3
Milford Meadow *BAUK* DL14 .... 27 F5
Milkwood Ct *DARLW* DL3 .... 115 F4 🔢
Millais Gv *BLGHM* TS23 .... 41 F3
Mill Bank *LOFT/ST* TS13 .... 112 B1
Millbank Cl *RHTLP* TS27 .... 10 C4 🔢
Millbank La *THNBY* TS17 .... 121 E2
Millbeck Wy *MTN/NUN* TS7 .... 101 D5
Millbrook Av *NORM/PKE* TS3 ..... 80 B5 🔢
Miller Cl *HTLP* TS24 .... 11 F4
Miller Crs *HTLP* TS24 .... 11 F4
Millfield Cl *EGG/EAG* TS16 .... 137 D5
  THNBY TS17 .... 96 A4
Millfield Rd *NORM/PKE* TS3 .... 99 E1
Millfields *NACLF* DL5 .... 55 D5

Millford Rd *NORTON* TS20 .... 74 B2 ▢
Millholme Cl *SALT/BTN/SK* TS12 .. 110 C1 ▢
Millholme Dr *SALT/BTN/SK* TS12 .... 110 C1
Millholme Ter *SALT/BTN/SK* TS12 .... 110 C1
Mill La *BAUK* DL14 .... 27 F4
  BLGHM TS23 .... 59 D5
  BLGHMW/WYN TS22 .... 41 D5
  DARLE DL1 .... 117 F4
  LOFT/ST TS13 .... 112 B3
  LOFT/ST TS13 .... 112 C1
  NACLF DL5 .... 52 B3
  NORTON TS20 .... 58 A5
Millpool Cl *HTLP* TS24 .... 13 E5 ▢
Mill Riggs *GTAY/STK* TS9 .... 152 C2
Mills Cl *NACLF* DL5 .... 54 B1
Mills St *MBORO* TS1 .... 4 A6
Millston Cl *HTLPW* TS26 .... 16 B3
Mill St *GUIS* TS14 .... 129 D3
  NORTON TS20 .... 74 C1
  SHIL DL4 .... 35 F4 ▢
Mill St East *STOCS* TS18 .... 7 H3
Mill St West *STOCS* TS18 .... 7 F3 ▢
Mill Vw *LOFT/ST* TS13 .... 113 D3
Mill Wynd *YARM* TS15 .... 137 D4 ▢
Milner Gv *HTLP* TS24 .... 18 A5 ▢
Milner Rd *DARLE* DL1 .... 132 D3
  NORTON TS20 .... 57 F5
Milne Wk *HTLPS* TS25 .... 22 B5
Milton Av *BAUK* DL14 .... 27 E1 ▢▢
Milton Cl *SALT/BTN/SK* TS12 .... 90 C4
Milton St *MBORO* TS1 .... 4 C4
Milton Rd *HTLPW* TS26 .... 2 B2 ▢
  HTLPW TS26 .... 17 F4
Milton St *DARLE* DL1 .... 133 D2
  SALT/BTN/SK TS12 .... 89 D2
Minch Rd *HTLPS* TS25 .... 30 B1
Minors Crs *DARLW* DL3 .... 114 B3
Minsterley Dr *ACK/BRKF* TS5 .... 122 C1
Mistral Dr *DARLE* DL1 .... 116 C1
Mitchell Av *THNBY* TS17 .... 121 F2
Mitchell St *HTLPW* TS26 .... 2 A3
Mitford Cl *MTN/NUN* TS7 .... 101 D5 ▢▢
Mitford Ct *SEDG* TS21 .... 29 D2
Mitford Crs *STOCN* TS19 .... 72 C3
The Moat *BLGHM* TS23 .... 60 A3
Moffat Cl *DARLE* DL1 .... 117 D2
Moffat Rd *HTLPS* TS25 .... 30 B1
Monach Rd *HTLPS* TS25 .... 30 C1
Monarch Gv *MTN/NUN* TS7 .... 126 A1
Mond Crs *BLGHM* TS23 .... 75 F1
Monkland Cl *MBORO* TS1 .... 5 E4
Monkseaton Dr
  BLGHMW/WYN TS22 .... 58 B1
Monks End *NACLF* DL5 .... 55 E5
Monkton Rd *BLGHMW/WYN* TS22 .. 30 B1
Monmouth Cl *EGG/EAG* TS16 ..... 137 E1
Monmouth Gv *HTLPW* TS26 .... 17 D1
Monmouth Rd *ESTON* TS6 .... 81 F5
Monreith Av *EGG/EAG* TS16 .... 137 E1
Montague St *HTLP* TS24 .... 19 E1
  MBORO TS1 .... 78 C4 ▢
Montagu's Harrier *GUIS* TS14 ...... 128 A3
Montgomery Gv *HTLPW* TS26 .... 17 D1
Montreal Pl *MGRV/ESTR* TS4 .... 98 C2 ▢
Montrose Cl *MTN/NUN* TS7 .... 125 E4
Montrose St *DARLE* DL1 .... 9 H2
  MBORO TS1 .... 5 C4
  SALT/BTN/SK TS12 .... 89 C3
Moorbeck Wy *MTN/NUN* TS7 ...... 101 D5
Moor Cl *YARM* TS15 .... 146 C5
Moorcock Cl *ESTON* TS6 .... 102 A3
Moore La *NACLF* DL5 .... 55 E1
Moore St *HTLP* TS24 .... 17 F2
  REDCAR TS10 .... 51 F4
Moorgate *ESTON* TS6 .... 102 C2 ▢
Moor Gn *MTN/NUN* TS7 .... 144 C1
Moorhead Wy *NACLF* DL5 .... 55 D3
Moorhen Rd *HTLPW* TS26 .... 16 C1
Moorlands Rd *DARLW* DL3 .... 115 D4
Moor La *SHIL* DL4 .... 36 C1
Moor Pde *HTLP* TS24 .... 19 E1
Moor Pk *EGG/EAG* TS16 .... 137 E2 ▢
  MTN/NUN TS7 .... 126 C5
Moorsholm Wy *REDCAR* TS10 ...... 68 A3
Moorside *SPEN* DL16 .... 14 B5
Moorston Cl *HTLPW* TS26 .... 16 B4 ▢
Moor Ter *HTLP* TS24 .... 19 F2
Moortown Rd *MARSKE* TS11 .... 86 B3
  MGRV/ESTR TS4 .... 98 B5
Moray Cl *DARLE* DL1 .... 117 D1
  MGRV/ESTR TS4 .... 98 C3 ▢
Moray Rd *NORTON* TS20 .... 74 B2
Mordales Dr *MARSKE* TS11 .... 88 A1
Moreland Av *BLGHM* TS23 .... 59 D2
Moreland Cl *BLGHMW/WYN* TS22 .. 41 E3 ▢
Moreland St *HTLP* TS24 .... 19 E1
Moresby Cl *MGRV/ESTR* TS4 .... 99 D4 ▢
Morgan Dr *GUIS* TS14 .... 128 C3
Morison Gdns *HTLP* TS24 .... 19 E3 ▢
Morlais Ct *THNBY* TS17 .... 138 B3 ▢
Morland Fell *REDCAR* TS10 .... 68 A2
Morland St *BAUK* DL14 .... 27 D4
Mornington La *DARLW* DL3 .... 115 E4 ▢
Morpeth Av *DARLE* DL1 .... 117 D3
  MGRV/ESTR TS4 .... 125 D2

Morpeth Cl *FYHL* DL17 .... 21 E1 ▢
Morpeth Gv *BAUK* DL14 .... 26 C3
Morrison Rd *GUIS* TS14 .... 129 E2
Morris Rd *ESTON* TS6 .... 102 A3 ▢
Mortain Cl *YARM* TS15 .... 147 D1
Mortimer Dr *NORTON* TS20 .... 74 B1 ▢
Morton Carr La *MTN/NUN* TS7 .... 127 E4
Morton Cl *GUIS* TS14 .... 128 B4
Morton St *HTLPW* TS26 .... 2 A1
Morvale Rd *ESTON* TS6 .... 102 A1 ▢
Morville Ct *THNBY* TS17 .... 139 D2 ▢
Moses St *NORM/PKE* TS3 .... 79 D5 ▢▢
Mosman Ter *NORM/PKE* TS3 .... 79 E5
Mossbank Gv *DARLE* DL1 .... 117 D3
Mossbrough Cl *STOCN* TS19 .... 73 F4 ▢
Mossmere *SPEN* DL16 .... 14 C1 ▢
Mosston Rd *STOCN* TS19 .... 73 D5
Moss Wy *STOCS* TS18 .... 120 A1
Mosswood Crs *ACK/BRKF* TS5 .... 123 D2
Motherwell Rd *HTLPS* TS25 .... 30 C1
Moule Cl *NACLF* DL5 .... 54 B2
Moulton Gv *STOCN* TS19 .... 92 C1
Mountbatten Cl *HTLP* TS24 .... 18 B1
Mount Gv *NORTON* TS20 .... 58 A5
Mount Leven Rd *YARM* TS15 .... 138 A5
Mount Pleasant Av *MARSKE* TS11 .. 70 C5
Mount Pleasant Gra *STOCS* TS18 .. 94 C4
Mount Pleasant Rd *NORTON* TS20 .. 75 D3
Mountstewart *BLGHMW/WYN* TS22.. 40 A2
Mountston Cl *HTLPW* TS26 .... 16 C3 ▢
Mowbray Dr *CNHM/HEM* TS8 ...... 123 E5
Mowbray Gv *STOCN* TS19 .... 72 C3
Mowbray Rd *HTLPS* TS25 .... 30 C2
  NORTON TS20 .... 75 D3
Mowden Cl *STOCN* TS19 .... 73 F4 ▢
Mowden Hall Dr *DARLW* DL3 ..... 114 C5
Mowden Ter *DARLW* DL3 .... 9 F1
Mowden Wk *DARLW* DL3 .... 114 B5 ▢
Moyne Gdns *HTLPS* TS25 .... 2 B5
Muff La *CNHM/HEM* TS8 .... 142 C5
Muirfield St *MARSKE* TS11 .... 86 C3 ▢
  RHTLP TS27 .... 11 E3
Muirfield Rd *EGG/EAG* TS16 .... 137 E1
Muir Gv *HTLPS* TS25 .... 30 C1
Muirkirk Gv *DARLE* DL1 .... 117 D2 ▢
Muker Gv *STOCN* TS19 .... 92 C2
Mulberry Ct *MGRV/ESTR* TS4 .... 98 B4 ▢
Mulgrave Ct *GUIS* TS14 .... 129 D1 ▢
  NACLF DL5 .... 39 D3
Mulgrave Rd *ACK/BRKF* TS5 .... 98 A3
  HTLPW TS26 .... 17 F4
Mulheim Cl *DARLW* DL3 .... 115 D3
Mullroy Rd *HTLPS* TS25 .... 22 B5 ▢
  HTLPS TS25 .... 30 B1 ▢
Munro Gv *HTLPS* TS25 .... 30 C1 ▢
Murdock Rd *NORM/PKE* TS3 .... 80 B5
Muriel St *LOFT/ST* TS13 .... 112 B1
  MBORO TS1 .... 98 B1
  REDCAR TS10 .... 51 F5
Murphy Crs *BAUK* DL14 .... 26 C4
Murrayfield Wy *DARLE* DL1 .... 117 F5
Murray St *HTLPW* TS26 .... 2 A2
Murray Wk *DARLW* DL3 .... 130 C1
Murton Cl *NACLF* DL5 .... 55 D5 ▢
Murton Ov *BLGHMW/WYN* TS22 .. 58 A1
Museum Rd *HTLP* TS24 .... 2 C2
Musgrave Ter
  BLGHMW/WYN TS22 .... 41 E3 ▢

N

Nab Cl *ESTON* TS6 .... 102 A3
Nairn Cl *DARLE* DL1 .... 117 F1
Nairnhead Cl *CNHM/HEM* TS8 .... 123 F5 ▢
Napier Cl *FYHL* DL17 .... 20 B2
Napier St *ACK/BRKF* TS5 .... 98 A1
  DARLB DL3 .... 8 C3 ▢
  ESTON TS6 .... 80 C3 ▢
  NORTON TS20 .... 75 D3 ▢
Naseby Ct *BLGHM* TS23 .... 42 C4
  SALT/BTN/SK TS12 .... 111 E3 ▢
Nash Gv *HTLPS* TS25 .... 23 D3
Navenby Gv *HTLPS* TS25 .... 30 C2
Navigation Wy *THNBY* TS17 .... 96 A2
Naylor Rd *SEDG* TS21 .... 29 D2
Neale St *FYHL* DL17 .... 20 B2 ▢
Neasham Av *BLGHM* TS23 .... 42 B4
  MTN/NUN TS7 .... 125 F5
Neasham Cl *STOCS* TS18 .... 7 H2
Neasham Ct *GTAY/STK* TS9 .... 152 A1
Neasham Dr *DARLE* DL1 .... 133 D4 ▢
Neasham Rd *DARLE* DL1 .... 132 C3
Neath Ct *THNBY* TS17 .... 138 B3

Nebraska Cl *DARLE* DL1 .... 116 C2
Nederdale Cl *YARM* TS15 .... 146 A2
Needles Cl *REDCAR* TS10 .... 68 A5
Neile Rd *NACLF* DL5 .... 39 D4
Nelson Sq *NORTON* TS20 .... 57 F5 ▢
Nelson St *BAUK* DL14 .... 27 D1
  ESTON TS6 .... 80 C3
  FYHL DL17 .... 21 F3 ▢
Nelson Ter *DARLE* DL1 .... 132 B3 ▢
  REDCAR TS10 .... 51 D5
  STOCS TS18 .... 7 F5
Nesbyt Rd *HTLP* TS24 .... 12 B4 ▢
Nesham Av *ACK/BRKF* TS5 .... 97 D3 ▢
Nesham Rd *HTLP* TS24 .... 19 E1
  MBORO TS1 .... 4 B6 ▢
Nestfield St *DARLE* DL1 .... 117 D4 ▢
Netherby Cl *YARM* TS15 .... 138 A5 ▢
Netherby Ga *HTLPW* TS26 .... 17 D3
Netherby Gn *NORM/PKE* TS3 ...... 100 A4
Netherby Ri *DARLW* DL3 .... 131 D2
Netherfields Crs *NORM/PKE* TS3 .. 100 C3
Netley Gv *NORM/PKE* TS3 .... 100 B4
Nevada Gdns *DARLE* DL1 .... 116 C2 ▢
Nevern Crs *THNBY* TS17 .... 138 A3
Neville Cl *SPEN* DL16 .... 15 E2
Neville Dr *SEDG* TS21 .... 29 D2
Neville Gv *GUIS* TS14 .... 128 B4
Neville Pde *NACLF* DL5 .... 55 D1
Neville Rd *DARLW* DL3 .... 8 A4
Neville's Ct *ACK/BRKF* TS5 .... 97 F4
Newark Rd *HTLPS* TS25 .... 30 C2
Newbank Cl *MTN/NUN* TS7 .... 127 D1
Newbiggin Rd *BLGHM* TS23 ...... 42 A3 ▢▢
Newburn Ct *NACLF* DL5 .... 38 D3
Newbury Av *ACK/BRKF* TS5 .... 97 D3 ▢
Newbury Rd *SALT/BTN/SK* TS12 .. 111 D1
Newbury Wy *BLGHM* TS23 .... 42 B5
Newby Cl *ACK/BRKF* TS5 .... 98 A5 ▢
  NORTON TS20 .... 74 C1 ▢
Newby Gv *THNBY* TS17 .... 95 F5 ▢
New Cl *NACLF* DL5 .... 39 E5
Newcomen Gv *REDCAR* TS10 .... 51 E4
Newcomen Rd *ESTON* TS6 .... 80 B4
Newcomen St *FYHL* DL17 .... 20 B1
Newcomen Ter *REDCAR* TS10 .... 51 D4
Newcommen Ter *LOFT/ST* TS13 .. 113 D3 ▢
Newfield Crs *ACK/BRKF* TS5 .... 123 D2
Newfoundland St *DARLW* DL3 ... 115 F4 ▢
Newgate *ESTON* TS6 .... 102 B2
Newgate St *BAUK* DL14 .... 27 D1
Newham Av *ACK/BRKF* TS5 .... 97 F5
Newham Crs *MTN/NUN* TS7 .... 125 F4
Newham Grange Av *STOCN* TS19 .... 6 A2
Newham Wy *CNHM/HEM* TS8 .... 124 C4
  CNHM/HEM TS8 .... 143 E1
Newhaven Cl *CNHM/HEM* TS8 ... 123 F5
Newholm Ct *HTLPS* TS25 .... 23 F5
Newholme Ct *GUIS* TS14 .... 128 C3 ▢
Newholm Wy *REDCAR* TS10 .... 68 A3
Newick Av *NORM/PKE* TS3 .... 99 F2
Newington Rd *MGRV/ESTR* TS4 .... 98 C4
Newlands Av *BAUK* DL14 .... 27 D3
  HTLPW TS26 .... 17 E5
  NORTON TS20 .... 75 D2
Newlands Gv *REDCAR* TS10 .... 68 A1
Newlands Rd *DARLW* DL3 .... 115 E4
  EGG/EAG TS16 .... 137 D2 ▢
  MBORO TS1 .... 78 C5
  SALT/BTN/SK TS12 .... 108 C4
New La *NACLF* DL5 .... 53 E5
Newley Ct *NORM/PKE* TS3 .... 100 C3
Newlyn Gn *NORM/PKE* TS3 .... 100 A4
Newlyn Wy *REDCAR* TS10 .... 69 E4
Newmarket Av *THNBY* TS17 .... 96 B3
Newmarket Rd *REDCAR* TS10 .... 68 C2
Newport Ct *DARLE* DL1 .... 117 F4 ▢
Newport Crs *MBORO* TS1 .... 5 F3
Newport Rd *ACK/BRKF* TS5 .... 77 D5 ▢
  MBORO TS1 .... 4 C5
Newport Wy *MBORO* TS1 .... 4 B4
Newquay Cl *CNHM/HEM* TS8...... 123 F5
  HTLPW TS26 .... 17 D2
New Rd *BLGHM* TS23 .... 75 F1
  GUIS TS14 .... 129 D3
New Row *GUIS* TS14 .... 105 F2
Newsam Crs *EGG/EAG* TS16 ...... 137 D2 ▢
Newsam Rd *EGG/EAG* TS16 .... 137 D2
Newstead Av *STOCN* TS19 .... 73 F4
Newstead Rd *MGRV/ESTR* TS4 ...... 98 C1
New St *THNBY* TS17 .... 95 E3
Newton Cl *ESTON* TS6 .... 102 B3
Newton Dr *THNBY* TS17 .... 121 F4
Newton Gv *BLGHMW/WYN* TS22... 58 A1
Newton La *RDARL* DL2 .... 114 A1
Newton Rd *GTAY/STK* TS9 .... 150 C1
  REDCAR TS10 .... 68 A3
Newton St *FYHL* DL17 .... 20 B1 ▢
Newtown Av *STOCN* TS19 .... 6 D2
Newtown Wy *HTLP* TS24 .... 12 A4
Nicklaus Dr *EGG/EAG* TS16 .... 137 F1
Nickerstream La *DARLW* DL3 ...... 114 C3
Nightingale Av *DARLE* DL1 .... 117 E3
Nightingale Cl *HTLPW* TS26 .... 16 B1
Nightingale Rd *ESTON* TS6 .... 101 F1
Nile St *TEESM* TS2 .... 5 E1

Nimbus Cl *MTN/NUN* TS7 .... 125 E3
Nine Acres *RHTLP* TS27 .... 10 A5
Ninefields *BAUK* DL14 .... 27 D1 🈂
Nolan Pl *STOCS* TS18 .... 7 E2
Nookston Cl *HTLPW* TS26 .... 16 C2
Norcliffe St *NORM/PKE* TS3 ...... 79 E5 🈂
Norfolk Cl *HTLPS* TS25 .... 24 A2
  REDCAR TS10 .... 68 A2 🈂
  SALT/BTN/SK TS12 .... 108 C2
Norfolk Crs *NORM/PKE* TS3 ...... 100 A4
Norfolk St *STOCS* TS18 .... 6 C6
Norfolk Ter *BLGHM* TS23 .... 59 E3 🈂
Normanby Hall Pk *ESTON* TS6 .. 101 E3
Normanby Rd *ESTON* TS6 .... 80 C2
  ESTON TS6 .... 101 E1
  MTN/NUN TS7 .... 100 C4
  NORM/PKE TS3 .... 101 D4
Norman Ter *ESTON* TS6 .... 80 B5
North Albert Rd *NORTON* TS20 ... 57 E5
Northallerton Rd *THNBY* TS17 ... 95 F5
North Av *SALT/BTN/SK* TS12 ...... 89 D2
North Bank Crs *MTN/NUN* TS7 .. 127 D1
Northbourne Rd *STOCN* TS19 .... 74 B4 🈂
Northbrook Ct *HTLPW* TS26 .... 17 D5
North Close Rd *SPEN* DL16 .... 15 D5
Northcote St *STOCS* TS18 .... 94 B3
Northcote Ter *DARLW* DL3 .... 115 F4
Northdale Ct *NORM/PKE* TS3 ... 100 A2 🈂
North Dr *HTLPW* TS26 .... 17 D4
  MTN/NUN TS7 .... 100 C5
  SPEN DL16 .... 14 B5
North Eastern Ter *DARLE* DL1 ... 9 H5 🈂
North End *SEDG* TS21 .... 29 D4
North End Gdns *BAUK* DL14 .... 27 D4
Northern Rd *ACK/BRKF* TS5 ...... 97 D2
North Fen *REDCAR* TS10 .... 68 A2 🈂
Northfield Cl *GTAY/STK* TS9 .... 152 A2 🈂
Northfield Dr *GTAY/STK* TS9 .... 152 E1
Northfield Rd *BLGHMW/WYN* TS22 .. 58 B1
  MARSKE TS11 .... 69 F5
Northfield Wy *NACLF* DL5 .... 54 B2
Northfleet Av *NORM/PKE* TS3 ... 100 A1
Northgate *DARLE* DL1 .... 9 F4
  GUIS TS14 .... 129 D2
  HTLP TS24 .... 19 D1
Northgate Rbt. *DARLW* DL3 .... 9 F3
Northgate Rd *ACK/BRKF* TS5 ..... 97 F4
Northiam Cl *CNHM/HEM* TS8 .. 123 F5 🈂
Northland Av *HTLPW* TS26 .... 17 E5 🈂
Northleach Dr *CNHM/HEM* TS8.. 123 F5
North Lodge Ter *DARLW* DL3 ...... 9 F3
North Ormesby Rd *MBORO* TS1 .. 78 C4
  MGRV/ESTR TS4 .... 78 C5 🈂
Northpark *BLGHM* TS23 .... 42 A3
North Park Rd *SEDG* TS21 .... 29 D5
Northport Rd *STOCS* TS18 .... 75 E5
North Ri *DARLW* DL3 .... 116 B3
North Rd *DARLE* DL1 .... 116 B5
  GTAY/STK TS9 .... 152 A2
  HTLPS TS25 .... 25 D4
  LOFT/ST TS13 .... 113 E3
  SPEN DL16 .... 15 F1
  TEESM TS2 .... 4 D2
North Rw *ESTON* TS6 .... 83 E5 🈂
Northside *NACLF* DL5 .... 37 D3
North St *FYHL* DL17 .... 20 C1 🈂
  SPEN DL16 .... 14 C3
  STOCS TS18 .... 7 F3
  TEESM TS2 .... 78 B2
North Ter *NACLF* DL5 .... 55 D5
  REDCAR TS10 .... 51 E4
Northumberland Av *BAUK* DL14.. 26 C3
Northumberland Gv
  NORTON TS20 .... 57 E4 🈂
Northumberland Rd *THNBY* TS17.. 95 E5
Northumberland St *DARLW* DL3 ... 9 E5
Northwold Cl *HTLPS* TS25 .... 31 D2
North Wd *ACK/BRKF* TS5 .... 97 F5🈂
Norton Av *NORTON* TS20 .... 74 C2
Norton Dr *STOCN* TS19 .... 72 C4
Norton Rd *NORTON* TS20 .... 75 D2
  STOCS TS18 .... 7 G3
Norwich Av *STOCN* TS19 .... 73 E4
Norwich Gv *DARLE* DL1 .... 117 F3 🈂
Norwich Rd *ACK/BRKF* TS5 ...... 98 A2
  REDCAR TS10 .... 69 E2
Norwood Cl *STOCN* TS19 .... 73 D4 🈂
Norwood Rd *NORM/PKE* TS3 ... 100 C2 🈂
Nottingham Dr *REDCAR* TS10 ... 69 D2 🈂
Nuffield Cl *DARLE* DL1 .... 116 C2 🈂
Nuffield Rd *BLGHM* TS23 .... 59 F2 🈂
Nugent Av *MBORO* TS1 .... 4 B6 🈂
Nuneaton Dr *CNHM/HEM* TS8 .. 123 F5
Nunnery Cl *DARLW* DL3 .... 130 C1 🈂
Nunnery La *DARLW* DL3 .... 130 C1
Nunnington Cl *THNBY* TS17 ..... 139 D1
Nuns Cl *BAUK* DL14 .... 27 F4
Nuns St *HTLP* TS24 .... 19 E2
Nursery Gdns *YARM* TS15 .... 146 C1
Nursery La *ACK/BRKF* TS5 .... 97 E2
  STOCS TS18 .... 6 A6
Nutfield Cl *CNHM/HEM* TS8 .... 123 F5 🈂
Nuthatch Cl *HTLPW* TS26 .... 16 C2
Nut La *MGRV/ESTR* TS4 .... 98 C1
Nutley Rd *BLGHM* TS23 .... 59 E2 🈂

O

Oak Av *MTN/NUN* TS7 .... 126 A4
Oakdale *MTN/NUN* TS7 .... 101 D5 🈂
Oakdale Rd *MARSKE* TS11 .... 86 C3 🈂
Oakdene Av *DARLW* DL3 .... 8 D6
  STOCS TS18 .... 94 A4
Oakdene Cl *STOCN* TS19 .... 101 F3
Oakenshaw Dr *ACK/BRKF* TS5 .. 123 E2
Oakesway *HTLP* TS24 .... 13 D5
Oakfield *NACLF* DL5 .... 54 A1
Oakfield Av *EGG/EAG* TS16 ...... 119 D5
Oakfield Cl *EGG/EAG* TS16 ...... 119 D5
Oakfield Rd *NORM/PKE* TS3 ...... 99 D1
Oak Gv *HTLP* TS24 .... 17 E2
Oak Hi *CNHM/HEM* TS8 .... 125 E5
Oakhurst Cl *THNBY* TS17 .... 139 E1 🈂
Oakhurst Rd *DARLW* DL3 .... 8 C2
Oakland Av *HTLPS* TS25 .... 23 F5
Oakland Gdns *DARLE* DL1 .... 116 B1
Oaklands *GTAY/STK* TS9 .... 150 B2
Oaklands Av *NORTON* TS20 ...... 75 D2 🈂
Oaklands Rd *ESTON* TS6 .... 101 F5
Oaklands Ter *DARLW* DL3 .... 9 E2 🈂
Oak Lea *SHIL* DL4 .... 36 A3
Oaklea Cl *NORTON* TS20 .... 74 C1
Oaklea Ter *BAUK* DL14 .... 27 D3
Oakley Cl *CNHM/HEM* TS8 .... 123 F5
  GUIS TS14 .... 129 E5
Oakley Gdns *HTLP* TS24 .... 17 F2
Oakridge *MTN/NUN* TS7 .... 101 D5 🈂
Oakrise *MTN/NUN* TS7 .... 101 D4 🈂
Oak Rd *EGG/EAG* TS16 .... 119 F3
  GUIS TS14 .... 129 D2
  REDCAR TS10 .... 69 E1
  SALT/BTN/SK TS12 .... 90 C4
Oaksham Dr *BLGHM* TS23 .... 42 A3
The Oaks *MTN/NUN* TS8 .... 123 F5 🈂
  FYHL DL17 .... 39 D2 🈂
Oak St *BLGHM* TS23 .... 61 D4
  ESTON TS6 .... 80 C3 🈂
  MBORO TS1 .... 5 H3
  NORM/PKE TS3 .... 79 F4
Oak Ter *BAUK* DL14 .... 27 E2
Oaktree Gv *STOCS* TS18 .... 93 D4 🈂
Oakwell Gdns *NORTON* TS20 .... 74 C1 🈂
Oakwell Rd *NORTON* TS20 .... 74 C1
Oakwood Cl *RHTLP* TS27 .... 11 E4
Oakwood Dr *DARLE* DL1 .... 116 C1
Oakworth Gn *MGRV/ESTR* TS4 .. 98 C4
Oatfields Ct *ESTON* TS6 .... 102 A3
Oban Av *HTLPS* TS25 .... 23 F2
Oban Rd *NORM/PKE* TS3 .... 99 F3
Occupation Rd *ESTON* TS6 .... 102 B4
Ocean Rd *HTLP* TS24 .... 11 E2
Ochil Ter *BAUK* DL14 .... 27 D3
Offerton Dr *CNHM/HEM* TS8 ... 123 F5
O Hanlan St *SPEN* DL16 .... 15 D2 🈂
Okehampton Dr *MTN/NUN* TS7 .. 125 E4
Oldbury Gv *CNHM/HEM* TS8 ... 124 A5 🈂
Old Cemetery Rd *HTLP* TS24 ..... 13 E5
The Olde Market *YARM* TS15 .... 137 D4 🈂
Oldford Crs *ACK/BRKF* TS5 ...... 123 E1
Oldgate *ESTON* TS6 .... 102 C2
Oldham Cl *SALT/BTN/SK* TS12 .. 109 E5 🈂
The Old Market *YARM* TS15 ..... 137 D4 🈂
Old Middlesbrough Rd *ESTON* TS6.. 80 B4
Old Rd *BLGHM* TS23 .... 58 C5
Old Station Rd *ESTON* TS6 .... 80 B2
Oldstead Ct *CNHM/HEM* TS8 ... 123 F5
Oliver St *ACK/BRKF* TS5 .... 97 F2
  ESTON TS6 .... 80 C4 🈂
Olive St *HTLP* TS24 .... 19 E2
Olliver St *REDCAR* TS10 .... 51 F5
Olympic St *DARLW* DL3 .... 115 E4
Ontario Crs *REDCAR* TS10 .... 68 B1
Orange Gv *NORTON* TS20 .... 74 C3
Orchard Cl *GTAY/STK* TS9 .... 150 C1
Orchard Gv *ESTON* TS6 .... 101 F2
Orchard Rd *ACK/BRKF* TS5 .... 97 F5
  DARLW DL3 .... 8 B1
  REDCAR TS10 .... 68 B1
  STOCN TS19 .... 93 D1
  THNBY TS17 .... 121 D2
The Orchard *SEDG* TS21 .... 29 E4 🈂
  SEDG TS21 .... 29 F4 🈂
Orchard Wy *MTN/NUN* TS8 ..... 100 C5
Orde Wingate Wy *STOCN* TS19 .... 7 F2
Ordsall Gn *NORM/PKE* TS3 ...... 100 A4
Oriel Cl *ACK/BRKF* TS5 .... 97 F4
Oriel Ct *DARLE* DL1 .... 116 C2
The Orlands *NACLF* DL5 .... 55 D5
Orleans Gv *MTN/NUN* TS7 .... 126 A3
Ormesby Bank *MTN/NUN* TS7 .. 127 D2
Ormesby Rd *ESTON* TS6 .... 101 E4
  HTLPS TS25 .... 23 F5
  NORM/PKE TS3 .... 79 E4
Ormston Av *NORM/PKE* TS3 ... 100 A4 🈂
Orpington Rd *NORM/PKE* TS3... 100 A4
Orton Gv *BLGHMW/WYN* TS22 ... 57 F1
Orwell Cl *SALT/BTN/SK* TS12 .. 109 F1 🈂
Orwell Gdns *STOCN* TS19 .... 93 D2 🈂
Orwell St *MBORO* TS1 .... 4 A6

Osborne Rd *ACK/BRKF* TS5 ...... 97 F2 🈂
  HTLPW TS26 .... 2 A4
  SPEN DL16 .... 14 C4
  STOCS TS18 .... 94 B3
Osborne St *SHIL* DL4 .... 35 E3 🈂
Osbourne Cl *CNHM/HEM* TS8 .. 123 F5
  DARLW DL3 .... 131 D1
Osprey Cl *NORTON* TS20 .... 58 A4
Osric Pl *NACLF* DL5 .... 38 B4
Ostler Cl *THNBY* TS17 .... 139 D1 🈂
Oswald Pl *FYHL* DL17 .... 20 C1 🈂
Oswestry Gn *MGRV/ESTR* TS4 .. 125 D2
Otley Av *NORM/PKE* TS3 .... 100 A4
Otley Ter *DARLW* DL3 .... 116 A4 🈂
Ottawa Rd *MGRV/ESTR* TS4 ...... 98 C1
Otterburn Cl *DARLE* DL1 .... 117 D2 🈂
Otterburn Gdns *ACK/BRKF* TS5 .. 123 F5
Otterburn Wy *BLGHM* TS23 ...... 42 B4 🈂
Otterhill Ct *CNHM/HEM* TS8 ... 123 F4 🈂
Otterington Cl *RHTLP* TS27 ...... 10 C4
Otterpool Cl *HTLP* TS24 .... 18 A1 🈂
Otter Wy *THNBY* TS17 .... 121 D5
Oughton Cl *YARM* TS15 .... 147 D1
Oulston Rd *STOCS* TS18 .... 93 F2
Ouseport Rd *STOCS* TS18 .... 75 E5 🈂
Outhwaite St *ACK/BRKF* TS5 .... 97 E1 🈂
Outram St *DARLW* DL3 .... 9 E4
  MBORO TS1 .... 4 C6
Oval Gra *HTLPW* TS26 .... 17 D4
The Oval *ACK/BRKF* TS5 .... 123 E4
  HTLPW TS26 .... 17 E4
  SHIL DL4 .... 35 E2
Overdale Cl *REDCAR* TS10 .... 68 B5
Overdale Rd *NORM/PKE* TS3 ..... 99 E3
Owens Rd *ESTON* TS6 .... 80 B4
Owen St *FYHL* DL17 .... 20 B2
Owington Gv *BLGHM* TS23 .... 42 B3
Owlets Ct *THNBY* TS17 .... 139 D5 🈂
Owton Cl *HTLPS* TS25 .... 23 E5
Owton Manor La *HTLPS* TS25 .... 23 E5
Oxbridge Av *STOCS* TS18 .... 93 F1
Oxbridge La *STOCS* TS18 .... 6 A6
Ox Close Crs *SPEN* DL16 .... 15 D2
Oxford Rd *ACK/BRKF* TS5 .... 97 E3
  HTLPS TS25 .... 23 E2
  SPEN DL16 .... 15 D2 🈂
  THNBY TS17 .... 95 E4
Oxford St *DARLE* DL1 .... 9 G2
  HTLPS TS25 .... 24 A2 🈂
  MBORO TS1 .... 97 F1
  SALT/BTN/SK TS12 .... 89 D2
  SALT/BTN/SK TS12 .... 109 D5
  SHIL DL4 .... 35 E4
  STOCS TS18 .... 7 F1
Oxford Ter *BAUK* DL14 .... 27 D1 🈂
Oxgang Cl *REDCAR* TS10 .... 68 B4
Oxley St *REDCAR* TS10 .... 51 F4

P

The Paddock *EGG/EAG* TS16 ..... 119 E5
  FYHL DL17 .... 39 D2
  GTAY/STK TS9 .... 152 B1
Padstow Cl *HTLPW* TS26 .... 16 C3
Page Gv *SPEN* DL16 .... 14 B4
Paignton Cl *CNHM/HEM* TS8 ... 125 D5
Paignton Dr *HTLPS* TS25 .... 31 E1
Palin Cl *MGRV/ESTR* TS4 .... 78 C4 🈂
Pallister Av *NORM/PKE* TS3 ..... 100 A1
Palmer Rd *NACLF* DL5 .... 55 D3
Palmerston St *STOCS* TS18 .... 7 E4
Palm Gv *STOCN* TS19 .... 93 D1
Palm St *MBORO* TS1 .... 5 H5
Palm Ter *TEESM* TS2 .... 61 D5
Pannel Cl *MARSKE* TS11 .... 86 B3 🈂
Pannell Av *ACK/BRKF* TS5 .... 97 D5
Pannell Cl *RHTLP* TS27 .... 11 E3 🈂
Pannierman La *GTAY/STK* TS9 .. 149 E2
The Parade *HTLPW* TS26 .... 17 D4
Paris Pl *MTN/NUN* TS7 .... 125 D3
Park Av *ESTON* TS6 .... 101 D1
  HTLPW TS26 .... 17 D4
  REDCAR TS10 .... 51 F5
  THNBY TS17 .... 95 F4
Park Av North *NORM/PKE* TS3 .. 100 B4
Park Av South *NORM/PKE* TS3 .. 100 C4
Park Ct *REDCAR* TS10 .... 51 F5
Park Crs *DARLE* DL1 .... 132 B4
Parkdale Wy *ACK/BRKF* TS5 ..... 98 A5 🈂
Park Dr *HTLPW* TS26 .... 16 C4
  STOCN TS19 .... 73 F3
Parkfield Av *ACK/BRKF* TS5 ...... 97 F5
Parkfield Rd *STOCS* TS18 .... 94 C3
Parkgate *DARLE* DL1 .... 9 H5
  ESTON TS6 .... 102 C2
Parkgate Rbt *DARLE* DL1 .... 9 G5
Parkin St *STOCS* TS18 .... 7 F3
Parkland Dr *DARLW* DL3 .... 114 B5
Parkland Gv *DARLW* DL3 .... 114 B5
Parklands Av *BLGHM* TS23 .... 58 C5
Parklands Cl *NORM/PKE* TS3 .... 99 F2 🈂

Parklands Wy HTLPW TS26 ...... 16 B5
Park La DARLE DL1 ...... 132 B3
   GUIS TS14 ...... 128 B3
   MBORO TS1 ...... 98 B1
Park Ms HTLPW TS26 ...... 17 D4
Park Pl DARLE DL1 ...... 9 H6
Park Rd ACK/BRKF TS5 ...... 98 A1
   HTLP TS24 ...... 2 B4
   HTLPW TS26 ...... 17 F5
   SALT/BTN/SK TS12 ...... 110 C1 [2]
   STOCS TS18 ...... 94 B3
   THNBY TS17 ...... 121 E1
Park Rd North MBORO TS1 ...... 98 A1 [1]
Park Rd South ACK/BRKF TS5 ...... 98 A2
   MGRV/ESTR TS4 ...... 98 B2
Parkside DARLE DL1 ...... 131 F4
   GUIS TS14 ...... 128 C2
   NORM/PKE TS3 ...... 126 A1
Park Sq HTLPW TS26 ...... 17 E3
Parkstone Cl MARSKE TS11 ...... 86 C3
Parkstone Gv HTLP TS24 ...... 11 F3 [2]
Parkstone Pl EGG/EAG TS16 ...... 137 D2
Park St BAUK DL14 ...... 27 E1
   DARLE DL1 ...... 9 G6
   MBORO TS1 ...... 5 F3
Park Ter SALT/BTN/SK TS12 ...... 111 D1 [2]
   STOCS TS18 ...... 7 F6
   THNBY TS17 ...... 95 E4
Park Vale Rd MGRV/ESTR TS4 ...... 78 C5
Parkview Rd East HTLPS TS25 ...... 24 B5
Parkview Rd West HTLPS TS25 ...... 24 A4
Parkway Dr ESTON TS6 ...... 101 F4
Parkway Gv NORM/PKE TS3 ...... 99 F2
The Parkway SALT/BTN/SK TS12 ...... 88 C2
Parkwood Dr STOCS TS18 ...... 93 F4 [1]
Parliament Cl STOCS TS18 ...... 94 C3 [3]
Parliament Rd MBORO TS1 ...... 4 C6
Parliament St STOCS TS18 ...... 94 C3
Parliament Wk STOCS TS18 ...... 94 C3 [3]
Parracombe Cl THNBY TS17 ...... 139 D4 [3]
Parrington Pl ESTON TS6 ...... 83 E5
Parsons Ct FYHL DL17 ...... 20 B2
Parton St HTLP TS24 ...... 18 A2
Partridge Av ACK/BRKF TS5 ...... 123 E3 [3]
Partridge Cl THNBY TS17 ...... 139 D1 [7]
Passfield Crs ESTON TS6 ...... 81 D3
Pasture Cl MARSKE TS11 ...... 69 F5
Pasture La ESTON TS6 ...... 83 E4
The Pastures CNHM/HEM TS8 ...... 143 E1
Pateley Moor Crs DARLE DL1 ...... 133 D5
Patten La GUIS TS14 ...... 129 E2 [1]
Patten St ESTON TS6 ...... 101 F3 [2]
Patterdale Av ACK/BRKF TS5 ...... 97 C5
   STOCS TS18 ...... 6 B1
Patterdale St HTLPS TS25 ...... 24 A2
Pattison St DARLE DL1 ...... 132 C2 [3]
Paulinus Rd NACLF DL5 ...... 54 B1
Pauntley Dr ACK/BRKF TS5 ...... 123 E4 [3]
Pavilion Cl HTLPS TS25 ...... 32 C1
Paxton Cl NACLF DL5 ...... 38 A4
   STOCS TS18 ...... 7 H2
Paxton St FYHL DL17 ...... 20 A1
Peabody St DARLW DL3 ...... 116 B2
Peacocks Cl GTAY/STK TS9 ...... 152 A1
Peakston Cl HTLPW TS26 ...... 16 C3
Pearl Rd THNBY TS17 ...... 95 F5
Pearl St MBORO TS1 ...... 5 E5
   SALT/BTN/SK TS12 ...... 89 E1
   SHIL DL4 ...... 35 E3
Pearson Cl STOCS TS18 ...... 94 C3
Pearson St MBORO TS1 ...... 4 B4
Pearson Wy THNBY TS17 ...... 95 E2
Pease St DARLE DL1 ...... 133 D2
Pease Wy NACLF DL5 ...... 54 B1
Peaton St NORM/PKE TS3 ...... 79 E5
Peel St BAUK DL14 ...... 27 E2
   DARLE DL1 ...... 132 C2 [2]
   MBORO TS1 ...... 5 E5
   THNBY TS17 ...... 95 E4
Pegman Cl GUIS TS14 ...... 129 E1 [3]
Peirse Cl MGRV/ESTR TS4 ...... 78 C4
Peirson St REDCAR TS10 ...... 51 D4
Pelham St HTLP TS24 ...... 17 F2
   MBORO TS1 ...... 5 H6
Pelton Cl BLGHM TS23 ...... 41 F3
Pemberton Crs MGRV/ESTR TS4 ...... 98 C4 [3]
Pemberton Rd NACLF DL5 ...... 38 C2
Pembroke Dr YARM TS15 ...... 138 B4
Pembroke Gv HTLPW TS26 ...... 17 D1
Pembroke Rd NORTON TS20 ...... 74 C2
Pembroke Wy REDCAR TS10 ...... 69 D1
Penberry Gdns THNBY TS17 ...... 138 B3
Penders La YARM TS15 ...... 147 D5
Penderyn Crs THNBY TS17 ...... 95 E3
Pendle Crs BLGHM TS23 ...... 59 D2 [2]
Pendleton Rd DARLE DL1 ...... 116 B3
Pendock Cl ACK/BRKF TS5 ...... 123 F3 [3]
Pendower St DARLW DL3 ...... 9 E1
Penhill Cl NORM/PKE TS3 ...... 99 E2
Penhill Rd STOCS TS18 ...... 93 D3
Penistone Rd NORM/PKE TS3 ...... 100 A4
Penllyn Wy CNHM/HEM TS8 ...... 123 F4
Pennard Gn NORM/PKE TS3 ...... 100 A2 [2]
Pennine Av STOCS TS18 ...... 76 B3
Pennine Cl DARLW DL3 ...... 115 D5

Pennine Crs REDCAR TS10 ...... 68 A2
Pennine Wy SALT/BTN/SK TS12 ...... 109 E1
   THNBY TS17 ...... 138 C4
Pennington Cl BLGHM TS23 ...... 42 A5 [2]
Pennyman Cl ESTON TS6 ...... 101 E3 [2]
Pennyman St NORM/PKE TS3 ...... 79 D4
Pennyman Wk MARSKE TS11 ...... 70 C5
Pennyman Wy CNHM/HEM TS8 .. 141 E1 [7]
Pennypot La EGG/EAG TS16 ...... 119 F2
Penrhyn St HTLPW TS26 ...... 2 B5
Penrith Cl REDCAR TS10 ...... 68 B2
Penrith Rd NORM/PKE TS3 ...... 99 F3
Penrith St HTLP TS24 ...... 18 C1
Penryn Cl SALT/BTN/SK TS12 ...... 109 F1
Pensbury St DARLE DL1 ...... 9 H6
Pensby Av MGRV/ESTR TS4 ...... 125 D2 [3]
Penshaw Cl THNBY TS17 ...... 139 E1 [3]
Penshaw Cl BLGHM TS23 ...... 42 A5 [7][2]
Penshurst Pl BLGHM TS23 ...... 59 E1 [3]
Pentilly St HTLP TS24 ...... 19 E1 [10]
Pentland Av BLGHM TS23 ...... 58 C2
   REDCAR TS10 ...... 67 F3
   SALT/BTN/SK TS12 ...... 109 E1 [3]
Pentland Gv DARLW DL3 ...... 130 C2
Penton Ct BLGHM TS23 ...... 42 A4 [3]
Penwick Cl YARM TS15 ...... 146 A1 [1]
Penyghent Wy THNBY TS17 ...... 139 D4
Percy Rd DARLW DL3 ...... 116 A2
Percy St BAUK DL14 ...... 27 D4
   HTLPW TS26 ...... 17 E3
   MBORO TS1 ...... 5 E6
Peregrine Ct GUIS TS14 ...... 128 A3
Perth Av THNBY TS17 ...... 121 F5
Perth Crs MTN/NUN TS7 ...... 125 F4
Perth Gv STOCS TS18 ...... 93 F3
Perth St HTLP TS24 ...... 18 A3 [3]
Pert Rd HTLP TS24 ...... 12 A4
Petch St STOCS TS18 ...... 7 E4
Peterhouse Cl DARLE DL1 ...... 116 C3
Petrel Crs NORTON TS20 ...... 57 F4
Petworth Crs THNBY TS17 ...... 139 D2
Pevensey Cl MGRV/ESTR TS4 ...... 98 C5
Peverell St BAUK DL14 ...... 27 F4 [3]
Peveril Rd BLGHM TS23 ...... 58 C1
Pexton Cl CNHM/HEM TS8 ...... 123 E5
Pheasant Cl THNBY TS17 ...... 139 D1 [3]
Phillida Ter ACK/BRKF TS5 ...... 98 B2 [3]
Phillips Av ACK/BRKF TS5 ...... 98 A3
Phoenix Cl HTLPS TS25 ...... 31 D1
Phoenix Pk CNHM/HEM TS8 ...... 124 A4
Phoenix Sidings STOCS TS19 ...... 7 E3
Phoenix Wk STOCS TS18 ...... 93 F2
Phyllis Mohan Ct NORM/PKE TS3 .. 99 F4 [7]
Pickering Gv HTLPS TS25 ...... 23 F5
Pickering Rd THNBY TS17 ...... 95 F5
Picton Av ACK/BRKF TS5 ...... 97 D4 [3]
   BLGHMW/WYN TS22 ...... 41 E5
Picton Crs THNBY TS17 ...... 121 D4
Picton Pl NORTON TS20 ...... 75 D1 [3]
Piercebridge Cl STOCS TS19 ...... 73 E4 [3]
Pierremont Crs DARLW DL3 ...... 8 A3
Pierremont Dr DARLW DL3 ...... 8 B2
Pierremont Gdns DARLW DL3 ...... 8 B3
Pierremont Rd DARLW DL3 ...... 8 B1
Pikeston Cl HTLPW TS26 ...... 16 C3 [3]
Pilgrim St HTLP TS24 ...... 3 F4
Pilkington St NORM/PKE TS3 ...... 79 E5 [13]
Pilmoor Gn DARLE DL1 ...... 133 D4
Pinder Cl NORTON TS20 ...... 74 C1 [3]
Pineda Cl ACK/BRKF TS5 ...... 123 F4
Pine Gv DARLW DL3 ...... 131 D5
   HTLP TS24 ...... 17 E1
Pine Hl CNHM/HEM TS8 ...... 125 E5
Pine Rd GUIS TS14 ...... 128 C2
   MTN/NUN TS7 ...... 101 D5
Pinero Gv HTLPS TS25 ...... 22 C3
The Pines YARM TS15 ...... 137 E5
Pine St MBORO TS1 ...... 5 G3
   NORM/PKE TS3 ...... 79 F4
   NORTON TS20 ...... 75 D1
Pine Tree Crs SHIL DL4 ...... 36 A3
Pinewood Av MGRV/ESTR TS4 ...... 98 B4
Pinewood Cl RHTLP TS27 ...... 11 E3
Pinewood Rd EGG/EAG TS16 ...... 119 E4
   MTN/NUN TS7 ...... 126 B3
Pinewood Wk GTAY/STK TS9 ...... 152 B1
Pinfold St STOCS TS18 ...... 7 C2
Piper Knowle Rd STOCN TS19 ...... 73 E1 [3]
Pipit Cl THNBY TS17 ...... 138 C1
The Pippins BLGHMW/WYN TS22 ...... 41 E3
Pirbright Gv CNHM/HEM TS8 ...... 124 A5
Planetree St MTN/NUN TS7 ...... 126 A3
Plantation Rd REDCAR TS10 ...... 68 B5
Player Ct EGG/EAG TS16 ...... 137 E1 [3]
Playlin Cl YARM TS15 ...... 138 A5
Plumer Dr NORTON TS20 ...... 74 C1 [3]
Plymouth Gv HTLPW TS26 ...... 17 D2
Pochin Rd ESTON TS6 ...... 82 A3 [3]
Polam La DARLE DL1 ...... 132 A3
Polam Rd DARLE DL1 ...... 132 A3
Poldon Ter BLGHM TS23 ...... 59 D3 [7]
Pond Field Cl DARLW DL3 ...... 130 C3
Pontac Rd MARSKE TS11 ...... 86 C2
Pope Gv HTLPS TS25 ...... 22 C2

Poplar Dr SPEN DL16 ...... 14 C4
Poplar Gv ESTON TS6 ...... 81 D5
   SALT/BTN/SK TS12 ...... 90 C5
Poplar Pl GUIS TS14 ...... 128 B2
Poplar Rd EGG/EAG TS16 ...... 137 D2 [7]
Poplars Rd ACK/BRKF TS5 ...... 98 A3
The Poplars BLGHMW/WYN TS22 ...... 41 E3
Poplar Ter TEESM TS2 ...... 61 D5 [3]
Poppy La STOCS TS19 ...... 73 E4
Porlock Rd BLGHM TS23 ...... 58 B1
Porrett Cl HTLP TS24 ...... 12 A3
Port Clarence Rd TEESM TS2 ...... 61 G5 [3]
Porter Cl NACLF DL5 ...... 39 D4 [3]
Porthleven Wy REDCAR TS10 ...... 69 E4
Portland Cl EGG/EAG TS16 ...... 137 E2 [7]
   MTN/NUN TS7 ...... 125 E4 [3]
   REDCAR TS10 ...... 68 B5 [3]
Portland Gv HTLPW TS26 ...... 11 F5 [3]
Portland Pl DARLW DL3 ...... 9 E4
Portman Ri GUIS TS14 ...... 129 D5
Portman Rd NORTON TS20 ...... 74 C2
Portman St MBORO TS1 ...... 5 E6
Portrack Back La STOCS TS18 ...... 75 F3
Portrack Grange Cl STOCS TS18 ...... 76 B3
Portrack Grange Rd STOCS TS18 .. 76 A4 [3]
Portrack La STOCS TS18 ...... 75 E5
Portrush Cl DARLE DL1 ...... 117 F2 [3]
   MARSKE TS11 ...... 86 B3 [10]
   MGRV/ESTR TS4 ...... 98 B5
Post Horn NACLF DL5 ...... 37 E4
Pottery St THNBY TS17 ...... 95 D4
Potto Cl YARM TS15 ...... 138 A5 [3]
Pounder Pl HTLP TS24 ...... 12 B5 [7]
Powburn Cl STOCN TS19 ...... 72 C4 [3]
Powell St HTLPW TS26 ...... 23 F1
Powlett Rd HTLP TS24 ...... 17 F1
Prebend Rw DARLE DL1 ...... 9 F4
Preen Dr ACK/BRKF TS5 ...... 97 D5
Premier Rd MTN/NUN TS7 ...... 126 C1
   NORM/PKE TS3 ...... 99 F2
   STOCN TS19 ...... 93 E1
Prescot Rd NORM/PKE TS3 ...... 100 B4 [3]
Prescott St DARLE DL1 ...... 116 C5
Preseli Gv THNBY TS17 ...... 138 B3
Preston La STOCS TS18 ...... 120 A2
Preston Rd NACLF DL5 ...... 54 B3
   STOCS TS18 ...... 93 E2
Preston St HTLPW TS26 ...... 17 F3 [3]
Preston Wy GTAY/STK TS9 ...... 152 A1
Prestwick Cl NORM/PKE TS3 ...... 100 B4
Prestwick Dr MGRV/ESTR TS4 ...... 98 B5
Prestwick Ct EGG/EAG TS16 ...... 137 E2 [3]
Preswick Cl MARSKE TS11 ...... 86 B3 [11]
Price Av ACK/BRKF TS5 ...... 97 D4
   BAUK DL14 ...... 26 C5
Price Rd REDCAR TS10 ...... 67 D2
Priestcrofts MARSKE TS11 ...... 71 D5
Priestfield Av NORM/PKE TS3 ...... 100 A5
Priestgate DARLE DL1 ...... 9 G4
Priestman Rd NACLF DL5 ...... 38 B5
Primitive St SHIL DL4 ...... 35 E2
Primrose Cl GUIS TS14 ...... 128 A4
   SPEN DL16 ...... 14 B4
Primrose St DARLW DL3 ...... 9 E5
   STOCN TS19 ...... 6 D1 [1]
Prince Pl REDCAR TS10 ...... 51 E4 [3]
Princeport Rd STOCS TS18 ...... 75 E5 [3]
Prince Regent St STOCS TS18 ...... 7 F5
Princes Rd MBORO TS1 ...... 4 D6
   SALT/BTN/SK TS12 ...... 89 E3
Princess Av STOCS TS18 ...... 7 G2
Princes Sq THNBY TS17 ...... 121 F4
Princess Sq HTLP TS24 ...... 19 E2
   SPEN DL16 ...... 14 C3 [3]
   TEESM TS2 ...... 5 F1
   THNBY TS17 ...... 95 E3
Prince's St BAUK DL14 ...... 27 D1
   DARLE DL1 ...... 132 C2 [3]
   MBORO TS1 ...... 5 E5
   SHIL DL4 ...... 35 D2
Princeton Dr THNBY TS17 ...... 95 E2
Prior Dene DARLW DL3 ...... 115 D4
Prior St DARLW DL3 ...... 115 D4
Priorwood Gdns THNBY TS17 ...... 139 D3
Priory Cl GUIS TS14 ...... 129 D2
Priory Dr CNHM/HEM TS8 ...... 141 E1
Priory Gdns NORTON TS20 ...... 74 C1
Priory Gv REDCAR TS10 ...... 50 C5
Priory Rd ACK/BRKF TS5 ...... 96 C4
Prissick St HTLP TS24 ...... 19 E2
Pritchett Rd NORM/PKE TS3 ...... 100 B4
Progress Wy DARLE DL1 ...... 9 G1
Prospect Pl DARLW DL3 ...... 116 A3
   NORTON TS20 ...... 75 D3 [10]
Prospect Ter MARSKE TS11 ...... 70 C5 [3]
The Prospect ACK/BRKF TS5 ...... 98 A4 [3]
Prospect Wy HTLPS TS25 ...... 24 A5
Protear Gv NORTON TS20 ...... 58 B5
Proudfoot Gv BAUK DL14 ...... 26 C5
Puddlers Rd ESTON TS6 ...... 80 C2
Pulford Gv NORTON TS20 ...... 74 B1
Pump La YARM TS15 ...... 147 D5
Punch St MBORO TS1 ...... 4 B4
Purfleet Av NORM/PKE TS3 ...... 80 A5
Purves St HTLP TS24 ...... 12 C5
Pym St ESTON TS6 ...... 80 C4 [3]

Pytchley Rd GUIS TS14 .... 129 D4

Q

Quaker La DARLE DL1 .... 9 E6
Quantock Cl DARLE DL1 .... 117 D3 ⑤
Quarry Bank Rd MARSKE TS11 .... 87 E5
Quarry Dr CNHM/HEM TS8 .... 141 E1
Quarry La MARSKE TS11 .... 87 F2
Quarry Rd STOCS TS18 .... 119 E4
Quarry St SHIL DL4 .... 35 E3
Quayside STOCS TS18 .... 7 G5
Quebec Gv BLGHM TS23 .... 42 A4 ⑤
    MGRV/ESTR TS4 .... 98 C2 ⑥
Quebec Rd STOCS TS18 .... 93 F4
Quebec St DARLE DL1 .... 9 G4
Queen Anne Ter STOCS TS18 .... 93 F3 ⑧
Queens Av THNBY TS17 .... 95 E3
Queensberry Av HTLPW TS26 .... 17 E5
Queensbury Cl REDCAR TS10 ...... 67 F4 ⑤
Queens Dr BLGHMW/WYN TS22 ...... 58 B1
    GTAY/STK TS9 .... 21 E3
    SEDG TS21 .... 28 C5
Queensland Av REDCAR TS10 .... 68 C1
Queensland Gv STOCS TS18 .... 93 F3 ⑥
Queensland Rd HTLPS TS25 .... 23 F5
Queensport Cl STOCS TS18 .... 75 F5
Queens Rd ACK/BRKF TS5 .... 97 F3
    BAUK DL14 .... 27 E2
    LOFT/ST TS13 .... 113 D2
Queen's Sq TEESM TS2 .... 5 G1
Queen's Ter TEESM TS2 .... 78 B1 ⑧
Queen St ESTON TS6 .... 80 C3
    ESTON TS6 .... 83 E5
    HTLP TS24 .... 18 C3
    HTLP TS24 .... 19 F2 ⑨
    HTLPS TS25 .... 25 D4
    LOFT/ST TS13 .... 112 B1
    REDCAR TS10 .... 51 D4
    SHIL DL4 .... 35 F2
    STOCS TS18 .... 7 G2
Queensway HTLPS TS25 .... 31 D4
    NORM/PKE TS3 .... 80 A4
    SALT/BTN/SK TS12 .... 88 C2
    SHIL DL4 .... 36 A3
Queen Ter HTLPS TS25 .... 25 D5 ⑥
Quenby Rd BLGHM TS23 .... 59 D1
Quorn Cl GUIS TS14 .... 129 D5

R

Raby Dr NACLF DL5 .... 39 D3 ⑦
Raby Gdns BAUK DL14 .... 27 D3 ⑫⑤
    HTLP TS24 .... 17 F2
Raby Rd FYHL DL17 .... 21 D1
    HTLP TS24 .... 17 F2
    HTLPW TS26 .... 2 B1
    REDCAR TS10 .... 69 D1
    STOCS TS18 .... 93 F2
Raby St DARLW DL3 .... 8 D5
    HTLP TS24 .... 19 E2
Raby Ter DARLW DL3 .... 9 E4 ⑩
Radcliffe Av STOCN TS19 .... 74 A2 ⑦
Radcliffe Crs THNBY TS17 .... 95 E2
Radcliffe Ter HTLP TS24 .... 19 F2
Radford Cl STOCN TS19 .... 56 C5 ⑥
Radlett Av STOCN TS19 .... 73 F2
Radnor Cl STOCN TS19 .... 74 A2 ⑥
Radnor Gn NORM/PKE TS3 .... 100 A5
Radnor Gv HTLPW TS26 .... 16 C2
Radstock Av STOCN TS19 .... 74 A1
Radyr Cl STOCN TS19 .... 56 B5
Raeburn St HTLPW TS26 .... 17 E4 ⑩
Rafton Dr RHTLP TS27 .... 11 F3
Raglan Cl STOCN TS19 .... 56 B5 ⑪
Ragpath La STOCN TS19 .... 73 F1
Ragworth Rd NORTON TS20 .... 74 C1
Railway Pl ESTON TS6 .... 81 F4 ⑨
Railway St BAUK DL14 .... 27 E2
    NORTON TS20 .... 75 D4
Railway Ter REDCAR TS10 .... 51 E5 ⑧
    SALT/BTN/SK TS12 .... 111 D1
    SHIL DL4 .... 35 E4
    THNBY TS17 .... 95 E3
Raincliffe Ct CNHM/HEM TS8 ...... 125 D5
Raine St BAUK DL14 .... 27 D1 ⑩
Rainford Av STOCN TS19 .... 74 A2
Rainham Cl NORM/PKE TS3 .... 100 C1
    THNBY TS17 .... 139 D3
Rainsford Crs NORM/PKE TS3 .... 100 B1
Rainton Av ACK/BRKF TS5 .... 123 E2
Rainton Dr THNBY TS17 .... 121 D3 ⑧
Rainton Gv STOCS TS18 .... 92 C3 ⑧
Raisbeck Cl MARSKE TS11 .... 70 B5 ⑥
Raisby Cl ACK/BRKF TS5 .... 123 D3
Raisdale Cl THNBY TS17 .... 121 F2
Raisegill Cl NORM/PKE TS3 .... 99 D2
Raithwaite Cl GUIS TS14 .... 128 C3
Rake Av STOCN TS19 .... 56 C5
Raleigh Cl MARSKE TS11 .... 88 B1 ⑤

Raleigh Ct TEESM TS2 .... 4 A1
Raleigh Rd NORTON TS20 .... 74 C2 ⑥
Ralfland Wy MTN/NUN TS7 .... 126 C5
Ralph Sq STOCN TS19 .... 73 F4 ⑧
Rampside Av STOCN TS19 .... 56 C5 ⑧
Ramsay Pl NACLF DL5 .... 39 D5
Ramsbury Av STOCN TS19 .... 73 F1
Ramsey Crs YARM TS15 .... 146 A1
Ramsey Dr FYHL DL17 .... 20 A2
Ramsey Rd REDCAR TS10 .... 67 E2
Ramsey Vw NORTON TS20 .... 75 E2
Ramsey Wk DARLE DL1 .... 117 E3 ⑧
Ramsgate STOCS TS18 .... 7 F5
Randolph St SALT/BTN/SK TS12 ..... 89 E3
Ranulf Ct NACLF DL5 .... 37 F4
Raskelf Av STOCN TS19 .... 73 F2 ⑥
Rathnew Av STOCN TS19 .... 73 E1 ⑥
Raunds Av STOCN TS19 .... 73 F2
Ravendale Rd NORM/PKE TS3 ...... 100 B4
Raven La NORTON TS20 .... 57 F5
Ravenscar Crs STOCN TS19 .... 74 B2
Ravenscroft Av ACK/BRKF TS5 .... 98 A4
Ravensdale Rd DARLW DL3 .... 131 E4
Ravensdale Wk DARLW DL3 ...... 131 E5 ⑧
Ravensworth Av BAUK DL14 ...... 27 D3 ⑪
    ESTON TS6 .... 101 E2
Ravensworth Crs HTLP TS24 .... 11 F2
Ravensworth Gv STOCS TS18 ...... 92 C3 ⑧
Ravensworth Rd BLGHM TS23 ...... 59 D1
    FYHL DL17 .... 21 E1
Ravenwood Cl RHTLP TS27 .... 11 D3
Rawcliffe Av ACK/BRKF TS5 .... 123 E4
Rawley Dr REDCAR TS10 .... 67 F4
Rawlings Ct HTLP TS24 .... 12 C5 ⑧
Rawlinson Av BLGHM TS23 .... 59 D5
Raydale CNHM/HEM TS8 .... 141 E1 ⑨
Raylton Av MTN/NUN TS7 .... 125 F5
Reading Rd NORTON TS20 .... 74 C3
Rectory Av GUIS TS14 .... 128 C3
Rectory Cl GUIS TS14 .... 128 C3
    HTLPS TS25 .... 33 D1
Rectory La GUIS TS14 .... 128 C3
Rectory Rw SEDG TS21 .... 29 E4
Red Barnes Wy DARLE DL1 .... 117 E5
Redbrook Av STOCN TS19 .... 73 F1 ⑥
Redcar Av MARSKE TS11 .... 70 A5
    STOCN TS19 .... 74 A2 ⑥
Redcar Cl HTLPS TS25 .... 2 A6
Redcar La REDCAR TS10 .... 51 F5
    REDCAR TS10 .... 68 C4
Redcar Rd GUIS TS14 .... 105 F1
    GUIS TS14 .... 129 D2
    MARSKE TS11 .... 69 F5
    REDCAR TS10 .... 69 D4
    THNBY TS17 .... 121 E1
Redcar Rd East ESTON TS6 .... 80 C3
Redcar St TEESM TS2 .... 5 G1
Redditch Av STOCN TS19 .... 74 A1
Redesdale Gv THNBY TS17 .... 138 C3 ⑨
Red Hall Dr DARLE DL1 .... 117 E5
Red Hall La YARM TS15 .... 147 F4
Redhill Rd STOCN TS19 .... 73 F2
Redland Cl STOCS TS18 .... 92 C2
Red Lion St REDCAR TS10 .... 51 E4
Redmayne Pl BLGHM TS23 .... 42 A5 ⑨
Redmire Cl DARLE DL1 .... 116 B3
Redmire Rd STOCS TS18 .... 6 A5
Redruth Av STOCN TS19 .... 74 A2 ⑥
Redstart Cl HTLPW TS26 .... 17 D1 ⑥
Redwing La NORTON TS20 .... 58 A4
Redwing Rising GUIS TS14 .... 128 A3 ⑧
Redwood Cl RHTLP TS27 .... 11 E3
Redwood Dr SALT/BTN/SK TS12 ..... 88 C3
Redworth Rd BLGHM TS23 .... 59 E1
    DARLW DL3 .... 114 C4 ⑩
    NACLF DL5 .... 52 B4
    SHIL DL4 .... 35 F4
Redworth Wy NACLF DL5 .... 54 C3
Reed Cl NORTON TS20 .... 75 E2 ⑧
Reedston Rd HTLPW TS26 .... 16 B3 ⑥
Reed St HTLP TS24 .... 3 E3
    THNBY TS17 .... 95 E3 ⑩
Reepham Cl STOCN TS19 .... 73 E1 ⑥
Reeth Moor Cl DARLE DL1 .... 133 F3
Reeth Rd NACLF DL5 .... 38 A4
Reeth Rd ACK/BRKF TS5 .... 97 E4
    STOCS TS18 .... 93 E4
Regal Dr DARLE DL1 .... 116 C1
Regency Av ESTON TS6 .... 101 F4
Regency Dr HTLPS TS25 .... 24 A4
Regency Pk THNBY TS17 .... 139 D3
Regent Cl ESTON TS6 .... 82 A5 ⑥
Regent Rd MGRV/ESTR TS4 .... 98 C3
Regent Sq HTLP TS24 .... 19 E2 ⑭
Regent St BAUK DL14 .... 27 E1
    HTLP TS24 .... 19 E2
    REDCAR TS10 .... 51 E4
    SHIL DL4 .... 35 D3
    STOCS TS18 .... 7 F4
Reid St DARLW DL3 .... 8 C1
Reid Ter GUIS TS14 .... 129 D2
Reigate Av ACK/BRKF TS5 .... 98 A4
Reigate Cl STOCN TS19 .... 73 F1

Reivaulx Dr ACK/BRKF TS5 .... 98 A5
Relton Wy HTLPW TS26 .... 17 D5
Rembrandt Wy NACLF DL5 .... 54 C4
Renfrew Cl NORTON TS20 .... 75 D1 ⑧
Rennie Cl DARLE DL1 .... 132 C1
Rennie Rd ESTON TS6 .... 80 B5
Rennie St FYHL DL17 .... 20 B2
Renown Wk ESTON TS6 .... 81 D5 ⑦
Renvyle Av STOCN TS19 .... 73 E1
Repton Av STOCN TS19 .... 73 F2
Repton Rd NORM/PKE TS3 .... 100 C1 ⑧
The Resolution MTN/NUN TS7 .... 126 C4
Resource Cl ESTON TS6 .... 81 D4
Retford Cl STOCN TS19 .... 73 F1 ⑧
Retford Gv HTLPS TS25 .... 31 D3 ⑦
Rettendon Cl STOCN TS19 .... 74 A1
Revesby Rd NORM/PKE TS3 .... 100 B4
Reynolds Ct BLGHM TS23 .... 41 F4 ⑦
Reynoldston Av STOCN TS19 .... 56 C5 ⑧
Rhinog Gv THNBY TS17 .... 138 B1
Rhobell Vw THNBY TS17 .... 138 A1
Rhondda Rd STOCN TS19 .... 74 A2
Rhoose Ga THNBY TS17 .... 122 A1 ⑧
Rhyl Cl STOCN TS19 .... 74 A1 ⑥
Ribble Cl BLGHMW/WYN TS22 ...... 40 C5 ⑧
Ribble Dr DARLE DL1 .... 132 A5
Ribbleton Cl MTN/NUN TS7 .... 126 B4 ⑧
Ribchester Cl STOCN TS19 .... 73 F1 ⑦
Riccarton Cl STOCN TS19 .... 73 E1 ⑧
Richardson Rd STOCS TS18 .... 94 B3
    THNBY TS17 .... 121 D1
Richardson St HTLPW TS26 .... 17 F3 ⑥
Richards St SALT/BTN/SK TS12 .... 110 B2
Richmond Av BAUK DL14 .... 26 B3
Richmond Cl DARLW DL3 .... 114 C3 ⑩
    ESTON TS6 .... 101 F2 ⑥
    FYHL DL17 .... 21 E2 ⑩
Richmond Ct ESTON TS6 .... 82 A5 ⑥
Richmond Crs BLGHM TS23 .... 59 D1 ⑧
Richmond Rd REDCAR TS10 .... 69 D2
    STOCS TS18 .... 94 A3
Richmond St HTLPS TS25 .... 24 A2 ⑥
    TEESM TS2 .... 78 A2
Ricknall Av NACLF DL5 .... 55 D3
Ricknall Cl ACK/BRKF TS5 .... 123 D3
Ricknall La NACLF DL5 .... 55 E2
The Ridge CNHM/HEM TS8 .... 143 D3
    SALT/BTN/SK TS12 .... 89 E4
Ridgeway CNHM/HEM TS8 .... 142 C1
    DARLW DL3 .... 116 A1
    NACLF DL5 .... 54 B3
Ridley Av ACK/BRKF TS5 .... 97 E5
Ridley Dr NORTON TS20 .... 74 B1
Ridley St HTLPW TS26 .... 17 F3 ⑥
    REDCAR TS10 .... 51 E4
Ridlington Wy HTLP TS24 .... 12 A3
Ridsdale Av STOCN TS19 .... 73 F2 ⑧
Ridsdale St DARLE DL1 .... 132 C2
Rievaulx Av BLGHM TS23 .... 58 C1
Rievaulx Cl STOCN TS19 .... 73 F1
Rievaulx Rd SALT/BTN/SK TS12 ... 109 F1
Rievaulx Wk ESTON TS6 .... 101 F2 ⑦
Rievaulx Wy GUIS TS14 .... 129 E3
Rifts Av SALT/BTN/SK TS12 .... 89 D2
Riftswood Dr MARSKE TS11 .... 70 A5
Riggston Pl HTLPW TS26 .... 16 B3
The Rigg YARM TS15 .... 146 B1
Riley St STOCS TS18 .... 6 C5
Rillington Cl STOCN TS19 .... 73 E1 ⑦
Rillston Cl HTLPW TS26 .... 16 C3
Rimdale Dr STOCN TS19 .... 72 C5
Rimswell Rd STOCN TS19 .... 72 C4
Ringway THNBY TS17 .... 122 A2
Ringwood Crs STOCN TS19 .... 74 A2
Ringwood Rd NORM/PKE TS3 .... 100 C2
Ripley Rd NORTON TS20 .... 57 E5
Ripon Cl STOCN TS19 .... 73 F2 ⑧
Ripon Dr DARLE DL1 .... 132 C4
Ripon Rd MTN/NUN TS7 .... 127 D4
    REDCAR TS10 .... 69 E2
    SALT/BTN/SK TS12 .... 91 E5
Ripon Wy ESTON TS6 .... 102 B1
The Rise DARLW DL3 .... 131 E3
    MTN/NUN TS7 .... 126 C1
Rishton Cl STOCN TS19 .... 73 F2 ⑧
Ritson Rd NACLF DL5 .... 54 B1
Rium Ter HTLP TS24 .... 2 B1
Riverdale Ct ACK/BRKF TS5 .... 97 D3 ⑧
Riverhead Av STOCN TS19 .... 73 F2
Riverside BAUK DL14 .... 14 A3
    STOCS TS18 .... 7 G4
Riverside Park Rd TEESM TS2 .... 4 A1
Riverside Rd TEESM TS2 .... 63 E4
Riverston Cl HTLPW TS26 .... 16 B3 ⑧
Riversway MTN/NUN TS7 .... 126 A3 ⑥
Robert Av STOCN TS19 .... 81 F3
Robert St SPEN DL16 .... 14 C4 ⑥
    THNBY TS17 .... 95 E3
Robin Cl THNBY TS17 .... 139 D1 ⑧
Robinson St LOFT/ST TS13 .... 113 F3
    SALT/BTN/SK TS12 .... 109 D1
Robson Av THNBY TS17 .... 139 F1
Robson Cl HTLP TS24 .... 17 F1 ⑧
Robson St BLGHM TS23 .... 60 C4 ⑧
    SHIL DL4 .... 35 E2

Rochdale Av *STOCN* TS19 .... **74** A1
Rochdale Rd *NORM/PKE* TS3 .... **99** F3 **1**
Rochester Cl *THNBY* TS17 .... **138** C3 **10**
Rochester Ct *THNBY* TS17 .... **138** C2
Rochester Dr *REDCAR* TS10 .... **69** D2 **1**
Rochester Rd *ACK/BRKF* TS5 .... **98** A3
  BLGHM TS23 .... **59** D1
  STOCN TS19 .... **74** A1
Rochester Wy *DARLE* DL1 .... **117** F4
Rockall Av *STOCN* TS19 .... **73** E1 **3**
Rocket St *DARLE* DL1 .... **132** C2 **3**
Rocket Ter *REDCAR* TS10 .... **50** C4 **1**
Rockferry Cl *STOCN* TS19 .... **73** E1 **5**
Rockingham St *DARLE* DL1 .... **132** B3 **6**
Rockliffe Rd *ACK/BRKF* TS5 .... **97** E3
Rockpool Cl *HTLP* TS24 .... **13** D5 **2**
Rockport Cl *STOCS* TS18 .... **75** E5 **6**
Rock Rd *SPEN* DL16 .... **14** C4
Rockwell Av *DARLE* DL1 .... **117** E3
Rockwood Cl *GUIS* TS14 .... **129** E4
Rodmell Cl *NORM/PKE* TS3 .... **100** C3
Rodney Cl *BLGHM* TS23 .... **75** F1
  SALT/BTN/SK TS12 .... **91** E5
Rodney St *HTLPW* TS26 .... **2** A1
Roebuck St *THNBY* TS17 .... **121** E5 **2**
Roecliffe Gv *STOCN* TS19 .... **73** D1
Roedean Dr *EGG/EAG* TS16 .... **137** E2
Rogeri Pl *HTLP* TS24 .... **12** B4
Roger La *CNHM/HEM* TS8 .... **140** B3
Rokeby Av *MGRV/ESTR* TS4 .... **98** C5
Rokeby St *HTLP* TS24 .... **13** E5
  STOCS TS18 .... **94** B3 **4**
Roker Cl *DARLE* DL1 .... **117** F5 **2**
Roker St *HTLPW* TS26 .... **2** B3
Roker Ter *STOCS* TS18 .... **94** B3
Rolleston Av *STOCN* TS19 .... **56** B5 **2**
  STOCS TS18 .... **73** E1 **10**
Romaine Pk *HTLP* TS24 .... **13** E5
Romaldkirk Rd *TEESM* TS2 .... **4** B1
Romanby Av *STOCN* TS19 .... **74** A2 **3**
Romanby Cl *HTLP* TS24 .... **13** E5 **2**
Romanby Gdns *ACK/BRKF* TS5 .... **124** A4 **8**
Roman Rd *ACK/BRKF* TS5 .... **97** F3
Romany Rd *GTAY/STK* TS9 .... **150** C2 **8**
Romford Rd *STOCN* TS19 .... **73** F1
Romney Cl *REDCAR* TS10 .... **69** D3
Romney Gn *BLGHM* TS23 .... **41** F4 **3**
Romney St *MBORO* TS1 .... **5** E6
Romsey Rd *STOCN* TS19 .... **74** A2
Ronaldshay Ter *MARSKE* TS11 .... **70** C5
Rook La *NORTON* TS20 .... **58** A4
Rookwood Hunt *NACLF* DL5 .... **37** F4
Rookwood Rd *MTN/NUN* TS7 .... **127** D4
Ropery Rd *HTLP* TS24 .... **18** B1
Ropery St *STOCS* TS18 .... **7** F4
Ropner Av *STOCS* TS18 .... **94** A3
Rosa St *SPEN* DL16 .... **14** C3
Roscoe Rd *BLGHM* TS23 .... **59** D5
Roscoe St *MBORO* TS1 .... **78** C5
Rosebank *HTLPW* TS26 .... **2** A1
Rosebay Ct *GUIS* TS14 .... **128** A4 **1**
Roseberry Av *GTAY/STK* TS9 .... **151** D2
  GTAY/STK TS9 .... **152** C1
Roseberry Crs *ESTON* TS6 .... **102** C1
  GTAY/STK TS9 .... **151** D1
  NORTON TS20 .... **58** A5
Roseberry Dr *CNHM/HEM* TS8 .... **141** E1 **2**
  GTAY/STK TS9 .... **150** C2
Roseberry Rd *BLGHM* TS23 .... **58** B2
  GTAY/STK TS9 .... **150** C2
  MGRV/ESTR TS4 .... **98** C1
  NORTON TS20 .... **58** A5
  REDCAR TS10 .... **67** F3
Roseberry Vw *THNBY* TS17 .... **95** E4
Rosebery Rd *HTLPW* TS26 .... **17** E4 **2**
Rosebery St *DARLW* DL3 .... **8** D1
Rosecroft Av *LOFT/ST* TS13 .... **113** D4
  MGRV/ESTR TS4 .... **98** B4
Rosedale *SPEN* DL16 .... **14** C2
Rosedale Av *HTLPW* TS26 .... **17** E5
  MGRV/ESTR TS4 .... **98** B2 **2**
Rosedale Cl *SEDG* TS21 .... **29** E3
Rosedale Crs *DARLW* DL3 .... **114** C4
  GUIS TS14 .... **128** A4
  LOFT/ST TS13 .... **113** D2
  SHIL DL4 .... **36** A3
Rosedale Gdns *BLGHM* TS23 .... **41** F5 **7**
  STOCN TS19 .... **73** F1 **5**
Rosedale Gv *REDCAR* TS10 .... **67** E2
Rosedale Rd *MTN/NUN* TS7 .... **127** D4
Rosehill *GTAY/STK* TS9 .... **150** C3
Rose Hill Dr *GTAY/STK* TS9 .... **152** A3
Rose Hill Wy *GTAY/STK* TS9 .... **152** A3
Roseland Dr *MTN/NUN* TS7 .... **126** A2
Rose La *DARLE* DL1 .... **117** F3
Rosemoor Cl *MTN/NUN* TS7 .... **125** E4
Rosemount Ct *BAUK* DL14 .... **27** F4
Rosemount Rd *BAUK* DL14 .... **27** F4
  MARSKE TS11 .... **86** B3
Roseneath Av *STOCN* TS19 .... **56** C5
Rose St *MBORO* TS1 .... **5** E3
The Roseway *SALT/BTN/SK* TS12 .... **89** E3 **1**
Rosewood Cl *MTN/NUN* TS7 .... **101** D5 **13**
Rosewood Ct *MTN/NUN* TS7 .... **125** F5
Rosgill *REDCAR* TS10 .... **68** A2

Roslyn Av *NORM/PKE* TS3 .... **99** F3
Roslyn St *DARLE* DL1 .... **132** B3
Rossall St *HTLPS* TS25 .... **23** F2
Rossendale Cl *MARSKE* TS11 .... **87** E1 **3**
Rosetti Wy *BLGHM* TS23 .... **41** F4
Ross Gv *HTLPS* TS25 .... **24** A5
Rosslare Rd *STOCN* TS19 .... **73** F1
Rossmere *SPEN* DL16 .... **14** C1 **3**
Rossmere Wy *HTLPS* TS25 .... **23** E5
Ross Rd *STOCS* TS18 .... **75** F5
Ross St *MBORO* TS1 .... **4** C6
Rossway *DARLE* DL1 .... **117** F1
Rosthwaite *ACK/BRKF* TS5 .... **123** D3 **3**
Rosthwaite Av *STOCN* TS19 .... **74** A1
Rosthwaite Cl *HTLP* TS24 .... **18** A1 **2**
Rostrevor Av *STOCN* TS19 .... **56** C5
Rothbury Av *STOCN* TS19 .... **73** F1
Rothbury Cl *THNBY* TS17 .... **139** D3
Rothbury Dr *DARLW* DL3 .... **114** C3
Rothbury Rd *NORM/PKE* TS3 .... **99** E3
Rothbury St *BLGHM* TS23 .... **58** C2 **1**
  STOCN TS19 .... **73** F2
Rothesay Dr *REDCAR* TS10 .... **69** D5 **2**
Rothesay Gv *MTN/NUN* TS7 .... **127** D3
Rothwell Crs *STOCN* TS19 .... **73** F2
Rothwell Ms *ESTON* TS6 .... **102** B2 **1**
Rottingdean Cl *STOCN* TS19 .... **73** F1 **6**
Roundhay Dr *EGG/EAG* TS16 .... **137** F3 **10**
Roundhill Av *THNBY* TS17 .... **138** B3
Rounton Gn *NORM/PKE* TS3 .... **99** E3 **1**
Rounton Gv *STOCN* TS19 .... **93** D2
Routledge Ct *HTLP* TS24 .... **17** F1 **1**
Routledge Rd *NORTON* TS20 .... **75** E5
Rowallane Gdns *THNBY* TS17 .... **139** D3
Rowan Av *GUIS* TS14 .... **128** A5
  SHIL DL4 .... **36** A3 **1**
Rowan Ct *DARLW* DL3 .... **131** D2 **1**
  SPEN DL16 .... **15** E3
Rowan Dr *GTAY/STK* TS9 .... **150** C2
Rowan Gv *CNHM/HEM* TS8 .... **141** D1 **4**
Rowan Pl *NACLF* DL5 .... **54** A1
Rowan Rd *EGG/EAG* TS16 .... **137** D2 **3**
  STOCN TS19 .... **74** C4 **7**
Rowell St *HTLP* TS24 .... **19** F2
Rowen Cl *THNBY* TS17 .... **138** B2 **3**
Rowland Keld *GUIS* TS14 .... **128** A5
Rowlands Gv *BLGHM* TS23 .... **42** C3 **1**
Roworth Rd *NORM/PKE* TS3 .... **100** B3
Roxburgh Cl *ESTON* TS6 .... **101** D1 **2**
Roxby Av *GUIS* TS14 .... **128** C5
  NORM/PKE TS3 .... **100** A5
Roxby Cl *HTLPS* TS25 .... **32** C1
  REDCAR TS10 .... **68** B3
  STOCN TS19 .... **73** F1
Roxby Moor Av *DARLE* DL1 .... **133** E4 **3**
Royal George Dr *EGG/EAG* TS16 .... **118** C5
Royal Oak Yd *DARLW* DL3 .... **9** F4 **1**
Royce Av *BLGHM* TS23 .... **60** A1
Royston Av *NORM/PKE* TS3 .... **100** A5
Royston Gv *HTLPS* TS25 .... **30** C2
Ruberry Av *STOCN* TS19 .... **73** E1 **11**
Ruby Rd *THNBY* TS17 .... **95** F5 **3**
Ruby St *DARLW* DL3 .... **116** B2
  MBORO TS1 .... **5** F4
  SALT/BTN/SK TS12 .... **89** E1
  SHIL DL4 .... **35** E3
Rudby Cl *YARM* TS15 .... **138** A5
Ruddock Av *BAUK* DL14 .... **26** C4
Rudston Av *BLGHMW/WYN* TS22 .... **57** F1
Rudston Cl *THNBY* TS17 .... **121** D3
Rudyard Av *STOCN* TS19 .... **73** F1
Rufford Cl *GUIS* TS14 .... **129** D5 **1**
  MTN/NUN TS7 .... **125** B4 **6**
  THNBY TS17 .... **139** E1
Ruff Tail *GUIS* TS14 .... **128** A3 **6**
Rugby Rd *STOCS* TS18 .... **6** C5
Rugby St *HTLPS* TS25 .... **23** F2
Rugby Ter *TEESM* TS2 .... **61** D5
Rugeley St *STOCN* TS19 .... **73** F2 **3**
Ruislip Cl *STOCN* TS19 .... **73** F2
Runciman Rd *HTLP* TS24 .... **12** B5
Runcorn Av *STOCN* TS19 .... **73** F1
Runfold Cl *STOCN* TS19 .... **56** B5
Runnymede *MTN/NUN* TS7 .... **126** C5
Runnymede Cl *STOCN* TS19 .... **73** F1 **8**
Runnymede Ct *BAUK* DL14 .... **27** E1 **3**
Runswick Av *ACK/BRKF* TS5 .... **123** E3
  REDCAR TS10 .... **67** F1
  STOCN TS19 .... **73** F2 **2**
Runswick Rd *ESTON* TS6 .... **102** B1
Rupert St *STOCS* TS18 .... **7** H2
Rushleigh Av *ACK/BRKF* TS5 .... **123** D1
Rushmere *CNHM/HEM* TS8 .... **144** A1
Rushmere Heath *EGG/EAG* TS16 .... **137** E2 **2**
Rushmoor *SPEN* DL16 .... **15** F2
Rushpool Cl *REDCAR* TS10 .... **68** A3
Rushyford Av *STOCN* TS19 .... **73** F2
Rushyford St *NACLF* DL5 .... **38** C4 **2**
Ruskin Av *ACK/BRKF* TS5 .... **123** D1
  SALT/BTN/SK TS12 .... **89** D2
  SHIL DL4 .... **35** E3
Ruskin Gv *HTLPS* TS25 .... **23** D2
Ruskin Rd *DARLE* DL1 .... **132** B5
Russell Ct *NACLF* DL5 .... **37** F3

Russell St *BAUK* DL14 .... **27** D1
  DARLE DL1 .... **9** C3
  HTLP TS24 .... **19** D1
  MBORO TS1 .... **5** H4
  MBORO TS1 .... **78** C4 **4**
  STOCS TS18 .... **7** E4
Russell Wk *HTLPS* TS25 .... **2** B6
Rustington Cl *STOCN* TS19 .... **73** F1 **8**
Rustland Dr *DARLW* DL3 .... **131** E3
Ruswarp Av *STOCN* TS19 .... **73** F2 **10**
Ruswarp Cl *ESTON* TS6 .... **102** B2
Ruswarp Gv *HTLPS* TS25 .... **33** D1
Ruswarp Rd *ESTON* TS6 .... **102** B2
Ruth Av *NORM/PKE* TS3 .... **100** A2 **3**
Ruthin Cl *STOCN* TS19 .... **74** A1
Rutland Av *BAUK* DL14 .... **27** D3 **10**
  MTN/NUN TS7 .... **125** E4
Rutland Cl *REDCAR* TS10 .... **68** A2
  STOCN TS19 .... **74** A1 **3**
Rutland Ct *MBORO* TS1 .... **5** H4
Ryan Av *STOCS* TS18 .... **7** G2
Ryan's Rw *MARSKE* TS11 .... **70** A5
Rydal Av *ACK/BRKF* TS5 .... **123** D3
  BLGHM TS23 .... **76** A1
  ESTON TS6 .... **82** B5
  REDCAR TS10 .... **68** A1
Rydal Rd *DARLE* DL1 .... **132** C3
  FYHL DL17 .... **20** C2
  SALT/BTN/SK TS12 .... **109** D1
  STOCS TS18 .... **6** B3
Rydal St *HTLPW* TS26 .... **2** A5
Ryder Cl *STOCN* TS19 .... **86** B3
Ryder Ct *FYHL* DL17 .... **38** B1
Ryde Rd *STOCN* TS19 .... **74** A2
Rye Cl *EGG/EAG* TS16 .... **137** D3
Rye Dl *GUIS* TS14 .... **128** A4
Ryedale Cl *YARM* TS15 .... **146** A2
Ryedale St *NORM/PKE* TS3 .... **79** E5 **10**
Rye Hl *DARLW* DL3 .... **115** E4
Ryehill Cl *MTN/NUN* TS7 .... **144** C1
Ryehill Gdns *HTLPW* TS26 .... **17** D3
Ryehills Dr *MARSKE* TS11 .... **71** D4
Rye Hill Wy *CNHM/HEM* TS8 .... **143** E5
Ryhope Av *STOCN* TS19 .... **73** F1 **7**
Rylstone Cl *NACLF* DL5 .... **38** A4 **2**
Rylstone Ct *MGRV/ESTR* TS4 .... **98** C4 **7**
Ryton Cl *THNBY* TS17 .... **121** D3

S

Sabatier Cl *THNBY* TS17 .... **95** E2
Sacriston Cl *BLGHM* TS23 .... **41** E5
Sadberge Gv *STOCN* TS19 .... **92** C1
Sadberge Rd *STOCS* TS18 .... **94** C4 **1**
Sadberge St *NORM/PKE* TS3 .... **79** E5 **20**
Saddler Cl *THNBY* TS17 .... **139** D1 **1**
  FYHL DL17 .... **20** B1
Saddler St *BAUK* DL14 .... **27** D1
The Saddlery *NACLF* DL5 .... **37** E4
Saddleston Cl *HTLPW* TS26 .... **16** C3
Sadler Dr *MTN/NUN* TS7 .... **125** E4
Sadler Forster Wy *THNBY* TS17 .... **121** F5
Sadler St *HTLPS* TS25 .... **3** F6
St Aidan's Crs *BLGHMW/WYN* TS22 .... **58** B3
St Aidans Dr *MBORO* TS1 .... **5** F4
St Aidan's St *HTLPS* TS25 .... **24** A2 **3**
  MBORO TS1 .... **5** E6
St Andrews Cl *DARLE* DL1 .... **117** E4
  EGG/EAG TS16 .... **137** E2
St Andrews Ct *FYHL* DL17 .... **38** B1 **1**
St Andrews Gv *RHTLP* TS27 .... **11** F3 **3**
St Andrew's La *SPEN* DL16 .... **15** E2
St Andrew's Pl *BAUK* DL14 .... **27** E2 **3**
St Andrew's Rd *BAUK* DL14 .... **27** D4
  MARSKE TS11 .... **86** C2
  MTN/NUN TS7 .... **125** F4
  SPEN DL16 .... **15** E2 **1**
St Andrew's Rd East *ESTON* TS6 .... **82** A4 **2**
St Andrew's Rd West *ESTON* TS6 .... **82** A4 **3**
St Andrew's St *DARLE* DL1 .... **116** B3 **3**
St Andrew's Ter *BAUK* DL14 .... **27** C2
St Annes Rd *MARSKE* TS11 .... **86** C3 **3**
St Ann's Ter *STOCS* TS18 .... **75** E5
St Arreck Cl *MARSKE* TS11 .... **86** B3 **12**
St Augustines Wy *DARLW* DL3 .... **9** E4
St Austell Cl *CNHM/HEM* TS8 .... **123** E5
St Barnabas' Rd *ACK/BRKF* TS5 .... **97** F2
St Bernard Rd *STOCS* TS18 .... **7** E5
St Columba's Av *BLGHMW/WYN* TS22 .... **58** B3
St Crispins' Ct *STOCN* TS19 .... **74** A4
St Cuthbert's Av *BLGHM* TS23 .... **58** B3 **1**
St Cuthbert's Rd *STOCS* TS18 .... **94** C3 **1**
St Cuthbert's Wy *HTLP* TS24 .... **19** D1 **1**
  NACLF DL5 .... **54** C1
St David's Cl *BLGHM* TS23 .... **58** B3
  SPEN DL16 .... **15** F1
St David's Rd *ESTON* TS6 .... **82** A3
St Edmunds Gn *SEDG* TS21 .... **29** E3 **7**
St Elizabeth's Cl *NACLF* DL5 .... **39** D2 **7**
St George's Crs *MARSKE* TS11 .... **86** C3

St George's Rd East *ESTON* TS6 ...... 82 A4
St Germain's Gv *MARSKE* TS11 ...... 70 C5 🔢
St Germain's La *MARSKE* TS11 ...... 70 C4
St Giles Cl *DARLW* DL3 ...... 130 B2 🔢
St Godrics Rd *NACLF* DL5 ...... 54 B1
St Helen's Cl *ESTON* TS6 ...... 101 F2
St Helen's St *HTLP* TS24 ...... 19 D1
St Hilda's Ter *LOFT/ST* TS13 ...... 112 C2
St Hild Cl *DARLW* DL3 ...... 130 C2
St Ives Cl *CNHM/HEM* TS8 ...... 125 D3
   REDCAR TS10 ...... 69 E4 🔢
St James Ct *ESTON* TS6 ...... 81 F3 🔢
St James Gv *RHTLP* TS27 ...... 10 B5 🔢
St Joan's Gv *HTLPS* TS25 ...... 24 A3
St Johns Cl *MGRV/ESTR* TS4 ...... 78 C5
   STOCS TS18 ...... 7 F2
St John's Crs *DARLE* DL1 ...... 132 C2
St John's Gv *REDCAR* TS10 ...... 68 C1
St John's Pl *DARLE* DL1 ...... 132 C2 🔢 🔢
St John's Rd *SHIL* DL4 ...... 35 F4
St John's Wy *STOCS* TS19 ...... 74 B3
St Josephs Ct *REDCAR* TS10 ...... 68 A1 🔢
St Leonards Rd *GUIS* TS14 ...... 128 B4
St Luke's Av *THNBY* TS17 ...... 95 F4
St Margaret's Gv *ACK/BRKF* TS5 ...... 97 F5 🔢
   ESTON TS6 ...... 81 D5
   HTLPS TS25 ...... 24 A3 🔢
   REDCAR TS10 ...... 68 C2
   THNBY TS17 ...... 121 F2 🔢
St Margaret's Wy
   SALT/BTN/SK TS12 ...... 91 D5
St Mark's Cl *MARSKE* TS11 ...... 70 B5 🔢
   STOCN TS19 ...... 73 D5 🔢
St Martins Cl *LOFT/ST* TS13 ...... 112 C4
St Martins Wy *YARM* TS15 ...... 146 C5
St Mary's Cl *BAUK* DL14 ...... 26 C4 🔢
   STOCS TS18 ...... 7 G2 🔢
St Mary St *HTLP* TS24 ...... 19 E2 🔢 🔢
St Mary's Wk *ACK/BRKF* TS5 ...... 97 F5
St Mawes Cl *HTLPW* TS26 ...... 16 C3
St Michael's Gv *NORTON* TS20 ...... 75 D5 🔢 🔢
St Nicholas Ct *ESTON* TS6 ...... 81 F3 🔢
St Nicholas Gdns *YARM* TS15 ...... 147 D1
St Ninian's Cl *DARLW* DL3 ...... 130 B2
St Oswalds Cl *BAUK* DL14 ...... 27 F3
St Oswalds Ct *NACLF* DL5 ...... 39 E4
St Oswald's Crs *BLGHM* TS23 ...... 58 B3 🔢
St Oswald's St *HTLP* TS24 ...... 18 A3 🔢
St Patrick's Cl *ESTON* TS6 ...... 82 A4 🔢
St Patrick's Rd *ESTON* TS6 ...... 82 A4
St Paul's Cl *SPEN* DL16 ...... 14 C3
St Paul's Pl *DARLE* DL1 ...... 116 B3 🔢
   MBORO TS1 ...... 4 D4
   STOCN TS19 ...... 6 D2 🔢
   THNBY TS17 ...... 95 E4
St Paul's St *SPEN* DL16 ...... 14 C3
   STOCN TS19 ...... 6 D3
St Paul's Ter *DARLE* DL1 ...... 116 B3
   SHIL DL4 ...... 35 F2
St Peter's Ct *REDCAR* TS10 ...... 68 C1
St Peter's Rd *STOCS* TS18 ...... 94 B3 🔢
St Thomas Gv *REDCAR* TS10 ...... 68 C1
St Vincent St *BLGHM* TS23 ...... 60 B3
Salcombe Cl *CNHM/HEM* TS8 ...... 125 D3
Salcombe Dr *HTLPS* TS25 ...... 31 E1
Salcombe Wy *REDCAR* TS10 ...... 69 D4
Salisbury Gv *REDCAR* TS10 ...... 69 E1 🔢
Salisbury Pl *BAUK* DL14 ...... 27 E2
Salisbury St *THNBY* TS17 ...... 95 F4 🔢
Salisbury Ter *DARLW* DL3 ...... 9 E1
   ESTON TS6 ...... 80 B3
   NORTON TS20 ...... 75 D3
   SHIL DL4 ...... 35 D3 🔢
Saltaire Ter *HTLPS* TS25 ...... 31 E5
Saltburn Gv *SALT/BTN/SK* TS12 ...... 89 F4
Saltburn Rd *SALT/BTN/SK* TS12 ...... 89 F2
   THNBY TS17 ...... 95 F5
Saltcote *MTN/NUN* TS7 ...... 126 A3
Salters Cl *DARLE* DL1 ...... 117 D2 🔢
Saltersgate Rd *DARLE* DL1 ...... 116 C1
Saltersgill Av *MGRV/ESTR* TS4 ...... 98 B4
   MGRV/ESTR TS4 ...... 125 D2
Saltersgill Cl *MGRV/ESTR* TS4 ...... 98 B4
Salters La *DARLE* DL1 ...... 133 F3
   SEDG TS21 ...... 29 E1
   SEDG TS21 ...... 29 E2
Salters La North *DARLE* DL1 ...... 117 D1
Salters La South *DARLE* DL1 ...... 117 D2
Saltholme Cl *TEESM* TS2 ...... 61 D5
Saltney Rd *NORTON* TS20 ...... 74 B1
Salton Cl *ACK/BRKF* TS5 ...... 97 D3
Saltram Cl *THNBY* TS17 ...... 139 D2 🔢 🔢
Saltram Gv *MTN/NUN* TS7 ...... 125 E3
Saltscar *REDCAR* TS10 ...... 69 D3
Saltview Ter *TEESM* TS2 ...... 78 C1
Saltwells Crs *MGRV/ESTR* TS4 ...... 79 D5
Saltwells Rd *MGRV/ESTR* TS4 ...... 79 C5
Salt Yd *DARLW* DL3 ...... 9 E4
Salutation Rd *DARLW* DL3 ...... 130 C3
Samaria St *ACK/BRKF* TS5 ...... 123 F3
Sambrook Gdns *ACK/BRKF* TS5 ...... 123 F4
Samphire St *TEESM* TS2 ...... 78 C1 🔢
Samsung Av *BLGHMW/WYN* TS22 ...... 40 C3
Samuel St *STOCN* TS19 ...... 6 D2

Sandalwood Ct *ACK/BRKF* TS5 ...... 124 A3 🔢
Sandbanks Dr *HTLP* TS24 ...... 11 F3
Sanderson Cl *NACLF* DL5 ...... 38 C4 🔢
Sanderson St *DARLE* DL1 ...... 9 H4
Sandford Cl *MGRV/ESTR* TS4 ...... 98 C5
Sandling Ct *MTN/NUN* TS7 ...... 126 A3
Sandmartin La *NORTON* TS20 ...... 58 A4 🔢
Sandmoor Cl *ESTON* TS6 ...... 102 A3 🔢
Sandmoor Rd *MARSKE* TS11 ...... 86 B3
Sandown Dr *FYHL* DL17 ...... 39 D2
Sandown Pk *REDCAR* TS10 ...... 68 C2
Sandown Rd *BLGHM* TS23 ...... 41 F5
Sandown Wy *THNBY* TS17 ...... 96 B3
Sandpiper Cl *REDCAR* TS10 ...... 69 D4
Sandriggs *DARLW* DL3 ...... 115 D5
Sandringham Rd *ESTON* TS6 ...... 82 A5 🔢
   HTLPW TS26 ...... 17 E4
   NORM/PKE TS3 ...... 99 F4
   STOCS TS18 ...... 6 B6
   THNBY TS17 ...... 95 F4
Sandsend Rd *ESTON* TS6 ...... 102 B1
   REDCAR TS10 ...... 67 F2
Sandwell Chare *HTLP* TS24 ...... 19 E2 🔢 🔢
Sandwich Gv *RHTLP* TS27 ...... 11 F3
Sandwood Pk *GUIS* TS14 ...... 128 A5
Sandy Bank *SEDG* TS21 ...... 28 A5
Sandy Flatts Ct *ACK/BRKF* TS5 ...... 124 A3
Sandy Flatts La *ACK/BRKF* TS5 ...... 124 A3
Sandy La *BLGHMW/WYN* TS22 ...... 40 B4
   BLGHMW/WYN TS22 ...... 58 A2
   GUIS TS14 ...... 85 F5
Sapley Cl *THNBY* TS17 ...... 121 E3
Sarah St *HTLPS* TS25 ...... 24 B2
Satley Rd *BLGHM* TS23 ...... 42 B3
Saunton Av *REDCAR* TS10 ...... 69 D4
Saunton Rd *BLGHM* TS23 ...... 59 E2
Sawley Cl *DARLW* DL3 ...... 114 A3 🔢
Sawley Gv *STOCS* TS18 ...... 92 C3
Sawtry Rd *NORM/PKE* TS3 ...... 100 B4 🔢
Saxby Rd *NORTON* TS20 ...... 75 D3
Saxonfield *CNHM/HEM* TS8 ...... 125 D5
Scalby Gv *REDCAR* TS10 ...... 69 D4
   STOCN TS19 ...... 92 C1
Scalby Rd *NORM/PKE* TS3 ...... 99 D2
Scalby Sq *THNBY* TS17 ...... 95 F5
Scaling Ct *GUIS* TS14 ...... 128 C2 🔢
Scampton Cl *THNBY* TS17 ...... 121 D3 🔢
Scanbeck Dr *MARSKE* TS11 ...... 70 C4
Scarborough St *ESTON* TS6 ...... 80 C4 🔢
   HTLP TS24 ...... 2 D2
   LOFT/ST TS13 ...... 112 C3 🔢
   THNBY TS17 ...... 95 E4 🔢 🔢
Scargill Dr *SPEN* DL16 ...... 15 D1 🔢
Scargilll *DARLE* DL1 ...... 133 D4
Scarteen *GUIS* TS14 ...... 128 C4
Scarth St *DARLW* DL3 ...... 8 D5
Scarth Wk *STOCS* TS18 ...... 7 E4
Scarthwood Cl *THNBY* TS17 ...... 139 E1 🔢
Scawfell Gv *HTLPS* TS25 ...... 24 A2 🔢
School Av *ACK/BRKF* TS5 ...... 97 D3
School Aycliffe La *NACLF* DL5 ...... 50 C5
School Cl *MARSKE* TS11 ...... 70 C5
   STOCS TS18 ...... 94 C3 🔢
School Cft *MBORO* TS1 ...... 5 H2 🔢
School La *LOFT/ST* TS13 ...... 112 C4
School St *DARLW* DL3 ...... 115 D4
Scotforth Cl *MTN/NUN* TS7 ...... 126 B4 🔢
Scotney Rd *BLGHM* TS23 ...... 58 C1 🔢
Scott Dr *NORTON* TS20 ...... 74 B1 🔢
Scotton Cl *STOCS* TS18 ...... 92 C4 🔢
Scott Rd *BAUK* DL14 ...... 27 D5
   ESTON TS6 ...... 101 D3
Scott's Rd *TEESM* TS2 ...... 78 C3
Scott St *REDCAR* TS10 ...... 51 E5
   SHIL DL4 ...... 35 E4
Scrafton Pl *MARSKE* TS11 ...... 70 C5 🔢
Scruton Cl *STOCS* TS18 ...... 93 D3 🔢
Scugdale Cl *YARM* TS15 ...... 146 A2 🔢
Scurfield Rd *STOCN* TS19 ...... 72 C2 🔢
Seaford Cl *REDCAR* TS10 ...... 69 D4
Seaham Cl *NORTON* TS20 ...... 57 D5
   REDCAR TS10 ...... 69 E4 🔢
Seaham St *NORTON* TS20 ...... 7 G1
Sealand Cl *THNBY* TS17 ...... 121 F4
Seamer Cl *ACK/BRKF* TS5 ...... 98 A5
Seamer Gv *STOCS* TS18 ...... 93 F3
Seamer Rd *CNHM/HEM* TS8 ...... 141 D2
Seathwaite *ACK/BRKF* TS5 ...... 123 D4 🔢
Seaton Carew Rd *TEESM* TS2 ...... 62 A1
   TEESM TS2 ...... 78 C1
Seaton Cl *REDCAR* TS10 ...... 69 E3 🔢
   STOCN TS19 ...... 92 C1 🔢
Seaton La *HTLPS* TS25 ...... 23 F5
Seaton St *MBORO* TS1 ...... 5 G6
Sea View Ter *ESTON* TS6 ...... 81 F2
   HTLP TS24 ...... 19 D1
Sedgefield Rd *ACK/BRKF* TS5 ...... 123 E3
Sedgefield Wy *STOCS* TS18 ...... 76 A4
Sedgemoor Rd *ESTON* TS6 ...... 102 A4
Sedgemoor Wy *BLGHM* TS23 ...... 42 C4
Sedgewick Cl *HTLP* TS24 ...... 12 C4
Sedgwick St *DARLW* DL3 ...... 115 F4 🔢
Sefton Rd *NORM/PKE* TS3 ...... 100 C2
Selbourne St *MBORO* TS1 ...... 4 D6 🔢
Selbourne Ter *DARLW* DL3 ...... 9 E2

Selby Crs *DARLW* DL3 ...... 114 B3
Selby Gv *HTLPS* TS25 ...... 23 F4 🔢
Selby Rd *MTN/NUN* TS7 ...... 127 D4
Selkirk Cl *MGRV/ESTR* TS4 ...... 98 B5
Selset Av *NORM/PKE* TS3 ...... 100 A5
Selset Cl *DARLE* DL1 ...... 133 D4 🔢
Selwood Cl *THNBY* TS17 ...... 121 F3 🔢
Selworthy Gn *THNBY* TS17 ...... 139 D4 🔢
Selwyn Dr *STOCN* TS19 ...... 73 D3
Semmerwater Gv *REDCAR* TS10 ...... 68 B1 🔢
Serpentine Gdns *HTLPW* TS26 ...... 17 D3
Serpentine Rd *HTLPW* TS26 ...... 17 D4
Severn Dr *GUIS* TS14 ...... 128 B4
Severn Gv *BLGHMW/WYN* TS22 ...... 40 C5
   SALT/BTN/SK TS12 ...... 109 E1
Severn Rd *REDCAR* TS10 ...... 50 C5
Severn Wy *DARLE* DL1 ...... 132 B5
Sewers Dr *CNHM/HEM* TS8 ...... 141 E1 🔢
Seymour Av *EGG/EAG* TS16 ...... 136 C3
Seymour Cl *MARSKE* TS11 ...... 88 A1
Seymour Crs *EGG/EAG* TS16 ...... 136 C2
Seymour Dr *EGG/EAG* TS16 ...... 136 C2
Seymour Gv *EGG/EAG* TS16 ...... 136 C3
Seymour St *BAUK* DL14 ...... 27 D3 🔢
Shackleton Cl *THNBY* TS17 ...... 121 F3
Shadforth Dr *BLGHM* TS23 ...... 42 B4
Shadwell Cl *ESTON* TS6 ...... 101 E5 🔢
Shaftesbury Rd *ESTON* TS6 ...... 101 E2
Shafto Rd *NACLF* DL5 ...... 55 D1
Shafto St *SPEN* DL16 ...... 15 D4 🔢
Shafto Wy *NACLF* DL5 ...... 39 D5
Shakespeare Av *ESTON* TS6 ...... 82 B5 🔢
   HTLPS TS25 ...... 23 F1
Shakespeare Rd *DARLE* DL1 ...... 132 B5
Shaldon Cl *REDCAR* TS10 ...... 69 E4 🔢
Shandon Rd *CNHM/HEM* TS8 ...... 143 F1
Shannon Ct *HTLPS* TS25 ...... 31 D4 🔢
Shannon Crs *STOCN* TS19 ...... 72 C5
Shannon Wy *DARLE* DL1 ...... 132 A5
Sharp Crs *HTLP* TS24 ...... 12 C5
Sharp Rd *NACLF* DL5 ...... 54 C1
Sharrock Cl *NORM/PKE* TS3 ...... 79 D5 🔢 🔢
Shawbrow Vw *BAUK* DL14 ...... 27 D5
   DARLW DL3 ...... 130 A1 🔢
Shaw Crs *ESTON* TS6 ...... 82 B5
Shawcross Av *ESTON* TS6 ...... 81 F4 🔢
Shearwater Av *DARLE* DL1 ...... 133 E1
Shearwater La *NORTON* TS20 ...... 57 F4
Sheepfoote Hl *YARM* TS15 ...... 137 D3
Sheerness Gv *HTLP* TS24 ...... 3 E4
Sheerness Wy *REDCAR* TS10 ...... 69 D4
Shelley Cl *BLGHM* TS23 ...... 41 F3 🔢
Shelley Crs *ESTON* TS6 ...... 101 E1 🔢
Shelley Gv *HTLPS* TS25 ...... 23 E2
Shelley Rd *DARLE* DL1 ...... 117 D5
   MGRV/ESTR TS4 ...... 98 B4
Shepherd Cl *THNBY* TS17 ...... 121 D1
Shepherdson Ct *ESTON* TS6 ...... 80 C3 🔢
Shepherdson Wy *TEESM* TS2 ...... 79 D3
Sheppards Cft *NACLF* DL5 ...... 53 E2
Shepton Cl *THNBY* TS17 ...... 122 A1
Sheraton Cl *NACLF* DL5 ...... 55 D1
Sheraton Pk *STOCN* TS19 ...... 74 A3
Sheraton Rd *NACLF* DL5 ...... 54 C1
Sheraton St *DARLW* DL3 ...... 116 A3 🔢
   STOCS TS18 ...... 6 C5
Sherborne Cl *DARLW* DL3 ...... 114 A4
Sherburn Av *BLGHM* TS23 ...... 42 B4
Sherburn Cl *ACK/BRKF* TS5 ...... 123 E3 🔢
Sheridan Gv *HTLPS* TS25 ...... 23 E2 🔢
Sheriff St *HTLPW* TS26 ...... 17 F4
Sheringham Ct *REDCAR* TS10 ...... 69 E4 🔢
Sherwood Cl *MTN/NUN* TS7 ...... 127 D2
Sherwood Dr *MARSKE* TS11 ...... 70 A5
Sherwood Rd *THNBY* TS17 ...... 121 E5
Shetland Cl *ACK/BRKF* TS5 ...... 123 F4
Shetland Dr *DARLE* DL1 ...... 117 E1
Shevington Gv *MTN/NUN* TS7 ...... 126 A4
Shibden Rd *NORM/PKE* TS3 ...... 99 E1 🔢
Shields Ter *HTLP* TS24 ...... 13 E5
Shield Wk *NACLF* DL5 ...... 39 D5
Shildon Cl *BLGHM* TS23 ...... 41 F5 🔢
Shildon Rd *NACLF* DL5 ...... 52 A3
Shildon St *DARLE* DL1 ...... 116 B3
Shincliffe Rd *BLGHM* TS23 ...... 42 B4 🔢
Shinwell Crs *ESTON* TS6 ...... 80 C4
Shipham Cl *REDCAR* TS10 ...... 69 D4
Ship Inn Yd *STOCS* TS18 ...... 7 F5 🔢
Shirley Av *ACK/BRKF* TS5 ...... 97 D3
Shoreham Cl *REDCAR* TS10 ...... 69 D4 🔢
Short Cl *STOCS* TS18 ...... 94 B5
Short St *BAUK* DL14 ...... 27 D4
Shotley Cl *BLGHM* TS23 ...... 41 F5 🔢
Shotton Ct *BLGHM* TS23 ...... 59 E1 🔢
Shrewsbury Rd *NORM/PKE* TS3 ...... 100 B5
Shrewsbury St *HTLPS* TS25 ...... 23 F1
Sid Chaplin Dr *NACLF* DL5 ...... 53 D2
Sidcup Av *NORM/PKE* TS3 ...... 100 A5
Sideling Tails *YARM* TS15 ...... 146 B4
Sidlaw Av *SALT/BTN/SK* TS12 ...... 109 E1 🔢
Sidlaw Rd *BLGHM* TS23 ...... 58 B1
Sidmouth Cl *CNHM/HEM* TS8 ...... 125 D2 🔢
Siemans St *FYHL* DL17 ...... 20 B1 🔢
Sildale Cl *DARLW* DL3 ...... 115 F4 🔢
Silkin Wy *NACLF* DL5 ...... 54 B1

Silton Gv *STOCS* TS18 .... 93 F3
Silverdale *MTN/NUN* TS7 .... 126 B5
Silverdale Pl *NACLF* DL5 .... 37 F5
Silver St *HTLP* TS24 .... 2 C4
  SPEN DL16 .... 15 D3 ◼
  STOCS TS18 .... 7 G4
  TEESM TS2 .... 78 B2 ◼
  YARM TS15 .... 137 D4
Silverton Rd *GUIS* TS14 .... 129 E5
Silverwood Cl *RHTLP* TS27 .... 11 E3
Simcox Ct *TEESM* TS2 .... 4 A1
Simonside Gv *THNBY* TS17 .... 139 D3
Simpasture Ga *NACLF* DL5 .... 54 B2
Simpson Cl *ESTON* TS6 .... 81 D4
Simpson St *ACK/BRKF* TS5 .... 98 A2
Sinclair Rd *HTLPS* TS25 .... 22 C3
Sinderby Cl *BLGHM* TS23 .... 42 A4 ◼
Sinnington Cl *GUIS* TS14 .... 129 D4
Sinnington Rd *THNBY* TS17 .... 121 E3
Sir Douglas Pk *THNBY* TS17 .... 121 E2 ◼
Siskin Cl *HTLPW* TS26 .... 16 B2
  NORTON TS20 .... 57 F4
Skeeby Cl *STOCS* TS18 .... 93 D4
Skeeby Rd *DARLE* DL1 .... 132 C3
Skeldale Gv *DARLW* DL3 .... 115 F4
Skeleton Ct *GUIS* TS14 .... 129 D1 ◼
Skelton Dr *MARSKE* TS11 .... 71 D5
  REDCAR TS10 .... 69 D2 ◼
Skelton Ellers *SALT/BTN/SK* TS12 .... 107 F3
Skelton Rd *SALT/BTN/SK* TS12 .... 110 C1
  THNBY TS17 .... 95 F5
Skelton St *HTLP* TS24 .... 12 B4
Skelwith Rd *NORM/PKE* TS3 .... 99 E3
Skerne Rd *HTLP* TS24 .... 12 C5
  NACLF DL5 .... 55 D3
  NORTON TS20 .... 74 C2
Skerries Crs *REDCAR* TS10 .... 68 A4
Skiddaw Cl *EGG/EAG* TS16 .... 119 D5 ◼
Skiddaw Ct *MTN/NUN* TS7 .... 126 B4
Skinnergate *DARLW* DL3 .... 9 E5
Skinner St *STOCS* TS18 .... 7 F5
Skinningrove Rd *LOFT/ST* TS13 .... 112 C2
Skiplam Cl *CNHM/HEM* TS8 .... 125 E5
Skipper's La *ESTON* TS6 .... 80 B4
Skipton Cl *FYHL* DL17 .... 21 E2
Skipton Gv *BAUK* DL14 .... 26 C3 ◼
Skipton Moor Cl *DARLE* DL1 .... 133 E4 ◼
Skipton Rd *BLGHM* TS23 .... 58 C1
Skirlaw Rd *NACLF* DL5 .... 55 D1
  YARM TS15 .... 146 A1
Skomer Ct *REDCAR* TS10 .... 69 D4
Skottowe Crs *GTAY/STK* TS9 .... 150 B2
Skottowe Dr *GTAY/STK* TS9 .... 150 B2
Skripka Dr *BLGHMW/WYN* TS22 .... 57 F1
Skylark Cl *HTLPW* TS26 .... 17 D1
Slater Rd *ESTON* TS6 .... 82 B5
Slater St *HTLPW* TS26 .... 17 F4 ◼
The Slayde *YARM* TS15 .... 146 B1
Sledmere Dr *ACK/BRKF* TS5 .... 98 A5
Sledwick Rd *BLGHM* TS23 .... 59 E1
Sleights Cl *GUIS* TS14 .... 129 D2 ◼
Sleights Ct *ESTON* TS6 .... 102 B1
Slingsby Cl *ACK/BRKF* TS5 .... 124 A1 ◼
Smithfield Rd *DARLE* DL1 .... 132 B3
Smith's Dock Park Rd *ESTON* TS6 .... 101 E3
Smith's Dock Rd *ESTON* TS6 .... 80 B1
Smith St *MBORO* TS1 .... 5 F4 ◼
  STOCS TS18 .... 7 F3
Smyth Pl *HTLP* TS24 .... 12 C4
Smythsons Cl *NACLF* DL5 .... 53 E3
Sneck Gate La *CNHM/HEM* TS8 .... 143 D5
Snipe La *RDARL* DL2 .... 131 F5
Snipe Rd *REDCAR* TS10 .... 50 A4
Snowberry Cl *NORTON* TS20 .... 74 B2
Snowden St *ESTON* TS6 .... 101 F1
Snowdon Crs *REDCAR* TS10 .... 68 A2
Snowdon Gv *HTLP* TS24 .... 11 F3
  THNBY TS17 .... 138 D1
Snowdon Rd *TEESM* TS2 .... 5 E1
Sober Hall Av *THNBY* TS17 .... 138 C4
Soho St *SHIL* DL4 .... 35 F4
Somersby Cl *HTLP* TS24 .... 13 E5 ◼
Somerset Crs *SALT/BTN/SK* TS12 .... 108 C2
Somerset Rd *ESTON* TS6 .... 82 A5
  GUIS TS14 .... 128 C4 ◼
  NORTON TS20 .... 74 D2
Somerset St *MBORO* TS1 .... 5 D2
Somerset Ter *BLGHM* TS23 .... 59 E3 ◼
Somerville Av *NORM/PKE* TS3 .... 100 B4
Soppett St *REDCAR* TS10 .... 51 E5
Sopwith Cl *STOCS* TS18 .... 94 B5
Sorbonne Cl *THNBY* TS17 .... 7 H6
Sorrel Cl *STOCN* TS19 .... 73 D4
Sorrel Ct *MTN/NUN* TS7 .... 125 E2
Sorrell Gv *GUIS* TS14 .... 128 A4 ◼
Sorrel Wynd *FYHL* DL17 .... 38 C2
Sotherby Rd *ESTON* TS6 .... 80 B4
  NORM/PKE TS3 .... 79 F5
Southampton St *DARLE* DL1 .... 116 B4 ◼
  REDCAR TS10 .... 51 F5
South Arden St *DARLE* DL1 .... 9 F6 ◼
South Av *BLGHM* TS23 .... 58 C5
  ESTON TS6 .... 67 D2
South Bank Rd *NORM/PKE* TS3 .... 79 E4

Southbrooke Av *HTLPS* TS25 .... 23 E3
Southburn Ter *HTLPS* TS25 .... 2 C5
South Church Rd *BAUK* DL14 .... 27 E2
South Crs *HTLP* TS24 .... 19 F2
Southdean Cl *CNHM/HEM* TS8 .... 124 A5 ◼
Southdean Dr *CNHM/HEM* TS8 .... 124 A4
South Dr *HTLPW* TS26 .... 17 D4
  MTN/NUN TS7 .... 100 C5
  MTN/NUN TS7 .... 125 F3
Southend Av *DARLW* DL3 .... 131 F3
Southend Pl *DARLW* DL3 .... 8 D6
Southfield Crs *NORTON* TS20 .... 75 E3
Southfield La *MBORO* TS1 .... 5 F5
Southfield Rd *MARSKE* TS11 .... 70 C5
  MBORO TS1 .... 5 F6
  NORTON TS20 .... 75 D3
Southgate *ESTON* TS6 .... 102 C2
  HTLP TS24 .... 19 F2
Southgate St *BAUK* DL14 .... 27 E1 ◼
Southland Av *HTLPW* TS26 .... 17 E5 ◼
Southlands Dr *MTN/NUN* TS7 .... 127 D3
Southlands Gdns *SHIL* DL4 .... 35 E2
Southmead Av *NORM/PKE* TS3 .... 100 A5 ◼
South Pde *HTLPS* TS25 .... 2 C6
South Pk *DARLE* DL1 .... 131 F4
South Park Av *ESTON* TS6 .... 101 F4
Southport Cl *STOCS* TS18 .... 75 F5 ◼
South Rd *HTLP* TS24 .... 2 B3
  HTLPW TS26 .... 2 A3
  NORTON TS20 .... 75 D1 ◼
South Side (Dean Rd) *FYHL* DL17 .... 20 C2
South St *DARLW* DL3 .... 116 A4
  ESTON TS6 .... 102 B3
  GUIS TS14 .... 128 C3
  SHIL DL4 .... 35 E4
  SPEN DL16 .... 15 D4
South Ter *BAUK* DL14 .... 27 E1
  DARLE DL1 .... 9 F6
  ESTON TS6 .... 80 C3 ◼
  REDCAR TS10 .... 51 F5
  SPEN DL16 .... 15 E2
South Town La *LOFT/ST* TS13 .... 113 F4
South Vw *DARLW* DL3 .... 58 C5
  EGG/EAG TS16 .... 136 C3 ◼
  RHTLP TS27 .... 10 B5
  SHIL DL4 .... 35 F2 ◼
South View Ter *NORM/PKE* TS3 .... 79 E5 ◼
Southware Cl *ESTON* TS6 .... 101 E5 ◼
South Wy *NORTON* TS20 .... 75 E2 ◼
Southwell Gn *DARLE* DL1 .... 117 F4
Southwell Rd *ACK/BRKF* TS5 .... 98 B3
Southwell Sq *ACK/BRKF* TS5 .... 98 B3 ◼
Southwood *CNHM/HEM* TS8 .... 143 D3
Sowerby Crs *GTAY/STK* TS9 .... 152 A2
Spalding Rd *HTLPS* TS25 .... 30 C2
Spark Sq *STOCN* TS19 .... 73 F4 ◼
Sparrow Hall Dr *DARLE* DL1 .... 117 D1
Sparrow La *GUIS* TS14 .... 129 E5
Spaunton Cl *CNHM/HEM* TS8 .... 123 E5
Speeding Dr *HTLP* TS24 .... 12 A3
Speedwell Cl *DARLE* DL1 .... 133 D2 ◼
Speeton Av *ACK/BRKF* TS5 .... 124 A1
Speeton Cl *BLGHM* TS23 .... 42 A3
Spell Cl *YARM* TS15 .... 138 B5
Spellman Gv *REDCAR* TS10 .... 67 D3
Spenborough Rd *STOCN* TS19 .... 73 F4
Spence Ct *GTAY/STK* TS9 .... 150 C2
Spencely St *SHIL* DL4 .... 35 E2 ◼
Spencer Cl *MARSKE* TS11 .... 70 B4
Spencerfield Crs *NORM/PKE* TS3 .... 100 B1
Spencer Gv *DARLE* DL1 .... 133 D4 ◼
Spencer Rd *ESTON* TS6 .... 101 F2
Spennithorne Rd *STOCS* TS18 .... 6 A4
Spenser Gv *HTLPS* TS25 .... 23 E2
Spilsby Cl *HTLPS* TS25 .... 31 D2
The Spinney *DARLW* DL3 .... 131 E5
  FYHL DL17 .... 38 C2
  HTLPW TS26 .... 16 B5
Spitalfields *YARM* TS15 .... 146 A1
Spital Ga *YARM* TS15 .... 146 B1 ◼
The Spital *YARM* TS15 .... 137 E5
Spitfire Cl *MARSKE* TS11 .... 70 A5 ◼
Spout La *SHIL* DL4 .... 36 A4
Springbank Rd *MTN/NUN* TS7 .... 127 D1
Spring Cl *THNBY* TS17 .... 95 E4
Spring Ct *DARLW* DL3 .... 115 D3
Springfield Ct *GTAY/STK* TS9 .... 152 B2
Springfield Av *SALT/BTN/SK* TS12 .... 110 C1
  STOCS TS18 .... 94 A4
Springfield Cl *EGG/EAG* TS16 .... 137 D1
Springfield Gdns *GTAY/STK* TS9 .... 152 B2
Springfield Gv *YARM* TS15 .... 147 D4
Springfield Rd *ACK/BRKF* TS5 .... 97 D2
  DARLE DL1 .... 117 D2
Springfields *NACLF* DL5 .... 53 E3 ◼
Spring Garden Ct *MTN/NUN* TS7 .... 127 D2
Spring Garden La *MTN/NUN* TS7 .... 126 C2
Spring Garden Rd *HTLPS* TS25 .... 24 A2
Springhead Ter *LOFT/ST* TS13 .... 113 E3
Spring Hi *DARLW* DL3 .... 9 D2 ◼
Springhill *MTN/NUN* TS7 .... 101 D5 ◼14
Springhill Gv *THNBY* TS17 .... 139 D3
Springholme *MTN/NUN* TS7 .... 101 D5 ◼15
Spring La *SEDG* TS21 .... 29 D5
Springlea *MTN/NUN* TS7 .... 101 D5 ◼16

Springmead *MTN/NUN* TS7 .... 101 D5 ◼17
Spring Ri *ESTON* TS6 .... 101 E5
Spring Rd *NACLF* DL5 .... 54 B5
Springston Rd *HTLPW* TS26 .... 16 C3
Spring St *STOCS* TS18 .... 94 B5
  TEESM TS2 .... 5 C1 ◼
Springvale Ter *ACK/BRKF* TS5 .... 97 D3
Spring Wy *STOCS* TS18 .... 94 A4
Springwell Cl *BLGHM* TS23 .... 42 B2 ◼
Springwell Ter *DARLE* DL1 .... 117 D3
Spruce Ct *SPEN* DL16 .... 15 D3 ◼
Spruce Gv *DARLW* DL3 .... 131 D1
Spruce Rd *STOCN* TS19 .... 74 A2
Spurrey Cl *THNBY* TS17 .... 121 D5 ◼
The Square *STOCS* TS18 .... 7 G3
Stadium Ct *ESTON* TS6 .... 80 C5
Stafford Cl *THNBY* TS17 .... 95 D4 ◼
  GUIS TS14 .... 128 C4
Stafford St *STOCS* TS18 .... 94 C3 ◼11
Stag La *NACLF* DL5 .... 39 F5
Staincliffe Rd *HTLPS* TS25 .... 25 D4
Staindale Cl *YARM* TS15 .... 138 A5 ◼
Staindale Rd *THNBY* TS17 .... 121 F1
Staindrop Ct *BLGHM* TS23 .... 41 E4 ◼
Staindrop Crs *DARLW* DL3 .... 115 D5
Staindrop Dr *ACK/BRKF* TS5 .... 123 E2
Staindrop Rd *DARLW* DL3 .... 114 B4
  DARLW DL1 .... 2 D4
Stainforth Gdns *THNBY* TS17 .... 139 E1
Stainmore Cl *STOCN* TS19 .... 6 C3
Stainmore Crs *NACLF* DL5 .... 37 F5
Stainsby Ga *THNBY* TS17 .... 96 A5
Stainsby Rd *ACK/BRKF* TS5 .... 97 D4
Stainsby St *THNBY* TS17 .... 95 E4
Staintondale *NACLF* DL5 .... 37 E4
Staintondale Av *REDCAR* TS10 .... 67 E2 ◼
Stainton Gv *NORTON* TS20 .... 74 C3 ◼
Stainton Rd *BLGHMW/WYN* TS22 .... 58 B1
Stainton St *NORM/PKE* TS3 .... 79 D3
Stainton Wy *CNHM/HEM* TS8 .... 141 E1
  MTN/NUN TS7 .... 126 A5
Staithes Rd *REDCAR* TS10 .... 67 E1
Stakesby Cl *GUIS* TS14 .... 128 C4
Stamford St *MBORO* TS1 .... 78 C5 ◼
Stamp St *STOCS* TS18 .... 7 F3
Stanfield Rd *NACLF* DL5 .... 39 D5
Stanford Cl *THNBY* TS17 .... 95 E3
Stanghow Rd *SALT/BTN/SK* TS12 .... 109 E2
Stanhope Av *HTLPW* TS26 .... 17 F5
Stanhope Cl *FYHL* DL17 .... 21 E1
  SPEN DL16 .... 15 E1
Stanhope Gdns *MGRV/ESTR* TS4 .... 99 D3
Stanhope Gv *ACK/BRKF* TS5 .... 97 F4
Stanhope Rd *BLGHM* TS23 .... 59 E1
  STOCS TS18 .... 6 A2
Stanhope Rd North *DARLW* DL3 .... 8 D3
Stanhope Rd South *DARLW* DL3 .... 8 D4
Stanhope St *SALT/BTN/SK* TS12 .... 89 E2 ◼
Stanley Cl *THNBY* TS17 .... 95 E4 ◼11
Stanley Ct *GTAY/STK* TS9 .... 148 C5
  REDCAR TS10 .... 51 F5
Stanley Rd *HTLPS* TS25 .... 24 A3
Stanley St *DARLE* DL1 .... 132 C2
  NORTON TS20 .... 74 C1
Stanmore Av *MGRV/ESTR* TS4 .... 98 C5
Stanmore Gv *HTLPS* TS25 .... 24 C5
Stannage Gv *THNBY* TS17 .... 121 E1 ◼
Stanstead Wy *THNBY* TS17 .... 122 A2
Stapleford Rd *NORM/PKE* TS3 .... 100 C4
Stapleton St *NORTON* TS20 .... 57 F4 ◼
Stapylton St *ESTON* TS6 .... 81 F3
Starbeck Wk *THNBY* TS17 .... 122 A4
Starbeck Wy *MTN/NUN* TS7 .... 101 D4
Starmer Crs *DARLE* DL1 .... 132 C4
Startforth Rd *TEESM* TS2 .... 77 F2
Statham Pl *DARLW* DL3 .... 116 B1 ◼
Station Av *HTLPS* TS25 .... 31 D4 ◼
Station Cl *MARSKE* TS11 .... 87 E1 ◼
Station Crs *BLGHM* TS23 .... 58 C3
Station La *HTLPS* TS25 .... 24 C5
Station Rd *BLGHM* TS23 .... 58 B2
  BLGHM TS23 .... 59 D5 ◼
  DARLW DL3 .... 9 F1
  DARLW DL3 .... 116 A4 ◼
  EGG/EAG TS16 .... 119 E4
  ESTON TS6 .... 102 A3
  GTAY/STK TS9 .... 150 C3
  GTAY/STK TS9 .... 152 C3
  HTLPS TS25 .... 31 D5
  LOFT/ST TS13 .... 113 D3
  NACLF DL5 .... 54 B5
  NORTON TS20 .... 57 F4
  REDCAR TS10 .... 51 E4
  SALT/BTN/SK TS12 .... 109 E1
  SEDG TS21 .... 28 C5
Station St *MBORO* TS1 .... 5 E2
  SALT/BTN/SK TS12 .... 89 E2 ◼
  SHIL DL4 .... 35 F4
  STOCS TS18 .... 7 G1
  THNBY TS17 .... 95 E3
Staveley Gv *STOCN* TS19 .... 74 A3
Stavordale Rd *STOCN* TS19 .... 6 C1
Stead Cl *NACLF* DL5 .... 38 B5
Steele Crs *ESTON* TS6 .... 81 D3

Steer Ct *BLGHM* TS23 ...... 41 F4
Stephenson St *DARLW* DL3 ...... 116 A4
  FYHL DL17 ...... 20 B1
  MBORO TS1 ...... 5 C5
  THNBY TS17 ...... 95 E3
Stephenson Wy *NACLF* DL5 ...... 38 A5
Stephens St *ESTON* TS6 ...... 81 D3
Stephen St *HTLPW* TS26 ...... 17 E3
Stevenage Cl *THNBY* TS17 ...... 96 A5
Stevenson Cl *YARM* TS15 ...... 138 A5
Stewart Rd *NORTON* TS20 ...... 75 D4
Stewart St *DARLW* DL3 ...... 115 F4
Stileston Cl *HTLPW* TS26 ...... 16 C3
Stirling Gv *DARLE* DL1 ...... 117 D1
Stirling Rd *REDCAR* TS10 ...... 69 D1
Stirling St *HTLPS* TS25 ...... 23 F2
Stirling Wy *THNBY* TS17 ...... 121 F4
The Stirrup *NACLF* DL5 ...... 37 E4
Stockdale Av *REDCAR* TS10 ...... 67 E2
Stockley Cl *DARLW* DL3 ...... 116 A1
Stocksmoor Cl *DARLE* DL1 ...... 133 D4
Stockton *ACK/BRKF* TS5 ...... 97 D1
  BLGHMW/WYN TS22 ...... 30 B4
  DARLE DL1 ...... 117 F3
  HTLPS TS25 ...... 2 B6
  SEDG TS21 ...... 29 E4
  THNBY TS17 ...... 96 B2
Stockton St *BLGHM* TS23 ...... 58 C4
  HTLP TS24 ...... 2 C3
  TEESM TS2 ...... 5 F1
Stockwell Av *THNBY* TS17 ...... 121 F5
Stockwith Cl *NORM/PKE* TS3 ...... 100 C4
Stokesley Crs *BLGHM* TS23 ...... 58 C3
Stokesley Rd *GUIS* TS14 ...... 128 B3
  HTLPS TS25 ...... D5
  MTN/NUN TS7 ...... 125 E2
Stoneacre Av *THNBY* TS17 ...... 139 D2
Stonebridge *DARLE* DL1 ...... 9 C5
Stonechat Cl *HTLPW* TS26 ...... 17 E1
  THNBY TS17 ...... 138 C1
Stonecliffe Dr *DARLW* DL3 ...... 131 D3
Stonecrop Cl *STOCS* TS18 ...... 93 F3
Stonedale Crs *DARLW* DL3 ...... 8 B3
Stonegate *ESTON* TS6 ...... 102 B2
Stonehaven Wy *DARLE* DL1 ...... 117 F1
Stonehouse Cl *YARM* TS15 ...... 146 C1
Stonehurst Dr *DARLW* DL3 ...... 131 D3
Stoneleigh Av *ACK/BRKF* TS5 ...... 97 D5
Stoneleigh Ct *NACLF* DL5 ...... 39 D3
Stonethwaite Dr *HTLP* TS24 ...... 18 A1
Stoneyhurst Av *ACK/BRKF* TS5 ...... 96 C4
Stooperdale Av *DARLW* DL3 ...... 115 D5
Stornaway Ct *STOCN* TS19 ...... 92 C1
Stotfold St *HTLPW* TS26 ...... 2 A3
Stoupe Gv *REDCAR* TS10 ...... 69 E3
Stowe St *MBORO* TS1 ...... 5 E6
Stowmarket Cl *HTLPS* TS25 ...... 31 E2
Strait La *CNHM/HEM* TS8 ...... 141 D1
Straker St *HTLPW* TS26 ...... 2 A1
Strand St *SHIL* DL4 ...... 35 E4
The Strand *REDCAR* TS10 ...... 69 E3
Stranton *HTLP* TS24 ...... 2 C5
Stranton St *BAUK* DL14 ...... 27 D1
  THNBY TS17 ...... 95 E4
Stratford Crs *ACK/BRKF* TS5 ...... 97 D2
Stratford Rd *HTLPS* TS25 ...... 23 F2
Strathaven Dr *EGG/EAG* TS16 ...... 137 F1
Strathmore Dr *YARM* TS15 ...... 146 C5
Stratton St *SPEN* DL16 ...... 14 C4
Strauss Rd *ESTON* TS6 ...... 81 D3
The Stray *DARLE* DL1 ...... 133 E2
Streatlam Rd *BLGHM* TS23 ...... 132 C5
  DARLE DL1 ...... 42 B5
Strensall Cl *MARSKE* TS11 ...... 86 C3
The Stripe *GTAY/STK* TS9 ...... 152 A2
Strome Cl *THNBY* TS17 ...... 139 E2
Stuart St *HTLP* TS24 ...... 18 A3
Stubbs Cl *BLGHM* TS23 ...... 41 F4
Studland Dr *HTLP* TS24 ...... 11 F3
Studland Rd *REDCAR* TS10 ...... 69 E4
Studley Rd *ACK/BRKF* TS5 ...... 97 E3
  HTLPS TS25 ...... 2 C6
  STOCN TS19 ...... 6 C1
  THNBY TS17 ...... 121 E1
Sturt Dr *NORTON* TS20 ...... 74 B1
Sudbury *MTN/NUN* TS7 ...... 126 A5
Sudbury Rd *NORTON* TS20 ...... 75 E1
Suffield St *TEESM* TS2 ...... 78 A2
Suffolk Cl *HTLPS* TS25 ...... 24 A2
Suffolk Rd *ACK/BRKF* TS5 ...... 98 B3
Suffolk St *STOCS* TS18 ...... 6 C6
Sugar Loaf Cl *THNBY* TS17 ...... 138 B2
Suggitt St *HTLPW* TS26 ...... 17 F4
Sulby Av *NORM/PKE* TS3 ...... 79 F4
Summerhouse Gv *DARLW* DL3 ...... 130 B1
Summerhouse Sq
  NORTON TS20 ...... 74 C1
Sunderland Rd
  BLGHMW/WYN TS22 ...... 41 F1
Sunley Av *MGRV/ESTR* TS4 ...... 98 C3
Sunningdale *FYHL* DL17 ...... 39 D2
Sunningdale Cl *ESTON* TS6 ...... 102 A3
Sunningdale Dr *EGG/EAG* TS16 ...... 137 E1
Sunningdale Gn *DARLE* DL1 ...... 117 F2

Sunningdale Rd *MARSKE* TS11 ...... 86 C3
  MGRV/ESTR TS4 ...... 98 B5
Sunningdale Wk
  EGG/EAG TS16 ...... 137 E1
Sunniside *HTLP* TS24 ...... 19 E2
Sunnybank Rd *MTN/NUN* TS7 ...... 127 D1
Sunnybrow Av *BLGHM* TS23 ...... 58 C4
Sunnyfield *MTN/NUN* TS7 ...... 100 C5
Sunnygate *ESTON* TS6 ...... 102 C2
Sunnyside *CNHM/HEM* TS8 ...... 124 B5
Sunnyside Av *MGRV/ESTR* TS4 ...... 98 B4
  SHIL DL4 ...... 35 F2
Sunnyside Gv *STOCS* TS18 ...... 93 E4
Sunstar Gv *MTN/NUN* TS7 ...... 125 E3
Sun St *BAUK* DL14 ...... 27 E2
  DARLW DL3 ...... 9 E3
  STOCS TS18 ...... 94 B3
  THNBY TS17 ...... 95 D4
Surbiton Rd *STOCN* TS19 ...... 72 B5
  STOCS TS18 ...... 92 B2
Surgery La *HTLP* TS24 ...... 12 C5
Surrey Rd *NORTON* TS20 ...... 75 E2
Surrey St *MBORO* TS1 ...... 97 F1
Surrey Ter *BLGHM* TS23 ...... 59 D3
Surtees Rd *NACLF* DL5 ...... 52 B4
Surtees St *BAUK* DL14 ...... 27 D1
  DARLW DL3 ...... 116 A4
  HTLP TS24 ...... 2 D3
  STOCS TS18 ...... 7 F6
Surtees Wk *NACLF* DL5 ...... 54 C2
Sussex St *HTLPS* TS25 ...... 24 A2
  TEESM TS2 ...... 5 F1
Sussex Wy *DARLE* DL1 ...... 117 D4
Sutcliffe Ct *DARLW* DL3 ...... 116 B1
Sutherland Gv *NORTON* TS20 ...... 57 F4
Sutton Cl *DARLW* DL3 ...... 130 B1
Sutton Pl *BLGHM* TS23 ...... 59 E1
Sutton Wy *MGRV/ESTR* TS4 ...... 98 B5
Swainby Rd *ACK/BRKF* TS5 ...... 124 A1
Swainby Rd *HTLPS* TS25 ...... 33 D1
  NORTON TS20 ...... 75 D4
Swainson St *HTLP* TS24 ...... 2 C2
Swainston Cl *ACK/BRKF* TS5 ...... 123 D2
Swale Av *THNBY* TS17 ...... 121 F1
Swalebrooke Av *HTLPS* TS25 ...... 23 E2
Swale Cl *EGG/EAG* TS16 ...... 137 D3
Swaledale Av *DARLW* DL3 ...... 115 D3
Swaledale Cl *THNBY* TS17 ...... 139 D3
Swaledale Crs *BLGHM* TS23 ...... 58 C3
Swale Rd *NORTON* TS20 ...... 74 C1
Swallowfields *CNHM/HEM* TS8 ...... 142 C2
Swallow La *NORTON* TS20 ...... 57 F5
Swanage Cl *CNHM/HEM* TS8 ...... 125 D3
Swanage Dr *REDCAR* TS10 ...... 69 E4
Swanage Gv *HTLP* TS24 ...... 11 F3
Swan St *DARLE* DL1 ...... 9 H5
Swan Wk *NACLF* DL5 ...... 55 D1
Swilly La *SALT/BTN/SK* TS12 ...... 109 C2
Swinburne Rd *DARLW* DL3 ...... 8 C5
  ECG/EAG TS16 ...... 119 E4
  HTLPS TS25 ...... 23 D3
Swinburn Rd *NORTON* TS20 ...... 74 C4
Swinton Rd *STOCS* TS18 ...... 93 D3
Swyfte Cl *SEDG* TS21 ...... 29 E4
Sycamore Cl *SALT/BTN/SK* TS12 ...... 89 C5
  THNBY TS17 ...... 121 E1
Sycamore Ct *STOCS* TS18 ...... 15 E3
Sycamore Crs *ESTON* TS6 ...... 101 E1
Sycamore Dr *SALT/BTN/SK* TS12 ...... 90 C5
Sycamore Rd *ACK/BRKF* TS5 ...... 98 A5
  EGG/EAG TS16 ...... 119 F5
  MTN/NUN TS7 ...... 127 D1
  STOCN TS19 ...... 74 A3
Sycamore Sq *SHIL* DL4 ...... 35 F3
The Sycamores *HTLPS* TS25 ...... 23 E3
Sycamore Ter *TEESM* TS2 ...... 61 D5
Sydenham Rd *HTLPS* TS25 ...... 24 B2
  STOCS TS18 ...... 94 B3
Sydney Cl *ACK/BRKF* TS5 ...... 97 D3
Sydney Rd *MTN/NUN* TS7 ...... 125 F4
Sydney St *STOCS* TS18 ...... 7 E4
Sylvan Gv *DARLW* DL3 ...... 8 A6
Symons Cl *STOCS* TS18 ...... 92 B2
Syon Gdns *NORTON* TS20 ...... 57 D5

T

Tailrigg Cl *STOCN* TS19 ...... 6 C2
Talbenny Gv *THNBY* TS17 ...... 138 B3
Talbot St *MBORO* TS1 ...... 78 C5
  NORTON TS20 ...... 75 D4
Talgarth Rd *NORTON* TS20 ...... 58 A5
Talisman Cl *EGG/EAG* TS16 ...... 118 C5
Talland St *RHTLP* TS27 ...... 11 E4
Tamarisk Cl *THNBY* TS17 ...... 121 E5
Tame Rd *NORM/PKE* TS3 ...... 79 E4
Tameside *GTAY/STK* TS9 ...... 152 A1
Tamworth Rd *BLGHM* TS23 ...... 42 A5
Tanfield Rd *HTLPS* TS25 ...... 23 F3
Tangmere *SPEN* DL16 ...... 14 C1
Tankersley Rd *MARSKE* TS11 ...... 86 C3
Tankerville St *HTLPW* TS26 ...... 17 F4

Tanner Cl *THNBY* TS17 ...... 139 D1
Tannery Yd *DARLE* DL1 ...... 9 H5
Tansley Av *NORM/PKE* TS3 ...... 100 A2
Tansley Gdns *DARLE* DL1 ...... 133 E3
Tanton Gv *BLGHMW/WYN* TS22 ...... 57 F1
Tanton Rd *GTAY/STK* TS9 ...... 152 B1
Tanwell Cl *STOCN* TS19 ...... 73 D4
Tanya Gdns *ACK/BRKF* TS5 ...... 124 A3
  STOCN TS19 ...... 93 E1
Tarnston Rd *HTLPW* TS26 ...... 16 C3
Tarran St *ACK/BRKF* TS5 ...... 97 E1
Tarring St *STOCS* TS18 ...... 7 E5
Tarr Steps *THNBY* TS17 ...... 139 D3
Tasman Dr *STOCS* TS18 ...... 93 D3
Tasmania Sq *MTN/NUN* TS7 ...... 126 A4
Tatham Cl *MTN/NUN* TS7 ...... 126 B5
Tattersall Cl *FYHL* DL17 ...... 39 D2
Taunton Cl *CNHM/HEM* TS8 ...... 125 D3
Taunton Gv *HTLPW* TS26 ...... 16 C2
Taunton V *GUIS* TS14 ...... 129 D5
Tavistock Rd *ACK/BRKF* TS5 ...... 97 F2
Tavistock St *ACK/BRKF* TS5 ...... 97 F2
Tawney Cl *ESTON* TS6 ...... 81 F5
Tawney Rd *ESTON* TS6 ...... 81 F5
Taybrooke Av *HTLPS* TS25 ...... 23 D3
Taylor Rd *BAUK* DL14 ...... 27 E3
Taylor Sq *BAUK* DL14 ...... 26 C4
Taylor St *MBORO* TS1 ...... 5 F4
Tayside *DARLE* DL1 ...... 117 F1
Teak St *MBORO* TS1 ...... 5 H5
Teal Rd *DARLE* DL1 ...... 133 F2
Teare Cl *MBORO* TS1 ...... 4 C5
Teasel Ct *STOCN* TS19 ...... 73 E4
Tebay Cl *MTN/NUN* TS7 ...... 100 C5
Tebay Rd *MTN/NUN* TS7 ...... 100 C5
Tedder Av *THNBY* TS17 ...... 121 F3
Ted Fletcher Ct *DARLE* DL1 ...... 117 E4
Tedworth Cl *GUIS* TS14 ...... 129 D5
Tees Bank Av *EGG/EAG* TS16 ...... 119 F4
Tees Barrage Wy *STOCS* TS18 ...... 96 A1
Tees Bridge Approach Rd
  BLGHM TS23 ...... 76 C4
Teesbrooke Av *HTLPS* TS25 ...... 23 E3
Tees Crs *SPEN* DL16 ...... 15 D2
Teesdale Av *BLGHM* TS23 ...... 58 C3
  DARLW DL3 ...... 130 C3
  HTLPW TS26 ...... 17 E5
Teesdale Bvd *THNBY* TS17 ...... 7 H4
Teesdale Ter *THNBY* TS17 ...... 95 F3
Teesdale Wk *SHIL* DL4 ...... 36 A3
Teesdale Wy *REDCAR* TS10 ...... 67 D1
  STOCS TS18 ...... 7 H6
  STOCS TS18 ...... 121 D2
  TEESM TS2 ...... 77 D4
Tees Dock Rd *ESTON* TS6 ...... 64 C3
Tees Dr *DARLE* DL1 ...... 132 B5
Teesgate *THNBY* TS17 ...... 122 A1
Tees Grange Av *DARLW* DL3 ...... 130 B2
Tees Link *GUIS* TS14 ...... 102 C5
  NORM/PKE TS3 ...... 79 F4
Tees Newport Bridge Approach Rd
  BLGHM TS23 ...... 77 D5
Tees Rd *GUIS* TS14 ...... 128 B4
  HTLPS TS25 ...... 33 D3
  REDCAR TS10 ...... 68 A1
Teesside Park Dr *THNBY* TS17 ...... 96 B3
Tees St *BLGHM* TS23 ...... 60 C4
  HTLPW TS26 ...... 2 B2
  LOFT/ST TS13 ...... 113 F5
Teesway *STOCS* TS18 ...... 76 B4
Telford Cl *HTLP* TS24 ...... 18 B1
Telford Dr *DARLE* DL1 ...... 132 C2
Telford Rd *NORM/PKE* TS3 ...... 80 A4
Temperance Av *SHIL* DL4 ...... 35 F2
Temperance Pl *DARLW* DL3 ...... 9 E3
Tempest Ct *DARLE* DL1 ...... 116 C1
Tempest Rd *HTLP* TS24 ...... 12 A4
Templar St *STOCS* TS18 ...... 94 B3
Templeton Cl *RHTLP* TS27 ...... 11 E4
Temple Wy *NACLF* DL5 ...... 38 A3
Tenby Cl *ESTON* TS6 ...... 102 A1
Tenby Wy *EGG/EAG* TS16 ...... 137 E2
Tennant St *STOCS* TS18 ...... 7 F3
Tennyson Av *ESTON* TS6 ...... 82 A4
  HTLPS TS25 ...... 23 E2
Tennyson Cl *HTLPS* TS25 ...... 82 A5
Tennyson Gdns *DARLE* DL1 ...... 132 B4
Tennyson Rd *BLGHM* TS23 ...... 41 F3
Tennyson St *MBORO* TS1 ...... 98 A1
Tenters St *BAUK* DL14 ...... 27 D1
Ternbeck Wy *THNBY* TS17 ...... 139 D1
Tern Gv *REDCAR* TS10 ...... 69 D3
Tetcott Cl *GUIS* TS14 ...... 129 D5
Tewkesbury Av *MTN/NUN* TS7 ...... 126 A5
Thackeray Gv *ACK/BRKF* TS5 ...... 97 F4
Thackeray Rd *HTLPS* TS25 ...... 22 C2
Thames Av *GUIS* TS14 ...... 128 B4
  HTLP TS24 ...... 17 F1
  THNBY TS17 ...... 121 F1
Thames Rd *BLGHMW/WYN* TS22 ...... 41 D5
  REDCAR TS10 ...... 67 F1
  SALT/BTN/SK TS12 ...... 109 C1
Thames Wy *DARLE* DL1 ...... 132 A5
Thatch La *THNBY* TS17 ...... 121 E5
Theakston Gv *STOCS* TS18 ...... 92 C3

Therby Cl *DARLW* DL3 .... 115 F3 ☑
Thetford Rd *HTLPS* TS25 .... 31 D2
Thinford Gdns *ACK/BRKF* TS5 ...... 123 F3
Thirlby Cl *NORM/PKE* TS3 .... 99 E3
Thirlmere *SPEN* DL16 .... 14 C1
Thirlmere Av *ACK/BRKF* TS5 .... 97 E5
Thirlmere Ct *BLGHM* TS23 .... 59 D5 ☑
Thirlmere Crs *ESTON* TS6 .... 101 F3 ☑
Thirlmere Dr *SALT/BTN/SK* TS12 .. 109 D2
Thirlmere Rd *DARLE* DL1 .... 132 C3
   FYHL DL17 .... 20 C2
   REDCAR TS10 .... 68 A1
Thirlmere St *HTLPW* TS26................ 2 A5
Thirsk Av *HTLPS* TS25 .... 24 A4
Thirsk Rd *GTAY/STK* TS9 .... 152 A4
   YARM TS15 .... 146 B1
Thirwall Dr *THNBY* TS17 .... 138 C2
Thistle Cl *SPEN* DL16 .... 14 B4
Thistle Gn *STOCS* TS18 .... 7 G3
Thistle Ri *CNHM/HEM* TS8 .... 124 B4
Thistle Rd *STOCN* TS19 .... 74 B2 ☑
Thistle St *MBORO* TS1 .... 5 H5
Thomas Cl *DARLE* DL1 .... 132 C2 ☑
Thomas St *DARLE* DL1 .... 132 C2 ☑
   NORM/PKE TS3 .... 79 E5 ☑
   SALT/BTN/SK TS12 .... 109 F2
   SHIL DL4 .... 35 F5 ☑
   SPEN DL16 .... 15 D3
   STOCS TS18 .... 7 F2 ☑
Thomlinson Rd *HTLPS* TS25 .... 24 B2
Thompson Gv *HTLP* TS24 .... 17 F1
Thompson Rd *BAUK* DL14 .... 27 E3 ☑
Thompsons Cl
   BLGHMW/WYN TS22 .... 41 E3 ☑
Thompson's Rd
   SALT/BTN/SK TS12 .... 108 C3
Thompson St *HTLP* TS24 .... 2 C5
   SPEN DL16 .... 15 D2 ☑
   STOCS TS18 .... 7 F2
Thompson St East *DARLE* DL1 .... 116 B2
Thompson St West *DARLW* DL3 .. 116 A2
Thomson Av *ACK/BRKF* TS5 .... 97 D2 ☑
Thomson St *GUIS* TS14 .... 128 C3
Thorgill Cl *MGRV/ESTR* TS4 .... 98 B4
Thorington Gdns *THNBY* TS17 .. 139 E2 ☑
Thornaby Pl *THNBY* TS17 .... 95 D3
Thornaby Rd *THNBY* TS17 .... 121 E1
Thornbrough Cl *STOCS* TS18 ...... 93 D4 ☑
Thornbury Cl *RHTLP* TS27 .... 11 E3
Thornbury Ri *DARLW* DL3 .... 115 D5
Thorn Cl *SPEN* DL16 .... 14 B5
   THNBY TS17 .... 121 D5
Thorndike Rd *ESTON* TS6 .... 102 A1
Thorndyke Av *MGRV/ESTR* TS4 ...... 98 C4
Thornfield Cl *EGG/EAG* TS16 ...... 136 C1
Thornfield Gv *ACK/BRKF* TS5 .... 97 E4
Thornfield Rd *ACK/BRKF* TS5 .... 97 E3
   DARLW DL3 .... 131 D1 ☑
Thornhill Gdns *HTLPW* TS26 .... 17 E3
   SHIL DL4 .... 35 E2
Thornley Av *BLGHM* TS23 .... 42 A3 ☑
Thorn Rd *STOCN* TS19 .... 74 A2
Thornside *THNBY* TS17 .... 121 D5
Thorn St *MBORO* TS1 .... 5 F4
Thornton Cl *CNHM/HEM* TS8 ...... 141 D2
Thornton Crs *BLGHMW/WYN* TS22 .. 58 A1
Thornton Garth *YARM* TS15 .... 146 B1
Thornton Gv *NORTON* TS20 .... 74 C3
Thornton Rd *CNHM/HEM* TS8 .... 141 D2
Thornton St *DARLW* DL3 .... 9 F2
   HTLPW TS26 .... 2 A3
   NORM/PKE TS3 .... 79 E5
Thornton V *CNHM/HEM* TS8 ...... 141 D2
Thorntree Av *NORM/PKE* TS3 ...... 100 A1
Thorntree Ct *THNBY* TS17 .... 121 F1 ☑
Thorntree Rd *THNBY* TS17 .... 95 E5
Thornville Rd *HTLPW* TS26 .... 17 F4
Thornwood Av *THNBY* TS17 .... 121 D5
Thorpe St *HTLP* TS24 .... 18 C1
Thorphill Wy *ACK/BRKF* TS5 .... 42 A4
Three Tuns Wynd *GTAY/STK* TS9 .. 152 A2 ☑
Throckley Av *ACK/BRKF* TS5 ...... 123 E2
Thropton Cl *BLGHM* TS23 .... 41 E4
Throstenest Av *DARLE* DL1 .... 117 D4
Throston Cl *HTLPW* TS26 .... 17 E1
Throston Grange La *HTLPW* TS26 .. 16 C2
Throston St *HTLP* TS24 .... 19 E2 ☑
Thrush Rd *REDCAR* TS10 .... 51 E5
Thrushwood Crs *MARSKE* TS11 .... 88 A1
Thruxton Wy *NORTON* TS20 .... 74 B1 ☑
Thurlestone *MTN/NUN* TS7 .... 126 B5 ☑
Thurlow Gv *NACLF* DL5 .... 38 B5
Thurlow Rd *SEDG* TS21 .... 29 E4
Thurnham Gv *MTN/NUN* TS7 ...... 126 A4
Thursby Cl *NACLF* DL5 .... 53 E2
Thursby Dr *MTN/NUN* TS7 .... 100 C5
Thursby Wy *HTLPS* TS25 .... 31 D2
Thurso Cl *STOCN* TS19 .... 92 B1 ☑
Thwaites Cl *NACLF* DL5 .... 38 A3 ☑
Thwaites La *REDCAR* TS10 .... 68 C1
Thweng Wy *GUIS* TS14 .... 128 B4
Tibbersley Av *BLGHM* TS23 .... 59 D5
Tibthorpe *MTN/NUN* TS7 .... 126 B4
Tidkin La *GUIS* TS14 .... 128 B4

Tilbury Rd *ESTON* TS6 .... 80 B3
Tilery Rd *NORTON* TS20 .... 75 D4
Timberscombe Cl *THNBY* TS17 .. 138 C4 ☑
Tindale Cl *YARM* TS15 .... 146 A2
Tindale Wk *ACK/BRKF* TS5 .... 123 E4 ☑
Tintagel Ct *RHTLP* TS27 .... 11 E4
Tintern Av *BLGHM* TS23 .... 58 C1
   DARLW DL3 .... 114 A3
Tintern Rd *SALT/BTN/SK* TS12 .... 109 F2
Tipton Cl *THNBY* TS17 .... 122 A1
Tirril Wy *MTN/NUN* TS7 .... 126 B5
Tithe Barn Rd *STOCN* TS19............ 72 C2
Tiverton Gv *HTLPW* TS26 .... 17 D2 ☑
Tivoli Pl *BAUK* DL14 .... 27 D3 ☑
Toddington Dr *NORTON* TS20 .... 74 A1
Todd St *SPEN* DL16 .... 14 C3
Tod Point Rd *REDCAR* TS10 .... 50 A4
Tofts Cl *MARSKE* TS11 .... 71 D5
Tofts Rd East *HTLPS* TS25 .... 32 C3
Tofts Rd West *HTLPS* TS25 .... 32 B3
Tollerton Cl *STOCN* TS19 .... 75 F5 ☑
Tollesby La *MTN/NUN* TS7 .... 125 E4
Tollesby Rd *ACK/BRKF* TS5 .... 98 A4
Tomlinson Wy *NORM/PKE* TS3 .. 100 B1 ☑
Tomlin St *SHIL* DL4 .... 35 E5
Topcliffe Dr *ACK/BRKF* TS5 .... 123 E3
Topcliffe Rd *THNBY* TS17 .... 122 A2
Topcliffe St *HTLPW* TS26 .... 17 E4
Topcroft Cl *NORM/PKE* TS3 .... 100 A5
Topham Gn *NORM/PKE* TS3 .... 99 E2
Topping Cl *HTLP* TS24 .... 13 F5 ☑
Torbay Cl *CNHM/HEM* TS8 .... 125 D2
Torbay Gv *HTLPW* TS26.................. 17 D2
Torcross Cl *RHTLP* TS27 .... 11 E4
Torcross Wy *REDCAR* TS10 .... 69 D4 ☑
Toronto Crs *MGRV/ESTR* TS4 .... 98 C2
Torquay Av *HTLPS* TS25 .... 31 E1
Torrance Dr *DARLE* DL1 .... 117 F1
Torver Mt *MTN/NUN* TS7 .... 126 B5
Torwell Dr *STOCN* TS19 .... 73 D5
Tothill Av *NORM/PKE* TS3.............. 100 C3
Totnes Cl *RHTLP* TS27 .... 11 E4
Tovil Cl *STOCN* TS19 .... 72 C3
Tower Cl *TEESM* TS2 .... 78 A2
Tower Rd *DARLW* DL3 .... 8 D2
Tower St *HTLP* TS24 .... 2 C5
   STOCS TS18 .... 7 G6
Town Wall *HTLP* TS24 .... 19 E2
Towthorpe *MTN/NUN* TS7 .... 126 B4
Trafalgar St *FYHL* DL17 .... 21 F3
Trafalgar Ter *DARLW* DL3 .... 115 F4
   REDCAR TS10 .... 51 D5
Trafford Cl *DARLE* DL1 .... 117 F4
Tranmere Av *NORM/PKE* TS3 ...... 100 A2
Tranter Rd *MGRV/ESTR* TS4 .... 98 B4
Travellers Ga *HTLPS* TS25 .... 24 A4 ☑
Travellers' Gn *NACLF* DL5 .... 55 D2
Trecastell *THNBY* TS17 .... 138 B3
Treelands *DARLW* DL3 .... 131 D2
Trefoil Cl *GUIS* TS14 .... 128 A4
Trefoil Ct *NORTON* TS20 .... 74 C3
Trefoil Wd *MTN/NUN* TS7 .... 125 E2
Tregarth Cl *MGRV/ESTR* TS4 .... 98 B4 ☑
Trenchard Av *THNBY* TS17 .... 121 F3
Trenholme Rd *MGRV/ESTR* TS4.... 99 D1
Trent Av *THNBY* TS17 .... 121 F1
Trentbrooke Av *HTLPS* TS25 .... 23 E3
Trentham Av *NORM/PKE* TS3 ...... 100 B3
Trent Pl *DARLE* DL1 .... 132 A5
Trent Rd *REDCAR* TS10 .... 67 F1
Trent St *NORTON* TS20 .... 74 C3
Trevarrian Dr *REDCAR* TS10.......... 69 D4
Trevino Ct *EGG/EAG* TS16 .... 137 E1 ☑
Trevithick Cl *DARLE* DL1 .... 132 C2 ☑
   EGG/EAG TS16 .... 119 D5 ☑
Trigo Cl *MTN/NUN* TS7 .... 125 E3 ☑
Trimdon Av *ACK/BRKF* TS5 .... 123 D2
Trinity Crs *NORM/PKE* TS3 .... 79 D4
Trinity Ms *THNBY* TS17 .... 95 E2
Trinity Rd *DARLW* DL3 .... 8 C4
Trinity St *HTLP* TS24 .... 19 E1 ☑
   STOCS TS18 .... 7 E6
Tristram Av *HTLPS* TS25 .... 23 E2
Tristram Cl *ESTON* TS6 .... 101 E3 ☑
Trident Cl *HTLP* TS24 .... 3 E2
Troisdorf Wy *REDCAR* TS10 .... 67 F2
Troon Av *DARLE* DL1 .... 117 F2
Troon Cl *BLGHMW/WYN* TS22 ...... 57 F1
   MGRV/ESTR TS4 .... 98 B5
Troutbeck Cl *SPEN* DL16 .... 14 C1 ☑
Troutbeck Rd *REDCAR* TS10 .... 68 A2
Trout Hall La *SALT/BTN/SK* TS12 .. 109 D3
Troutpool Cl *HTLP* TS24 .... 18 B1
Troutsdale Cl *YARM* TS15 .... 146 A2
Trueman Gv *DARLW* DL3 .... 116 B1 ☑
Trunk Rd *ESTON* TS6 .... 66 A4
   ESTON TS6 .... 80 C5
   ESTON TS6 .... 82 A4
   REDCAR TS10 .... 67 D1
Truro Cl *DARLE* DL1 .... 117 F3
Truro Dr *HTLPS* TS25 .... 31 E1
Tubwell Rw *DARLE* DL1 .... 9 F5
Tunstall Av *BLGHM* TS23 .... 42 B3
   HTLPW TS26 .... 17 D3
Tunstall Gv *HTLPW* TS26 .... 17 D3

Tunstall Rd *NACLF* DL5 .... 54 B1
   STOCS TS18 .... 93 D4
Tunstall St *NORM/PKE* TS3 .... 79 E5 ☑
Turford Av *NORM/PKE* TS3.......... 100 A1
Turnberry Av *EGG/EAG* TS16 ...... 137 E2
Turnberry Dr *MARSKE* TS11 .... 86 B4
Turnberry Gv *RHTLP* TS27 .... 11 E3
Turnberry Wy *CNHM/HEM* TS8 .. 144 A1
Turnbull St *HTLP* TS24...................... 18 A3
Turner Cl *BLGHM* TS23 .... 41 F4
Turner St *REDCAR* TS10 .... 51 E4
The Turnstile *ACK/BRKF* TS5 ...... 97 F1 ☑
Turton Rd *YARM* TS15 .... 146 A1
Tuson Wk *HTLP* TS24 .... 18 A3
Tweed Av *THNBY* TS17 .... 121 F1
Tweed Pl *DARLE* DL1 .... 132 B5
Tweedport Rd *STOCS* TS18 .... 75 C5
Tweed Rd *REDCAR* TS10 .... 67 F1
   SPEN DL16 .... 15 F1
Tweed St *LOFT/ST* TS13 .... 113 F3
   SALT/BTN/SK TS12 .... 89 E2
Tyne Cl *ESTON* TS6 .... 80 C5
Tyne Crs *DARLE* DL1 .... 132 B5
   SPEN DL16 .... 15 D2
Tynedale St *STOCS* TS18 .... 6 C5
Tynedale Wk *SHIL* DL4 .... 36 A4 ☑
Tyne Rd *REDCAR* TS10...................... 68 A1
Tyne St *LOFT/ST* TS13 .... 113 F3
Tyrone Rd *STOCN* TS19 .... 72 C5

U

Uldale Dr *EGG/EAG* TS16 .... 137 D2
Ullapool Cl *STOCN* TS19 .... 92 B1 ☑
Ulla St *MBORO* TS1 .... 5 F6
Ullswater Av *ACK/BRKF* TS5.......... 97 E5
Ullswater Cl *ESTON* TS6 .... 82 B5
   SPEN DL16 .... 15 F2 ☑
Ullswater Dr *SALT/BTN/SK* TS12 .. 109 D1
Ullswater Gv *REDCAR* TS10............ 68 B1
Ullswater Rd *BLGHM* TS23 .... 59 D5 ☑
   FYHL DL17 .... 20 C2
   HTLPS TS25 .... 24 B2
   STOCS TS18 .... 6 A3
Union Pl *DARLE* DL1 .... 132 C2
Union Rd *HTLP* TS24 .... 18 B1
Union Sq *STOCS* TS18 .... 7 F3
Union St *BAUK* DL14 .... 27 E2
   DARLW DL3 .... 9 F3
   GUIS TS14 .... 129 D3
   HTLP TS24 .... 19 E2
   MBORO TS1 .... 4 C6
Union St East *STOCS* TS18 .... 75 C5 ☑
University Bvd *THNBY* TS17 .... 95 E2
Uplands Rd *DARLW* DL3 .... 8 C5
Upleatham St *SALT/BTN/SK* TS12 .. 89 E2
Upleatham Gv *STOCN* TS19 .... 93 D2
Upper Archer St *DARLW* DL3 ...... 9 E3 ☑
Upper Branch St *ESTON* TS6 .... 80 C3 ☑
Upper Garth Gdns *GUIS* TS14 .... 129 D3
Upper Graham St *ESTON* TS6 .. 80 C3 ☑
Upper Green La *THNBY* TS17 ...... 121 E2
Upper Napier St *ESTON* TS6.......... 80 C3
Upper Oxford St *ESTON* TS6 .... 80 C3
Upper Princess St *ESTON* TS6 ...... 80 C3
Upper Russell St *DARLE* DL1 ...... 9 H3 ☑
Uppingham St *HTLPS* TS25 .... 23 F2 ☑
Upsall Dr *DARLW* DL3 .... 131 F3
Upsall Gv *STOCN* TS19 .... 93 D2
Upsall Rd *MTN/NUN* TS7 .... 127 D4 ☑
   NORM/PKE TS3 .... 99 F2 ☑
Upton Ct *THNBY* TS17 .... 138 C2
Upton St *MBORO* TS1 .... 5 G6
Upton Wk *HTLPS* TS25 .... 31 D2
Urford Cl *YARM* TS15 .... 147 D1
Urlay Gv *ACK/BRKF* TS5 .... 123 F2
Urlay Nook Rd *EGG/EAG* TS16 .... 118 B5
Usk Ct *THNBY* TS17 .... 138 B2
Usworth Rd *HTLPS* TS25.................. 24 A4
Uvedale Rd *ESTON* TS6 .... 81 D4

V

Vale Dr *THNBY* TS17 .... 96 A5
The Vale *HTLPW* TS26 .... 16 C5
   MGRV/ESTR TS4 .... 98 B4
   STOCN TS19 .... 73 E4
Valiant Wy *THNBY* TS17 .... 121 E4 ☑
Valley Cl *HTLPW* TS26 .... 16 B5
   MARSKE TS11 .... 70 B4
   YARM TS15 .... 137 F5
Valley Dr *HTLPW* TS26.................... 22 B1
   YARM TS15 .... 137 F5
Valley Gdns *EGG/EAG* TS16 .... 136 C2
   STOCN TS19 .... 73 F4
Valley Rd *MGRV/ESTR* TS4 .... 98 B3
Valley St North *DARLE* DL1 .... 9 G3
Valley View Ct *SHIL* DL4 .... 35 D1

Vancouver Gdns
  MGRV/ESTR TS4 .... 98 C1 [1]
Vane Rd *NACLF* DL5 .... 39 D5
Vane St *HTLP* TS24 .... 19 D1
  STOCS TS18 .... 7 F4
Vane Ter *DARLW* DL3 .... 8 D4
Van Mildert Rd *NACLF* DL5 .... 55 D1 [3]
Varo Ter *STOCS* TS18 .... 6 D6
Vart Rd *BAUK* DL14 .... 27 D4
Vasser Wy *THNBY* TS17 .... 7 H5
Vaughan St *DARLW* DL3 .... 116 B1
  SALT/BTN/SK TS12 .... 110 A2
  SHIL DL4 .... 34 C3
Vaynor Dr *THNBY* TS17 .... 138 B2
Venables Rd *GUIS* TS14 .... 128 C2
Ventnor Av *HTLPS* TS25 .... 23 F3
Ventnor Rd *ACK/BRKF* TS5 .... 97 F3
Verity Ri *DARLW* DL3 .... 116 A3 [3]
Verner Cl *HTLP* TS24 .... 11 E2
Verner Rd *HTLP* TS24 .... 11 E2
Vernon Ct *CNHM/HEM* TS8 .... 141 E1
Veronica St *NORM/PKE* TS3 .... 79 D5 [7]
Verwood Cl *STOCN* TS19 .... 72 C3
Veryan Rd *BLGHM* TS23 .... 59 E1 [1]
Vicarage Av *STOCN* TS19 .... 6 D3
Vicarage Gr *MARSKE* TS11 .... 70 C5
Vicarage Rd *DARLE* DL1 .... 116 C5 [3]
Vicarage Rw *HTLPS* TS25 .... 31 D4 [3]
Vicarage St *STOCN* TS19 .... 6 D2
Vickers Cl *MARSKE* TS11 .... 70 A4
  STOCS TS18 .... 120 B1
Vickers St *BAUK* DL14 .... 27 D1
Victoria Av *BAUK* DL14 .... 27 E1 [7]
  NORTON TS20 .... 74 C3
  REDCAR TS10 .... 68 C1
Victoria Cl *MARSKE* TS11 .... 86 C2
Victoria Emb *DARLE* DL1 .... 132 A3
Victoria Gdns *SPEN* DL16 .... 14 C4
Victoria Gv *STOCN* TS19 .... 73 E5 [5]
Victoria Pl *HTLP* TS24 .... 19 E2
Victoria Rd *DARLE* DL1 .... 9 E6
  EGG/EAG TS16 .... 119 E5 [11]
  ESTON TS6 .... 81 F3
  HTLP TS24 .... 2 B2
  HTLPW TS26 .... 2 A2
  MBORO TS1 .... 5 F6
  SALT/BTN/SK TS12 .... 89 E4
  STOCN TS19 .... 73 E5
  THNBY TS17 .... 95 E4
Victoria St *DARLE* DL1 .... 132 C2 [1]
  ESTON TS6 .... 80 C3
  HTLP TS24 .... 2 B2
  HTLPS TS25 .... 25 D5 [11]
  MBORO TS1 .... 4 B5
  SHIL DL4 .... 35 F4
  SPEN DL16 .... 14 C4
  STOCS TS18 .... 7 F3
Victoria Ter *HTLP* TS24 .... 3 E1
  SALT/BTN/SK TS12 .... 89 E3
  TEESM TS2 .... 78 B1 [1]
Victor Wy *THNBY* TS17 .... 121 E3
Victory Ter *REDCAR* TS10 .... 51 D5
Viewley Centre Rd
  CNHM/HEM TS8 .... 124 A5
Viewley Hill Av *CNHM/HEM* TS8 .... 124 B5
Village Cl *NACLF* DL5 .... 39 D3
Village Paddock *STOCS* TS18 .... 93 F4
Villa St *SPEN* DL16 .... 14 C4
Villiers Cl *DARLW* DL3 .... 130 C1
Villiers St *HTLP* TS24 .... 2 B3
  SPEN DL16 .... 15 D2
Vincent Rd *ACK/BRKF* TS5 .... 98 B3
  BLGHM TS23 .... 41 F4
Vincent St *HTLP* TS24 .... 13 E5
Vine Cl *GUIS* TS14 .... 129 C4
Vine St *DARLW* DL3 .... 8 B1
  SPEN DL16 .... 15 D2
  TEESM TS2 .... 5 F1
Violet Gv *DARLE* DL1 .... 133 D1 [2]
Virginia Cl *STOCN* TS19 .... 73 F3 [5]
Virginia Gdns *ACK/BRKF* TS5 .... 123 F5
Vollum Ri *HTLP* TS24 .... 19 D1 [2]
Voltigeur Dr *RHTLP* TS27 .... 10 C3
Vulcan St *DARLE* DL1 .... 116 C4 [3]
  TEESM TS2 .... 78 B2
Vulcan Wy *THNBY* TS17 .... 121 F4
Vyners Cl *SPEN* DL16 .... 15 E4
Vyner St *SPEN* DL16 .... 14 C3

W

Waddington St *BAUK* DL14 .... 27 D3 [11]
Wade Av *STOCS* TS18 .... 7 G2
Wadham Gv *DARLW* DL3 .... 116 B2
Waine Crs *BAUK* DL14 .... 27 D4
Wainfleet Rd *HTLPS* TS25 .... 30 C2
Wainstones Cl *GTAY/STK* TS9 .... 150 C4
Wainstones Dr *GTAY/STK* TS9 .... 150 B4
Wainwright Cl *HTLPS* TS25 .... 25 D3
Wakefield Rd *ACK/BRKF* TS5 .... 98 A2 [2]
Wake St *NORM/PKE* TS3 .... 79 E5 [14]
Walcher Rd *NACLF* DL5 .... 38 C5

Waldon St *HTLP* TS24 .... 2 B4
Waldridge Gv *BLGHM* TS23 .... 42 C3 [2]
Waldridge Rd *STOCN* TS19 .... 73 D2
Waldron St *BAUK* DL14 .... 27 D1
Wales St *DARLW* DL3 .... 116 A3
Walker Dr *BAUK* DL14 .... 26 C5
Walker La *NACLF* DL5 .... 54 C2
Walker's La *NACLF* DL5 .... 37 D5
Walkers Rw *GUIS* TS14 .... 129 D2
Walker St *REDCAR* TS10 .... 51 E4
  THNBY TS17 .... 95 E4
Walkley Av *THNBY* TS17 .... 121 E1 [2]
Wallas Rd *NACLF* DL5 .... 54 C1
Wallington Dr *SEDG* TS21 .... 29 D3
Wallington Rd *BLGHM* TS23 .... 42 A3
Wallington Wy *BLGHM* TS23 .... 42 A4 [7]
Wallis Rd *ESTON* TS6 .... 80 B5
Walmer Av *BAUK* DL14 .... 26 C3
Walmer Crs *MARSKE* TS11 .... 86 B3
Walnut Cl *THNBY* TS17 .... 121 E1
Walnut Gv *REDCAR* TS10 .... 69 D1
Walpole Rd *HTLPS* TS25 .... 23 D2
Walpole St *MBORO* TS1 .... 4 D5
Walsham Cl *STOCN* TS19 .... 73 E4 [2]
Walsingham Ct *BLGHM* TS23 .... 59 D5 [5]
Walter St *SHIL* DL4 .... 35 F5 [7]
  STOCS TS18 .... 94 B3
Waltham Av *STOCS* TS18 .... 93 E2
Waltham Cl *DARLW* DL3 .... 114 C4
Walton Av *ACK/BRKF* TS5 .... 97 F4
Walton St *DARLE* DL1 .... 132 C3
  STOCS TS18 .... 75 F5
Walton Ter *GUIS* TS14 .... 129 D3 [6]
Walworth Cl *REDCAR* TS10 .... 69 D2
Walworth Crs *DARLW* DL3 .... 115 D3
Walworth Gv *ACK/BRKF* TS5 .... 123 D2
Walworth Rd *NACLF* DL5 .... 54 C4
  STOCN TS19 .... 73 E2 [2]
Wand Hl *SALT/BTN/SK* TS12 .... 109 E5
Wandhill Gdns *SALT/BTN/SK* TS12 .... 109 E5
Wandhills Av *SALT/BTN/SK* TS12 .... 110 A1
Wansbeck Gdns *HTLPW* TS26 .... 17 F5
Wansford Cl *BLGHM* TS23 .... 42 B3
Wanstead Cl *MARSKE* TS11 .... 70 B4 [2]
Warbler Cl *THNBY* TS17 .... 138 C1
Warburton Cl *NACLF* DL5 .... 39 D5
Warcop Cl *MTN/NUN* TS7 .... 126 B5
Wardale Av *ACK/BRKF* TS5 .... 123 E3
Ward Cl *STOCS* TS18 .... 7 E5
Wardell Cl *YARM* TS15 .... 146 C1
Warden Cl *STOCN* TS19 .... 73 E2
Wardley Cl *STOCN* TS19 .... 73 E2
Wardman Crs *REDCAR* TS10 .... 69 D1
Warelands Wy *MGRV/ESTR* TS4 .... 99 D1
Ware St *NORTON* TS20 .... 75 D4 [2]
Warkworth Av *BAUK* DL14 .... 26 C3
Warkworth Dr *HTLPW* TS26 .... 16 C4 [2]
Warkworth Rd *BLGHM* TS23 .... 41 E5
Warner Gv *DARLW* DL3 .... 116 B1 [1]
Warren Cl *HTLP* TS24 .... 17 F1
Warrenport Rd *STOCS* TS18 .... 75 E5
Warren Rd *HTLP* TS24 .... 12 B5
  NACLF DL5 .... 54 C3 [1]
Warren St *DARLW* DL3 .... 8 D2
  HTLP TS24 .... 19 D1
  MBORO TS1 .... 4 D5
Warrior Dr *HTLPS* TS25 .... 24 C4
Warsett Crs *SALT/BTN/SK* TS12 .... 110 A2
Warsett Rd *MARSKE* TS11 .... 71 D5
Warton St *NORM/PKE* TS3 .... 79 E5
Warwick Cl *EGG/EAG* TS16 .... 137 D3 [2]
  SPEN DL16 .... 15 E1
Warwick Crs *BLGHM* TS23 .... 59 E3 [4]
Warwick Gv *HTLPW* TS26 .... 17 E5
  NORTON TS20 .... 75 D2
Warwick Pl *HTLP* TS24 .... 2 D1
Warwick Rd *BAUK* DL14 .... 26 C3
  GUIS TS14 .... 128 C4
  REDCAR TS10 .... 69 D2
Warwick Sq *DARLW* DL3 .... 114 C3 [2]
Warwick St *ACK/BRKF* TS5 .... 97 F1 [7]
  ESTON TS6 .... 80 C4 [4]
  MBORO TS1 .... 4 D5
Wasdale Cl *HTLP* TS24 .... 18 A1
Wasdale Dr *EGG/EAG* TS16 .... 137 E2
Wasdale Gv *STOCN* TS19 .... 74 A3 [6]
Washbrook Dr *DARLW* DL3 .... 116 B1
Washford Cl *THNBY* TS17 .... 138 D5
Washington Crs *NACLF* DL5 .... 39 D4
Washington Gv *NORTON* TS20 .... 74 B2
Waskerley Cl *STOCN* TS19 .... 73 E2 [2]
Waterford Rd *NORTON* TS20 .... 74 C3
Waterford Ter *MBORO* TS1 .... 97 E1 [1]
Water La *LOFT/ST* TS13 .... 113 E3
Waterloo Rd *MBORO* TS1 .... 5 F6
Waterloo Ter *SHIL* DL4 .... 35 D2
Waterside *DARLE* DL1 .... 115 D5
Watersmeet Cl *THNBY* TS17 .... 139 D5
Watling Cl *NORTON* TS20 .... 74 B1
Watling Rd *BAUK* DL14 .... 27 D2
Watness Av *SALT/BTN/SK* TS12 .... 110 A1
Watson Gv *THNBY* TS17 .... 95 D4 [2]
Watson Rd *NACLF* DL5 .... 54 B2
Watson St *MBORO* TS1 .... 5 H4
Watton Cl *HTLPS* TS25 .... 31 D3 [2]

Watton Rd *THNBY* TS17 .... 122 A1
Watt St *FYHL* DL17 .... 20 B1
Waveney Gv *SALT/BTN/SK* TS12 .... 109 F1
Waveney Rd *REDCAR* TS10 .... 67 F2
Waverley St *MBORO* TS1 .... 4 D5
  STOCS TS18 .... 94 B3 [5]
Waverley Ter *DARLE* DL1 .... 9 G6
  HTLPS TS25 .... 23 E2
Wayland Ter *DARLW* DL3 .... 115 E3
Waymar St *ACK/BRKF* TS5 .... 97 E3
Wayside Rd *DARLE* DL1 .... 116 C1 [4]
  NORM/PKE TS3 .... 100 C1 [1]
Wear Ct *ESTON* TS6 .... 80 B5
Wear Crs *EGG/EAG* TS16 .... 137 D3
Weardale Crs *BLGHM* TS23 .... 58 C4
Weardale Gv *ACK/BRKF* TS5 .... 98 A4 [4]
Weardale Pl *STOCS* TS18 .... 6 B2
Weardale Wk *SHIL* DL4 .... 36 A3 [2]
Wear St *SPEN* DL16 .... 15 D4
Weastell St *ACK/BRKF* TS5 .... 98 A2 [2]
Weatherhead Av *ACK/BRKF* TS5 .... 97 D4
Weaver Cl *THNBY* TS17 .... 121 E5
Weaverham Rd *NORTON* TS20 .... 74 B2
Weavers Ct *CTAY/STK* TS9 .... 152 A2
Weaver's Wy *DARLE* DL1 .... 9 G3
Weaverthorpe *MTN/NUN* TS7 .... 126 B4
Webb Cl *NACLF* DL5 .... 38 B5
Webb Rd *ESTON* TS6 .... 80 B4
Webster Av *ACK/BRKF* TS5 .... 98 B3 [4]
Webster Cl *STOCS* TS18 .... 7 E5
Webster Rd *ESTON* TS6 .... 102 A3
Webster St *STOCS* TS18 .... 7 E6
Wederly Cl *DARLW* DL3 .... 116 A4
Weir St *DARLE* DL1 .... 9 G3
Welbeck Av *DARLE* DL1 .... 117 E3
Welbeck Ct *SALT/BTN/SK* TS12 .... 109 F1
Welbeck St *DARLE* DL1 .... 132 B3 [7]
Welburn Av *MGRV/ESTR* TS4 .... 98 C3
Welburn Gv *MTN/NUN* TS7 .... 100 C5
Welbury Cl *STOCS* TS18 .... 93 D3
Welbury Gv *NACLF* DL5 .... 39 E5
Welbury Wy *NACLF* DL5 .... 54 C5
Welland Cl *ACK/BRKF* TS5 .... 123 E3
Welland Crs *STOCN* TS19 .... 73 D4
Welland Rd *HTLPS* TS25 .... 31 D2
  REDCAR TS10 .... 67 F2
Wellbrook Cl *THNBY* TS17 .... 139 E2 [2]
Wellburn Rd *STOCN* TS19 .... 92 C1
Welldale Crs *STOCN* TS19 .... 73 D5
Welldeck Gdns *HTLPW* TS26 .... 17 E4
Welldeck Rd *HTLPW* TS26 .... 17 E4
Wellesley Rd *MGRV/ESTR* TS4 .... 78 C2
Well House Ride *NACLF* DL5 .... 38 B3
Wellington Cl *MARSKE* TS11 .... 70 A5
Wellington St *STOCS* TS18 .... 7 E4
  TEESM TS2 .... 5 F1
Wellmead Rd *NORM/PKE* TS3 .... 100 B1 [1]
Wells Av *HTLP* TS24 .... 12 C5
Wells Cl *DARLE* DL1 .... 117 F3 [7]
  ESTON TS6 .... 102 A2
Wells Gv *REDCAR* TS10 .... 69 E2
Wellspring Cl *ACK/BRKF* TS5 .... 123 D2
Wells St *HTLP* TS24 .... 19 E1
Wembley Ct *STOCS* TS18 .... 6 C5
Wembley St *MBORO* TS1 .... 4 B6
Wembley Wy *ESTON* TS6 .... 101 E5 [5]
  STOCS TS18 .... 6 C5
Wembury Cl *REDCAR* TS10 .... 69 D4 [4]
Wensleydale Cl *SALT/BTN/SK* TS12 .. 109 D1 [1]
Wensleydale Gv *THNBY* TS17 .... 139 D3
Wensleydale Rd *DARLE* DL1 .... 116 B3
Wensleydale St *HTLPS* TS25 .... 24 A2
Wensley Rd *STOCS* TS18 .... 93 F2
Wentworth Ct *ESTON* TS6 .... 102 A3 [6]
Wentworth Crs *MARSKE* TS11 .... 86 B3 [13]
Wentworth Gv *RHTLP* TS27 .... 11 E4
Wentworth St *MBORO* TS1 .... 4 D5
Wentworth Wy *DARLW* DL3 .... 114 B3
  EGG/EAG TS16 .... 137 E2
Wesleyan Rd *SPEN* DL16 .... 15 D5
Wesley Gv *BAUK* DL14 .... 27 D2
Wesley Pl *NORTON* TS20 .... 74 C2
Wesley St *DARLE* DL1 .... 132 C2 [16]
West Auckland Rd *BAUK* DL14 .... 34 A2
  DARLW DL3 .... 115 D2
  SHIL DL4 .... 34 C3
West Av *BLGHM* TS23 .... 58 C5
  SALT/BTN/SK TS12 .... 89 D2
Westbank Rd *MTN/NUN* TS7 .... 127 D1
Westbeck Gdns *ACK/BRKF* TS5 .... 98 A4
West Beck Gv *DARLW* DL3 .... 130 B1
West Beck Wy *CNHM/HEM* TS8 .... 125 D5
Westborough Gv *STOCS* TS18 .... 92 C3 [3]
Westbourne Gv *DARLW* DL3 .... 8 B5
  ESTON TS6 .... 81 D5
  NORM/PKE TS3 .... 79 D5 [17]
  REDCAR TS10 .... 51 E4 [6]
Westbourne St *HTLPS* TS25 .... 23 F2
  STOCS TS18 .... 94 B3
Westbrook *DARLW* DL3 .... 9 F1
Westbrooke Av *HTLPS* TS25 .... 23 F3
Westbrooke Gv *HTLPS* TS25 .... 23 F3 [1]
Westbury St *THNBY* TS17 .... 95 E3

Westcliffe Ct *DARLW* DL3 .... 8 D6 [1]
West Cl *SHIL* DL4 .... 35 D3 [3]
West Coatham La *REDCAR* TS10 ... 66 C2
Westcott St *STOCS* TS18 .... 94 C3
West Crs *ACK/BRKF* TS5 .... 97 D3
  DARLW DL3 .... 8 D3
Westcroft Rd *ESTON* TS6 .... 81 F3
Westdale Rd *THNBY* TS17 .... 121 F2 [2]
West Dyke Rd *REDCAR* TS10 ...... 51 E4 [10]
  REDCAR TS10 .... 67 F4
West End *GTAY/STK* TS9 .... 152 A3
  GUIS TS14 .... 128 C3
  SEDG TS21 .... 29 D4
West End Av *GUIS* TS14 .... 128 C3
West End Gdns *EGG/EAG* TS16 .... 137 D3 [5]
Westerby Rd *NORM/PKE* TS3 .... 79 F4
Westerdale *SPEN* DL16 .... 14 C2
Westerdale Av *STOCN* TS19 .... 6 A1
Westerdale Ct *DARLW* DL3 .... 115 D2 [9]
Westerdale Gdns *SHIL* DL4 .... 36 A3 [4]
Westerdale Rd *HTLPS* TS25 .... 32 C1
  NORM/PKE TS3 .... 99 E2
Westerham Gv *MGRV/ESTR* TS4 ... 98 C5
Westerhope Ct *DARLW* DL3 .... 115 D3
Westerleigh Av *STOCN* TS19 .... 93 D1 [7]
Westerton Rd *BLGHM* TS23 .... 42 A3 [14]
Westfield Av *DARLW* DL3 .... 51 E5
Westfield Cl *ESTON* TS6 .... 101 D3 [8]
Westfield Ct *STOCN* TS19 .... 74 A4 [1]
Westfield Crs *STOCN* TS19 .... 74 A3
Westfield Dr *DARLW* DL3 .... 131 D1
Westfield Rd *BAUK* DL14 .... 27 D3
  ESTON TS6 .... 101 E3
  GTAY/STK TS9 .... 152 A2
  MARSKE TS11 .... 69 F5 [8]
West Flds *NACLF* DL5 .... 53 E3
Westfield Ter *LOFT/ST* TS13 .... 113 D3
Westfield Wy *LOFT/ST* TS13 .... 113 D2
  REDCAR TS10 .... 67 D2
Westgarth Cl *MARSKE* TS11 .... 70 A5
Westgarth Ter *DARLE* DL1 .... 117 D5
Westgate *EGG/EAG* TS16 .... 137 D3
  GUIS TS14 .... 129 D2
Westgate Crs *DARLW* DL3 .... 115 D2
Westgate Rd *ACK/BRKF* TS5 .... 97 E4
  DARLW DL3 .... 115 D2
  GUIS TS14 .... 129 D2
West Hartlepool Rd
  BLGHMW/WYN TS22 .... 41 E3
Westholme Ct *BLGHM* TS23 .... 42 B5 [3]
Westkirk Cl *DARLW* DL3 .... 115 D2
Westland Av *HTLPW* TS26 .... 23 E1 [2]
Westlands *YARM* TS15 .... 146 C5
Westlands Av *NORTON* TS20 .... 75 D2 [6]
Westlands Rd *DARLW* DL3 .... 115 E4
  EGG/EAG TS16 .... 137 D2 [9]
Westland Wy *STOCS* TS18 .... 94 B5
  ESTON TS6 .... 81 F3
Westlea Av *BAUK* DL14 .... 27 E3
Westlowthian St *TEESM* TS2 .... 78 B1
Westminster Cl *ESTON* TS6 .... 102 A1
Westminster Rd *ACK/BRKF* TS5 .... 98 A2
  DARLE DL1 .... 133 E4
Westmoor Cl *SPEN* DL16 .... 14 B4
West Moor Cl *YARM* TS15 .... 138 A5
West Moor Rd *DARLE* DL1 .... 133 D5
Westmoreland St *DARLW* DL3 .... 116 A3
Westmorland Cl *SPEN* DL16 .... 15 F1
Westmorland Gv *NORTON* TS20 ... 57 E4 [4]
Westmorland Rd *ACK/BRKF* TS5 ... 97 F2 [6]
  REDCAR TS10 .... 68 B2
Westmorland Wy *NACLF* DL5 .... 58 B5
Weston Crs *NORTON* TS20 .... 75 D3
West Pk *HTLPW* TS26 .... 16 C5
West Park Av *LOFT/ST* TS13 ...... 113 D3
Westpark Dr *DARLW* DL3 .... 115 D2
West Park La *SEDG* TS21 .... 29 D4
Westpoint Rd *THNBY* TS17 .... 7 H6
Westport Cl *STOCS* TS18 .... 75 E5 [7]
West Powlett St *DARLW* DL3 .... 8 D5
Westray *CNHM/HEM* TS8 .... 144 A1
Westray St *LOFT/ST* TS13 .... 112 B1
West Rd *BAUK* DL14 .... 27 D1
  BLGHM TS23 .... 58 C5
  LOFT/ST TS13 .... 113 D3
  SHIL DL4 .... 35 D3
West Rw *ACK/BRKF* TS5 .... 97 D3 [8]
  DARLE DL1 .... 9 F5
  HTLPS TS25 .... 31 D5
  STOCS TS18 .... 75 E4
West Scar *REDCAR* TS10 .... 68 C3
West St *DARLW* DL3 .... 9 E5
  ESTON TS6 .... 101 F3
  ESTON TS6 .... 102 B2 [9]
  TEESM TS2 .... 78 B1 [9]
  YARM TS15 .... 137 D4
West Ter *NORM/PKE* TS3 .... 79 D5
  REDCAR TS10 .... 51 E4
  SPEN DL16 .... 14 B4
West View Rd *HTLP* TS24 .... 12 A4
West View Ter *EGG/EAG* TS16 .... 137 D2
Westwood Av *ACK/BRKF* TS5 .... 98 A4

MTN/NUN TS7 .... 127 D4 [3]
Westwood La *THNBY* TS17 .... 139 E2
Westwood Wy *RHTLP* TS27 .... 11 E4
Westworth St *YARM* TS15 .... 147 D1 [9]
Wetherall Av *YARM* TS15 .... 146 A2
Wetherby Cl *STOCS* TS18 .... 76 A4
Wetherell Cl *MARSKE* TS11 .... 88 A1
Wetherfell Cl *THNBY* TS17 .... 138 C4 [4]
Weymouth Av *CNHM/HEM* TS8 ... 125 D3
Weymouth Dr *HTLP* TS24 .... 11 F3 [4]
Weymouth Rd *STOCS* TS18 .... 93 E2 [9]
Whaddon Cha *GUIS* TS14 .... 129 E4
Wharfdale *SALT/BTN/SK* TS12 ..... 89 E5
Wharfdale Av *BLGHM* TS23 .... 58 C4
Wharfedale Cl *THNBY* TS17 .... 139 D4 [10]
Wharfe Wy *DARLE* DL1 .... 132 B5 [2]
Wharf St *STOCS* TS18 .... 7 G6
Wharton Ct *YARM* TS15 .... 147 D1 [9]
Wharton St *HTLPW* TS26 .... 2 B2
  SALT/BTN/SK TS12 .... 110 B2
Wheatear Dr *REDCAR* TS10 .... 68 C4
Wheatear La *THNBY* TS17 .... 138 C1
Wheatlands *GTAY/STK* TS9 .... 150 C2
Wheatlands Cl *GUIS* TS14 .... 129 E4
Wheatlands Dr *MARSKE* TS11 .... 70 B5
Wheatlands Pk *REDCAR* TS10 .... 68 C4
Wheatley Cl *ACK/BRKF* TS5 .... 123 F5
Wheatley Rd *STOCN* TS19 .... 73 D2
Wheeldale Av *REDCAR* TS10 .... 67 E2 [8]
Wheeldale Cl *DARLE* DL1 .... 117 D5
Wheeldale Crs *THNBY* TS17 .... 121 F2
Whernside *MTN/NUN* TS7 .... 126 B5
Whernside Crs *THNBY* TS17 .... 139 D4
Whessoe Rd *DARLW* DL3 .... 116 A4
  STOCN TS19 .... 73 E2
Whickham Cl *NORM/PKE* TS3 .... 79 D4
Whickham Rd *STOCN* TS19 .... 73 D2
Whinbank Rd *NACLF* DL5 .... 54 B3
Whinbush Wy *DARLE* DL1 .... 117 F1
Whinchat Cl *HTLPW* TS26 .... 17 D1
  THNBY TS17 .... 139 D1 [2]
Whinchat Tail *GUIS* TS14 .... 128 A3
Whinfell Av *EGG/EAG* TS16 .... 119 D5
Whinfell Cl *MTN/NUN* TS7 .... 126 B5
Whinfield Cl *STOCN* TS19 .... 72 C4 [3]
Whinfield Dr *NACLF* DL5 .... 54 C5
Whinfield Rd *DARLE* DL1 .... 117 F1
Whinflower Dr *NORTON* TS20 .... 57 E5 [4]
Whingroves *THNBY* TS17 .... 96 B5 [5]
Whinlatter Cl *STOCN* TS19 .... 6 C3
Whinlatter Pl *NACLF* DL5 .... 53 F1
Whinney Banks Rd *ACK/BRKF* TS5 .. 96 C3
Whinston Cl *HTLPW* TS26 .... 16 B5 [3]
Whinstone Dr *CNHM/HEM* TS8 .. 141 E1 [11]
Whinstone Vw *GTAY/STK* TS9 ..... 150 C2
Whin St *MBORO* TS1 .... 5 F4
Whisperdale Ct *NORM/PKE* TS3 .. 100 A2 [7]
Whitburn Rd *STOCN* TS19 .... 73 D2
Whitburn St *HTLPS* TS25 .... 2 B5
Whitby Av *ESTON* TS6 .... 102 A1
  GUIS TS14 .... 129 E3
Whitby Cl *SALT/BTN/SK* TS12 .... 109 F2
Whitby Crs *REDCAR* TS10 .... 69 E2 [3]
Whitby Rd *GUIS* TS14 .... 129 E3
  LOFT/ST TS13 .... 113 F3
  MTN/NUN TS7 .... 127 D4
  THNBY TS17 .... 95 F5 [4]
Whitby St *HTLP* TS24 .... 2 D2
Whitby Wk *HTLP* TS24 .... 2 D2 [6]
Whitby Wy *DARLW* DL3 .... 114 B3
Whitebeam Ct *MGRV/ESTR* TS4 ... 98 B4 [11]
Whitebridge Dr *DARLE* DL1 .... 117 D1
White Hart Crs *DARLE* DL1 .... 117 F5
White House Dr *SEDG* TS21 .... 29 E4
Whitehouse Dr *STOCN* TS19 .... 73 F5
White House Rd
  BLGHMW/WYN TS22 .... 40 C5
Whitehouse Rd *SPEN* DL16 .... 15 D4
White House Rd *THNBY* TS17 .... 121 D4 [1]
Whitehouse St *ACK/BRKF* TS5 .... 97 D1
Whiteley Gv *NACLF* DL5 .... 38 C4
Whitemeadows *DARLW* DL3 ...... 131 D1 [2]
White Stone Cl *REDCAR* TS10 ...... 69 E3 [3]
White St *NORM/PKE* TS3 .... 99 E1 [8]
Whitfield Cl *EGG/EAG* TS16 .... 137 D1 [1]
Whitfield Dr *HTLPS* TS25 .... 24 A3
Whitfield Rd *NORTON* TS20 .... 57 E5
Whithorn Gv *CNHM/HEM* TS8 .... 124 A4
Whitley Rd *THNBY* TS17 .... 121 F3
Whitrout Rd *HTLP* TS24 .... 12 A4
Whitton Cl *ACK/BRKF* TS5 .... 123 D1 [6]
Whitton Ct *NACLF* DL5 .... 39 D3
Whitton Rd *STOCN* TS19 .... 73 D2
Whitwell Cl *STOCS* TS18 .... 94 C3 [13]
Whitwell Rd *DARLE* DL1 .... 133 E2
Whitwell Ter *GUIS* TS14 .... 129 D2 [8]
Whitworth Av *NACLF* DL5 .... 54 B4
Whitworth Cl *SPEN* DL16 .... 14 B4
Whitworth Dr *NACLF* DL5 .... 54 C4
Whorlton Cl *GUIS* TS14 .... 128 C5 [3]
Whorlton Moor Crs *DARLE* DL1 .. 133 E4
Whorlton Rd *BLGHMW/WYN* TS22 . 58 A1
  STOCN TS19 .... 73 D2

Wibsey Av *NORM/PKE* TS3 .... 99 F5
The Wickets *HTLPS* TS25 .... 33 D1
Wicklow St *MBORO* TS1 .... 97 F1
Widdowfield St *DARLW* DL3 .... 9 E1
Widdrington Ct *STOCN* TS19 ...... 72 C3 [2]
Widecombe Wk *FYHL* DL17 .... 21 F2
Widgeon Rd *DARLE* DL1 .... 133 F2
Wigton Sands *ACK/BRKF* TS5 .... 123 D4 [8]
Wilbore Cft *NACLF* DL5 .... 53 E2 [3]
Wilder Gv *HTLPS* TS25 .... 22 C2 [5]
Wilfred St *STOCS* TS18 .... 6 D6
Wilken Crs *GUIS* TS14 .... 129 D2
Wilkes St *DARLW* DL3 .... 9 F1
Wilkinson Rd *NACLF* DL5 .... 55 D1 [1]
Wilkinson St *NORTON* TS20 .... 75 D4
Willey Flatt La *YARM* TS15 .... 146 A1
William Crossthwaite Av
  THNBY TS17 .... 139 F2
Williamfield Wy *NACLF* DL5 .... 38 A5
Williams Av *ACK/BRKF* TS5 .... 97 D3
Williams St *SALT/BTN/SK* TS12 ... 110 B2
William St *DARLW* DL3 .... 116 A3
  ESTON TS6 .... 102 B2 [3]
  HTLP TS24 .... 2 D3
  REDCAR TS10 .... 51 F5
  SALT/BTN/SK TS12 .... 109 F2
  STOCS TS18 .... 7 F5
  TEESM TS2 .... 5 F1
Willington Rd *STOCN* TS19 .... 73 D2
Willowbank *CNHM/HEM* TS8 ...... 143 D1
Willow Cl *SALT/BTN/SK* TS12 ...... 88 C3
  THNBY TS17 .... 121 E1
Willowdene Av *STOCS* TS18 .... 94 A4 [3]
Willow Dr *ESTON* TS6 .... 101 E4
  SALT/BTN/SK TS12 .... 110 C1
Willow Gv *HTLP* TS24 .... 17 F2
Willow Ms *NORTON* TS20 .... 57 F4 [3]
Willow Rd *DARLW* DL3 .... 115 E4
  FYHL DL17 .... 21 D1
  GUIS TS14 .... 129 D2
  SPEN DL16 .... 14 A5
  STOCN TS19 .... 74 B4
Willow Rd East *DARLW* DL3 .... 115 F4
Willows Av *CNHM/HEM* TS8 .... 140 B2
Willows Rd *ACK/BRKF* TS5 .... 98 A3
The Willows *BAUK* DL14 .... 27 E1
  MTN/NUN TS7 .... 126 A3
  REDCAR TS10 .... 69 D1 [3]
  STOCN TS19 .... 73 F4 [12]
Willow Ter *TEESM* TS2 .... 61 D5 [4]
Wilmire Rd *BLGHMW/WYN* TS22 .. 58 A1
Wilson St *DARLW* DL3 .... 116 A4
  GUIS TS14 .... 128 C3
  HTLPW TS26 .... 17 E4
  MBORO TS1 .... 5 E2
  SALT/BTN/SK TS12 .... 111 D1
  THNBY TS17 .... 95 F3
Wilstrop Gn *NORM/PKE* TS3 .... 99 F5
Wilton Av *HTLPW* TS26 .... 17 E5
  REDCAR TS10 .... 66 C2
Wilton Bank *SALT/BTN/SK* TS12 ... 88 C3
Wilton Cl *DARLW* DL3 .... 130 C1
  Wilton Ct *NACLF* DL5 .... 37 E5
Wilton Dr *DARLW* DL3 .... 130 C1
Wilton Gn *ESTON* TS6 .... 83 D5
Wilton La *ESTON* TS6 .... 84 A4
  GUIS TS14 .... 105 F5
Wilton Rd *HTLPW* TS26 .... 17 F5
Wilton St *MBORO* TS1 .... 58 A1
  REDCAR TS10 .... 51 E4 [10]
Witton Wy *ESTON* TS6 .... 102 B1
Wiltshire Rd *SALT/BTN/SK* TS12 .. 108 C2 [2]
Wiltshire Wy *HTLPW* TS26 .... 17 D2
Wimbledon Cl *DARLE* DL1 .... 117 E5
Wimbledon Rd *ACK/BRKF* TS5 ...... 97 E4 [8]
Wimborne Cl *DARLW* DL3 .... 114 B3
Wimpole Rd *STOCN* TS19 .... 72 B5
Wincanton Rd *REDCAR* TS10 .... 68 C2
Winchester Rd *ACK/BRKF* TS5 ...... 98 B2
  REDCAR TS10 .... 69 E2
  SALT/BTN/SK TS12 .... 91 E5
Winchester Wy *DARLE* DL1 .... 117 F4
Windermere *SPEN* DL16 .... 14 C1 [3]
Windermere Av *BLGHM* TS23 ...... 59 D5
  REDCAR TS10 .... 68 B1
Windermere Ct *DARLE* DL1 .... 132 C3
Windermere Dr
  SALT/BTN/SK TS12 .... 109 D1
Windermere Rd *ACK/BRKF* TS5 ..... 97 E3
  FYHL DL17 .... 20 C2
  HTLPS TS25 .... 24 A3 [3]
  STOCS TS18 .... 6 A3
Windleston Cl *STOCN* TS19 .... 73 D2 [8]
Windleston Dr *NORM/PKE* TS3 ..... 99 F5
Windlestone Rd *BLGHM* TS23 ...... 59 E1
Windmill Ter *NORTON* TS20 .... 75 D3
Windrush Gv *DARLE* DL1 .... 116 C1 [8]
Windsor Av *FYHL* DL17 .... 21 D1
Windsor Cl *FYHL* DL17 .... 39 E2
Windsor Ct *BAUK* DL14 .... 27 D1 [8]
  ESTON TS6 .... 82 A5
  SHIL DL4 .... 35 E4
Windsor Crs *MTN/NUN* TS7 .... 126 C4
Windsor Gdns *SHIL* DL4 .... 35 F3
Windsor Ov *THNBY* TS17 .... 121 E1 [7]

Windsor Rd *ACK/BRKF* TS5 .... 97 F2
   ESTON TS6 .... 101 F3
   REDCAR TS10 .... 69 D1
   SALT/BTN/SK TS12 .... 89 E2
   STOCS TS18 .... 94 A3
   THNBY TS17 .... 121 E1
Windsor St *BLGHM* TS23 .... 60 C4
   DARLE DL1 .... 116 B4 ⬚
   HTLPW TS26 .... 2 B4
   MBORO TS1 .... 5 E5
Windsor Ter *SHIL* DL4 .... 35 F2
Windy Hill La *MARSKE* TS11 .... 70 C5
   MARSKE TS11 .... 88 C1
Wingate Av *BLGHM* TS23 .... 42 B4
Wingate Rd *STOCN* TS19 .... 73 D1
Winlaton Cl *STOCN* TS19 .... 73 D2 ⬚
Winpenny Cl *YARM* TS15 .... 147 D1 ⬚
Winsford Ct *THNBY* TS17 .... 139 D4 ⬚
Winston Av *BLGHM* TS23 .... 42 A4 ⬚
Winston Churchill Cl
   THNBY TS17 .... 121 F3 ⬚
Winston Dr *ESTON* TS6 .... 102 A2
Winston St *DARLW* DL3 .... 9 E4
   STOCS TS18 .... 94 B3 ⬚
Winterbottom Av *HTLP* TS24 .... 12 C5
Winter Cl *HTLPS* TS25 .... 24 A3 ⬚
   YARM TS15 .... 146 A2
Wintersweet Gdns *NORTON* TS20 .... 74 B2
Winthorpe Gv *HTLPS* TS25 .... 30 C2
Wisbech Cl *HTLPS* TS25 .... 30 C3 ⬚
Wiseman Wk *NACLF* DL5 .... 39 D4
Wiske Cl *STOCN* TS19 .... 73 D4 ⬚
Witbank Rd *DARLW* DL3 .... 8 C2
Witham Av *EGG/EAG* TS16 .... 119 E4
Witham Gv *HTLPS* TS25 .... 31 D2
Witton Cl *BLGHM* TS23 .... 59 E1 ⬚⬚
Witton Crs *DARLW* DL3 .... 114 C3
Witton Dr *SPEN* DL16 .... 15 D1
Woburn Av *DARLW* DL3 .... 114 A3 ⬚
Woburn Gv *HTLPS* TS25 .... 31 F1
   NORM/PKE TS3 .... 100 B4 ⬚
Woking Cl *ESTON* TS6 .... 101 F5 ⬚
Wolfe Rd *NORTON* TS20 .... 74 C2 ⬚
Wollaton Rd *BLGHM* TS23 .... 59 E1
Wolseley St *FYHL* DL17 .... 21 F3
Wolsey Cl *NACLF* DL5 .... 39 D4
Wolsey Dr *NORTON* TS20 .... 57 D5
Wolsingham Cl *STOCN* TS19 .... 73 D2 ⬚
Wolsingham Dr *ACK/BRKF* TS5 .... 123 F3
   THNBY TS17 .... 122 A2
Wolsingham Ter *DARLE* DL1 .... 117 D5
Wolviston Back La *BLGHM* TS23 .... 42 A3
Wolviston Cl *NACLF* DL5 .... 38 A4
Wolviston Mill La
   BLGHMW/WYN TS22 .... 40 C5
Wolviston Rd *BLGHM* TS23 .... 58 B3
   BLGHMW/WYN TS22 .... 41 E5
   HTLPS TS25 .... 23 F2
Woodbank Rd *MTN/NUN* TS7 ...... 127 D2
Woodbine Cl *GTAY/STK* TS9 .... 150 C2 ⬚
Woodborough La *STOCN* TS19 .... 73 F4
Woodbrook Cl *MARSKE* TS11 .... 86 B3
Woodburn Cl *CNHM/HEM* TS8 .... 124 A4 ⬚
Woodburn Dr *DARLW* DL3 .... 131 D3
Woodcock Cl *ESTON* TS6 .... 102 A3
Woodcrest Rd *DARLW* DL3 .... 131 E3
Woodford Cl *MARSKE* TS11 .... 70 A5
Woodford Gn *EGG/EAG* TS16 ...... 137 E2
Woodford Wk *THNBY* TS17 .... 121 E4
Woodgate Cl *HTLPS* TS25 .... 31 D4
Woodhall Gv *STOCS* TS18 .... 93 D4 ⬚
Woodham Ga *NACLF* DL5 .... 38 B2
Woodham Rd *BLGHM* TS23 .... 42 A4 ⬚
   NACLF DL5 .... 54 C4
Woodham Wy *FYHL* DL17 .... 38 C2
Woodhay Av *ACK/BRKF* TS5 .... 96 C4 ⬚
Woodhouse La *BAUK* DL14 .... 26 C4
Woodhouse Rd *GUIS* TS14 .... 128 B3
Woodland Ms *SEDG* TS21 .... 29 E2
Woodland Rd *DARLW* DL3 .... 8 A2
Woodlands Dr *ESTON* TS6 .... 102 A5
   YARM TS15 .... 137 F5

Woodlands Gv *HTLPW* TS26 .... 16 C4
Woodlands Rd *BAUK* DL14 .... 27 E2
   ESTON TS6 .... 101 F5
   MBORO TS1 .... 5 G6
The Woodlands *DARLW* DL3 .... 8 B3
   MTN/NUN TS7 .... 145 D1
   THNBY TS17 .... 121 E2
Woodland St *STOCS* TS18 .... 94 B3 ⬚⬚
Woodlands Wk *GTAY/STK* TS9 .... 152 B1
Woodland Ter *DARLW* DL3 .... 8 A3
Wood La *FYHL* DL17 .... 21 D1
Woodlea *CNHM/HEM* TS8 .... 143 D1 ⬚
Woodley Gv *MTN/NUN* TS7 .... 127 D2
Woodmere Rd *STOCN* TS19 .... 73 F5
Woodrow Av *MTN/NUN* TS7 .... 125 F4
   SALT/BTN/SK TS12 .... 89 D2
Woodrush *CNHM/HEM* TS8 .... 143 E3
Woodside *MTN/NUN* TS7 .... 100 B5
   REDCAR TS10 .... 68 B4
   SALT/BTN/SK TS12 .... 90 C5
   THNBY TS17 .... 121 D5 ⬚
Woodside Dr *DARLW* DL3 .... 131 F3
Woodside Gv *STOCS* TS18 .... 93 E4
Wood Sq *BAUK* DL14 .... 26 C4 ⬚
Woodstock Wy *RHTLP* TS27 .... 11 E3
Wood St *ESTON* TS6 .... 82 A3 ⬚
   HTLP TS24 .... 19 F2
   HTLPS TS25 .... 3 F6
   MBORO TS1 .... 5 G2
Woodvale *CNHM/HEM* TS8 .... 125 F5
Woodvale Rd *DARLW* DL3 .... 131 E3
Wood Vw *LOFT/ST* TS13 .... 113 E3
Woodville Av *MGRV/ESTR* TS4 ..... 98 B4
Wood Vue *SPEN* DL16 .... 15 D1
Woolcotts Cl *THNBY* TS17 .... 138 C4 ⬚
Wooler Rd *HTLPW* TS26 .... 17 D4
Wooler St *DARLE* DL1 .... 9 G2
Worcester Gdns *HTLPS* TS25 .... 24 A2 ⬚
Worcester St *MBORO* TS1 .... 97 F1
Wordsworth Av *HTLPS* TS25 .... 23 E2
Wordsworth Cl *BLGHM* TS23 .... 41 F3 ⬚
Wordsworth Rd *DARLE* DL1 .... 132 B4
   ESTON TS6 .... 101 F1 ⬚
Wordsworth V *ACK/BRKF* TS5 .... 123 D1 ⬚
Works Rd *NORM/PKE* TS3 .... 79 F4
   SPEN DL16 .... 15 F2
Worsall Cl *YARM* TS15 .... 137 D4
Worsall Gv *STOCS* TS18 .... 93 E3 ⬚
Worsley Cl *EGG/EAG* TS16 .... 119 F3
Worsley Crs *MTN/NUN* TS7 .... 125 F5
Worthing St *STOCS* TS18 .... 7 E6
Worton Dr *DARLE* DL1 .... 132 C4
Wray St *MGRV/ESTR* TS4 .... 78 C4 ⬚
Wrekenton Cl *STOCN* TS19 .... 73 D2 ⬚
Wren Av *DARLE* DL1 .... 117 E2
Wren Cl *NACLF* DL5 .... 39 E4
   STOCS TS18 .... 6 C5
Wrensfield Rd *STOCN* TS19 .... 6 C2
Wren St *LOFT/ST* TS13 .... 113 F3 ⬚
   STOCS TS18 .... 6 C6
Wrentree Cl *REDCAR* TS10 .... 68 C4
Wright Cl *NACLF* DL5 .... 38 B5
Wrightson St *NORTON* TS20 .... 75 D2 ⬚
Wroxham Cl *STOCN* TS19 .... 73 E4 ⬚
Wroxton Av *ACK/BRKF* TS5 .... 97 E4 ⬚
Wroxton Cl *ACK/BRKF* TS5 .... 97 D4
Wrynose Gdns *STOCN* TS19 .... 6 C3
Wycherley Av *ACK/BRKF* TS5 .... 97 E4
Wycherley Cl *MTN/NUN* TS7 .... 127 D2
Wychgate *ESTON* TS6 .... 102 C2
Wychwood Cl *THNBY* TS17 .... 121 F3 ⬚
Wycliffe Cl *NACLF* DL5 .... 39 E4 ⬚
Wycliffe Wy *DARLW* DL3 .... 130 B2
Wycombe St *DARLW* DL3 .... 8 D4
Wye Cl *STOCN* TS19 .... 73 D4
Wykeham Av *GUIS* TS14 .... 128 C5
Wykeham Cl *BLGHMW/WYN* TS22 .... 57 F1
   REDCAR TS10 .... 68 A4
Wykeham Wy *CNHM/HEM* TS8 .... 125 D4
Wykes Cl *SEDG* TS21 .... 29 E4 ⬚
Wylam Av *DARLE* DL1 .... 117 D2
Wylam Cl *SHIL* DL4 .... 35 F4

Wylam Rd *NORTON* TS20 .... 74 C2
Wylam St *MBORO* TS1 .... 4 D6
The Wynde *STOCN* TS19 .... 72 C4
The Wynd *CNHM/HEM* TS8 .... 141 D1 ⬚
   MARSKE TS11 .... 70 B5
Wynnstay Gdns *HTLP* TS24 .... 17 F2
Wynyard Ct *NACLF* DL5 .... 37 F4
Wynyard Ms *HTLPS* TS25 .... 23 D5 ⬚
Wynyard Rd *BLGHMW/WYN* TS22 .... 41 D4
   HTLPS TS25 .... 22 C5
   SEDG TS21 .... 56 B3
Wynyard St *NORTON* TS20 .... 7 G1 ⬚
Wyverne Ct *HTLPS* TS25 .... 23 F4 ⬚

Y

Yale Crs *THNBY* TS17 .... 95 D3
Yarm Back La *SEDG* TS21 .... 72 B5
Yarm Cl *HTLPS* TS25 .... 23 F3
Yarm La *GTAY/STK* TS9 .... 149 D3
   STOCS TS18 .... 7 F6
Yarmouth Cl *HTLPS* TS25 .... 31 D3 ⬚
Yarm Rd *DARLE* DL1 .... 133 E2
   EGG/EAG TS16 .... 137 E1
   STOCS TS18 .... 94 A5
   YARM TS15 .... 137 D3
Yarm St *STOCS* TS18 .... 7 F6
Yarrow Ct *FYHL* DL17 .... 38 C2
Yeadon Gv *THNBY* TS17 .... 122 A2
Yearby Bank *MARSKE* TS11 .... 85 E3
Yearby Cl *ACK/BRKF* TS5 .... 123 D1
   ESTON TS6 .... 102 A3 ⬚
Yearby Crs *MARSKE* TS11 .... 71 D5
Yearby Rd *REDCAR* TS10 .... 85 D3
Yeoman St *REDCAR* TS10 .... 51 F5
   SALT/BTN/SK TS12 .... 109 E1
Yeoman Ter *MARSKE* TS11 .... 70 B5 ⬚
Yew Cl *SPEN* DL16 .... 14 C4
Yew St *MBORO* TS1 .... 5 E5
Yew Tree Av *REDCAR* TS10 .... 67 F4
Yewtree Av *SHIL* DL4 .... 36 A3
Yew Tree Gv *MTN/NUN* TS7 .... 126 B3
Yiewsley Dr *DARLW* DL3 .... 130 B1
Yoden Ct *NACLF* DL5 .... 37 F4
Yoredale Av *DARLW* DL3 .... 115 D5
Yoredale Cl *THNBY* TS17 .... 139 D3 ⬚
York Crs *BLGHM* TS23 .... 59 D4
York Hill Crs *SPEN* DL16 .... 15 F1
York Hill Rd *SPEN* DL16 .... 15 F1
York Pl *HTLP* TS24 .... 19 E3
York Rd *ACK/BRKF* TS5 .... 98 B3
   HTLPW TS26 .... 2 B3
   MTN/NUN TS7 .... 127 D4
   REDCAR TS10 .... 50 B4
   SALT/BTN/SK TS12 .... 91 E5
York St *DARLE* DL1 .... 116 C4
   STOCS TS18 .... 7 F6
Yorkway *THNBY* TS17 .... 95 E3
Young St *HTLPW* TS26 .... 2 A1
Yukon Gdns *MGRV/ESTR* TS4 ..... 98 C1 ⬚

Z

Zetland Hunt *NACLF* DL5 .... 37 E4
Zetland Pl *MBORO* TS1 .... 5 G2
Zetland Rd *HTLPW* TS26 .... 17 E4
   LOFT/ST TS13 .... 113 D3
   MARSKE TS11 .... 70 C5 ⬚
   MBORO TS1 .... 5 F7
   REDCAR TS10 .... 69 E2
   STOCN TS19 .... 74 B4
Zetland St *DARLW* DL3 .... 116 A3
Zetland Ter *SALT/BTN/SK* TS12 .... 89 E2

Abbey County Infant School
  DARLW DL3 8   A6
Abbey Hill School
  STOCN TS19 73   F3
Abbey Junior School
  DARLW DL3 8   A5
A B C Cinema
  DARLE DL1 9   G2
Abingdon Junior & Infant School
  MBORO TS1 5   H5
Acklam Grange Secondary School
  ACK/BRKF TS5 123   D1
Acklam Whin Primary School
  ACK/BRKF TS5 123   E3
Alderman Leach Junior School
  DARLW DL3 115   D3
Alderman William Jones
  Primary School
  ESTON TS6 81   F4
Alliance Industrial Estate
  DARLE DL1 116   C4
All Saints Industrial Estate
  SHIL DL4 36   A5
Archibald Primary School
  ACK/BRKF TS5 97   E1
Ark Grove Industrial Estate
  STOCS TS18 75   F4
Art Gallery
  STOCS TS18 7   F4
Art Gallery & Library
  DARLE DL1 9   G4
The Art Gallery
  DARLE DL1 9   G5
Ash Trees School
  BLGHM TS23 41   F5
Askham Bryan College
  GUIS TS14 129   E2
Atkinson Industrial Estate
  HTLPS TS25 3   E6
Attlee Road Primary School
  ESTON TS6 82   A5
The Avenue Primary School
  MTN/NUN TS7 126   C4
Aycliffe Industrial Estate
  NACLF DL5 54   B4
Aycliffe School
  NACLF DL5 39   F4
Aycliffe Village Primary School
  NACLF DL5 55   E5
Ayresome School
  MBORO TS1 97   F1
Bader Primary School
  THNBY TS17 121   E3
Badger Hill Primary School
  SALT/BTN/SK TS12 91   E5
Bankfields Infant School
  ESTON TS6 102   A3
Bankfields Primary School
  ESTON TS6 102   A3
Barnard Gallery
  STOCS TS18 7   G4
Barnard Grove Primary School
  HTLP TS24 11   F3
Barnfield Community
  Mental Health Centre
  SPEN DL16 15   E2
The Barwick Medical Centre
  THNBY TS17 139   D1
Bassleton School
  THNBY TS17 121   F2
Bassleton Secondary School
  THNBY TS17 122   A1
Beaumont Hill School
  DARLE DL1 116   C1
Beckfield Medical Centre
  THNBY TS17 139   E2
Bede Sixth Form College
  BLGHM TS23 42   A5
Beech Grove Junior &
  Infant School
  ESTON TS6 81   D5
Beechwood Infant School
  MGRV/ESTR TS4 98   C4
Belasis Business Centre
  BLGHM TS23 59   F3
Belle Vue Sports Centre
  HTLPS TS25 24   B2
Belmont Primary School
  GUIS TS14 129   D4
Berwick Hills Primary School
  NORM/PKE TS3 99   E2
Bessemer Park Infant School
  SPEN DL16 15   E2

Beverley School
  MGRV/ESTR TS4 98   B5
Bewick Crescent Surgery
  NACLF DL5 54   C1
Bewley Infant School
  BLGHM TS23 42   C4
Bewley Junior School
  BLGHM TS23 42   C4
Billingham Art Gallery
  BLGHM TS23 58   C2
Billingham Cricket Club
  BLGHM TS23 59   D5
Billingham Golf Club
  BLGHMW/WYN TS22 57   F2
Billingham Health Centre
  BLGHM TS23 58   C2
Billingham Reach Industrial Estate
  BLGHM TS23 77   D2
Billingham South Junior &
  Infant School
  BLGHM TS23 59   D4
Bishop Auckland College
  NACLF DL5 54   C1
Bishop Auckland Cricket Club
  BAUK DL14 27   E1
Bishop Auckland Football Club
  BAUK DL14 27   E1
Bishop Auckland General Hospital
  BAUK DL14 27   D2
Bishop Auckland Hospitals
  NHS Trust
  BAUK DL14 27   D1
Bishop Auckland R U F C
  BAUK DL14 26   C1
Bishop Barrington
  Comprehensive School
  BAUK DL14 26   B3
Bishopgate Medical Centre
  BAUK DL14 27   D2
Bishopsgarth School
  STOCN TS19 72   B4
Bishopsmill School
  NORTON TS20 58   A5
Blackwell Golf Club
  DARLW DL3 131   E5
Blakeston School
  STOCN TS19 56   B5
Borough Road Industrial Estate
  DARLE DL1 9   H3
Bowesfield Industrial Estate
  STOCS TS18 120   C1
Boys Welfare Rugby Club
  HTLPW TS26 17   E2
Brackenhoe Secondary School
  MGRV/ESTR TS4 99   D5
Brambles Primary School
  NORM/PKE TS3 100   A1
Branch Surgery
  HTLPS TS25 23   E4
Branksome
  Comprehensive School
  DARLW DL3 114   B4
Breckon Hill Primary School
  MGRV/ESTR TS4 79   D5
Brierton Medical Centre
  HTLPS TS25 22   C4
Broom Cottages County
  Primary School
  FYHL DL17 21   D2
Broom Primary School
  FYHL DL17 21   D1
Brougham Junior & Infant School
  HTLP TS24 18   A3
Bus Station
  MBORO TS1 5   E3
Bydales School
  MARSKE TS11 70   B4
Caldicotes Primary School
  NORM/PKE TS3 100   C1
Captain Cook
  Birthplace Museum
  MTN/NUN TS7 125   F2
Captain Cook Primary School
  MTN/NUN TS7 125   F3
Captain Cooks
  Schoolroom Museum
  GTAY/STK TS9 150   C3
Carlow Street Health Clinic
  MBORO TS1 97   E1
Carmel RC Aided
  Comprehensive School
  DARLW DL3 130   C2
Carmel Surgery
  DARLW DL3 131   D1

Carter Bequest Hospital
  ACK/BRKF TS5 97   F4
Catcote School
  HTLPS TS25 23   D1
Central House Durham C C &
  Registry Office
  DARLW DL3 9   F2
Century Business Centre
  STOCS TS18 76   B4
Chandlers Ridge Primary School
  MTN/NUN TS7 126   C5
Chilton industrial Estate
  FYHL DL17 20   B5
Christ the King RC
  Primary School
  THNBY TS17 122   A3
Civic Centre
  MBORO TS1 5   G3
Civic Centre Square
  SHIL DL4 35   E3
Civic Centre Surgery
  SHIL DL4 35   E3
Clairville Stadium
  MGRV/ESTR TS4 98   B1
Clavering Primary School
  RHTLP TS27 11   E4
Cleveland Business Centre
  MBORO TS1 5   H3
Cleveland College of Art & Design
  ACK/BRKF TS5 97   H3
Cleveland County Council
  MBORO TS1 5   H4
Cleveland County Council
  MBORO TS1 5   G2
Cleveland County Council
  NORM/PKE TS3 100   B4
Cleveland Health Centre
  MBORO TS1 5   F3
Cleveland Shopping Centre
  MBORO TS1 5   F3
Club House
  DARLE DL1 117   E1
Club House
  FYHL DL17 38   B1
Club House
  REDCAR TS10 51   D4
Coatham C of E Primary School
  REDCAR TS10 50   C4
Coatham Surgery
  REDCAR TS10 51   D4
Cockerton C of E
  Primary School
  DARLW DL3 114   C4
Cockton Hill Junior &
  Infant School
  BAUK DL14 27   E3
Co Durham Priority
  Services NHSTrust
  BAUK DL14 27   D3
College of Art
  HTLP TS24 2   C3
Combined Courts
  MBORO TS1 5   H3
Community Cen & Library
  ACK/BRKF TS5 97   D3
Community Centre
  MBORO TS1 4   C5
Conyers School
  YARM TS15 146   B2
Cornmill Centre
  DARLE DL1 9   F4
Corporation Road Primary School
  DARLW DL3 9   E1
Corpus Christi RC Junior School
  NORM/PKE TS3 100   A1
Coulby Newham
  Secondary School
  CNHM/HEM TS8 124   C5
Council Offices
  BLGHM TS23 59   E1
Council Offices
  CNHM/HEM TS8 124   A5
Council Offices
  ESTON TS6 81   D4
County Infant School
  MARSKE TS11 86   B3
County Infant School
  NACLF DL5 54   A1
County Junior & Infant School
  SEDG TS21 29   E4
Cromwell Road Primary School
  ESTON TS6 80   C4
Crooksbarn Primary School
  NORTON TS20 57   F4

Index - featured places 187

Crossfell Health Centre
 NORM/PKE TS3 .... 99 F2
Crystal Galleries
 NORM/PKE TS3 .... 79 D5
Dale Road Trading Estate
 SHIL DL4 .... 36 A4
Darlington Borough Council
 DARLE DL1 .... 9 F5
Darlington Borough Council
 DARLE DL1 .... 116 C5
Darlington Borough Council
 DARLE DL1 .... 117 F2
Darlington Borough Council
 DARLE DL1 .... 133 D2
Darlington Civic Theatre
 DARLE DL1 .... 9 H4
Darlington College of Technology
 DARLW DL3 .... 8 B4
Darlington F C
 DARLE DL1 .... 132 A3
Darlington Memorial Hospital
 NHS Trust
 DARLW DL3 .... 8 C2
Darlington Railway
 Centre & Museum
 DARLW DL3 .... 116 A4
Darlington Retail Park
 DARLE DL1 .... 133 F2
Darlington Rugby Football Club
 DARLE DL1 .... 131 F5
Darlington Technical College
 DARLW DL3 .... 8 D5
Dean Bank Primary School
 FYHL DL17 .... 20 B1
De Brus School
 SALT/BTN/SK TS12 .... 109 D1
The Dene Secondary School
 THNBY TS17 .... 122 A1
Dockside Road Industrial Estate
 NORM/PKE TS3 .... 79 E3
Dodmire Junior & Infant School
 DARLE DL1 .... 132 C3
Dolphin Centre
 DARLE DL1 .... 9 F5
Dorman Museum
 ACK/BRKF TS5 .... 98 A1
Dormanstown Clinic
 REDCAR TS10 .... 67 D2
Dormanstown Primary School
 REDCAR TS10 .... 67 D2
Dr Ramaswamy Surgery
 STOCS TS18 .... 7 F6
Dr Stephen & Partners
 THNBY TS17 .... 121 F2
Drug & Alcohol Abuse Clinic
 NORM/PKE TS3 .... 79 D5
Durham County Council
 BAUK DL14 .... 27 E1
Durham County Council
 BAUK DL14 .... 27 D3
Durham County Council
 NACLF DL5 .... 54 B4
Durham Lane Primary School
 EGG/EAG TS16 .... 136 C1
Dyke House Learner
 Swimming Pool
 HTLP TS24 .... 17 F2
Dyke House Secondary School
 HTLP TS24 .... 17 F2
Eaglescliff Health Centre
 EGG/EAG TS16 .... 137 E1
Eastbourne
 Comprehensive School
 DARLE DL1 .... 133 D1
Easterside Day Centre & Clinic
 MGRV/ESTR TS4 .... 125 D1
Easterside Primary School
 MGRV/ESTR TS4 .... 125 D2
Egglescliffe C of E School
 EGG/EAG TS16 .... 137 D3
Egglescliffe School
 EGG/EAG TS16 .... 136 C2
Eldon Grove Sports Centre
 HTLPW TS26 .... 17 E5
Elmfield Primary School
 NACLF DL5 .... 54 A1
The Empire Theatre
 MBORO TS1 .... 5 G3
Enfield Shopping Centre
 GUIS TS14 .... 129 D4
English Martyrs R C Voluntary
 (Aided) Comprehensive School
 HTLPS TS25 .... 23 D1

Errington County Primary School
 MARSKE TS11 .... 70 C5
Eston Baths
 ESTON TS6 .... 81 E5
Eston Park School
 ESTON TS6 .... 101 F1
Eston Sports Centre
 ESTON TS6 .... 81 E5
Etherley Lane County School
 BAUK DL14 .... 27 D2
Fairfield County Junior School
 STOCN TS19 .... 92 C1
Fairfield Infant School
 STOCN TS19 .... 92 C1
Fairfield Medical Health Centre
 STOCN TS19 .... 92 C1
Ferryhill & Cleves Cross
 Junior & Infant School
 FYHL DL17 .... 21 E1
Ferryhill & District
 Maternity Clinic
 FYHL DL17 .... 20 C1
Ferryhill Leisure Centre
 FYHL DL17 .... 21 E2
Ferryhill Medical Practice
 FYHL DL17 .... 20 C1
Ferryhill Station Primary School
 FYHL DL17 .... 21 F4
Fifield Industrial Estate
 HTLPS TS25 .... 24 A4
Fire Station
 ACK/BRKF TS5 .... 98 B2
Fire Station
 DARLE DL1 .... 9 C5
Firth Moor Junior School
 DARLE DL1 .... 133 F4
Fleetham College of Art
 MBORO TS1 .... 4 D5
The Forum Theatre
 BLGHM TS23 .... 59 D2
Frederick Nattrass
 Primary School
 NORTON TS20 .... 74 C1
Freemasons Hall
 DARLW DL3 .... 9 E3
Gables Clinic
 MGRV/ESTR TS4 .... 98 C2
Galley Hill Primary School
 GUIS TS14 .... 128 A4
Gas Holders
 MBORO TS1 .... 4 B4
Gillbrook Technology College
 ESTON TS6 .... 101 E1
Gladstone Industrial Estate
 THNBY TS17 .... 95 E3
Godstone House Surgery
 HTLPW TS26 .... 2 A2
Golden Flatts Primary School
 HTLPS TS25 .... 32 A1
The Grange Business Centre
 BLGHM TS23 .... 59 E4
Grangefield County
 Secondary School
 STOCS TS18 .... 93 F1
Grange Primary School
 HTLPS TS25 .... 30 C1
Grangetown Primary School
 ESTON TS6 .... 82 A4
Greatham C of E Primary School
 HTLPS TS25 .... 31 D5
Greenfield
 Comprehensive School
 NACLF DL5 .... 37 E5
Green Gates Primary School
 REDCAR TS10 .... 68 A4
Green Lane Primary School
 ACK/BRKF TS5 .... 97 F4
Greythorpe Industrial Estate
 HTLPS TS25 .... 32 C5
Guisborough Cricket Club
 GUIS TS14 .... 129 E3
Guisborough General Hospital
 GUIS TS14 .... 129 D2
Guisborough Health Centre
 GUIS TS14 .... 129 E3
Guisborough Rugby Union
 Football Club
 GUIS TS14 .... 129 E4
Gurney Pease Primary School
 DARLE DL1 .... 116 C4
Hackworth Girls School
 SHIL DL4 .... 35 E4
Hackworth Junior & Infant School
 SHIL DL4 .... 35 E4

Hallgarth Comprehensive School
 ACK/BRKF TS5 .... 123 F1
Hall Garth Surgery
 SHIL DL4 .... 35 E2
Halls of Residence
 MBORO TS1 .... 98 B1
Hambleton District Council
 CTAY/STK TS9 .... 152 A2
Hardwick Health Centre
 STOCN TS19 .... 73 E2
Hardwick Primary School
 SEDG TS21 .... 29 E3
Hardwick Primary School
 STOCN TS19 .... 73 D1
Harewood Infant School
 THNBY TS17 .... 95 F5
Harrogate Hill Junior School
 DARLW DL3 .... 116 B2
Harrowgate Hill County
 Infant School
 DARLW DL3 .... 116 B2
Harrow Gate Primary
 Infant School
 STOCN TS19 .... 73 F2
Harry Dack Infant School
 LOFT/ST TS13 .... 113 D3
Hartburn Primary School
 STOCS TS18 .... 93 F3
Hartlepool Art Gallery
 HTLP TS24 .... 2 D2
Hartlepool Borough Council
 HTLP TS24 .... 2 C2
Hartlepool Borough Council
 HTLP TS24 .... 12 C5
Hartlepool Borough Council
 HTLP TS24 .... 19 E2
Hartlepool Borough Council
 HTLPS TS25 .... 3 E5
Hartlepool Borough Council
 HTLPS TS25 .... 23 D5
Hartlepool Borough Council
 HTLPS TS25 .... 24 A5
Hartlepool Borough Council
 HTLPS TS25 .... 24 A4
Hartlepool Borough Council
 HTLPS TS25 .... 25 E5
Hartlepool College of
 Further Education
 HTLP TS24 .... 2 D3
Hartlepool County Court
 HTLPW TS26 .... 2 B2
Hartlepool Hospital Management
 Committee
 HTLP TS24 .... 17 E1
Hartlepool Magistrates Court
 HTLPW TS26 .... 2 C2
Hartlepool Museum Service
 HTLP TS24 .... 2 C2
Hartlepool Old Boys R F C
 Mayfield Park
 HTLP TS24 .... 12 B5
Hartlepool & Peterlee
 Hospitals NHS Trust
 HTLP TS24 .... 17 E1
Hartlepool Power Station
 Visitor Centre
 HTLPS TS25 .... 33 F5
Hartlepool Rovers Rugby
 Football Club
 HTLP TS24 .... 13 E5
Hartlepool Sixth Form College
 HTLPS TS25 .... 23 E1
Hartlepool Yacht Club
 HTLP TS24 .... 3 G1
Hart Primary School
 RHTLP TS27 .... 10 B4
Haughton
 Comprehensive School
 DARLE DL1 .... 117 E3
Healthfield Primary School
 DARLE DL1 .... 133 E1
Heighington C of E
 Primary School
 NACLF DL5 .... 52 C5
Hemlington Hall School
 CNHM/HEM TS8 .... 141 E1
Hemlington Health Centre
 CNHM/HEM TS8 .... 124 A5
Hemlington Lake &
 Recreation Centre
 CNHM/HEM TS8 .... 141 F1
Henknowle County
 Primary School
 BAUK DL14 .... 27 E4

Henry Smith Secondary School
HTLP TS24 .... 12 B3
High Clarence Primary School
TEESM TS2 .... 78 A1
High Tunstall
Comprehensive School
HTLPW TS26 .... 16 B4
Hill St Shopping Centre & Market
MBORO TS1 .... 5 E2
Hollywood Bowl
THNBY TS17 .... 96 C2
Holmwood E S N School
MGRV/ESTR TS4 .... 98 B5
Holy Family RC Primary School
DARLW DL3 .... 115 D4
Holy Trinity Church of England
(Aided) Primary School
HTLPS TS25 .... 25 D5
Holy Trinity C of E Junior School
STOCN TS19 .... 92 C2
Horndale Infant School
NACLF DL5 .... 37 F5
Hospital
NACLF DL5 .... 53 F4
Hospital of God
HTLPS TS25 .... 31 D4
Hummersea Primary School
LOFT/ST TS13 .... 113 D2
Hummersknott
Comprehensive School
DARLW DL3 .... 130 B2
Hundens Day Hospital
DARLE DL1 .... 133 D2
Huntcliff School
SALT/BTN/SK TS12 .... 89 D3
Ian Ramsey C of E School
STOCN TS19 .... 93 D2
Industrial Estate
TEESM TS2 .... 78 B2
Ingleby Mill Primary School
THNBY TS17 .... 138 C2
Jamiah Al Bilal Mosque
STOCS TS18 .... 94 C3
Jesmond Road School
HTLPW TS26 .... 17 E3
John Emmerson Batty
Primary School
REDCAR TS10 .... 69 D1
Junction Farm Primary School
EGG/EAG TS16 .... 137 D1
Kader Primary School
ACK/BRKF TS5 .... 123 E2
Keldholme
Comprehensive School
NORM/PKE TS3 .... 100 A3
Kemplah Primary School
GUIS TS14 .... 128 C5
Kiltonthorpe School
SALT/BTN/SK TS12 .... 90 C5
King James I
Comprehensive School
BAUK DL14 .... 27 E2
King Oswy Learner
Swimming Pool
HTLP TS24 .... 11 F3
Kingsley Primary School
HTLPS TS25 .... 23 E3
Kings Manor
Comprehensive School
ACK/BRKF TS5 .... 97 F5
King Street Junior & Infant School
SPEN DL16 .... 15 D2
Kingsway Medical Centre
BLGHM TS23 .... 59 D2
Kirkleatham Hall School
REDCAR TS10 .... 85 D1
Kirkleatham Old Hall Museum
REDCAR TS10 .... 84 C1
Kirklevington County
Primary School
YARM TS15 .... 147 D5
Lady Eden Hospital
BAUK DL14 .... 27 D2
Lakes Primary School
REDCAR TS10 .... 68 B2
Langbaurgh School
NORM/PKE TS3 .... 100 A3
Larchfield Sports Centre
DARLW DL3 .... 8 D5
Laurence Jackson School
GUIS TS14 .... 129 E1
Layfield Primary School
YARM TS15 .... 146 A2

Letitia Industrial Estate
ACK/BRKF TS5 .... 77 D5
Levendale Primary School
YARM TS15 .... 138 A5
Lingfield Primary School
MTN/NUN TS7 .... 125 F5
The Links Primary School
EGG/EAG TS16 .... 137 E1
Linthorpe Infant School
ACK/BRKF TS5 .... 97 F3
Linthorpe Junior School
ACK/BRKF TS5 .... 97 F2
Little Theatre
ACK/BRKF TS5 .... 98 A4
Loftus Clinic
LOFT/ST TS13 .... 113 E3
Loftus Cricket Club
LOFT/ST TS13 .... 113 F3
Loftus Junior School
LOFT/ST TS13 .... 113 D3
Loftus Leisure Centre
LOFT/ST TS13 .... 112 C2
Loftus Town Hall
LOFT/ST TS13 .... 113 E3
Longfield Comprehensive School
DARLW DL3 .... 116 A1
Low Grange Infant School
BLGHM TS23 .... 42 B5
Lynnfield Primary School
HTLPW TS26 .... 17 F4
Macmillan College
ACK/BRKF TS5 .... 97 D1
Mandale Mill Primary School
THNBY TS17 .... 95 E5
Manor Park Clinic
HTLPS TS25 .... 23 D5
Manor School
HTLPS TS25 .... 31 D1
Market Hall
DARLE DL1 .... 9 F5
Marsh House Medical Centre
BLGHM TS23 .... 42 A5
Marske Clinic
MARSKE TS11 .... 70 B5
Marske Cricket Club
MARSKE TS11 .... 70 C5
Marton Cricket Club
MTN/NUN TS7 .... 125 E3
Marton Grove Primary School
MGRV/ESTR TS4 .... 98 B2
Marton Manor Primary School
MTN/NUN TS7 .... 125 E3
Marwoods C of E Infant School
GTAY/STK TS9 .... 150 B3
Merrington Industrial Estate
SPEN DL16 .... 15 F4
Middlesbrough Art Gallery
MBORO TS1 .... 98 A1
Middlesbrough Borough Council
ACK/BRKF TS5 .... 97 D4
Middlesbrough Borough Council
CNHM/HEM TS8 .... 125 E5
Middlesbrough Borough Council
MBORO TS1 .... 5 F3
Middlesbrough Borough Council
NORM/PKE TS3 .... 79 F5
Middlesbrough Borough Council
NORM/PKE TS3 .... 99 F2
Middlesbrough College
ACK/BRKF TS5 .... 97 F3
Middlesbrough College
ACK/BRKF TS5 .... 123 F1
Middlesbrough Football Club
NORM/PKE TS3 .... 79 D3
Middlesbrough Football Club
TEESM TS2 .... 77 F1
Middlesbrough General Hospital
ACK/BRKF TS5 .... 97 E1
Middlesbrough Municipal
Golf Club
ACK/BRKF TS5 .... 124 C3
Middlesbrough Rugby &
Cricket Clubs
ACK/BRKF TS5 .... 97 E4
Midwife Clinic
CNHM/HEM TS8 .... 125 D4
Mill House Swimming Baths
HTLP TS24 .... 2 B1
Moorlands Surgery
DARLW DL3 .... 115 D4
Mosque
STOCS TS18 .... 7 E5
Mosque
THNBY TS17 .... 95 E4

Most Holy Rosary RC
Primary School
BLGHMW/WYN TS22 .... 58 B1
Mount Pleasant Primary School
DARLW DL3 .... 114 B3
Mowden Infant School
DARLW DL3 .... 130 C1
Mowden Junior School
DARLW DL3 .... 114 C5
Museum
GTAY/STK TS9 .... 150 C3
Museum of Hartlepool
HTLP TS24 .... 18 B3
National Gallery
MBORO TS1 .... 5 E6
Newburn Bridge Industrial Estate
HTLPS TS25 .... 3 F5
Newcomen Primary School
REDCAR TS10 .... 67 F2
Newham Bridge Primary School
ACK/BRKF TS5 .... 98 A5
Newland Community
Mental Health Centre
REDCAR TS10 .... 50 C5
New Marske Primary School
MARSKE TS11 .... 86 B3
Newport Bridge
TEESM TS2 .... 77 D5
Newport Primary School
MBORO TS1 .... 4 D5
Newstead Primary School
GUIS TS14 .... 128 B5
Newton Aycliffe Leisure Centre
NACLF DL5 .... 38 C5
Newton Aycliffe Sports Club
NACLF DL5 .... 55 E1
Newtown Junior & Infant School
STOCN TS19 .... 6 B1
Normanby Primary School
ESTON TS6 .... 101 F4
Northfield School
BLGHMW/WYN TS22 .... 41 D5
Northgate Junior School
GUIS TS14 .... 129 D1
North Ormesby Health Centre
NORM/PKE TS3 .... 79 D5
North Ormesby Primary School
NORM/PKE TS3 .... 79 E5
North Riding Infirmary
MBORO TS1 .... 4 D4
North Road (Darlington)
Primary School
DARLE DL1 .... 116 B3
North Road Industrial Estate
DARLW DL3 .... 116 A4
North Road Junior School
SPEN DL16 .... 15 F2
North Tees General Hospital
STOCN TS19 .... 73 E3
Norton Primary School
NORTON TS20 .... 75 E3
Nuffield Hospital
NORTON TS20 .... 57 D5
Nunthorpe
Comprehensive School
MTN/NUN TS7 .... 127 E4
Nunthorpe Primary School
MTN/NUN TS7 .... 127 E4
Oakland Comprehensive School
ACK/BRKF TS5 .... 97 D4
Odeon Theatre
MBORO TS1 .... 5 H3
Old Billingham Business Centre
BLGHM TS23 .... 58 C5
The Open University
ACK/BRKF TS5 .... 97 F4
Ormesby Primary School
MTN/NUN TS7 .... 100 C5
Our Lady & St Bede
Comprehensive School
STOCN TS19 .... 73 E5
Owton Manor Primary School
HTLPS TS25 .... 22 C5
Oxbridge Lane Primary School
STOCS TS18 .... 6 B6
Oxclose Primary School
SPEN DL16 .... 14 C2
Pallister Park Primary School
NORM/PKE TS3 .... 99 F2
Park End Clinic
NORM/PKE TS3 .... 99 F4
Park End Primary School
NORM/PKE TS3 .... 100 A4

Parkgate Health Centre
DARLE DL1....................................... **9** H5
Park Lane Infant School
GUIS TS14 .... **128** C2
Parkview East Industrial Estate
HTLPS TS25 .... **24** A5
Park View Medical Centre
MGRV/ESTR TS4 .... **98** C1
The Pease Way Medical Centre
NACLF DL5 .... **54** B1
Pennyman Primary School
NORM/PKE TS3 .... **100** C4
The Picture Gallery
HTLPW TS26 .... **2** A4
Polam Hall School
DARLE DL1.................................... **132** A3
Police HQ
CNHM/HEM TS8 .... **124** C3
Police Station & Law Courts
MBORO TS1 .... **5** C4
Poole Hospital
MTN/NUN TS7 .... **145** D3
PO Sorting Office
DARLE DL1....................................... **9** G6
PO Sorting Office
MBORO TS1 .... **4** D3
Preston Farm Industrial Estate
STOCS TS18 .... **120** B1
Preston Hall Museum
STOCS TS18 .... **119** F3
Preston Primary School
EGG/EAG TS16............................ **119** E3
Primary School
MGRV/ESTR TS4 .... **78** C5
Prior Pursglove College
GUIS TS14 .... **129** E2
Priors Mill C of E Primary School
BLGHMW/WYN TS22 .... **41** D5
Priory Wood School
NORM/PKE TS3 .... **101** D3
Prissick Sports Centre
MGRV/ESTR TS4 .... **99** D5
Queen Elizabeth Sixth
Form College
DARLW DL3 .... **8** C4
Queens Court Surgery
MBORO TS1 .... **5** E3
Queens Park Medical Centre
STOCS TS18 .... **7** F2
Queen Street Shopping Centre
DARLW DL3 .... **9** F4
Ravensthorpe
Preparatory School
DARLW DL3 .... **131** D2
Ravensworth Junior School
ESTON TS6 .... **101** E2
Redcar Borough Council
REDCAR TS10 .... **51** E4
Redcar & Cleveland
Borough Council
ESTON TS6 .... **80** C4
Redcar & Cleveland
Borough Council
ESTON TS6 .... **82** B4
Redcar & Cleveland
Borough Council
REDCAR TS10 .... **51** D5
Redcar & Cleveland
Borough Council
REDCAR TS10 .... **67** D1
Redcar & Cleveland
Borough Council
SALT/BTN/SK TS12 .... **109** D2
Redcar & Cleveland College
REDCAR TS10 .... **51** D5
Redcar & Cleveland College
REDCAR TS10 .... **68** C3
Redcar Cricket Club
REDCAR TS10 .... **51** D5
Redcar Leisure Centre
REDCAR TS10 .... **51** D4
Redcar Station Business Centre
REDCAR TS10 .... **51** E4
Red Hall Primary School
DARLE DL1.................................... **117** F4
Red House School
NORTON TS20 .... **57** F5
Reid Street Primary School
DARLW DL3 .... **8** D1
Rift House Primary School
HTLPS TS25 .... **23** D2
Rise Carr Primary School
DARLW DL3 .... **116** A2

Riverbank Trading Estate
DARLE DL1.................................... **116** B4
River Tees Port Health Authority
MBORO TS1 .... **5** F5
River View Industrial Estate
DARLE DL1.................................... **117** D4
Rosa Street Primary School
SPEN DL16...................................... **14** C3
Roseberry Clinic
REDCAR TS10 .... **68** A3
Roseberry CP School
GTAY/STK TS9 .... **151** D2
Rosecroft School
LOFT/ST TS13 .... **113** D4
Rosehill Infant School
STOCN TS19 .... **93** D3
Rose Wood Primary School
CNHM/HEM TS8 .... **143** D2
Roseworth Primary School
STOCN TS19 .... **73** F1
Rossmere County Primary &
Infant School
HTLPS TS25 .... **23** E5
Rossmere Learner
Swimming Pool
HTLPS TS25 .... **23** D5
Rye Hills School
REDCAR TS10 .... **69** D2
Sacred Heart RC
Primary School
ACK/BRKF TS5 .... **97** F1
Sacred Heart RC School
HTLPW TS26 .... **17** E3
Sacred Heart RC School
REDCAR TS10 .... **51** D5
St Aidans Church of England
(Aided) Memorial
Primary School
HTLPS TS25 .... **23** F3
St Albans RC Primary School
REDCAR TS10 .... **68** A4
St Alphonsus RC Primary School
NORM/PKE TS3 .... **79** E5
St Andrews RC Primary School
ESTON TS6 .... **81** D5
St Annes C of E School
BAUK DL14...................................... **26** C3
St Anns Industrial Estate
STOCS TS18 .... **75** E5
St Anthonys RC
Secondary School
NORM/PKE TS3 .... **100** A2
St Augustines RC Junior &
Infants School
DARLW DL3 .... **8** D6
St Augustines RC Primary School
CNHM/HEM TS8 .... **125** E5
St Bedes RC Primary School
DARLE DL1.................................... **117** D2
St Bedes RC Primary School
MARSKE TS11 .... **70** B5
St Bedes RC Primary School
STOCN TS19 .... **6** C1
St Begas RC Primary School
HTLP TS24 .... **13** F5
St Bernadettes RC
Primary School
MTN/NUN TS7 .... **126** B4
St Clare's Abbey
DARLW DL3 .... **131** D2
St Clares RC Primary School
ACK/BRKF TS5 .... **123** D3
St Cuthberts RC Primary School
HTLPS TS25 .... **24** A2
St Cuthberts RC Primary School
STOCS TS18 .... **94** C3
St Davids Secondary School
ACK/BRKF TS5 .... **123** F2
St Dominics RC Primary School
REDCAR TS10 .... **68** A1
St Edwards RC Primary School
ACK/BRKF TS5 .... **98** A3
St Francis C of E Junior School
NACLF DL5 .... **37** F5
St Francis Primary School
ACK/BRKF TS5 .... **97** D4
St Gabriels RC Primary School
MTN/NUN TS7 .... **100** C4
St Gerards RC Primary School
CNHM/HEM TS8 .... **124** B5
St Helens Primary School
HTLP TS24 .... **19** D1
St Johns C of E Primary School
DARLE DL1.................................... **133** D3

St Johns C of E School
SHIL DL4... **35** F3
St Johns RC Comprehensive School
BAUK DL14...................................... **26** C4
St John the Baptist Primary School
STOCN TS19 .... **74** B3
St John the Evangelist RC
Primary School
BLGHM TS23 .... **59** D4
St John Vianny RC
Primary School
HTLP TS24 .... **12** A4
St Josephs RC Junior &
Infant School
NACLF DL5 .... **38** A5
St Josephs RC Primary School
BLGHM TS23 .... **42** B5
St Josephs RC Primary School
HTLP TS24 .... **2** D3
St Josephs RC Primary School
LOFT/ST TS13 .... **113** D4
St Josephs RC Primary School
MGRV/ESTR TS4 .... **98** C1
St Josephs RC Primary School
NORTON TS20 .... **74** C1
St Lukes Hospital
MGRV/ESTR TS4 .... **99** D3
St Marks C of E (Aided)
Junior School
STOCN TS19 .... **73** D5
St Marys Cathedral
CNHM/HEM TS8 .... **143** D1
St Marys Gate Business Park
NORTON TS20 .... **7** G1
St Marys RC Junior School
ESTON TS6 .... **81** F4
St Marys RC Primary School
NACLF DL5 .... **39** D5
St Marys Sixth Form College
MGRV/ESTR TS4 .... **124** B1
St Michaels RC
Comprehensive School
BLGHM TS23 .... **42** C5
St Patricks Junior School
STOCN TS19 .... **93** D1
St Patricks RC
Comprehensive School
THNBY TS17 .... **121** F1
St Patricks RC Primary School
STOCN TS19 .... **93** D1
St Patricks RC Primary School
THNBY TS17 .... **95** E4
St Paulinas RC Primary School
GUIS TS14 .... **128** A4
St Pauls RC Primary School
BLGHMW/WYN TS22 .... **40** C5
St Peters C of E Primary School
SALT/BTN/SK TS12 .... **90** B5
St Peters RC Primary School
ESTON TS6 .... **81** D5
St Peters RC School
ESTON TS6 .... **81** D4
St Pius X RC Primary School
NORM/PKE TS3 .... **99** F3
St Teresas RC Primary School
DARLE DL1.................................... **133** E3
St Teresas RC Primary School
HTLPS TS25 .... **23** E5
St Therese of Lisieux
Primary School
THNBY TS17 .... **138** C2
St Thomas Mores RC
Primary School
MGRV/ESTR TS4 .... **124** C2
St Wilfreds RC School
BAUK DL14...................................... **26** C4
Saltburn Primary School
SALT/BTN/SK TS12 .... **89** E2
Saltburn Sports Centre
SALT/BTN/SK TS12 .... **89** D3
Seaton Carew Cricket Club
HTLPS TS25 .... **33** D1
Sedgefield Borough Council
NACLF DL5 .... **55** D3
Sedgefield Community College
SEDC TS21 .... **29** E3
Sedgefield Magistrates Court
NACLF DL5 .... **38** C5
Sedgefield Racecourse
SEDC TS21 .... **28** B5
Shildon Primary School
SHIL DL4... **35** D2
Showcase Cinemas
THNBY TS17 .... **96** C2

Sikh Temple
MBORO TS1 .... **4** C5
Sikh Temple
THNBY TS17 .... **122** A2
Skelton Castle
SALT/BTN/SK TS12 .... **108** C1
Skelton Health Centre
SALT/BTN/SK TS12 .... **109** F2
Skelton Infant School
SALT/BTN/SK TS12 .... **109** F1
Skelton Junior School
SALT/BTN/SK TS12 .... **109** F1
Skerne Park County
Infant School
DARLE DL1 .... **132** A4
Skerne Park County
Junior School
DARLE DL1 .... **132** A4
South Bank Business Centre
ESTON TS6 .... **80** C2
South Cleveland Hospital
MGRV/ESTR TS4 .... **99** D4
South Durham Health Care
BAUK DL14 .... **26** C2
South Durham Health Care
DARLW DL1 .... **9** E3
South Durham NHS Trust
SPEN DL16 .... **15** D3
South Grange Medical Centre
ESTON TS6 .... **81** D5
South Park Sixth Form College
ESTON TS6 .... **101** F4
Spennymoor
Comprehensive Lower School
SPEN DL16 .... **14** C5
Spennymoor
Comprehensive School
SPEN DL16 .... **14** B4
Spennymoor United
Football Club
SPEN DL16 .... **15** D1
Springfield County
Primary School
DARLE DL1 .... **117** D3
Springwell School
HTLPW TS26 .... **17** D2
Stead Memorial Hospital
REDCAR TS10 .... **51** D5
Stephenson Way Primary School
NACLF DL5 .... **38** A5
Stockton & Billingham College of
Further Education
BLGHM TS23 .... **58** C1
Stockton & Billingham College of
Further Education
STOCS TS18 .... **93** F1
Stockton Borough Council
BLGHM TS23 .... **58** C2
Stockton Borough Council
STOCS TS18 .... **7** G3
Stockton Borough Council
THNBY TS17 .... **95** E5
Stockton Borough Council
THNBY TS17 .... **121** F3
Stockton Business Centre
STOCS TS18 .... **7** E5
Stockton Council
THNBY TS17 .... **121** F2
Stockton on Tees
Borough Council
STOCN TS19 .... **73** F1
Stockton on Tees
Borough Council
STOCS TS18 .... **7** E5
Stockton on Tees
Borough Council
THNBY TS17 .... **121** F2
Stockton on Tees
Borough Council
THNBY TS17 .... **122** A4
Stockton Sixth Form College
STOCN TS19 .... **73** F5
Stockton Sports Centre
NORTON TS20 .... **75** D4
Stokesley CP School
GTAY/STK TS9 .... **152** B2
Stokesley Health Centre
GTAY/STK TS9 .... **152** A2
Stokesley Leisure Centre
GTAY/STK TS9 .... **152** C3
Stokesley School
GTAY/STK TS9 .... **152** C3
Stranton Primary School
HTLPS TS25 .... **2** C6

Sugar Hill County Junior &
Infant School
NACLF DL5 .... **54** C1
Sunningdale School
MGRV/ESTR TS4 .... **125** D2
Sunnydale
Comprehensive School
SHIL DL4 .... **36** A2
Sunnyside Primary School
CNHM/HEM TS8 .... **124** C5
Tedder Primary School
THNBY TS17 .... **122** A3
Tees Bay Business Park
HTLPS TS25 .... **32** C4
Tees Bay Retail Park
HTLPS TS25 .... **24** B4
Tees Health Authority
MTN/NUN TS7 .... **145** D2
Teeside Tertiary College
MGRV/ESTR TS4 .... **99** E5
Teesside High School
EGG/EAG TS16 .... **119** F5
Teesside Tertiary College
(Longlands Campus)
MGRV/ESTR TS4 .... **98** C1
Teesville Infant School
ESTON TS6 .... **101** D1
The Temple
MBORO TS1 .... **5** D1
Terry Dicken Industrial Estate
GTAY/STK TS9 .... **152** C4
The Theatre Club
ACK/BRKF TS5 .... **98** A3
The Theatre
STOCS TS18 .... **7** F6
Thornaby C of E Primary School
THNBY TS17 .... **121** F1
Thornaby Cricket Club
THNBY TS17 .... **96** A4
Thornaby Swimming Baths
THNBY TS17 .... **95** D5
Thornaby Village Primary School
THNBY TS17 .... **121** E1
Thornby Health Centre
THNBY TS17 .... **121** F2
Thornhill School
HTLPW TS26 .... **16** B4
Thorntree Primary School
NORM/PKE TS3 .... **100** C2
Throston Medical Centre
HTLPW TS26 .... **16** C2
Throston Primary School
HTLPW TS26 .... **17** D2
Tofts Farm Industrial Estate West
HTLPS TS25 .... **32** C2
Tollesby E S N School
MGRV/ESTR TS4 .... **98** B5
Tom Leonards Museum
LOFT/ST TS13 .... **112** C1
Trident Business Centre
TEESM TS2 .... **77** C2
Tudhoe RC Junior & Infant School
SPEN DL16 .... **15** E1
University
ESTON TS6 .... **102** A5
University College Stockton
STOCS TS18 .... **95** F1
University College Stockton
THNBY TS17 .... **7** H6
University of Teesside
MBORO TS1 .... **5** G5
Vane Road County
Junior & Infant School
NACLF DL5 .... **39** D5
Veterinary Hospital
MBORO TS1 .... **4** B5
Viewley Hill School
CNHM/HEM TS8 .... **142** A1
The Village Medical Centre
ACK/BRKF TS5 .... **98** A2
Walworth School
NACLF DL5 .... **38** A4
Ward Jackson Primary School
HTLP TS24 .... **2** D4
Warsett School
SALT/BTN/SK TS12 .... **90** C5
Warwick Road School
BAUK DL14 .... **26** C3
Wear Valley District Council
BAUK DL14 .... **26** C4
West Acklam Clinic
ACK/BRKF TS5 .... **123** F2
Westbury County Junior School
THNBY TS17 .... **95** F4

Westgarth County
Primary School
MARSKE TS11 .... **70** A5
Westlands School
THNBY TS17 .... **122** A3
West Lane Hospital
ACK/BRKF TS5 .... **97** E2
West Park Primary School
HTLPW TS26 .... **16** B4
West Redcar School
REDCAR TS10 .... **67** F2
West View Primary School
HTLP TS24 .... **12** B5
Whale Hill County
Primary School
ESTON TS6 .... **102** B1
Wheatlands Primary School
REDCAR TS10 .... **69** D4
Whinfield Road Junior &
Infant School
DARLE DL1 .... **117** F2
Whinfield Surgery
DARLE DL1 .... **117** E2
Whinstone Primary School
THNBY TS17 .... **139** D1
Whitecliffe Primary School
LOFT/ST TS13 .... **112** B1
Whitworth School
SPEN DL16 .... **14** C4
Wilton Castle
ESTON TS6 .... **84** A5
Wilton County Primary School
ESTON TS6 .... **83** E5
Wilton Works (Chemicals)
ESTON TS6 .... **83** E1
Windsor Road Clinic
ESTON TS6 .... **101** F3
Wolviston Primary School
BLGHMW/WYN TS22 .... **41** E3
Woodham Burn County
Junior & Infant School
NACLF DL5 .... **38** A5
Woodham
Comprehensive School
NACLF DL5 .... **39** D4
Woodhouse Close County
Junior School
BAUK DL14 .... **26** C5
Woodhouse Close
Leisure Complex
BAUK DL14 .... **27** D4
Woodlands Family Medical Centre
STOCS TS18 .... **6** D6
Wynyard Road Doctors Surgery
HTLPS TS25 .... **23** D5
Yarm County Junior School
YARM TS15 .... **146** B1
Yarm Medical Centre
YARM TS15 .... **137** D5
Yarm School
YARM TS15 .... **137** D5
Yorkshire NHS Trust
ESTON TS6 .... **101** E4
Zetland County Primary School
REDCAR TS10 .... **51** F5
Zetland Lifeboat Museum
REDCAR TS10 .... **51** F4

Page 7

E6
1 Lawson St

Page 9

E5
1 Beaumont St West

Page 17

F3
1 Hawkridge Cl
2 Hopps St
3 Jobson St
4 Preston St
5 Richardson St
6 Ridley St

F4
1 Bentick St
2 Briar Wk
3 Christopher St
4 Elcho St
5 Elliott St
6 Grosvenor St
7 Hartley Cl
8 Hunter St
9 Laburnum St
10 Mary St
11 Slater St
12 Tankerville St
13 Young St

F5
1 Benson St
2 Bentley St
3 Campion St

Page 19

E2
1 Abbey St
2 Back Throston St
3 Bedford St
4 Brig Open
5 Darlington St
6 Gladstone St
7 Groves St
8 The Lawns
9 Londonderry St
10 Manners St
11 Marine Crs
12 Marquis St
13 Middlegate
14 Regent Sq
15 St Mary St
16 Sandwell Chare
17 Throston St
18 Victoria St

Page 23

F5
1 Ballater Gv
2 Balmoral Ct
3 Banff Gv
4 Barra Gv
5 Beauly Gv
6 Brechin Gv
7 Buckie Gv

Page 27

D1
1 Adelaide St
2 Bishop St
3 The Clarence
4 George St
5 Ninefields
6 Oxford Ter
7 Raine St
8 Stranton St
9 Windsor Ct

D3
1 Barnard Av
2 Beaumont St
3 Bell St
4 Brewer St
5 Byron Av
6 Caroline St
7 Chatsworth Av
8 Conway Gv
9 High Melbourne St
10 Linden Rd
11 Milton Av
12 Raby Gdns
13 Ravensworth Av
14 Rutland Av
15 Seymour St
16 Tivoli Pl
17 Waddington St

Page 35

F4
1 Blake St
2 Magnet St
3 Mill St

Page 39

D2
1 Beechers Gv
2 Campion Ct
3 Epsom Ct
4 Fallow Rd
5 Fawn Cl
6 The Oaks
7 Saint Elizabeth's Cl

Page 41

F5
1 Annfield Cl
2 Deal Rd
3 Deighton Gv
4 Dudley Rd
5 Hetton Cl
6 Laxton Cl
7 Rosedale Gdns
8 Shildon Cl
9 Shotley Cl

Page 42

A3
1 Atwick Cl
2 Betjeman Cl
3 Budworth Cl
4 Butsfield Wy
5 Byron Cl
6 Dryden Cl
7 Escombe Rd
8 Halton Cl
9 Herrington Rd
10 Lowell Cl
11 Newbiggin Rd
12 Penshaw Ct
13 Thornley Av
14 Westerton Rd

A4
1 Aislaby Gv
2 Barlow Ct
3 Barmton Rd
4 Penton Ct
5 Quebec Gv
6 Sinderby Cl
7 Wallington Wy
8 Winston Av
9 Woodham Rd

Page 51

E4
1 Central Ter
2 Cleveland St
3 Clifford St
4 Dundas St
5 Grant St
6 Milbank Ter
7 North Ter
8 Prince Pl
9 Westbourne Gv
10 West Dyke Rd
11 Wilton St

Page 59

D1
1 Balmoral Av
2 Brough Rd
3 Coleshill Cl
4 Conway Av
5 Croxdale Rd
6 Knole Rd
7 Lumley Rd
8 Richmond Crs

Page 73

D2
1 Chopwell Cl
2 Dawdon Cl
3 Denton Cl
4 Dunford Cl
5 Dunston Rd
6 Windleston Cl
7 Winlaton Cl
8 Wolsingham Cl
9 Wrekenton Cl

E2
1 Instow Cl
2 Kelloe Cl
3 Walworth Rd
4 Waskerley Cl

F3
1 Hesledon Cl
2 Hulam Cl
3 Humbledon Rd
4 Virginia Cl

F4
1 Aireborough Cl
2 Chatsworth Ct
3 Daylight Rd
4 Kedleston Cl
5 Mexborough Cl
6 Mossbrough Cl
7 Mowden Cl
8 Ralph Sq
9 Spark Sq
10 The Willows

F5
1 Tollerton Cl

Page 74

A2
1 Radcliffe Av
2 Radnor Cl
3 Redcar Av
4 Redruth Av
5 Romanby Av

A5
1 Bilsdale Rd

C1
1 Cameron St
2 Chantry Cl
3 Colpitt Cl
4 The Garth
5 Mallory Rd
6 Newby Cl
7 Oakwell Gdns
8 Pinder Cl
9 Plumer Dr
10 Summerhouse Sq

C4
1 Azalia Rd
2 Cherry Ct
3 Daphne Rd
4 Eastbourne Rd
5 Larch Rd
6 Midbourne Rd
7 Rowan Rd

C5
1 Balaclava St
2 Craggs St
3 Ezard St
4 Farrer St
5 Ford Pl
6 Hume St
7 Nolan Pl
8 Thomas St

Page 75

D5
1 Bone St
2 Buxton Rd
3 Carbutt St
4 Haffron Av
5 Maritime Cl
6 Paxton Cl
7 Pinfold St
8 Rupert St
9 Ryan Av
10 St Mary's Cl
11 Wynyard St

E5
1 Essexport Rd
2 Gooseport Rd
3 Knightport Rd
4 Ouseport Rd
5 Princeport Rd
6 Rockport Ct
7 Union St East
8 Westport Cl

Page 77

F5
1 Carey Cl
2 Faraday St
3 Garrett Wk
4 Gough Cl
5 Gresham Rd
6 Selbourne St
7 Teare Cl
8 Warren St
9 Waverley St
10 Wentworth St

Page 78

A3
1 Acklam St South
2 Boundary Rd
3 Cathedral Gdns
4 Princess St
5 Sussex St
6 Vine St
7 William St

A4
1 Beaufort St
2 Dale St
3 Eshwood Sq
4 Gilkes St
5 Harris St
6 Head St
7 Hill St
8 Johnson St
9 Monkland Cl
10 Newport Crs
11 Rose St
12 St Aidans Dr
13 Smith St
14 Taylor St
15 Whin St
16 Yew St

A5
1 Barritt St
2 Coral St
3 Fleetham St
4 King Edward's Rd
5 Manor St
6 Palmer St
7 Peel St
8 St Aidan's St
9 Waterloo Rd

B3
1 Albert Rd
2 Bridge St East
3 Brook St
4 Brunswick St
5 Dundas Ms
6 Dundas St
7 Exchange Sq
8 Lower Gosford St
9 Queen's Sq
10 Redcar St
11 Spring St
12 Zetland Pl

C5
1 Blenheim Rd
2 Brine St
3 Ely St
4 North Ormesby Rd
5 Stamford St

Page 79

D5
1 Basil St
2 Benedict St
3 Breen Cl
4 Colliers Gn
5 Constance St
6 Cromwell St
7 Elizabeth Ter
8 Forum Ct
9 Hankin Rd
10 Kings Ms East
11 Kings Ms West
12 Magdalen St
13 Margaret St
14 Moses St
15 Sharrock Cl
16 Veronica St
17 Westbourne Gv

E5
1 Beaumont Rd
2 Bristow St
3 Cadogan St
4 Calvert Cl
5 Coltman St
6 Coronation St
7 Deacon St
8 Derwent St
9 Dorothy St
10 Frederick St
11 Herbert St
12 Hovingham St
13 Jefferson St
14 Kindersley St
15 Maltby St
16 Maria St
17 Norcliffe St
18 Pilkington St
19 Ryedale St
20 Sadberge St
21 South View Ter
22 Thomas St
23 Tunstall St
24 Wake St

F4
1 Maple St

Page 86

B3
1 Abridge Cl
2 Ainsdale Cl
3 Appleby Cl
4 Cawdor Cl
5 Downfield Wy
6 Eaglescliffe Cl
7 Greenock Cl
8 Hunstanton Gv
9 Pannel Cl
10 Portrush Cl
11 Preswick Cl
12 St Arreck Cl
13 Wentworth Crs

Page 93

D2
1 Orwell Gdns

F4
1 Fraser Rd
2 Parkwood Dr

Page 94

B4
1 Arncliffe Av
2 Hazeldene Av

C1
1 Bakery St
2 Burgess St
3 California Cl
4 California St
5 Cobden St
6 Corporation St
7 Derby St
8 Dovecot St
9 Durham St
10 Frederick St
11 Hutchinson St
12 Inkerman St
13 Laing St
14 Middle St
15 Milbank Ct
16 Milbank St
17 Nelson Ter
18 Palmerston St
19 Parkin St
20 Russell St
21 Scarth Wk
22 Stamp St
23 Tennant St
24 Union Sq
25 Vane St

Page 95

E3
1 Archer St
2 Barnard Cl
3 Bridge St
4 Chelmsford St
5 Cranworth St
6 Frederick St
7 Georgiana Cl
8 Glasgow St
9 Middleway
10 Reed St

F4
1 Belvedere Rd
2 Camelon St
3 Cheltenham Av
4 Ellerburne St
5 Salisbury St

Page 97

D3
1 Agecroft Gdns
2 Ascot Av
3 Curran Av
4 Nesham Av
5 Newbury Av
6 Riverdale Ct
7 Sydney Cl
8 West Rw

E3
1 Bisham Av
2 Hanover Gdns
3 Studley Rd

F5
1 Church La
2 Langdale Gv
3 St Margaret's Gv

Page 98

A2
1 Binks St
2 Chesham St
3 Emmerson St
4 Wakefield Rd
5 Weastell St

C3
1 Balmoral Dr
2 Barnard Ct
3 Birchwood Av
4 Farndale Ct
5 Farndale Crs
6 Hadleigh Crs
7 Headingham Cl
8 Howard Ct
9 Moray Cl
10 Sunley Av

C4
1 Ainderby Wy
2 Bretby Cl
3 Harwell Cl
4 Hurworth Rd
5 Marsden Cl
6 Pemberton Crs
7 Rylstone Ct

Page 99

F5
1 Highmead Wk

Page 100

A2
1 Bruntons Manor Ct
2 Elvington Gn
3 Linmoor Av
4 Northdale Ct
5 Pennard Gn
6 Ruth Av
7 Whisperdale Ct

B3
1 Copperwood
2 Crinklewood
3 Crosskirk Cl

C5
1 Alwinton Ct
2 Church Cl
3 The Hall Cl
4 Tebay Rd

Page 101

E1
1 Elm Cl
2 Laburnum Rd
3 Shelley Crs

F3
1 Clifton Pl
2 Consett Dryden Cl
3 Grosvenor Gdns
4 Hewley St
5 The Jennings
6 Lambton St
7 Mason St
8 Patten St
9 Thirlmere Crs

Page 116

A2
1 Elmtree St
2 Kitching Gv
3 Mewburn Ct

B1
1 Botham Gv
2 Garden Pl
3 Hendren Cl
4 Lynne Cl
5 Melrose Av
6 Statham Pl
7 Sutcliffe Ct
8 Trueman Gv
9 Warner Gv

Page 117

D2
1 Boston Cl
2 Furness St
3 Muirkirk Gv
4 Otterburn Cl
5 Salters Cl

F3
1 Brecon Side
2 Canterbury Gv
3 Guildford Cl
4 Leicester Gv
5 Norwich Gv
6 Stockton Rd
7 Wells Cl

Page 121

D3
1 Barton Cl
2 Brighton Cl
3 Rainton Dr
4 Scampton Cl

F2
1 Fawcett Rd
2 Manning Cl
3 St Margarets Gv
4 Westdale Rd

F4
1 Hastings Cl

Page 123

D2
1 Hunwick Cl

F5
1 Holey Cl
2 Nairnhead Cl
3 Northiam Cl
4 Nutfield Cl
5 The Oaks

Page 124

A1
1 Biggin Cl
2 Boltby Cl
3 Ellerton Cl
4 Haxby Cl
5 Kepwick Cl
6 Levisham Cl
7 Slingsby Cl
8 Swainby Cl

Page 132

A1
1 Archer St
2 Holly St
3 Kendrew St
4 King St
5 Lowe St
6 Maude St
7 Portland Pl
8 Royal Oak Yd
9 Salt Yd
10 Temperance Pl
11 Union St
12 Upper Archer St
13 Winston St
14 Wycombe St

A2
1 Bakehouse Hl
2 Beaumont St West
3 Bull Wynd
4 Chancery La
5 Church Rw
6 East Rw
7 Feethams South
8 Northumberland St
9 Primrose St
10 South Arden St

B1
1 Brunswick St North
2 Coburg St
3 Hilda St
4 Ianson Sq
5 John Dobbin Rd
6 Middleton St
7 Priestgate
8 Quebec St
9 Sanderson St
10 Steeplejack Wy
11 Tannery Yd
12 Upper Russell St
13 Weaver's Wy

Page 137

D2
1 Aspen Rd
2 Butterfield Cl
3 Esk Gn
4 Langdale Cl
5 Newlands Rd
6 Newsam Crs
7 Poplar Rd
8 Rowan Rd
9 Westlands Rd

E1
1 Blairmore Gdns
2 Brae Head
3 Casper Ct
4 Crosby Ct
5 The Fairway
6 Hazel Slade
7 Highfield Gdns
8 Hindhead
9 Player Ct
10 Roundhay Dr
11 Sunningdale Wk
12 Trevino Ct

Page 139

D1
1 Copse La
2 Eider Cl
3 Farrier Cl
4 Hanbury Cl
5 Lorimer Cl
6 Ostler Cl
7 Partridge Cl
8 Pheasant Cl
9 Robin Cl
10 Saddler Cl
11 Tanner Cl
12 Whinchat Cl

Notes

Notes

Notes

Notes